Confessions of a
Tax Collector

Confessions of a Tax Collector

ONE MAN'S TOUR OF DUIY

INSIDE THE IRS

Richard Yancey

HarperCollins*Publishers*

HarperCollins books may be purchased for educational, business, or sales promotional use. For information, please write: Special Markets Department, HarperCollins Publishers Inc., 10 East 53rd Street, New York, NY 10022.

FIRST EDITION

Designed by Laura Lindgren

Printed on acid-free paper

Library of Congress Cataloging-in-Publication Data is available upon request.

ISBN 0-06-055560-2

04 05 06 07 08 ❖/RRD 10 9 8 7 6 5 4 3

For the Revenue Officers

ACKNOWLEDGMENTS

This book would not exist if not for the real people who occupy its pages. They were more than coworkers during my time with the Service. They were also my friends. I have struggled to portray them accurately and to the best of my recollection. Much time has passed since those days. Memory fades, but not the fondness I have for all of them. God bless and Godspeed.

I am extraordinarily fortunate to have Marjorie Braman, vice president and executive editor at HarperCollins, as my editor. Perceptive, empathetic, an enthusiastic lover of stories well told, she has been coach, cheerleader, and most avid fan throughout the entire process. All writers should be as lucky.

Brian DeFiore, my agent, advocate, and guide, championed the book. Always positive, but with stern pragmatism, he never hesitated in the early days of this project to take up my banner and recklessly charge up the hill.

I thank my three boys, who endured my mood swings and evening absences with grace, understanding, and patience. A father could not ask for better sons.

There are not enough words in the language to express my gratitude to my wife. I am convinced there is no one on the face of the planet with more courage, honesty, or unselfish devotion—particularly toward this most difficult of husbands. Brian charged up the hill, but she was ever the light on top of it, guiding me home.

CONTENTS

AUTHOR'S NOTE

No name in this book, with the exception of my own, belongs to anyone I know. I have changed the names of all other characters and have altered their personal appearances and histories. I have taken particular pains to protect the identities of those taxpayers with whom I dealt during my years of service, changing appearance, occupation, and, in some circumstances, gender.

I have also taken liberties with the arrangement of incidents, for clarity and to facilitate the narrative flow. I did not keep contemporaneous notes of my conversations with taxpayers, coworkers, or any other persons. I have relied on my own memory, such that it is, to reconstruct conversations. Throughout, however, I have striven to record the spirit of what was said, if not the actual words.

The Service is the largest civilian employer in the federal government. To claim that my experiences are common to all within it would not only be grossly inaccurate but monumentally unfair. This is the story of one employee among the thousands who serve.

CAST OF CHARACTERS

JIM NEYLAND, Grade 14 Branch Chief, Tampa Branch, Jacksonville District, Southeast Region

BETH, Grade 12 Revenue Officer, Lakeside post-of-duty

GINA TATE, Grade 13 Supervisory Revenue Officer (Group Manager), Lakeside post of duty

MELISSA CAVANAUGH, Grade 12 Revenue Officer and On-the-Job Instructor, Lakeside post-of-duty

HENRY, Grade 11 Revenue Officer, Lakeside post-of-duty

ALLISON, Grade 7 Revenue Officer Trainee, Lakeside post-of-duty

RACHEL, Grade 7 Revenue Officer Trainee, Lakeside post-of-duty

DEE, Grade 7 Revenue Officer Trainee, Lakeside post-of-duty

CAROLINE, Grade 7 Revenue Officer Trainee, Lakeside post of duty

TOBY PETERSON, Grade 12 Revenue Officer and Union Steward, Lakeside post-of-duty

CINDY SANDIFER, Grade 12 Revenue Officer and On-the-Job Instructor, Lakeside post-of-duty

BONNY, Grade 5 Group Clerk, Lakeside post-of-duty

BRYON SAMUELS, Grade 15 Collection Division Chief, Jacksonville District, Southeast Region

SAM MASON, Grade 12 Revenue Officer and lead instructor, RO Basic Training, Tampa post-of-duty

LARRY SIMON, Grade 12 Offer-in-Compromise Specialist and Basic Training Instructor, Panama City post-of-duty

WILLIAM CULPEPPER, Grade 12 Revenue Officer and On-the-Job Instructor, Lakeside post-of-duty

JENNY DUNCAN, Grade 13 Supervisory Revenue Officer (group manager) and Acting Branch Chief, Orlando Branch

HOWARD STEVENS, Grade 13 Special Agent-in-Charge, Criminal Investigation Division, Tampa post-of-duty

BOB CAMPBELL, Grade 14 Branch Chief, Orlando Branch, Jacksonville District, Southeast Region

FRED NEWBERRY, Grade 12 Occupational Development Specialist, Jacksonville District

ANNIE DeFLORIO, Grade 13 Supervisory Revenue Officer (group manager), Orlando and (later) Lakeside post-of-duty

THE SERVICE

THE ORGANIZATION (C. 1991)

The American Taxpayer

The President of the United States

The Secretary of the Treasury

The Commissioner of the Internal Revenue Service

The Regional Directors

The District Directors

The Collection Division Chiefs

The Branch Chiefs

The Group Managers

The Revenue Officers

The American Taxpayer

THE OCCUPATION*

Description of the Work
Internal Revenue Officers focus on the collection of delinquent taxes and functions directly related to that work. Cases, called taxpayer delinquent

---

* From "Position Classification Standard for Internal Revenue Officer, Series GS-1169," Office of Personnel Management, 1993.

accounts (TDA) or taxpayer delinquent investigations (TDI) are assigned to a revenue officer for resolution...

Revenue officers have extensive face-to-face personal contacts with taxpayers, attorneys, accountants, and other representatives and spend a major portion of their time in fieldwork...

The Difficulty of the Work
Conditions affecting the difficulty and responsibility of revenue officer work include:

- pressure to resolve delinquent cases within deadlines;
- applying complex statutes, regulations, and judicial decisions to complicated situations;
- dealing with fearful, hostile, and defensive individuals and organizations;
- working in unstructured environments such as high crime areas; and
- dealing with prominent taxpayers or similar circumstances subject to news media coverage.

THE FOUR PROTOCOLS

"You will learn there are things you may say and things you may not say, and it is those things you may not say that are the essence of your work here."

THE FIRST PROTOCOL: *Find where they are*

THE SECOND PROTOCOL: *Track what they do*

THE THIRD PROTOCOL: *Learn what they have*

THE FOURTH PROTOCOL: *Execute what they fear*

PART ONE

The Trainee

Some years ago—never mind how long precisely—having little or no money in my purse, and nothing particular to interest me on shore, I thought I would sail a little and see the watery part of the world.

—*Moby-Dick*

CHALLENGER

For most of the past thirteen years, I have used a different name, chosen by me and approved by our government, to perform the task appointed to me by the people of the United States. This name, my professional name, I will not tell you.

I am a foot soldier in the most feared, hated, and maligned agency in the federal government.

I work for the Treasury. I execute Title 26 of the United States Code, for the Internal Revenue Service—or the Service, as we in the trenches call it.

I collect taxes, but don't call me a tax collector. Nobody wants to be a tax collector. Call me what the Service calls me. Call me a revenue officer.

And hear my confession.

NOVEMBER 1990

"Okay, Rick, let's start. Why do you want to be a revenue officer?"

I was sitting in a small conference room in Tampa, across the table from Jim Neyland, chief of the Tampa branch of the Jacksonville District of the Internal Revenue Service. It was after-hours. His tie was loose around his neck and his shirtsleeves rolled to his elbows. He was about fifty, with thinning salt-and-pepper hair and a bushy black mustache. I had just turned twenty-eight, and was wearing a ten-year-old suit with a ten-day-old dark blue tie. The interview had been scheduled to begin an hour earlier, but I had waited in the reception area of the branch office, while his secretary fussed at her desk and his loud voice boomed throughout the office as he made dinner arrangements on the phone. There were no magazines to read, no television to stare blankly at while I waited. In one corner sat a dusty plastic palm tree. The carpeting was dark blue. The divider separating the secretary's workstation from the waiting area was white. The ceiling was white. On the white wall directly opposite me were two large framed photographs, one of the Sunshine Skyway Bridge and another of the space shuttle *Challenger*. The bridge had collapsed into Tampa Bay in 1980, killing thirty-five people. *Challenger* had exploded in 1986, seconds after the photograph was taken.

Jim Neyland did not want Chinese. He wanted barbecue. He had been thinking about it all day, and his heart was set on barbecue. He hated Chinese; he was always hungry again thirty minutes later. He wanted some barbecue pork and some beans and corn on the cob and some coleslaw and he didn't give a good goddamn what everybody else wanted. No, not Italian, either. There would be no compromise where he was concerned. It was barbecue or nothing. The secretary flashed an apologetic smile in my direction and buzzed him again. "Mr. Yancey is here for his interview." He apparently didn't hear her. I examined my new tie for any picks, stains, or hitherto unnoticed blotches. I had to urinate, but knew the moment I bolted for the bathroom, Jim Neyland would turn the corner from the inner recesses of his office, looking for me. I stared at the picture of *Challenger*. Like most Americans, I could remember exactly where I was and what I was doing when I heard the news. How long ago that seemed—a lifetime or two. And now I was here, four months after answering an ad in the newspaper, more on a whim than design. My destination, my mission, was not as clearly defined as *Challenger*'s, but in its own way was no less perilous.

"I need the job," I answered. I had decided not to repeat the preface I had used in my second interview, which had taken place two weeks prior to this one: *Well, I never dreamed of being a tax collector when I grew up.* This had not gone over well with one of my interrogators. "And it sounds like very interesting work."

"Well, you'll never be bored," Jim Neyland said. He picked up a folder and opened it. I could see my name printed on its face in large black letters: Yancey, John Richard. Inside were my application and notes from the first two interviews. I folded my hands in my lap, rubbing the tips of my thumbs against my slick palms. There was a motel-room quality print of a beach scene on the wall behind Jim Neyland, with a lone seagull perched on a picket fence, staring out over the dark ocean.

"So, you went to law school." His hair was thinning at the crown, a perfectly round bald spot about the size of a golf ball. Curly black hair carpeted his forearms.

"For a year."

"What happened?"

"I left."

"You dropped out?"

"I dropped out."

"Why did you drop out?"

"I decided it wasn't for me."

"It took you a year to figure that out?"

"I was kind of trying to live up to someone else's expectations." My father was a lawyer, as was my brother.

"Need a job to pay off the loans?" His tone was friendly; he seemed genuinely interested.

"Among other things."

He turned a page. "Boy, you've had quite a few jobs over the years."

"Well, the application said list everything for the past ten years." I stopped. I sounded defensive.

He ignored me. "Typesetter. Drama teacher. English professor... your degree is in English?"

"That's right."

"What the hell did you think you were going to do with *that*?" The question was rhetorical. He continued, "Dramaturge... what the hell is a dramaturge?"

"Someone who analyzes drama."

"They pay you to analyze that?"

"Not much."

"Playwright. Convenience store manager. Ranch hand. Ranch hand?"

"Sort of the family business."

"Get along li'l doggies!"

I managed to laugh.

"Anything you haven't done?"

"Singing telegrams."

"Anything you won't do?"

"Singing telegrams."

"What's your deal, Rick, besides comedy? I mean, what do you want to be when you grow up?"

He slapped the file closed and leaned back in his chair, cupping the back of his head with both hands, fingers laced. For a balding man, his hair appeared extraordinarily thick. It grew in tangled knots between his knuckles and the back of his hands. I had hoped the interview would not turn existential. I was about to lose control of my bladder. I argued with myself, what's it going to hurt, to ask if I could be excused? I was afraid the temptation to flee would be too great, once I left the room.

"I'm a writer. It's all I ever wanted to be, since I was a little kid."

"But it doesn't pay the bills."

"It doesn't pay mine."

"You married, Rick?"

"Engaged."

"Ah, say no more. I get it. Playtime is over."

"Maybe something like that."

"Well, let me tell you something about the IRS. When we bring people on board, we put them through hell. Don't mistake me, Rick: if we bring you inside, we bring you *all the way* inside—you understand what I mean? We *try* to make you quit. You wanna know why we do that? Why we try to make you quit?"

"To see if I have the right stuff?"

"Maybe something like that."

"I have the right stuff."

"We don't want quitters."

"I'm not a quitter."

"You quit law school."

"I left law school."

"You dropped out."

"To weigh my options."

"You bailed, buddy."

"I guess I bailed."

"You will hate this job. Some mornings you'll come to work and you'll think, 'Why the hell did I ever take this stinking job?' You'll want to put your fist through a wall. You'll think you're having a nervous breakdown. Some people *do* have nervous breakdowns, by the way. I've been to many a hospital ward. Do you think I'm making this up?"

"No."

"You're damn right I'm not making this up," he said pleasantly. I was having trouble reading him. His words were harsh but his tone was playful. A big raven-haired cat. He said, "I like that, 'the right stuff,' like we're astronauts or something. No, we will try to break you. Crush you. Push you to the brink. Because that's what we do. You know what we do, don't you?"

"I do."

"So if your manager comes to you and says, 'We're gonna seize this guy's house,' you think you could do that?"

"Take somebody's house?" I was just buying time, and he knew it.

"We put people on the street for not paying their taxes. You understand that? So could you do that? Could you take somebody's house?"

"I think I could."

"He's got a wife. Two little kids. You're going to put two little kids in a homeless shelter for something like *taxes*?"

"Maybe he could live with a relative."

"He's an orphan."

"He could use the money he was paying on the mortgage for rent."

"His dead mother left him the house, free and clear. There is no mortgage."

I took a deep breath. We were playing dueling scenarios, and I wasn't sure why. I was fairly sure, however, what answer he was looking for.

"Yes, Mr. Neyland."

"No."

"No?"

"Call me Jim."

"Yes—Jim—I think I could do that."

"Why?"

I gave the best answer I could. It was the first answer I gave, the only answer I had. "I need the job."

"Everybody needs a job," he said, waving his hand. "I'm talking about *this* job. The job of taking people's houses."

"Yes, I think I could."

"Think you could you sleep that night?"

"Which night?"

"That night. That night. The night you took it."

"I don't—I don't know."

"You see, Rick, the kind of people I'm looking for seize houses even if it means they *can't* sleep at night. Anyway, I don't want you to have a false impression of what you're getting into. Look around you, Rick. I mean, literally, don't look at me, look around this room. You see up there, that molding up there, and that baseboard down there? Go ahead, check out that baseboard. You notice anything special about that baseboard? Come on, this isn't a test. See how it's a different color? The walls are off-white, kind of an eggshell, but the baseboards are white, bright white, a brilliant white. See how carefully those baseboards have been painted, and the trim around the top? Not just anybody could do that. It takes a *professional* to do that, somebody with an incredible eye for detail. So what do you think?"

"About the baseboard?" I wasn't being sarcastic; I had fallen off the conversational train and was stumbling down the tracks, trying to catch up.

"If you had to seize someone's house, if it was the right thing to do for the case, for the good of your country—could you do that?"

"Yes. Yes, I could." I had no idea if I could, but he had made it clear seizing someone's house was a patriotic act.

"Not many people do—revenue officers, I mean. A few years back the law changed and all personal residence seizures had to be approved by the District Director. All of a sudden, nobody was doing them anymore. No one wanted the DD to look at the case." He drummed his fingers on the tabletop. "So . . . tell me something about yourself, Rick."

o   o   o

The ad copy did not contain the words "collection" or "IRS." It was styled as an invitation to an open house, a get-acquainted party. The starting salary was printed in bold type at the bottom. It was the starting salary that caught my eye, and the job requirements. It sounded too good to be true.

The day I found the ad—or the day the ad found me—I showed it to my live-in fiancée, Pam. After four years of living together, it had become apparent that, unless something changed, we would stay engaged for the duration of the relationship. Pam was tired of bearing the financial burden while I worked a series of menial jobs that barely paid for my upkeep. "Why should I marry you?" she often asked. "You can't even hold down a job." Marriage also came at a price: Pam was a widow and received a government annuity that would terminate when she remarried. In other words, marrying me could hit her hard in the pocketbook. The house we shared on a small lake in Clearview was hers. The furniture was hers. The plates and cups and glasses and utensils were hers. The towels and linens and curtains were hers. The pictures on the walls and knickknacks on the shelves were hers. I had some clothes, my rattletrap of a car, and a collection of paperback books. I was twenty-four and living with my parents when Pam and I met at the local community theater. I had recently returned to Florida, after earning my four-year degree in a mere seven years. Pam was six years older than I, and had taken a maternal interest in me from the moment we first spoke. Six months later, we were living together, officially engaged. Four years later, we were still living together and still officially engaged.

"You want to work for the IRS?" she asked incredulously.

"The ad says the Department of the Treasury."

"That's what the IRS is, dummy."

"But look at this. All I need is a degree and a 3.5 GPA. And look at the starting salary. That's almost triple what I made last year."

"What the hell do you know about taxes?"

"It doesn't say I—"

"Or accounting? Or auditing tax returns?"

"It doesn't talk about that."

"Why don't you go back to work for the college? You liked teaching."

"They won't hire me full-time without a master's, you know that. We've talked about that." Two years before, in one of my frequent episodes of near-adolescent angst, I calmly informed her I was moving to Tampa to return to school for my masters degree. She responded by slugging me as hard as she could in the middle of my back. A year later, when I actually made good on my threat to move to St. Petersburg to attend law school, she greeted the news by slapping me so hard my glasses flew across the room. Pam had abandonment issues.

"This is a very bad idea, Rick," she said.

"Oh, it won't last long," I said. "Just something to pay the bills till I can sell something."

"Sell something? Sell what? You hardly write at all anymore."

"Maybe this job will be so horrible it'll motivate me."

"It *will* be horrible."

"Then I will be motivated."

o   o   o

The open house was held at the federal building in downtown Lakeside. The building was small, one-storied, brick, resembling the old county courthouses so prominent in the South. Four Doric columns stood at the entrance. Behind it, across the alley, towered the tallest building in town, the ten-story Wesley Building. In high school I had worked in the Wesley; my father's company owned it. I had been a glorified handyman, changing lightbulbs, fiddling with the twenty-year-old air-conditioning system, running errands for my father. He had since sold the building to a bank, which had performed extensive renovations after succeeding in having the Wesley declared a national historical landmark. It dominated the landscape downtown; its marble facade glittered in the streetlights as I pulled into a parking space across the street. Since this was not a formal interview, I had dressed comfortably in jeans and my lucky flannel shirt.

I stepped into the foyer and immediately fought the desire to hightail it home. About a dozen people were milling about sipping punch from Dixie cups, eating pretzels, wandering from display table to display table—

and wearing their formal business attire. Heads turned. A man about my age with the physique of a boxer and a haircut like the sergeant from *Gomer Pyle* frowned in my direction. *Hey, buddy, deliveries in the rear!* A large woman in a loud floral print pants suit touched my elbow.

"Hi, are you here for the open house?"

I considered replying I had just popped in to use the rest room. I said, "Yes."

"Hi, my name's Beth."

She extended her hand. It was surprisingly small and delicate, given her size. I shook it gently. Her hand was icy cold.

"I'm a revenue officer," she said.

"Oh. What's a revenue officer?"

"The job you're here for. There's refreshments in the conference room down the hall to your left, some chips and pretzels and punch, but stay away from the bean dip."

"Okay. Thanks for the tip."

"And watch out for the little woman in the black dress."

"The little woman in the black dress?"

"That's right."

"Why should I watch out for the little woman in the black dress?"

"Lots of reasons, but tonight mainly because she made the bean dip."

"Oh. Gotcha."

"We have some material for you to look over at the tables over there against that wall. The program starts in five minutes." She spoke rapidly, like someone who was used to being interrupted. "You know you need a college degree."

"I have one."

"And a 3.5 GPA or higher."

"Have that too."

"You know what a revenue officer does?"

"That's what I'm here to find out."

"It's the IRS. I don't know why they didn't put that in the ad."

"I figured it was."

"You'd be surprised how many people didn't. They walked in tonight, took one look at that door, and walked right out."

She nodded to the glass double-doors on her right. Stenciled in chipped gold paint were the words INTERNAL REVENUE SERVICE.

"They did it on purpose," she said.

"Who did?"

"Whoever put the ad in the paper."

"Didn't the IRS put the ad in the paper?"

"Well, I doubt it was the FBI."

I nodded. She had totally lost me. "Kind of like the old bait-and-switch, only in reverse," she added.

I nodded. I didn't get it. "Maybe I'll have some punch."

"Don't forget about the bean dip."

Nothing made with beans seemed like a good idea at a meet-and-greet. Later, I learned it was the manager of the collection office, Gina, who had brought the dip. Gina brought bean dip to every office function. Her famous bean dip, she called it. It was sitting in a cake pan beside the punch bowl and the stack of Dixie cups. This was the office conference room. About a dozen chairs were arranged in two rows before a television that rested on a roll-away cart pushed against the far wall. A short woman wearing a black dress with very dark hair and Prince Valiant bangs intercepted me as I headed for the punch bowl.

"Hi, welcome, I'm Gina Tate."

"Rick Yancey."

"I was about to ask you something stupid, like if you were here for the open house. Don't tell me, somebody has already asked you that question."

"As a matter of—"

"We have punch and cookies and pretzels and chips and crackers and you have to try the bean dip."

I began to say I'd been warned off the bean dip, but she barreled on. "It doesn't surprise me. Some of them aren't the ripest apples off the tree. You look like a lumberjack, though too skinny, really. Are there skinny lumberjacks? You think of lumberjacks and you think of Paul Bunyan. What did he have as a sidekick, a yak?"

"I think it was a—"

"No, it was a bull or an ox. Bright blue, or that may be something Disney has imprinted on our collective memories. You did know this is the IRS, right?"

I nodded. It was easier just to nod. I kept nodding at the appropriate places as she led me to the table and handed me a paper plate.

"Forgive the paper. We don't have much of a budget. That's something you'll learn quickly if you come on board. We're a bunch of pack rats. Pens, paper clips, staples. Currently there's a shortage of staples. I'm keeping a box in my desk and I'm doling them out, one little row at a time. I'm the manager here; I'm the official doler. This is collection, you know."

Nod.

"We're Collection. In the IRS there's Examination, Collection, Criminal Investigation, Inspection, and Taxpayer Service. That's excluding the Service Centers, of course. Examination examines, Collection collects, CI investigates, Inspection inspects, and Taxpayer Service serves. We're Collection."

Nod.

"You're a 3.5, I presume. You know, they tried this a couple of years ago—this Outstanding Scholars Program—not in Lakeside, but in Orlando—Tampa, too, I think; anyway, they seemed really pleased with the results. Some high-caliber people. And not all of them with business or accounting degrees. You don't need one to be a revenue officer, you know."

Nod. She had taken the plate from me and was filling it with bean dip. It suddenly occurred to me that, if by some miracle I came to work here, this woman would be my boss.

"Well, the turnout is about what I expected. The economy is too good right now. We do better hiring in a recession—which is ironic since there's not as much to collect. Is that enough dip? You want some punch? Now, here's the drill. We do the video in about five minutes, then a Q&A and then, for anyone left standing, some one-on-one. If we like you, we invite you back for an interview. How old are you, Rick?"

I told her.

"You don't look that old. You have a very babyish face. Have you ever thought about growing facial hair? I bet you look about ten without your glasses. I have myopia, but I am also vain. Hard to understand, to look at me. Oh, and there's a questionnaire on the table right by the front doors. Don't forget to fill one out before you go. Thanks for stopping by tonight!"

She hurried away. A thin woman with big Farrah Fawcett hair was leaning in the doorway. Her nose was sharp, her eyes small and hard. Gina Tate took her by the elbow and led her out of the room, whispering something in her ear. I left my paper plate on the serving table and carried my Dixie cup to a chair in the back row. I was not a mingler, and decided to wait in the conference room for the video. The boxer stepped into the room, followed by one or two other suits. They took the front row. A middle-aged woman ducked her head in, then pulled it out again. I sipped my punch. What was I doing here? I checked my watch. Four or five others took their seats. Gina stepped back into the room, herding people in front of her. Behind her were Beth and the thin woman with the eighties haircut. A short man hovered in the doorway. He was nattily dressed in a blue cardigan and brown slacks. He stood with his hands folded over his crotch, as if fearing a devastating blow.

Gina stepped to the front of the room, Beth and the thin woman flanking her. She introduced herself and thanked us for coming. She introduced Beth, then the thin woman, Melissa. They were here to answer any questions we might have after seeing the short video prepared by National Office. The little man in the doorway, as if on cue, reached over and flipped off the lights.

"Turn the lights on, Henry," Gina said, in a tone clearly reserved for small children, animals, and half-wits. The fluorescents flickered back on.

She turned and pressed the play button on the VCR. A white badge against a blue background appeared on the screen. The badge was set in the center of a circle of gold. In gold lettering above the badge were the words U.S. TREASURY. And below the badge, wrapping halfway up the circle on either side, INTERNAL REVENUE SERVICE. The scales of justice occupied the top half of the badge; a large golden key the lower half. The image lingered for a minute, then faded into a picture of the American flag, flying on a cloudless day, snapping smartly in the breeze. Aaron Copeland's *Fanfare for the Common Man* began to play. The camera slowly panned right, revealing an imposing, monolithic, glittering skyscraper. In a rich baritone, a narrator intoned, "Welcome to the Internal Revenue Service." I shuddered. He sounded like the guy from *Outer Limits*.

An attractive young woman emerged from the shadow of the building into the brilliant sunlight. Her dress was red; her hair golden blond.

Announcer: "This video will introduce you to the revenue officer position. After the conclusion of this video, your facilitators will be available to answer any questions you may have . . . please hold your questions until the conclusion of this video." The woman in the video was carrying a leather satchel. Her expression was one of gritty determination. She was beautiful. She radiated vitality, power, confidence, grit. The camera followed her to a sleek silver sports car that appeared to be parked illegally on the plaza. She opened the door, tossed the satchel inside, and pulled a U-turn, disappearing from view. The camera panned back to the monolith. Announcer: "The revenue officer position offers a rewarding, yet challenging, career, with opportunities for advancement, while serving the people of the United States by collecting the revenue necessary to run the government." Fade back to flag. "The American people rely on the revenue officer to ensure full, fair, and honest enforcement of the tax laws." Cut to the blond woman in the red dress walking into an office. She flashes an ID at the startled man behind the desk.

BLOND WOMAN: Mr. Pierce . . .
MR. PIERCE: Hey, I was just going to call you!
BLOND WOMAN: Mr. Pierce, I'm here today about the taxes your company owes.

The rest of their scene is played in pantomime as the announcer continues. "Revenue officers have the opportunity to work with all segments of the American taxpaying public. Individuals, businesses, public and private institutions. They deal with many people from many backgrounds. A revenue officer should be adept at handling negotiations and, in some rare cases, confrontations."

Mr. Pierce is now standing, shaking his finger at the blond woman's perfect nose. She shakes her head sadly, reaches into her briefcase, and removes some paperwork.

BLOND WOMAN: Mr. Pierce, I'm here to seize your business for nonpayment of internal revenue taxes.
MR. PIERCE: You're here to do what?

The scene cuts to a man in blue overalls standing beside the blond woman outside the business's doors. When he turns around, the words LARRY'S LOCKSMITHS appears, stenciled across the back of his overalls. He appears to be changing the locks on the doors. The hapless Mr. Pierce is at the blonde's elbow, appearing to beg her for mercy. She is grimly determined, though pleasant enough. She places a three-by-five card on the door that reads: WARNING INTERNAL REVENUE SEIZURE.

MR. PIERCE: I don't like this, but I understand you have to do it. If only I had paid my taxes like I should have!

The scene slowly fades back to the American flag, still waving. The message so far is clear: revenue officers were attractive, they made good money, and they took things.

After the video concluded, Gina conducted a brief question-and-answer session. Most people sat silently while one or two asked about health insurance, retirement benefits, promotion potential, how many people they were looking to hire. Gina explained that the office was authorized to hire up to five new revenue officer trainees. "Your training period lasts for one year. You're what's called a *probationary employee*." To each trainee would be assigned a seasoned revenue officer like Beth or Melissa, as his or her On-the-Job Instructor, or OJI. "At the end of the year, if your performance meets the standards, you're automatically promoted to Grade nine Revenue Officer." Grade 9 referred to the federal government's pay scale. Revenue Officers were either Grade 9, or journeyman level, Grade 11 or Grade 12. No one asked what happened to Grade 10. Grade 12 was the highest a revenue officer could rise without entering management. "Every promotion after the training year is competitive," she said. Melissa and Beth walked around the room while she spoke, handing out a packet of information enclosed in a glossy folder, the cover of which was embossed with the same Treasury symbol from the video. I set mine on the chair beside me without opening it. I had already decided this wasn't for me.

"If you hate the idea of a desk job, this is the career for you," Gina said. "Revenue Officers are field officers—we do most of our work outside the office, calling on taxpayers. You're behind your desk maybe two or three days a week, at the most."

The square-jawed boxer man turned in his chair, thrusting a legal pad in my direction. Now, what was this? Gina said, "We're passing around a sign-up list if you're interested in talking to us some more tonight. Those of you who are staying can wait in here—we'll call you out, one by one."

There were only four other names on the list. The last was Freddy Listrom. The boxer man. I stared at the pad resting in my lap. Gina said, "Signing up will not commit you to anything."

Ah, well, if she was going to put it *that* way.

I waited for my name to be called. I am not accomplished at waiting, though much of life consists of it. I watched as Freddy Listrom helped himself to another cup of punch. If they called us out in order, I would be the last person summoned. This filled me with an unreasonable fear of being alone in the room. It occurred to me that I was almost twenty-eight years old and had no life insurance, no health insurance, no retirement plan, and no other plans that I could think of. What had happened? Why was I sitting here in a federal building wearing a flannel shirt and blue jeans, cradling my little Dixie cup in my lap? Dixie cups reminded me of my childhood, of birthday parties and after-school snacks. Presently Freddy's was called, and I was alone. Time to bolt. I would rededicate myself to writing. I had an idea for a screenplay I was toying around with. I could try selling a story to a magazine. At sixteen, I started writing a second book inspired by the runaway success of *Jaws*, about a killer bull running amok in the wilds of rural Florida. That went nowhere.

I couldn't shake the feeling that there was a reckoning coming for all the years I had wasted. The decision to attend law school had brought a certain relief from the unrelenting pressure created by the conviction that I was somehow above the fray, outside the stream of normal society, where people fretted over insurance, retirement, job security, getting their kids into the right college. It was as if I had turned the canoe around and entered the main channel; all I had to do was rest my oar and be swept along effortlessly to the terminus of my journey. It had not panned out that way. Now, as I neared my twenty-eighth birthday, I was starting over—again. Soon, I would be too old for fresh starts.

My name was called. I rose and followed the little man named Henry into the corridor and through the glass doors with the words INTERNAL REVENUE SERVICE stenciled on their face. A rack of forms was against the wall on my left. To my right were three rows of armless green chairs facing a counter at the rear of the room. This was the Taxpayer Service office, the portal through which the public entered the world of the IRS. For some reason the lights in the room were dimmed. Gina was sitting in one of the green chairs. Henry sat beside her. I had a choice: to sit beside Henry or to sit one row in front of them, which would necessitate turning awkwardly in the chair to talk. I sat directly in front of Henry, preferring awkwardness to intimacy.

"So Rick," Gina began, "what was your major in college?"

I told her. She beamed. "I was an English major, too!"

Henry's narrow eyes became even narrower. "Why you want this job, then? Why ain't you teachin' or somethin'?"

"Hard to find work, even at the high school level."

Gina said, "What else do you do?"

I told them I worked at the theater in Clearview, teaching and writing children's plays. I also acted occasionally.

"You an actor?" Henry asked. He sounded flabbergasted, as if I had just confessed to murder.

"That's what great about this new hiring program," Gina said. "We're getting people from all backgrounds."

"I have an MBA," Henry said archly.

"That stands for Mainly a Bullshit Attitude," Gina leaned in and whispered, then clapped her hands with delight. Henry scowled. She said, "Henry's family business is embalming."

"There's more to it than dead people," Henry said.

There seemed to be nothing to do but nod.

"Why you want to be a RO?" Henry demanded.

"Revenue officer," Gina translated for me.

"That's right," Henry said. "Rev-eh-new off-ih-*sir.*"

"I need stable employment. I'm a little tired of freelancing." And, I might have added, there was a reckoning coming.

"Well, lemme tell you somethin'," Henry said. "If they hire you they gonna go over your file with a fine-combed toothpick."

"With a—a what?"

"This is just between me and you and the stop sign, but when you come on board they sniff you out. Gonna audit you, you know."

Gina said helpfully, "That's standard for all new-hires. We audit your past three years' 1040s."

"And they find *anything* wrong . . ." He drew a finger slowly across his throat.

"Where are you from, Rick?" Gina asked.

"Lakeside. I'm a native."

"You don't meet too many of those," Gina said.

"Why would an actor want to work for the IRS?" Henry demanded. He was troubled by the concept.

"Oh, I don't know. Maybe the rent needs paying," Gina said.

"They look at that, too," Henry said. "They look at everythin'. And you don't have all this together," he patted his stomach, "they fire you."

"Henry exaggerates," Gina said.

He folded his arms across his chest and sat back in his chair. For some reason I have never understood, he said, "And you can put that where the moon don't shine."

On Monday of the following week, I was called for a second interview. This time I left the flannel at home. I had trouble with the tie and the coat hung loosely on me; it drooped from my shoulders and bunched into folds between my shoulder blades; I had lost weight in the six years since I had purchased it. I said to Pam, "I can always tell how a jacket in the store is going to look on me: the same as it does on the hanger." Pam did not think I was funny.

"Your tie's crooked," she said. "Are you sure you want to go through with this?"

"What's wrong with this?"

"I don't have a good feeling about it."

"You're right. I should rely on other people to take care of me the rest of my life."

The interview was conducted by Gina Tate and Melissa Cavanaugh, the thin, pinched-faced woman with the teased bottle-blond hair. They sat on one side of the conference table and me on the other. Gina opened by wondering aloud why someone with my background would want to work for the IRS. I answered I had not grown up dreaming of being a tax collector, at which point Gina laughed and Melissa scowled. Then I added that I felt it was time to settle into something more stable than the arts; that I needed a good job with good benefits (and government benefits were superb); that the job itself sounded interesting, exciting, challenging, different from your average nine-to-five, blah, blah, blah. The women across the table made copious notes. I would not know until much later that the Service required all interviewers to record *every single word* of an applicant's answers. Recording devices were not used, on the assumption they might inhibit the respondents.

"Don't get me wrong, Rick," Gina said, perhaps in reaction to my slightly defensive tone. "It's just we don't usually get applicants from people of your—background."

"You got an English degree," Melissa reminded her.

"I *have* an English degree," Gina corrected her.

"I'm glad you said that," I said to Gina. It brought the desired response: she laughed, but Melissa did not. Melissa, it was clear, had taken an instant dislike to me. It was as if she thought this artsy-fartsy guy was trying to pull a fast one on her.

I did very little talking in this interview. I learned later that Gina had already made up her mind about recommending me for the final interview with Jim Neyland. Gina talked, Melissa scowled, and I concentrated on not saying anything completely moronic. Gina asked again, perhaps for the third or fourth time, if I understood this was *collection*. I assured her I understood. She explained how the selection process worked: if I "passed" this interview, the branch chief in Tampa would conduct the third and final interrogation. If I passed that, I would be hired, contingent upon my background check. "We fingerprint you, you know," she said. I said that was fine with me—I was not aware of any felonies in my past. The "new-hires," as we would be called, would spend two weeks in something called "pre-Phase," in Lakeside, before going to Tampa for four weeks of Phase One, or basic training.

"It's during Phase One that you truly begin to understand what we do here," Gina said. "But I hope by this point you do understand that we *collect taxes?*"

She mentioned again that the trainees would be assigned a coach, called an OJI, by the Service.

"Melissa has already volunteered to take on at least two or three of the newbies," Gina said. "And you can't ask for anyone better. Melissa is one of the best revenue officers who ever worked for me."

"I came on-board in 1980, before there was such a thing as the Outstanding Scholars Program," Melissa said. Her tone was derisive. "Started as a clerk and worked my way up to Grade Twelve. Busted my ass."

"That's great," I said, meaning her achievement, but as she scribbled I realized the notes might reflect that I was referring to her ass. I began to panic, but there was really no way to fix it. Melissa was frowning—and scribbling. I would learn that most revenue officers are determined, if not obsessive, documenters. Conversely, they are also prolific shredders. They had to be to survive.

"We want to get away from the stereotype," Jim Neyland said. "You know, geeky little four-eyed pencil-necked pencil-pushers sitting in windowless rooms." He seemed oblivious to the fact that he had just described me. "Lazy, corrupt, livin' off the government, bullying taxpayers. That's the whole idea behind this Outstanding Scholars Program. There was a lot of resistance to the whole idea, at least down here at the local level, but I'm a hundred percent for it. For too long the Service has hired—and promoted, God help us—old cops, old grunts, old clerks with nowhere else to go. It's time for some fresh ideas, some new blood. A new image! Don't you think we should change our image?"

"Sure, I—"

"Why, what's wrong with our image?"

"What's wrong with it?"

"Come on, Rick, that's a cheap ploy. You're smarter than that!"

"Well, I guess most people are afraid of—"

"Huh? Afraid? Shouldn't they be afraid? What, you think most people pay taxes out of a sense of patriotism? That's what you think, Rick?"

"That's why I pay mine."

"Good answer! But you're wrong. It's fear. So the question becomes, is fear so bad? Maybe the reason we need to change our image is people don't fear us *enough*. There's a helluva lot of taxpayers, attorneys, CPAs who've got our number, who know how to play the system better than we do. You think I'm kidding, but your average shyster knows how to run rings around your average revenue officer. Why do you think we've been authorized to hire five thousand more? We're coming after these bastards dull as butter knives when we should glitter like daggers! Let me make it easy for you. Let me play Barbara Walters for a minute. If you were a tree, what kind of tree would you be?"

"Seriously?"

"Yeah. Seriously."

"I guess I would be...I don't know, some kind of hard wood. Is mahogany hard? I don't know that much about trees."

"Why a hard wood?"

"Well, you know, something tough."

"Tough doesn't matter. Smart matters."

"I don't know of any smart trees."

"I'm not talking about trees right now. I've known many good ROs who weren't what you'd call tough, but they were smart. Smart will get you a lot farther than tough. Tough helps. Next question: What would you want on your tombstone?"

That's a good question, I thought, *because you are fucking killing me.* I had not peed my pants since kindergarten. Not in twenty-two years. It was tough to sit there while my bladder threatened to explode. Tough, but not smart. I tried to concentrate. *Don't give him the answer you think he wants. Just be honest.* But the honest answer was I thought quotes on tombstones were stupid. He isn't being literal, I told myself. He doesn't intend to record it for posterity. I said the first thing that came to mind.

" 'He worked very hard.' "

Now, what a moronic thing to hang over your head for all eternity: *He worked very hard.* I crossed my legs and the pressure moved upward, into my stomach.

"You've quit a lot of jobs, Rick. What makes you think you won't quit this one? No, the real question is, what's gonna make *me* think you won't?"

"I don't know how to answer that, Mr. Neyland," I said. "A lot of things about the job appeal to me. There's independence, opportunities to advance. I like that it's not your typical nine-to-five desk job."

"Lemme tell you something, Rick: you are gonna *loathe* it. Everybody hates it, some more and some less, but especially during the training year you're gonna say to yourself, 'Why the hell did I listen to that SOB Neyland and take this stinkin' job?' You're gonna be confused and upset and dreading getting up in the morning." A smile slowly spread across his narrow face. "But then, one day, and I can't tell you when, but one day you're gonna be sitting at your desk and it's gonna hit you, and you're gonna say, 'Jesus Christ, this is the easiest job in the whole damn world!' You won't believe the government pays you forty, fifty thousand dollars a year to collect taxes. Most attorneys in this country don't make that much. What's the most you've ever made in a year, Rick?"

I guessed. "Eleven, twelve thousand."

"And you busted your butt for that twelve grand, I bet. Long nights, weekends. At the ranch ripping your hands on the barbed wire, stomping in the cow patties. You understand what I'm getting at. Dollar for dollar, this is the easiest job ever invented by man. You don't believe me, but you will. I promise you will. So here's the bottom line, Rick. You want this job? Last chance. You want it?"

"I want it."

"No going back. You'll shatter my faith. I'm batting a thousand: no one I've hired has yet to leave the Service. My gut is always right, and my gut is telling me something about you, Mr. Yancey. My gut is *screaming* at me to do something to you."

"What—what are you going to do to me?"

"I'm going to hire you, man!"

He leapt to his feet and thrust his hand toward me. I accepted his iron grip immediately.

"Let me be the first to congratulate you, Mr. Yancey. Welcome aboard the Internal Revenue Service!"

Twilight had come and, with it, a fine, misting rain. I was on the interstate, heading home. I had driven my father's GMC pickup to the interview, my old rattletrap having suffered another breakdown. I was in a state of shock. If someone had told me just a month before that I would soon be a tax collector for the largest employer in the federal government, I would have laughed. Me? The IRS? Never! It must be fate, I told myself. There was no other explanation. Fate had brought the Service and me together. The world had gone monochrome, and along the interstate the towering pines cast no shadow. I drove nine miles over the speed limit, the volume on the radio set to speaker-busting levels, and thought of towering white sails shimmering ghostlike upon slate-gray seas, of men neither bold nor foolish but merely cognizant of the brutal practicalities of life. Did the crew know fear as they rode the metal cage to the top of *Challenger*? These launches had become routine. How could there be any dread in their hearts? Nerves, of course, and a certain quivery anticipation of stepping through a magic doorway to the wonderland on the other side. But the other side on that particular day had been oblivion.

Every great undertaking balances on the edge of disaster. Yet those commuters on the Sunshine Skyway Bridge were upon no great undertaking. They were going to work, to shop, to visit relatives, to see a doctor. . . disaster stalks even our most trivial decisions. I had not hesitated to take Jim Neyland's hand because the alternative, as the *Challenger* crew and the drivers on the bridge understood, was paralysis, a kind of acquiescence to failure and death. That failure resulted did not matter. What mattered was climbing into the car for the trip. What mattered was stepping into the cage for the ride to the top.

Welcome aboard.

②

SHOOT THEM ALL

When I was in college, the remake of *The Fly* starring Geena Davis and Jeff Goldblum was released. The movie, about a man who slowly changes into a giant man-eating fly, thus ruining any possibility of true love, deeply disturbed me, on a level beyond the stomach-churning special effects. One scene played repeatedly in my mind for days, of Jeff Goldblum collapsing into the arms of his lover and whispering desperately into her ear, "Help me. Help me be human." His own ear had just come off in his hand.

I borrowed some money from my father and purchased five neckties, one for each day of the week. Three button-down Oxford shirts, white, blue, and tan, three pairs of slacks, and two pairs of shoes, one brown and one black. (I forgot socks and had to return to the store the next day.) The shoes were size tens; the salesman tried to sell me a ten and a half. I tried on the larger size, but thought my feet looked too big in them. They looked like clown feet. I jammed the tens on and walked about, wincing. I had not worn dress shoes in over ten years. "You really should go with the ten and a half," the salesman said.

"They'll stretch," I said. "I'll break 'em in." He looked at me dubiously, then shrugged. *Help me be human.*

One afternoon I drove down to Powell, the county seat, to have myself fingerprinted. My fingerprints would be sent to FBI headquarters in Washington as part of my background check. I thought of that unpaid speeding ticket in Chicago five years before—or had I paid it? Jim Neyland wanted detail-oriented people, not speeders and definitely not speeders who can't remember if they paid the fine. I had two library books about six years overdue, but I didn't see how running my prints could implicate me.

"So you're going to work for the IRS, huh?" the clerk at the sheriff's office asked.

"I guess I am," I said.

She made a face, an expression not unlike Geena Davis's when Jeff Goldblum's ear came off. "Ugh," she said.

I walked back to my car, hands jammed deep into my pockets: I didn't want anyone to see the stains on my fingertips and assume the worst. I wondered if the clerk ever had said to anyone, "So you just murdered your girlfriend, huh? Ugh!"

My fingerprints were now on file with the Federal Bureau of Investigation. I would never be able to commit a felony with any spontaneity and get away with it. For every door that opens, another closes.

I contacted my alma mater in Chicago and instructed it to forward a copy of my transcripts to the Internal Revenue Service in Lakeside, Florida. I drove to the federal building that same day with my diploma: the Service wanted proof that I had actually earned one. A man wearing a pocket protector answered my knock on the door.

"This is a private office," he said. "You want Taxpayer Service down the hall."

I showed him my diploma.

"Oh, so you're one of *those*," he said. He shut the door in my face, taking my diploma with him. I waited in the hall, feeling awkward and strangely exposed, like a man who has ducked into the women's room by accident. The big man appeared after a moment and handed the diploma back to me.

"Okay, I made a copy of it," he said. "English degree, huh?" He laughed, shook his head, and shut the door in my face. I wasn't allowed in yet.

That night I dug through the trunk of my car, the last repository of all things I couldn't find. Pam came outside and stood behind me, looking over my shoulder.

"What now?" she asked.

"I'm looking for something."

"Good luck."

"My tax returns for the past three years."

"Oh. Why?"

"They're going to audit me."

"They won't audit me, will they?"

"Pam, why would they audit you? We don't file together."

"But we live together."

"They don't know that."

"The address on the returns is the same."

"You think they cross-reference every address?"

"Oh, you bet I do. They better not audit me, Rick."

"They won't audit you."

"You'll stop them?"

"Pam, trust me. They won't audit you. Well, I supposed they might audit you, but it would have nothing to do with me."

"What makes you so sure?"

"I'm only being audited because I'm going to work there."

"You know what's so annoying about you? You say everything with such conviction. And the more uncertain you are, the more certain you sound. The truth is the truth, Rick, you can't believe something into being."

"Okay. I'll make a note of that."

She watched me pawing through the debris for another moment, then said, "I don't even remember you filing last year."

"Well, I did."

"Did you make enough money to file?"

"I had to pay, remember?" I remembered the exact amount: $256.74, for self-employment tax based on my theater income. Pam had been livid: I was broke, and she paid the tax for me.

"Well, I guess now you'll be able to pay me back." she said.

JANUARY 13, 1991

"All right. This is it," Gina Tate said. "After this, there's no turning back. You are about to be inducted into service to the United States of America. If you have any second thoughts at all, speak now or forever hold your peace.... Raise your right hand and repeat after me: 'I do solemnly swear...that I will support and defend the Constitution of the United

States ... against all enemies, foreign and domestic ... that I will bear true faith and allegiance to the same ... that I take this obligation freely without any mental reservation or purpose of evasion ... and that I will well and faithfully discharge the duties ... on which I am about to enter ... So help me God.' Congratulations, and welcome aboard."

The five new-hires of the Lakeside post-of-duty gathered in the conference room—the same room in which the video was shown on the night of the open house. We had introduced ourselves moments before taking the oath, over coffee and orange juice.

There was Allison, the youngest, only a couple years out of college. She'd had only one other job, as a bookkeeper for a local trucking company. Of the five of us, Allison was the only one with a business degree. Her features were round and pasty white, based on some dubious advice from the clerk at the Clinique counter at the mall. Her hair was jet black and teased upward to give an impression of height: she was about five foot four, in heels.

Rachel, the oldest, was in her mid-forties, married to a drug company rep. The mother of two, Rachel was returning to work now that the youngest was out of elementary school. She seemed, on first impression, to be much too kind and gentle to be a tax collector.

Dee was a year older than Allison and three years younger than I. She was thin, with a pageboy haircut and a childlike, freckly face. Her degree was in psychology. "I'm not staying with this very long," she confided. "Just till I save up enough to money to get back into school. I love school. Don't you love school? I wish it had never ended." I agreed, and told her I liked it so much I spent seven years at it, to maximize my pleasure. She did not laugh, though I meant it as a joke. Her brows came together. Oh, God, I thought. She's analyzing me. Never use the words *maximize* and *pleasure* in the presence of a psych major.

Caroline had been a major in the army reserves before leaving to complete her government service with the IRS. She was painfully thin, with a high forehead, a birdlike nose, and a pointy chin. Married, with two small children, Caroline was earnest to a fault. Her immediate supervisor in the reserves was Colonel Richard Brane. His nickname was Dick. Caroline never saw the humor in this or, if she did, never acknowledged it. She was very excited about the job. "Did you hear we get to spend three weeks in Tampa—all expenses paid?"

I didn't recognize any of them from the open house, which made me wonder, not for the first time, if a mistake had been made—perhaps not on a cosmic scale, but that I had been plucked from the wrong pool of applicants. Where was Freddy Listrom? It seemed extraordinary that I had made the cut and Freddy Listrom had not.

We sat at the large conference tables and spent two hours filling out forms. W-4s, life and health insurance declarations, security systems clearance certificates. Forms for savings bonds, the Thrift Savings Plan—the IRS version of a 401(k)—Union enrollment forms.

"Everyone is entitled to representation by NTEU," Gina said.

"What's NTEU?" Allison asked.

"The National Treasury Employees Union," a voice boomed from the doorway. Towering there was a corpulent black man wearing a short-sleeve dress shirt and Sansabelt pants that terminated two inches above his scuffed shoes.

"Ah, right on cue," Gina said. "Folks, this is Toby Peterson. He's another of my senior Grade Twelve revenue officers. He is also a Union Steward."

"Why is there a union?" Rachel asked. "I thought federal workers couldn't strike."

"That's a good question," Toby said. "And I'll get to it soon as she's out of here."

"She" was Gina, who ducked her head and hurried from the room, a small, secretive smile playing on her lips. Toby pulled up a chair and sat down, his enormous thighs jutting over the edge of the seat. He folded his arms over his chest and said, "Damn, you all just a bunch of babies!"

"Thank you!" Rachel said.

"My name is Toby Peterson and I'm the Union Steward for this post-of-duty. I'm the one person you need when the shit goes down, and the shit *will* go down." He looked at Allison. "No, we can't strike, child. But we do have certain rights under a contract between NTEU and the IRS. In that mountain of crap in front of you is a copy of the contract. If you do just one thing tonight, take that contract home and read it. It's the only lifeline you got, 'cause you all in deep water now, whether you know it or not."

"What happens if we don't join the Union?" Allison asked.

"Then your ass is grass. In some cases, we'll still represent you, but only to enforce the contract. This POD has one hundred percent enrollment 'cause management here is one hundred percent FOS"

"FOS?" Caroline asked.

"Full of shit," Rachel translated for her. There were, it seemed, acronyms for profanity.

"That's right," Toby said. "So my advice would be to sign up. It's only ten bucks a pay period. Think of it as an insurance policy—you don't really need it till you really need it." He glanced at the door and leaned toward us. His booming voice dropped to a hoarse whisper. "I feel sorry for you all. They gonna do things to you. Things you won't even believe. Shit, things I won't believe. Half of you won't be here by this time next year." He pulled a piece of paper from his pocket and unfolded it. He held it up for us to see the words, written in large block letters: THEY'RE LISTENING. He jabbed a finger at the ceiling tiles above us. He flipped the paper over. On the other side was written, PHONES TOO.

"But you hang in there," he boomed, causing us to jump in our chairs. "Anybody want to talk to me, today or anytime, I'm in that little suite down the hall, last door on your right. Give your enrollment forms to me. Be the most important form you fill out your entire career—and, believe me, you're gonna be fillin' out a helluva lot of forms."

He stuffed the paper back in his pocket and lumbered from the room. There was a silence, then Rachel said, "Well, that was encouraging." Gina returned with the same small smile she took with her. Following her, like obedient ducklings, were Henry, Melissa, Beth, and a tall middle-aged blonde I had not seen before.

"Well," Gina said brightly. "You've met Toby, and here's the rest of the group, with the exception of Mr. Culpepper, who's on special assignment."

"He's always on some kind of *assignment*," Henry said.

Gina ignored him. "I think you already know Beth and Melissa from the open house. And Henry, of course. This is Cindy Sandifer. She's a recent transfer from the New Orleans District."

"Welcome aboard," Cindy Sandifer said. "Now, please, y'all don't tell me your names all at once. I'll never keep 'em straight."

"I know 'em all already," Henry said. He pointed at Dee, "Anabelle." At Allison, "Rachel." At Rachel, "Caroline." At Caroline, "And . . . Caroline." He laughed. Perhaps he realized his mistake or recognized the oddity of two of the trainees having the same name. He did not say my name.

"I'm Allison," Allison said.

"Dee."

"Rachel."

"He got my name right," Caroline said.

"Rick," I said.

"He's an *actor*," Henry said to Cindy in a stage-whisper.

"We suspect he may be simply here to research a role," Gina said.

Beth said, "Welcome aboard, everyone," and left the room. Henry said he had an important call to make, and left. Melissa said, "This is very important: never go to Henry for help. Never ask him a question. If he gives you any advice, just nod and say, 'Uh-huh,' then find me—or Cindy."

"Cindy and Melissa will be your On-the-Job Instructors," Gina said. "Dee, Rachel, and Caroline will work with Cindy. Allison and Rick, you're Melissa's."

Melissa smiled humorlessly at me. I lowered my eyes. I did not want to be Melissa's. My impression from the second interview, in which I indirectly corrected her grammar, was she didn't like me.

"Melissa and Cindy will review all your work—before it comes to me for final approval. They are your coaches and first point-of-contact during the training year. Always check with your OJI first—that's what they're here for. They will accompany you to the field, sit in on interviews, monitor your phone calls, review all correspondence—at least until you're comfortable and *we're* comfortable with your progress. During these next two weeks, they will familiarize you with our procedures and some of the basic elements of the job—what we do here. In front of you is a booklet entitled 'Revenue Officer Pre-Phase Training.' "

Caroline fingered the edge of the booklet. Melissa said sharply, "Don't touch that yet!" and Caroline snatched her hand away, smiling apologetically in Melissa's direction.

Gina said, "You'll work through this material until you leave for Tampa. Oh, and by the way, we don't have listening devices in the ceiling and your phones are not tapped. Any questions?"

Yes, I thought, *how did you know what was on Toby's paper?*

Allison asked, "When do we get to see our offices?"

We did not have offices. Five desks had been arranged in a large room at the rear of the building. There were two extra desks for our OJIs. We were not allowed to pick where we would sit. Rachel would be directly behind me, Allison to my right. Dee and Caroline would sit on the other side of the room. The desks were government-issued, at least twenty years old.

"Where does everyone else sit?" Allison asked.

"There's a suite of offices beside this room," Gina said.

"Everyone else gets a private office?"

"We're not trainees," Melissa snapped at her.

"You don't know how lucky you are," Gina told Allison. "In the Stone Age, when I came on board, four ROs shared one church-social type folding table, with a single phone in the middle. We had to stare at each other all day and take turns with the phone. On the upside, it encouraged fieldwork."

"Speaking of the field," Melissa said to Gina, "I've got those FTD Alerts."

"On their first day?" Cindy asked.

Dee asked, "What's a FTD Alert?"

"Why not?" Melissa turned to Cindy. "You know what Jim said."

"What did Jim say?" Rachel asked.

Then Caroline, "Who's Jim?"

"I didn't go to the field until I got back from Phase One," Cindy said.

"Jim Neyland," Allison said. "The man who hired us."

"That was *your* district," Melissa was saying to Cindy. "This is the *Jacksonville* District."

"They don't have commissions," Cindy said.

"What's a commission?" Caroline asked.

"Why do they need commissions?" Melissa demanded. "They'll be with me."

"Well," Cindy said. "Maybe if you want to take *your* trainees."

"We should expose them as soon as possible."

"Expose us to what?" Allison asked.

"DBs."

"Melissa!" Gina said sharply.

"Okay," Melissa said. "Tax . . . pay . . . ers."

Caroline asked, "What's a DB?"

"Never mind," Gina said.

"Dumb bastards?" Rachel tried.

"Deadbeats," Melissa said, with a defiant flip of her hair in Gina's direction.

"We are not allowed to call them that," Gina said. She was trying to be stern.

"I didn't actually use the word," Melissa said.

"It's not politically correct," Gina said.

"I don't give a shit," Melissa said. "If it were up to me, I'd line 'em all up against a wall and shoot them."

We trailed behind Gina into the secretary's office, adjacent to our common room. Melissa and Cindy remained, to continue their argument. Gina introduced us to Bonny, the group's clerk. Bonny was a pleasant woman with large, expressive eyes and a gentle voice.

"Welcome aboard," she said.

"Behind every great revenue officer is a great group clerk," Gina said. "Get to work, Bonny. Ha-ha! This way."

She led us through a door into a huge room that ran the length of the building. We weaved between five-foot-tall dividers as heads popped up, like prairie dogs out of burrows, to ogle us.

"This is Examination," Gina said. "You know, the geeks." She introduced us to those present. I left that day without remembering a single name. Each welcomed us aboard and wished us luck. As a whole, Tax Examiners were a quiet, introspective lot, the true number crunchers of the IRS. Most revenue officers held them in contempt and resented them for setting up assessments, sometimes in the millions of dollars, which we had no hope of collecting.

Next we toured Taxpayer Service, also called "Walk-In" by revenue officers, because taxpayers literally walked in, without an appointment, to obtain forms, ask tax questions, complain about a refund, or seek guidance with one of the mystifying letters issued by a computer in the Service Center. Today the room was nearly full. Gina explained that traffic began to pick up in mid-January and would continue to grow until it reached its peak in April.

"By April First this place will be standing room only," she said. "By the fifteenth, they'll be out the door, in the hall, and standing on the street."

We returned to the conference room. Gina clapped her hands and said, "Okay, it's eleven-thirty. Lunch!" She reminded us of the breaks allowed under the contract: thirty minutes for lunch, plus a fifteen-minute break in the morning and one in the afternoon. Dee asked if the two short breaks could be combined and taken with the lunch. Gina answered no, of course not. She left the room.

"I'm taking this up with Toby," Rachel said.

"There's no place to eat downtown," Allison said. "Where are we supposed to go for lunch?"

"I brought my lunch," Caroline said.

"I'm not hungry," Dee said.

"Well, I could eat a horse," Rachel said.

"I think we should all go to lunch together," Allison announced. "We need to bond." She clearly saw herself as the natural leader of our little group. She asked our opinion on the bonding issue. Caroline repeated that she had brought her lunch and intended to eat in the break room. Rachel suggested the restaurant located in the Burdines department store two blocks to the south. Dee said nothing. I had the impression she had a definite opinion about bonding but chose not to express it. I said I didn't know anything about bonding, but I was hungry and now we had only twenty-five minutes. Rachel asked what would happen if we took more than thirty minutes—would they shoot us at the door? Caroline left. We were floundering already; after just three and a half hours of someone telling us what to do, we had lost the ability to make the simplest of decisions. I jammed my hands in my pockets, rocked back on my heels, and studied the ceiling tiles. Somewhere, perhaps, a squirrelly little man was wearing earphones in a windowless bunker, listening, the reel-to-reel humming at his elbow.

·   ·   ·

We were gone forty minutes. The Burdines restaurant was not crowded at that hour, but our waitress did not share our sense of urgency. We would discover that few people outside the Service did: revenue officers are not known for their patience. At lunch we learned Rachel's husband had once played drums for the band that would become AC/DC. Allison's husband worked for the local grocery store chain. Dee was single, between boy-friends. I offered that I was single, too, but between the ring and the altar. Then I spilled mustard on my new tie.

We walked back to the office. "I'll take up the rear," Rachel said. "In case they do shoot us." No one laughed.

Dee said, "Anyone ever have one of those anxiety dreams, where you go to school in your underwear?"

"Why would you go to school in your underwear?" Allison asked.

Melissa was waiting for us in the conference room. Caroline was with her. Allison's attitude toward her turned icy—she had betrayed us, broken ranks on the very first day.

"We're late," Rachel announced. "We had an-eighty-year-old waitress who didn't split the check right."

Melissa ignored her. "Follow me," she said. She was carrying a stack of blue file folders. We followed her into the common room, to a little nook behind my cubicle wall. Melissa slapped the file folders on a small table beside a computer terminal. Her thin fingers flew over the keys. Mustard-colored letters shimmered on the black screen, reminding me of the stain on my tie; I placed my hand awkwardly over the spot. Even while seated, Melissa seemed to be in motion, a dervish of nervous energy. She had that air of someone who is perpetually running behind with no time to finish everything on her plate. "Melissa even *sleeps* in a hurry," Gina would later tell me.

"What are you doing?" Allison asked.

"Pulling these accounts," Melissa said, jerking her head toward the folders by her right elbow. "This is IDRS, the Integrated Data Retrieval System. It's linked to the mainframe in Martinsburg."

She hit the ENTER key. A message appeared on the screen:

INTEGRATED DATA RETRIEVAL SYSTEM
WILLFUL UNAUTHORIZED ACCESS OR INSPECTION OF ANY TAX-
PAYER INFORMATION IS EXPRESSLY PROHIBITED. ACCESS TO
THIS SYSTEM IS RESTRICTED TO THOSE EMPLOYEES WHO HAVE
AN AUTHORIZED, WORK-RELATED REASON TO ACCESS AND
INSPECT TAXPAYER INFORMATION. WILLFUL, UNAUTHORIZED
ACCESS OR INSPECTION OF THE TAXPAYER INFORMATION CON-
TAINED IN THIS SYSTEM MAY SUBJECT THE OFFENDER TO CRIM-
INAL PROSECUTION UNDER 18 USC 1030 OR 26 USC 7213.

She referred to the first folder on the stack, then typed a string of numbers. "Here's the sequence: command code, taxpayer ID number, entry code." *Click-u, click-u, click-u.* She slapped the enter key again. Shimmering yellow numbers popped onto the black background. She tapped one of her long, tapered nails on the glass as she described what each set of numbers represented. "MFT, period, DLN, amount, lien indicator, freeze code."

"I see," Allison said, appearing absolutely fascinated. She had bulled her way to a position just behind Melissa's right shoulder.

Rachel said, "I'm clear so far on everything except MFT, period, DLN, lien indicator, and freeze code."

"Master File Transaction, tax period, Document Locator Number... you know what a tax lien is? If it says 'lien' in this field, that means we've filed a lien."

"And if it's blank, we haven't?" Allison asked.

Melissa stared at her for a moment. "Yes," she said through gritted teeth. "That's right."

"What's a master file? That sounds ominous," Dee said.

"Does everyone have a master file?" Caroline asked.

"Master File is our reference for kind of tax. For example, these two numbers represent Form 941, the employment tax return."

"Wouldn't it be easier just to use the form numbers?" Rachel asked. "Why use two numbers to represent three other numbers?"

"I never thought about it," Melissa said. "It's just the way it is."

"Oh," Rachel said.

"Probably has something to do with memory," Dee said.

"It won't help me remember," Caroline said.

"Computer memory, Caroline," Dee said. "Computer memory."

Melissa shrugged. "The next set of numbers is the tax period. This, 8903, is code for March Thirty-first, 1989. So the MFT is Form 941, the tax period is the first quarter."

"Cool," Allison said.

"This long series of numbers is the Document Locator Number. Every form filed with the Service is assigned a Document Locator Number."

"Why?" Caroline asked.

"So they can locate the document," I said.

"We, Rick," Rachel said. "We."

"Right," Melissa said, without a trace of irony. "So we can locate the document in our system. The next figure is the dollar amount."

"Oh!" Caroline said. "I see the decimal now!"

"Good," Melissa said. "There's the lien indicator, and that last field is for a freeze code, if there happens to be one on the module. You're going to cover all this in Phase One—I didn't want to get bogged down. I want to get to the field on these Alerts."

She pressed another button and the ancient printer beside the terminal began to jerk and whine. Melissa slapped it on the side with the flat of her hand. She raised her voice to be heard over the protests of the machine.

"All our shitty equipment is ten years obsolete."

"So every return ever filed is in this—what did you call it?" Rachel asked.

"IDRS. And the answer is yes and no."

"Pretty common answer around here," Dee whispered to me.

Melissa continued, "The main thing to remember right now is IDRS is a revenue officer's chief research tool. We capture every bit of information on a tax return, individual and business, as well as information sent to us by payers—you know, 1099 and W-2 information."

"Wow," Rachel said. "Hey, can you pull me up?"

"I could, if I wanted to get fired," Melissa said. "And you can, if you want to. You are not allowed, ever, under any circumstances, to pull your account information, your relatives', your friends', celebrities', spouse's, ex-spouse's, boyfriends', *anyone* not assigned to you."

Caroline had gone pale. "But what if it's an accident?"

"Then you tell Inspection it's an accident."

"Inspection," Rachel said. "I've heard that name before, but nobody's explained what it is. What is Inspection?"

Melissa was scribbling something in the file folder.

"We don't have time for that now, Rachel," she said. "Anyway, I thought Toby would talk about that this morning."

"He said we were being bugged," Allison said.

"Well, then he did talk about Inspection."

There are exceptions to every rule, and I would learn during my training year that there was an exception to the strict prohibition against "browsing" on IDRS. While it was true we could not access unassigned accounts, we were allowed to use IDRS to locate third-party information. For example, if an informant told us the taxpayer's ex-girlfriend's name, we could look her up on IDRS in order to ask her for information. This exception aside, the Service was serious about controlling access to IDRS, for obvious reasons. "Unauthorized access," as it was called, was the leading cause for termination. For some, the temptation is simply too great. Why not look up how much Michael Jordan earned last year? Who's it going to hurt? Or a friend asks you to see what her ex claimed as income on his tax return because she believes he's lying to the judge. Or a buddy calls you asking about the status of his refund. With an IDRS password, you had access to information that *no one else* had access to, not the president of the United States, not the FBI, not the CIA. You were only a half-dozen keystrokes away from generating false refunds in the millions of dollars. You could find anyone, anywhere in the country, and sometimes anywhere in the world. The implications of access to IDRS are staggering. Give me your name and in thirty seconds I would have your Social Security number. Give me your Social Security number and in five minutes I would know how old you were, where you lived, what you did for a living, how many children you have, how many times you've been married, how much you make, what your investments are, if you are generous, sick, permanently disabled, or recently relocated; if you graduated from college, served in the military, pay alimony, live with your parents, had a recent sex-change operation. For most people, this means I would know more about them than they know themselves.

"Okay, since you wanted to know: FTD stands for Federal Tax Deposit. Alert means just what it says. Alert. So FTD Alert means Federal Tax Deposit Alert."

"Oh," Allison said. "Yes, I see now."

"I still don't get it—what *is* an FTD Alert?" Rachel asked.

"It's an alert, Rachel, an *alert*. Means we got to get out there fast. They're issued every quarter by the Service Center and we have fifteen days to make contact."

We were racing down the interstate, packed shoulder to shoulder in Melissa's 1987 Corolla. Allison was in the middle between Melissa and Rachel. I was on the right in the rear, with Dee's hip pressing into mine. From my vantage point, I could see the speedometer. Eighty-six miles per hour.

"I didn't want to be your OJI," Melissa said abruptly. "Being an OJI gets you nothing. They take your inventory away, but give your trainees seventy cases. So I've gone from managing forty cases to managing seventy. They say that's okay because all of you are 3.5s and you'll pick it up quick. Well, I don't care what your GPA is, this isn't fucking college."

"It sure isn't," Rachel said.

"I wanted Billy to take you."

"Who's Billy?" Allison asked.

"Billy Culpepper. Only never call him Billy. He was my OJI, and if I had to take him, you should."

William Culpepper was the office star, according to Melissa, the one RO in Lakeside who seemed destined for upper management, perhaps even an executive position in Washington.

"And he's a fucking maniac. I mean, I think he really might be crazy. When I was a trainee he took my case file and set fire to it."

"Why?" Caroline asked.

"Because he wanted to scare me."

"He scares me and I haven't even met him," Dee said.

"I would avoid him if I were you."

I had begun to shut down mentally: too much information had been
thrown at me in six hours to absorb it all. The only things I had pretty clear
by this point were Inspection was probably something bad, the Union was
probably something good, and thirty minutes for lunch was definitely something unreasonable. Despite Gina having told me more than a dozen times
that my job was collecting taxes, I still wasn't entirely sure what my job was.
The bright January sun cast a glare on Melissa's dirty windshield and I wondered how she could see the road. Maybe she couldn't. Maybe she navigated
by sonar, like a bat. The car had a funny smell, similar to the smell of decay-
ing paper. I tuned out the conversation while I watched the fields and orange
groves glide by outside my window. This was my hometown, the place in
which I was raised; we were actually not far from my father's cattle ranch on
the far north side of town, where I had spent every summer of my youth,
daydreaming of future conquests, of glories to come when I reached the
full age of maturity. Where would I be, I wondered then, when the time for
daydreams expired, when the freedom finally came to make my own way in
the world? Packed into a car with strangers, destination unknown, with a
mustard stain on my tie, being driven, at a death-defying speed of eighty-
five miles per hour, by a revenue officer of the Internal Revenue Service.

The answer startled me.

"Don't say anything," Melissa instructed us. "Let me do all the talking.
Don't make eye contact with him and don't—"

"Make any sudden moves?" Rachel asked.

"*Interrupt me.*"

"Sorry."

"If he asks a question, don't say you don't know the answer. Just keep
your mouths shut and I'll answer. You're here to watch and learn."

She whipped into a parking place before a small brick building. A sign
by the door read NEWMAN, CRAIG & PAUL, ATTORNEYS AT LAW.

"It's a law firm?" Caroline asked.

"No," Dee whispered in my ear. "It's a taxidermist."

Melissa stepped out of the car and flipped her hair over her collar. We
stood behind her as she opened the trunk and removed her briefcase and
her purse. She pulled out something that resembled a large, thin wallet

covered in black leather. She flipped it open, laying her finger in the crease, and held it up. Her picture, of slightly better quality than a driver's license photo, occupied the top right half. Beside it was a drawing of the Treasury Building in Washington, D.C. On the top were the words, in ornate script, DEPARTMENT OF THE TREASURY/INTERNAL REVENUE SERVICE.

"Somebody asked what a commission was," Melissa said. "This is a commission. Some people call them 'credentials.'"

"Oh," Caroline said. "It's like our badge."

"It's not a badge," Melissa said. "Because they won't let us carry guns."

She slapped the commission closed but did not return it to her purse. We followed her to the door. Rachel said, "Well, I'm disappointed about the gun thing. I kind of wanted to pack some heat." I heard Allison whisper to her, "Shhh. Melissa told us not to talk."

"I'm too busy fighting the urge to goosestep," Dee said.

We trooped into the dark-paneled foyer, furnished with soft leather chairs, a glass-topped coffee table, and potted palm trees. Muzak was piped through speakers hidden, it sounded, within the palms. I was inexplicably nervous. Melissa went directly to the receptionist, who sat behind a glass partition. Allison shadowed her, standing directly behind her while the rest of us hovered near the coffee table. Rachel picked up a magazine. Melissa said, "I'm here to see one of the partners."

"Which one?" the receptionist asked. She was smacking a piece of gum.

"I'd rather talk to the senior partner, if he's in."

"He's not in. How about an associate? There's about a billion of those around."

"It has to be an officer."

"Do you have an appointment?"

"I have this."

Melissa held up her commission. The receptionist's expression did not change, but she stopped smacking her gum.

"So tell me who's in."

"Mr. Paul is in court."

"I asked who was in."

"Mr. Paul handles the taxes. Would you like to make an appointment to see Mr. Paul?" She flipped through a calendar on the desk.

"No, I don't want an appointment with Mr. Paul. I want to see an officer. I asked who was in, not who is out."

"Who's on first," Rachel muttered. She was eyeing a recipe for chocolate truffles in the December issue of *Ladies' Home Journal*.

"Well, Mr. Newman is hardly ever here. He's about ninety years old, you know, but of course they keep his name on the door."

"What about Craig? Is Craig here?"

"Mr. Craig," the receptionist said. "His last name is Craig."

"I don't care if his last name is George Bush," Melissa said. "If he's an officer and if he's here, I need to see him. Right now."

"Let me check."

The receptionist picked up the phone. She pulled the wad of gum from her mouth and, presumably, dropped it into the trash can located somewhere underneath the desk. Melissa tapped the edge of her commission on the little ledge in front of her.

"Mr. Craig? Oh, you are in. There's someone here to see you. No, they don't have an appointment." She lowered her voice slightly. "It's the IRS." She listened for a moment. "All right, I'll tell them." She hung up and smiled at Melissa. "He'll be right out."

"Thanks."

Melissa had turned and taken one step toward the leather chairs when a door beside the receptionist's office flew open and a man lunged into the room. He was tall, athletic, perfectly tanned. His blue eyes sparkled as he extended his hand in Melissa's direction. Melissa raised the black leather-bound commission in her left hand while she accepted his hand in her right.

"Mr. Craig, I'm Revenue Officer Melissa Cavanaugh."

"Please, call me Bernie."

"I'm with the Internal Revenue Service."

"Pleasure to meet you, Melissa." He looked over her shoulder to us, still hovering around the coffee table.

"These are my associates," she said.

"Oh, your associates. Of course."

He took a step in our direction. Melissa said, "Is there someplace private we can talk?"

"Private? Sure. You mean, all of you?"

"Yes."

"Um, okay. How about our conference room? Would that be okay?"

"That's fine."

Melissa followed him through the door and we followed Melissa. Since I was covering the rear, I closed the door behind us. The entire office complex was blessed, it appeared, with the soothing, yet contemporary, sounds of Muzak. We followed Bernie Craig down a couple of halls, turning left, then right, then cutting back left again. Heads turned, people stopped what they were doing and stared. I fought the urge to whisper to one, "Class action suit," and thought that if I had not bolted from law school, this would be my milieu. I would be tan and fit and play golf three times a week and bill $75 per hour, just like Bernie Craig. Thus Bernie Craig was a cruel mockery of what I might have become. A Rolex glittered on his wrist; a plain gold ring shone on his left hand. His white shirt was pressed and starched and there was a diamond stud in his fourteen-carat tiepin and diamonds on his cuff links. The ornamentation on my tie was a mustard stain about the size of a dime.

We filed into a large room dominated by a huge mahogany table. Floor-to-ceiling bookshelves displayed the firm's law library. The plush carpeting was dark blue. Bernie Craig waved us toward the table.

"Have a seat, have a seat," he said. "Can I get anyone anything? We have soda, Perrier, coffee."

Rachel started to answer, and Melissa cut her off.

"No thanks."

"No? Nothing? All right then."

We sank into the leather armchairs. Bernie Craig's smile had not disappeared since he met us in the foyer. His teeth appeared to be capped and were brilliantly white.

"Jeez," he said. "I didn't know the IRS came with so much—force."

Melissa pulled a file from her briefcase.

"I mean," he said, eyes on Melissa. "You guys are a just short of a battalion."

Melissa opened the file and removed a computer printout. She studied it. Bernie Craig kept talking.

"I didn't know you guys just showed up like this. I mean, I thought only Publishers Clearinghouse and the Jehovah's Witnesses paid surprise visits. I don't remember getting any notices or anything. Don't you usually send a notice or something? I've gotten them in the past. But no one's ever showed up at the door. Not even one guy from the IRS. Is there some kind of trouble?"

"That's what you're gonna have to tell me," Melissa said.

"Maybe I should get Marie in here. She's the office manager."

He started to get up. Melissa said, "I don't need to see Marie, unless Marie is an officer. Is Marie an officer?"

"No, Marie is not an officer."

"I need to speak with an officer."

"We seem to be doing a lot of that, but we're not saying very much. Do you mind telling me why you're here, Ms. Cavanaugh?"

Now he was getting down to it, though the dazzling smile remained fixed, masklike, and the blue eyes danced. He was accustomed to deposing hardened criminals and corporate big shots. He wasn't about to let this skinny, big-haired pencil-pusher from the IRS get the best of him.

"I'm here because of the payroll taxes."

"We're all paid up, as far as I know."

"We monitor your federal tax deposits, and our records indicate a significant drop in the fourth quarter."

"The last quarter?"

"Yes, Mr. Craig. The fourth quarter of anything would be the last quarter."

Point for Cavanaugh. Bernie Craig said, "Like I said, our office manager handles the tax deposits. Why are you monitoring our deposits?"

"We monitor everybody's deposits."

"Well, of course you do."

"And when there is a change, we want to know why."

"That's very thorough."

"We want to know why you're not depositing the same amount."

"Well, all I can say is our liability usually goes up in the fourth quarter. That's the quarter we pay out bonuses."

"Your deposits are twelve thousand dollars less than the third quarter."

"For the fourth quarter?"

"Yes, Mr. Craig, for the fourth quarter—isn't that the quarter we've been talking about?" She had removed a pen from her purse, but had made no notes. She slapped the pen down on the desk.

"I think you better bring your records in here."

"What records?"

"Your payroll records."

"Why, are you auditing me?"

"This isn't an audit. I'm a revenue officer, not a tax examiner. I want to see your payroll records to verify you aren't twelve thousand dollars in the hole for the fourth quarter."

"If you're a revenue officer, who are these people?" He waved a hand in our direction. "And why don't they say anything? It's really starting to give me the creeps, to tell you the truth."

"Are you refusing to let me see your payroll records?"

"I don't recall refusing to let you see anything."

"Because if you are refusing, I can issue a summons to produce them. I have one right here in my briefcase."

"Ms. Cavanaugh, I would be happy to show you the records. Can I have five minutes?"

"In a minute," Melissa said. "I wanted to ask you about your personal taxes."

"My personal taxes?"

"Your 1040 taxes."

"I know what personal taxes are."

"Are you current?"

"What's that mean?"

"Have you filed and paid?"

"Yes."

"Is there any year that you haven't filed or paid?"

"Of course not."

"What's your Social Security number?"

"Why do you want my Social Security number?"

"To verify you've filed and paid your personal income taxes."

"I thought you were here about the payroll taxes."

"We're required to address *all* taxes with everyone we contact."

"Even the mailman? Never mind. I'm just giving you a hard time. Fun, isn't it? That was rhetorical." He told her his Social Security number and left the room.

"You see his face when I asked for his SSN?" she asked us. "They all think they're so fucking smart."

"Who thinks they're smart?" Caroline asked.

"Lawyers," Melissa said. "We like to catch 'em quick."

"Lawyers?" Rachel asked.

"Taxpayers. Any collector will tell you the quicker you can get to 'em, the more you'll collect. So the Service tracks payroll tax deposits. If the deposits drop off suddenly, it issues an FTD Alert to the field for a revenue officer to take early intervention. If there's a problem, we're there at the beginning, not after all the assets are gone and there's no hope of collecting."

"So we're like the shock troops," Rachel said.

"I got no idea what that means," Melissa said.

Bernie Craig reentered the room with a ledger book in his hands. He set it before Melissa and slipped back into his chair without saying a word. For the next twenty minutes she quizzed him about the size of the firm's payroll, how the bonuses were recorded, who was responsible for getting the money deposited through the bank. She had removed a form from her briefcase and was asking him questions, fired like bullets toward his smooth brown forehead. Who were the officers? Did he know their Social Security numbers? Who signed the payroll checks? Were taxes ever discussed in meetings and, if they were, what was discussed? Did he have the authority to hire and fire employees? Who signed the tax returns? Who reviewed them? Who prepared them?

He finally interrupted her. His cheerful, commanding veneer was wearing thin. He was frustrated that she refused to speak to Marie, the one person in the office who could clear up the matter in minutes.

"May I ask why we're going into all this right now?"

"I'm trying to figure out who is responsible for paying the taxes."

"I'll save you some time. I am. I'm responsible."

"Because we'll come after you, too."

"Come after me?"

"You personally. You. Your assets. Your stuff, like that Rolex on your wrist right there. We can assess the taxes your business withheld from the employees against you personally and seize your assets."

"You are—you're going to seize my Rolex?"

"I didn't say that. I said we could, if we have to."

"Believe me, you won't have to."

Melissa shrugged. She returned to the payroll records. Bernie Craig abruptly rose from his chair and sped from the room.

"What's the matter, is he sick?" Caroline asked.

He returned in a moment with a manila folder that he slapped in front of Melissa.

"I should have thought of this right away," he said. "See, we've already filed the fourth quarter. We filed it early, and here's a copy. See? Everything matches."

"That doesn't answer my question," Melissa said. "Why have the deposits dropped?"

"Your question is moot. We don't owe anything."

"I can't leave here until I know. You said yourself your payroll is usually higher in the fourth quarter." She slapped the ledger book closed.

Bernie Craig blinked rapidly. The smile was completely gone now. The tie was loose around his neck. He seemed to have developed a twitch in his left hand; his buffed fingernails slid back and forth across the varnished table.

"I don't have an explanation," he said slowly. He appealed to us trainees silently with his devastatingly blue eyes. "All I know is this is the tax on the return and this is the total of our deposits. We don't owe anything for the fourth quarter. That's all I know."

"But I know what you said."

"What I said?"

"I know you said you paid bonuses in the fourth quarter, but on this return the liability is actually lower than the third quarter."

"Okay. I'll grant you that."

"And so I have to know—why?"

"Maybe we fired somebody. Maybe somebody got demoted. Like I said, I don't handle personnel issues."

"But you are aware of the bonuses."

"Bonuses?"

Melissa heaved an exaggerated sigh. "Did you get a bonus last year, Mr. Craig?"

"Yes."

"And the other partners?"

"Of course."

"You're a lawyer, you're pretty smart, you gotta understand what I'm getting at."

He nodded. I watched him nod and was glad he understood, because I had no idea what she was getting at.

"And I take offense at the suggestion, Ms. Cavanaugh."

"I'm not trying to offend you. I'm trying to get an answer to a simple question: Why did the taxes go down and what part of those taxes reflect these huge bonuses?"

"Now wait a minute. That's two questions, and I never said the bonuses were huge."

"Well, I guess there's only one way I'm gonna find out."

She reached into her briefcase and I watched as Bernie Craig's tan bled from his face. He looked like he was going to be sick.

"This is a summons to appear before me, in my office, and produce the complete bank records for the business for the last three months of 1990," Melissa said as her hand flew across the form. "If you choose not to appear and do not file a motion to quash in federal court, we will enforce the summons before a magistrate, at which time if you still choose to deny us the records, we will throw you in jail for contempt."

"First my Rolex and now jail time? Jesus Christ, the return shows we don't owe anything!"

"Exactly," Melissa said. "And the Service wants to know why."

I expected him to come over the table at her, but he rallied the charm instead. He acquiesced, promising to deliver the bank records precisely on his appearance date. Somehow, Melissa had beaten him down. He was ready to be led to the wall. He was ready for the blindfold.

On the way back to the office, Rachel asked her, "So what did you do before you worked for the IRS?"

Melissa shrugged. "Finished high school."

③

DANCE LESSONS

We spent the majority of "pre-Phase" training in the conference room, plowing through the training booklet, or enduring incomprehensible lectures from Cindy and Melissa.

Melissa: "Documentation is everything. Document, document, document. If it isn't in your case history, it didn't happen. If it didn't happen, you didn't do it. If you didn't do it, you failed to do it."

Cindy: "We work with two basic kinds of assignments: TDAs and TDIs. TDA is Taxpayer Delinquency Accounts—the tax has been assessed and you must collect it. TDI is Taxpayer Delinquency Investigation—no returns have been filed and you must secure them or verify they don't have to be filed. The easy way to remember it is TDA means money and TDI means returns."

Melissa: "Shred every day. Shred everything. And don't let your shredding pile up in a drawer. Never leave anything on your desk with taxpayer information on it. That's disclosure. Disclosure will get you into big trouble. And be careful around that shredder. It's about four hundred fucking years old and it will suck your fingers in, rip them right off your hand. Rick better be real careful. A revenue agent leaned over to grab a stack of paper by the shredder and it ate his tie. Almost pulled his head into the shredder."

Cindy: "Remember the three Cs in 'collection.' Cause, cure, compliance. Cause: What did the TP do—or not do—to fall behind or not file? Cure: What can the TP do—or you do—to bring the taxpayer back into compliance? Compliance: Is the TP current? If it's a business, are the owners current? Is every entity they have an interest in current? Check everything, across the board."

Melissa: "Always make demand. Demand, demand, demand. Don't write in your history: 'Asked TP to pay.' Always write, '*Demanded* full-pay.' That's how I begin every history: 'Issued Pub 1* and demanded full-pay.' "

Cindy: A lien is automatic. It arises as a matter of law after the tax goes unpaid for ten days. A *Notice* of Federal Tax Lien is a document filed in the county courthouse that perfects our lien, the lien that already exists . . . out there. Out there in, I don't know, limbo somewhere. A lien is not a levy. Sometimes a TP will call in and say, 'You put a lien on my bank account!' No, you placed a *levy* on his bank account. The NFTL† attaches to everything; a levy is specific. Bank account, wages, savings, tangible assets—that would be a seizure, though it's still a levy. Seizures are levies but not all levies are seizures, though technically we are seizing the actual money in the bank account. The lien grabs anything and everything the taxpayer owns now or in the future, but it doesn't do anything with it. The lien just sits there, at the courthouse, letting everybody know we're in there, like a mortgage or a judgment, but those people have to go to court to enforce their interest; we don't. We just go in and levy the assets under the authority of our lien. Though you don't need a lien down to issue a levy to a bank account, say, or someone's wages, because the statutory lien is floating around out there. So don't get confused about liens or levies. Levy, lien. Lien, levy. You'll get it straight."

At home, Pam asked how it was going.

"I really don't know."

"What do you mean? How can you not know?"

"I don't know because I don't have a clue what we're doing."

"Rick, why are you wasting your time with this? You're like an elephant taking flying lessons."

I decided to ignore the remark. "How many Cs in collection?" I asked.

---

* Publication 1: Your Rights as a Taxpayer.
† Notice of Federal Tax Lien.

"What?"

"How many Cs are there in collection?"

"Two."

"You're wrong. In the IRS, there are three Cs in collection. And did you know that a tax lien floats around in limbo, that there's a purgatory for tax liens? Then you have your liens that don't float. They stick. Stick and grab. Sticky, grabby liens, leeching onto everything you have."

"I hate taxes," she said.

"I'm staying at least through Phase One."

"It's a waste of time."

"But they're paying me a helluva lot of money just to sit there and be bored and confused."

"Okay. I can see the appeal of that."

"Are you coming with me to Tampa?"

"Why the hell would I do that?"

"It might be fun."

"Look, Rick, you chose to get into this. I told you not to and you did it anyway. This is your gig, not mine."

"Just a suggestion. I'll only be home on the weekends, you know."

"Fine. But if I find out you've screwed any of those weirdos, I'll super-glue your dick to your leg."

JANUARY 29, 1991, IRS TRAINING CENTER, TAMPA

Byron Samuels, Chief of Collection for the Jacksonville District, opened Revenue Office Unit 1 Basic Training with these remarks:

"I just wanted to take this opportunity to welcome all of you on board. This is an exciting time for the Service, the most ambitious and massive hiring initiative we've ever undertaken and I know you won't disappoint us."

We were sitting in a large classroom, two to a table. Caroline was my tablemate. She had brought a plastic hotel cup filled with grapes with her. For someone so thin, Caroline was constantly eating. Seated directly in front of us were Rachel and Allison. Dee sat in the front of the room beside one of the new-hires from Tampa. The majority of the trainees in this room were fresh from college, making Rachel and me two of the oldest people in the room.

"When you return to your PODs* in March, you will have forty cases sitting on your desk waiting for you. You're gonna feel lost, confused, overwhelmed, and, some of you, very, very afraid. By this time next year, if you trust the statistics, half of you will no longer be employed by the Service. But I promise those of you who will be, as a former RO myself, if you stick with it, if you hang on through the training year, you'll find this the most challenging and rewarding work you could ever hope to find. I guarantee that. The first few months are gonna be tough. We make them tough, because we want tough people in the job. We want bright, yes. We want ambitious, yes. But we also want tough. We want tough because without tough our entire government collapses."

Byron Samuels was about sixty, with a bone-white crew cut and thick horn-rimmed glasses, wearing a wrinkled short-sleeve shirt and speaking barely above a whisper. He was a living legend within the Service. Brilliant, mercurial, eccentric, he once told his managers, "You gotta get out once in a while or you'll go nuts. I'm never hanging a manager out to dry for jumping into the car every now and then and doing ninety on the highway." A devout teetotaler, he cursed like a sailor in private meetings, we heard, often berating his underlings until they fled the room in tears.

"Basic Training will teach you the fundamentals of the job," he said. "The mechanics. That is, the 'how,' not the 'why.' *Why* do we do things the way we do them? Because our tax system is based, in theory at least, on self-assessment and voluntary compliance. That's the first two rails of our system: self-assessment and voluntary compliance. They are interrelated, in that you can't have self-assessment without voluntary compliance and you can't have voluntary compliance without self-assessment. I suppose, being 3.5s, you all can guess what the 'third rail' of our tax system is." He flashed a smile. "Enforcement. You. Without you, our system collapses. Because no matter how fair the system is, no matter how much resources and energy we pour into education and taxpayer service, there has been

---

* Posts-of-Duty.

and there always will be a portion of the population who will not pay."

He smiled again. This smile lasted at least fifteen seconds.

"So. Make 'em pay."

Sam Mason, our lead instructor, had been with the Service for fifteen years. His reputation was sterling as a technician and scandalous as a playboy. Even in the brisk Florida winters, he favored Hawaiian shirts that displayed his copious chest hair. He liked to brag that he never slept. In 1981, before the advent of airbags, he slammed his car into a light pole, suffering severe injuries to his head and neck. Those who knew him before the accident said the portion of his brain that governed personality had been permanently damaged. He spent his evenings, after the bars closed, at a twenty-four-hour restaurant, where he drank coffee until dawn and hit on the waitresses. Several clerks now with the Service owed their jobs to Sam Mason. He considered himself a creative person or, as he put it, a "right-brainer in a left-brained job." He painted. He sculpted. He wrote poetry. During the second week of Phase One, he drew me aside and said, "I hear you're a writer. I want to show you something." He pulled a tiny square piece of paper and carefully unfolded it. "It's better if you read it aloud," he said. "But probably not a good idea in here." It was an erotic poem to his latest conquest. The first lines ran: "As I lower my face / Between your wide-spread thighs."

"Well, what do you think?" he asked. He seemed eager to hear my opinion. "I really struggled with that second line. I had 'betwixt' before I changed it to 'between.' Don't you think 'betwixt' is too archaic?"

"You don't hear it very often," I said.

"But you hear the phrase, 'betwixt and between.' What the hell does that phrase mean anyway? So you like it?"

"You know," I said. "Emily Dickinson used to fold her poems into tiny squares like that."

"Really?" He seemed thrilled he had something in common with Emily Dickinson. "Didn't she try to kill herself or something?"

Dee, with an undergraduate degree in psychology, diagnosed Sam as "bipolar." She didn't have enough training or experience, she said, to know if his disorder had anything to do with the accident.

Sam's co-instructor was Larry Simon. Larry Simon was something called an Offer-in-Compromise Specialist. During Phase One, I was never entirely clear on exactly what Offer-In-Compromise Specialists did, except that they seemed to spend a lot of time inside people's houses, pawing through their drawers. Larry liked to tell the story of finding a $50,000 check rolled up in a pair of socks, thus thwarting the taxpayer's plan to put one over on the Service. On the first day of class, after Bryon Samuels's speech, Larry played a homemade video for us starring Mister Bill from *Saturday Night Live*. Mister Bill was a taxpayer (the revenue officer was a voice-over part, played with strained ferocity by Larry Simon). The scenario was a seizure of Mister Bill's car: "Oohhhh noooo, Mister Taxman, please don't take my car. Ahhhhhhh!" Larry liked white short-sleeve shirts and wore colorful clip-on neckties. He punctuated his lectures by bouncing on the balls of his feet. "When we file a Notice of Federal Tax Lien [*bounce*], we have perfected [*bounce*] our lien interest [*bounce, bounce*]. We have made our lien *choate* [*bounce, bounce, bounce*]." Behind his back, we called him Tigger. He was a fixture at the bars we haunted each night after class. His taste ran to the over-thirty set, which severely limited his chances, given the average age of our class was twenty-four. He liked Rachel, called her his "honey-pie," but Rachel did not return his affections. "What a freak," she said, watching him on the dance floor, still in his short-sleeve shirt and clip-on necktie, gyrating his widening hips across from Crystal, the former Tampa Bay Bucs cheerleader.

"He's creepy," Dee agreed. She was sitting next to me, drinking a piña colada, slowly.

"Rick," Rachel leaned over and whispered, "why don't you dance with Dee?"

"Because I can't dance," I said.

"I don't believe that."

"I don't like to dance. I never know what to do next."

"Rachel," Dee said, "Rick is engaged."

"Rick is engaged in word only."

"I won't dance with my fiancée either."

"Why not? Larry would."

"Larry would dance with a corpse," Dee said.

"Why won't Pam come over and stay for a couple nights?" Rachel asked.

"She has a full-time job, Rachel."

I had asked her to. Her reply: "Why would I want to party with those weirdos?"

Larry returned to our table, trailing Crystal. Crystal was a native of Tennessee and was fond of miniskirts and low-cut blouses that accentuated her perfect tan. Crystal frightened me. Tall, with angular, masculine features, her body was gym-hardened and constantly on display. In the coming year, she would be counseled repeatedly for showing up at work wearing what most people would consider more appropriate for a streetwalker.

"Whew!" Larry said. "This girl will wear you *out*."

He winked at Rachel. "What about it, Rachel? You want a turn? The night is young."

"But you're not, Larry," Rachel said. "You look like you're about to have a heart attack."

"Bullshit! I feel great! I feel just great!" He drummed on the tabletop. *Tap-tap, tap-tap-tap-tap, tap-tap.* "I'm the kinda guy who can go all night." With another wink at Rachel.

"Larry," Dee said, "you're the kind of guy who talks in bad song lyrics."

I laughed. Dee turned to me, smiling. Our eyes met. She arched one thin eyebrow. I grabbed my drink and finished it in a single swallow. I was not attracted to her. She struck me as boyish, with her short haircut and freckly nose. Rachel whispered something to Dee, who did not respond.

"What's the matter with Rick?" Larry asked. "All these lovely ladies and he hasn't danced once."

"Rick can't dance," Rachel said. "But Dee's going to teach him how."

"Oh, that isn't dancing," Larry said, jerking his head toward the dance floor. "That's air-fucking."

"You *are* desperate," Rachel said.

o   o   o

Much of our time in class was devoted to the mechanics of filling out the dozens of forms the IRS relied on to keep millions of taxpayer accounts in order. Sam would remind us, though, that only three documents closed a

case that we could not collect in full: Form 433-D, used to set up installment agreements; Form 3870, used to abate taxes and penalties; and Form
53, used to report taxes as currently not collectible. "But don't get caught
up in all these damn forms," he admonished us. "It isn't how you fill out
forms. A Grade Three clerk can fill out a form. We're paying you for your
judgment, not how well you can fill out a form."

Our training followed a student guide constructed by a team of upper-
level analysts in Washington. Each lesson—or *module*—was illustrated by
a case scenario, followed by a series of questions, such as "How would you
close this case?" "Which asset should have been addressed before closing
the case as CNC?*" "Should the NFTL be filed in this case? How does filing, or nonfiling, the lien affect the outcome?" Modules had titles such
as "Initial Contact," "Lien Priorities," and "Enforcement Tools." Sam
described the ideal taxpayer contact: introduce yourself, give Publication
One, make demand, secure all the necessary financial information, set a
deadline, enforce when the deadline was missed. It sounded simple. I
stopped taking notes. Repeatedly Sam, Larry, and the material referred us
to the Internal Revenue Manual, a thousand-page-plus document, the
Bible of the IRS, derived from Title 26, the Internal Revenue Code.

"It's all in the manual," I whispered to Caroline one morning during
our second week.

"What is?" She was eating a doughnut. The glaze shone on her sharp
chin.

"How we do things."

"What things?"

I gave up.

"Be careful how you explain CNC to a TP," Sam said. "Make sure the
taxpayer understands we aren't writing off or forgiving the debt. The debt
remains. The interest continues to run until the statute blows." He was
referring to the statute of limitations on collecting back taxes. Under the
law, the IRS has ten years to collect on its assessments.

Sam enjoyed relieving the tedium by telling war stories from his years
in the trenches. Once a taxpayer had jabbed his finger in Sam's face and

* Currently-Not-Collectible.

snarled at him, "Next time you show up at my door, Mason, you better bring a fucking army with you." So the next time he called, Sam brought some buddies from the National Guard, dressed in full uniform. "Hi!" he said. "I'm back, and I brought the fucking army with me." He was full of helpful tips, too: "When no one answers the door I drop my card for them to call in at eight o'clock the next morning. When they don't call, at eight-fifteen I've got the levy in the mail."

By law, the IRS cannot levy assets without first giving the taxpayer a "final notice," either delivered by hand or sent to the last known address by certified mail. It was common practice, though not mandated by any regulation or the Manual, for a revenue officer to issue final notice before even meeting with the taxpayer. "Because," Sam explained, "we are paid to close cases. If you wait thirty days to make contact, then issue a thirty-day notice, you've wasted two whole months. Issue the final notice on initial receipt and you've shaved thirty days off the life of the case." This reflected the Service's obsession with "overage," those cases that had been in the field more than twelve months. Revenue officers were under constant pressure to close cases and close them quickly. Those who quickly "rolled over" their inventories were promoted over those who anguished over each closure, as if their decision meant life or death for the taxpayer.

"But it does sometimes, doesn't it?" Rachel asked.

"Doesn't it what?" Sam asked.

"Life or death. I mean, is it about closing a case or doing the right thing for the taxpayer?"

"Doing the right thing for the taxpayer? Rachel, we don't work for the taxpayer. One of the critical elements of your job is 'protecting the government's interest.' You are a federal agent, not a public advocate."

"But what if the government's interest is wrong?"

"Our interest is never wrong or right. It just *is*. A defense attorney doesn't question the guilt or innocence of his client—that's irrelevant. The Service is paying you to be its zealous advocate."

During a break, Rachel announced, "Sam can say what he wants. I can't be a zealous advocate if it means hurting people."

"They made their own bed, Rachel," Allison said. "And it's not fair. I pay my taxes."

"I see my job as trying to help them get straight with Uncle Sam."

"Service," Dee said. "It's still in our name."

Sam also supplied supplemental material to enrich our basic training experience. One little booklet was entitled *Assaults & Threats: A Guide for Your Personal Safety*. The title was printed in bright red ink. At the bottom of the cover was the disclaimer, common on many internal forms: CAUTION: THIS DOCUMENT IS FOR CONFIDENTIAL USE OF INTERNAL REVENUE SERVICE EMPLOYEES ONLY. As if we had been given Top Secret Clearance and to leak the information might be a breach of national security. The book contained helpful tidbits such as, "Upon entering the residence or business, be alert to your surroundings. Look for exits, windows, and potential weapons. In a rural setting, it may be perfectly normal to have a rifle, shotgun, or other weapon in the house. A weapon elsewhere should be a warning to you." And, "Consider ending the interview if the taxpayer remains hostile." And, "Remove objects such as ashtrays, staplers, and other taxpayer files from the room when interviewing a taxpayer in an IRS office. Sit near the exit so you can escape if trouble occurs." The book proposed nine simple rules for not getting yourself killed:

TREAT ALL TAXPAYERS FAIRLY AND COURTEOUSLY

DO NOT PERSONALIZE COLLECTION EFFORTS

LISTEN CAREFULLY

DO NOT THREATEN, SCOLD, OR PATRONIZE

RECOGNIZE YOUR OWN ATTITUDES AND ELIMINATE THOSE THAT ARE
    COUNTERPRODUCTIVE

TREAT TAXPAYERS AS YOU WOULD WANT TO BE TREATED

KNOW WHERE THE EXITS ARE

AVOID GETTING TRAPPED

USE FORCE ONLY SUFFICIENT TO DISENGAGE

"These are, of course," Sam concluded, "also the rules for marriage."

Investigative Techniques. Potentially Dangerous Taxpayers. Effective Inventory Management. Disclosure. Superpriorities. Discharge & Subordination of the Fed-

eral Tax Lien. Seizure & Sale. There were times in class when I was totally lost, repeating to myself, "It's all in the manual. It's all in the manual." I spent some evenings in my hotel room, pouring over the lesson, working through the problems. *Establishing Equity. Securing the Financial Statement. Interview Techniques.* A test loomed at the end of the three weeks. It was never explicitly stated, but somehow understood that if you did not pass the test, you would not be returning to your post-of-duty. Sam: "During the first year you are considered a conditional employee. The Service can fire you whenever they like for whatever reason they like." I was determined to pass the test. I had always prided myself on my academic skills; it was just in real life that I was averaging a C-. *Suit to Set Aside a Fraudulent Conveyance. Suit to Foreclose the Notice of Federal Tax Lien. Suit to Enforce a Notice of Levy. Nominee, Transferee & Alter Ego Doctrine.* That's exactly what I needed to implement: an alter ego doctrine. Success would not ride on whether I could pretend to be someone I'm not; I must find the part of me that already *was* a revenue officer.

Foreclosure & Right of Redemption. That was it. A right of redemption. That's all I wanted. An opportunity to learn the dance.

March was unusually warm that year. One afternoon, the temperature hit eighty degrees. Over lunch, plans were laid to hit the hotel pool immediately after class.

"I didn't bring my suit," Allison said.

"You can wear one of mine," Dee offered.

"Excuse me, but I don't think it would fit," Allison said.

"I didn't bring a suit either," I said. The thought of swimming with people who were practically strangers to me was abhorrent.

"I can't swim," Rachel said.

"Oh, Rachel, you can swim," said Allison.

"No, I really can't. I'm so fat I sink right to the bottom."

Dee said, "Rachel just skinny-dips."

"*Shhh,*" Rachel said. "Only Larry's supposed to know."

"I bet Larry has something you could wear, Rick," Allison said.

"He probably has two or three extra pairs of Speedos lying around," Dee said.

"Larry's swimming trunks are clip-on, like his ties," Rachel said. That broke everyone up. I felt a hand on my knee, a quick squeeze, and the hand was gone.

Dee.

I watched a movie in my room and ate Chinese takeout. I called home during a commercial and got the answering machine. I was dozing off, cartons piled around me on the bed, when the phone rang.

"Rick? Hi, this is Dee."

"Hi."

"I'm sorry, were you sleeping?"

"No."

"Oh, good. Hey listen, everybody's meeting in my room for pizza, you wanna come?"

"Thanks, but I just ate."

"Rachel's bringing daiquiri mix and Caroline is bringing Twister."

"I'm sorry, she's bringing what?"

"Twister. You know, the game, Twister."

"Why would Caroline bring Twister to training?"

"Come on, it'll be fun. You know how important it is for us to bond."

I tried calling Pam again. My own voice on the answering machine enraged me. I hung up the phone without leaving a message. I smoked a cigarette and walked about the room in the nude. I would never smoke inside Pam's house—or walk around nude in it. I wondered why the Service spent so much money to bring everyone to Tampa for three weeks, paying our room and board and our transportation, when it would have been much easier—and cheaper—to train us in our individual PODs. When I lived in Chicago, the Moonies occupied a building at the end of my block, a kind of combination commune and recruiting center. One friendly Moonie stopped me regularly to gently ask if I wanted to watch a movie with them that night or share a hot meal. They wanted to draw me inside, cut me off from my friends and family, so *they* could become my friends and family. Already in class, we fell into the strange language of the Service, without realizing it. *Do we file the NFTL on every account we CNC? If the TP isn't coded PDT, do we use a 4844 to input the TC?* Why did the Service use code words, when the real words would do just as well? Why did we say "MFT" when we meant "return"? Why did we say "NFTL" when we meant "tax lien"? Everything was encoded, encrypted, "for official, confidential use only." Why was that? January 13, 1991, was not my starting date or my first day on the job; it was my *EOD*, my "Entrance-on-Date." What the hell did "Entrance-on-Date" mean? We were learning a second language, the odd nomenclature of Byzantium, where even taxes we collected weren't called "taxes" but "modules." Where no one else could understand us and where anyone from the outside would be, by custom, language, and tradition, a foreigner.

"You're being paranoid," I told my thin, naked reflection in the closet mirror. Then, with bitterly satisfying self-deprecation: "Hey, didn't I see you in an appeal for famine relief?"

I dressed quickly and took the elevator up two flights to Dee's room.

She answered the door wearing a leopard-print robe. She was barefoot. Her hair was still wet from the pool. She was alone.

"Where is everyone?" I asked.

"Allison's not coming," she said. "Has a headache. And Rachel is always late for everything. I haven't heard from Caroline. You want something to drink?"

She waved me toward the sofa. Dee had a suite with a gas fireplace. "It's over per diem," she had said. "But I figure for ten extra bucks, why not a fireplace?" I sat on the sofa while she stepped into the kitchenette and rummaged in the refrigerator.

"How was the pool?"

"Great. I just got back. I was just about to jump into the shower."

I stood up. "Okay. Well, I'll just go back to my room and when Rachel—"

"That's crazy. You just got here."

She handed me a glass of white wine. I did not drink wine, but decided this was not the moment to tell her that. I set the glass on the coffee table. Dee collapsed on the sofa beside me.

"God, don't you love it, how your body feels after a swim? Soooo relaxed."

Her robe had come open, exposing the length of her left leg, sitting four inches away from mine. She stretched, arching her back, her long arms over her head. I had not been the object of many seductions, but I had seen enough movies and read enough books to know when I was in the middle of one. I saw the phone sitting at my elbow and grabbed the receiver.

"I'll call Rachel and see what's keeping her."

"Are you nervous, Rick?"

"Constantly."

"You're an intellectual."

"Huh?"

"Intellectuals are nervous people. Intellectuals are never in the moment. They're always thinking. You know I'm attracted to you. Everyone's noticed. Even Caroline's noticed, and she hardly notices anything."

"*I* didn't notice."

"Are you in love with Pam?"

"I'm engaged to Pam."

"I think you just answered my question. Some men think I'm too skinny."

"Some people think I am too."

"Oh, I like lean men. Allison said you used to be a cowboy."

"Not in the traditional sense. I never rode a horse or roped a steer or—"

"Rachel has a theory you might be gay."

"I'm not gay."

"I didn't think you were. But her theory goes your relationship with Pam is just a cover."

"No. I have a real relationship with Pam."

"Are you attracted to me?"

"I—I don't really know you, Dee."

"I didn't ask if you knew me or not. I asked if you were attracted to me."

At that moment, mercifully, the phone rang. I yanked it up. It was Rachel.

"Where's Dee?" she asked.

"Right here," I said. Dee took my free hand and pressed my knuckles to her lips. "Where's the daiquiris?"

"What daiquiris?"

"Just as I thought," I said into the phone. "A setup. Did Caroline bring Twister to training?"

"Bring what?"

Dee released my hand. "Give me the phone," she snapped. "Rachel, I've got to call you back." She handed the phone back to me. "She's not there," she said when I put it to my ear. I hung up the phone and stood up.

"I've got to go," I said. "I don't want to hurt your feelings." Always the good student, I was applying something I had learned from class: DO NOT THREATEN, SCOLD, OR PATRONIZE.

RECOGNIZE YOUR OWN ATTITUDES AND ELIMINATE THOSE THAT ARE COUNTERPRODUCTIVE: "I guess I'm just a loyal person." AVOID GETTING TRAPPED. I headed for the door. KNOW WHERE THE EXITS ARE.

"No," she said. "A loyal person wouldn't have come here in the first place."

I never told Pam about my encounter with Dee. I never told anyone. Dee and I did not speak of it, not in the four years we worked together in the Service. That was fine with me. I could think of no worse fate than falling in love with someone who worked, as I did, for the Internal Revenue Service. I didn't realize at the time, however, that within the Service there are far worse temptations than those of the flesh, and that love, wherever we might find it, often proves to be our only hope of salvation.

THE PRINCE OF POWER

On the morning of our return from Phase One training, Gina summoned Allison and me to her office for a private conference. She was
wearing a black dress, black hose and black soft-soled Rockport shoes. "I
have terrible feet," she had explained to the puzzled women of the office.
She wore a diamond-encrusted pin over her right breast: an Egyptian
scarab. Gina was fond of jewelry that drew its inspiration from the insect
world. Crueler tongues than mine made reference to her large, protruding
eyes as having a decidedly entomological slant, hence her affinity for wearing bugs on her breasts. Others said it had nothing to do with her appearance: wearing insect-inspired jewelry was a form of religious expression,
Gina being a Wiccan, a modern-day witch. The Wiccan rumor was persistent and altogether baseless, the dyed-black hair, black clothes, and the
onyx spider ring notwithstanding.

"Melissa is gone," she said. She did not elaborate. "I'm reassigning
both of you to Culpepper."

Allison and I exchanged an apprehensive glance. We had met William
Culpepper on our first day and had seen him occasionally before we shipped
off to Tampa, but had not spoken more than five minutes with him. Melissa
had told us to avoid him. My foremost impression of him was that he was
an extremely snappy dresser. He was, at least in Florida, a living legend inside
the Service, having made his bones early in his career by taking down five
car salesmen in a bribery case. The case had involved undercover surveil-
lance, midnight dead-drops, phone taps, and hidden microphones, and

resulted in prison time for the offenders. Culpepper was destined for great-
ness, a rising star. His reputation for technical expertise was exceeded only
by his reputation for bureaucratic brutality.

"He isn't happy about being assigned to you," Gina added.

"Why?" Allison asked. She was the more aggressive of the two of us. I
had no personal experience in the matter, but I was of the opinion you
don't get into the face of a Wiccan.

"Culpepper wants to move into management," Gina said. "Being an
OJI is a step down for him. But I've made him promise to refrain from
taking it out on you guys. Anyway, he's waiting for you now, in the conference room."

Her words rang in my head as I followed Allison down the hall to the
conference room: *I've made him promise to refrain from taking it out on you.* I
was consumed with envy of our fellow trainees, assigned to the gentle, if
somewhat obtuse, Cindy Sandifer. And what was the deal with Melissa?
Like so many things that happened inside the Service, there were few facts
and many rumors. One rumor had it that she had had a disastrous romance
with an IRS middle manager. Another that she couldn't bear to be separated
from her on-again, off-again bartender boyfriend named Butch, who lived
in Tampa. Who knew? Everyone seemed to and nobody confessed to.
Knowledge is power and, as I was about to learn, power is everything.

Culpepper was sitting at the head of the large conference table. Before him
were two stacks of blue file folders, each about two feet high: our cases. I
felt something about the size of a grapefruit rise in my throat. He rose
upon our entrance. He seemed taller than his five feet ten inches, probably
because he held himself so stiffly erect and his body had been hardened
from his four-hour daily workouts. Culpepper's passion was bodybuilding,
his profession mind-molding. His uniform that morning consisted of suit
by Brooks Brothers, tie by Armani, shoes by Nunn Bush, hair gel by Sas-
soon. His nails shone from a fresh manicure. He waved us toward the
chairs but he himself remained standing. He slid one stack of file folders
before Allison and another stack in front of me. Then, with no preamble
whatsoever, he said, "I don't intend to teach you anything. What you need
to know about tradecraft can be easily learned by reading the manual,

reviewing your training material, or consulting with SPf.* In this sense, 'instructor' is a misnomer. I am your trainer. My job is to prepare you to succeed. Whether you actually succeed is, of course, entirely up to you."

He paced around the table as he talked, completing a circuit, pausing at the head of the table, his starting point, then beginning again, moving in the opposite direction. He reminded me of Robert De Niro as Al Capone in *The Untouchables*, circling the dining table with the baseball bat.

"I've read your personnel files. I have every confidence one of you has what it takes to make an outstanding revenue officer. About the other, I have my doubts." He gave no indication who he thought was doomed. I felt he didn't need to. My face burned with shame even as Allison turned her eyes toward me. She felt he didn't need to either. "But I've been wrong before. Once. These are your cases. As you know, you only have thirty days to make initial contact on each. That isn't much time. You'll have one hour to choose the five that need immediate contact, and then we go."

"Go where?" Allison had the temerity to ask.

"To the field."

"We're going to the field . . . today?"

"We hired you to be field officers," Culpepper said. "If you wanted to sit behind a desk and talk on the phone you should have applied for ACS."† He resumed his route around the table. "As you review these cases, I want you to keep one thing in the forefront of your mind: you are a revenue officer now. Whatever you were on the outside before you came here doesn't exist anymore. You are a revenue officer. What does that mean? That means you are the last stop on the line. There is no step in the system after the revenue officer. Keep in mind that these people have had many opportunities to resolve their tax issues before their case landed in your inventory. We've sent them notices, we've mailed them letters, we've called them on the phone, and still they are waiting for us—they are waiting for *you*. And you are going to give them exactly what they expect."

Allison spoke. "What do they expect?"

---

* Special Procedures function: technical wizards in district headquarters consisting of experts in various subject matters.

† Automated Collection Service.

He paused, turned his icy-blue eyes upon her, and she actually flinched. I caught myself sinking lower into my chair and willed myself to sit erect.

"When I first came on board, a senior revenue officer took me aside and showed me a sign someone had made. He kept this sign hidden in his desk, because if it was seen outside his desk he would have been reprimanded. You will learn there are things you may say and things you may not say, and it is those things you may not say that are the essence of your work here."

He sat at the head of the table and laced his fingers together. The silence dragged out until I couldn't take it any longer.

"What did the sign say?" I asked.

"It was entitled 'The Four Protocols,'" Culpepper said, still looking at Allison. "They are the rules that we may not say." He counted the Four Protocols on his fingers. "Find where they are. Track what they do. Learn what they have. Execute what they fear."

William Culpepper was a native Floridian, raised in the comfort of suburbia. He attended a small, private university near Miami, where he earned a bachelor's degree in business administration, and after graduation moved north to make his mark on the world. He didn't get very far north or make much of a mark. He eventually settled in Lakeside, where all his ventures ended in utter failure: the clothing store, the restaurant, the watch-repair shop. At twenty-five, he was selling hotdogs wrapped in Pillsbury crescent rolls from a cart at the Joker Marchant Stadium, home to the Lakeside Tigers, the triple-A farm team for Detroit. "Billy's Pigs in a Blanket." He was also experimenting with various syrups with an eye on cornering the slushy market. His life changed abruptly and irrevocably when he answered an ad in the local paper.

He often said the IRS had "discovered" him—had plucked him from obscurity—and it was inside the Service that William Culpepper discovered his true calling, his passion and, ultimately, his damnation: the occupation of revenue officer.

o   o   o

Once we settled into Allison's car, Culpepper began to hold forth. "I have been spat on, kicked, punched, pushed down, my hair yanked, and had a gun pulled on me. I have been called Nazi, Gestapo, pig, and other names that would make a marine blush. I've had doors slammed in my face and once somebody tried to run me over with a car. I go home at night and my wife tells me I drink too much and brood too much and don't get enough sleep. I haven't spoken to my parents in two years. My friends from college don't call me anymore. People at my church cross the sidewalk so they can pretend they don't see me. My neighbors call me 'Mr. Culpepper.' Three years ago, every strand of hair on my body, from the top of my head to those little hairs that grow on the top of my feet, fell out. Just fell out. I was bald all over. I was stripped completely bare. I looked like I was made out of wax. So I bought a toupee and the first thing I noticed was how much nicer people were to me, since they assumed I was undergoing chemo. Then one day my hair just started growing back, and it came in this dark; it came in *black*. Before it fell out it was brown. Now it's black. . . . You are exceeding the speed limit, Allison. You get a ticket on the job and I'll write you up. I'll fire your ass. You are a federal officer. Henceforward you will be held to higher standard. And, while you are under me, you will be held to the *highest* standard . . . Be proud of what you do. Be proud you're a revenue officer. Not some number-cruncher, not some fucking accountant or CPA who can't make it in private practice. You are a revenue officer. There are only ten thousand others like you in the whole country, and you are the best of the breed. The United States has the most efficient tax system in the world, because of one thing. Don't forget the fourth protocol. . . . You're turning right in less than a hundred feet; signal your turn. Make known your intentions. Always make known your intentions. Learn to detest the unexpected. Hate surprises. Surprises will get you killed. The highest award a revenue officer can receive from the government is named after the only revenue officer who was killed in the line of duty. Ambushed by a protestor. A few years back they actually put it to a vote whether ROs should carry guns. The overwhelming majority voted it down. I don't think I need to tell you how I voted."

I thought of Melissa and her opening remarks my first day on the job: "If it were up to me, I'd line 'em all up against a wall and shoot them." I sat in the backseat of Allison's Audi and thanked all the gods of collection that he had chosen her cases to take to the field that opening day.

Our first stop was a mortuary, the first stop of dead people. As we approached the door, Culpepper said, "Remember the third protocol. Never go into a business thinking, 'Am I going to have to seize this place?' Always go in thinking, '*What* am I going to seize in this place?'" He said it with no trace of irony. I prayed that what we saw inside was limited to caskets and flowers. The fact remained that Culpepper had chosen this as the first case and Culpepper never wasted an opportunity to signal his intentions.

The day had not gone well for Allison. She had become flustered, tongue-tied, bound by minutiae. She clearly thought she should have performed better and would not stop beating herself up for it. The owner of the mortuary was a stooped octogenarian named Mr. Rose and he spoke with a soft, babyish lisp. He was pitiful. Allison was pitiful. The whole damned thing was pitiful. Culpepper was intensely interested—or at least he pretended to be—in the esoteric intricacies of embalming. He assumed the lead in this and the other two of Melissa's cases we called on that first day. At the end of it, after we had returned to the office, I looked through the window and saw her hurrying to her car, head bowed, and I was shocked to realize that Allison was crying.

Back in the office, Culpepper tossed a three-inch-thick case file before me and said, "Look this over. We're calling on it tomorrow." He added, "One of Melissa's dogs." A "dog" was an old case, either overworked or under-collected. Dogs were nearly impossible to close. "You'll notice it flunks the thickness test."

"The thickness test?"

"The thicker the case, the harder it is to close. The little sucker is choking on all the paper. You never want a case file over an inch thick. Under an inch, you're a superstar. Over an inch, you're a fucking loser." It was clear from his tone what category he thought Melissa belonged to. "Look it over tonight."

My first homework assignment. I dutifully brought the file home and spent three hours poring through Melissa's history and the dozens of forms, computer printouts, letters, and sticky-notes pasted throughout.

At the beginning of the case, some two years before, Melissa's handwriting was large and flowing, almost flowery. By the eighteenth-month anniversary of its assignment to her, her handwriting had deteriorated to an almost illegible scrawl, like some desperate lifer scribbling on the cell wall. The last entry was over two months old. She had written, "TP stll nt curr. Sts needs add. time to consol. debt & refin. DL in 2 wks to supply new CIS." Most histories are written in this kind of shorthand. Translated, it read, "The taxpayer [is] still not current [with making tax deposits]. States needs additional time to consolidate debt and refinance. [Gave] deadline in two weeks to supply new Collection Information Statement." The deadline came and went without Melissa securing the new information from Ms. Marsh. That, I supposed, was up to me, under the guiding hand and watchful eye of William Culpepper. I comforted myself that I would not be alone: at least Allison would be there and could be counted on to draw some of Culpepper's fire.

"Allison's called in sick," Culpepper informed me when I walked through the door the following morning. "It's just you and me today. Grab your cases. You're driving."

He lowered himself into my little car and shifted his bulk this way and that in the bucket seat, trying to get comfortable. That was not a possibility for someone his size in a Nissan Sentra. He looked around the confines of the interior, unable to disguise his distaste. Culpepper drove a Ford Probe, jet black, low to the ground and immaculately kept. My car was not immaculately kept. Old newspapers, plastic lids from convenience-store fountain drinks, yellow napkins from Wendy's, gum wrappers, loose change, all littered the tiny backseat and floorboards. He shifted his feet, trying to clear a spot. I dropped the case files into the seat behind me, slid down into the driver's seat, buckled my seat belt, placed my hands on the steering wheel, and waited for the entire universe to come undone and crash upon my head. The stories of Culpepper's cruelty were legion; they were recounted in Phase One training with gleeful abandon, like ghost stories told around a campfire to frighten little children. Melissa had told us about the time he set fire to her case file. Then there was the time he told a trainee he would make it his mission in life to get him fired and back on the unemployment line where he belonged—then did. And the time he took three trainees into the conference room and spent three hours screaming at them until one poor woman fled from the building, never to be seen again. And the time he humiliated another trainee on a field call, joining the taxpayer's rep in mocking her for her lack of expertise until she burst into tears and quit right on the spot. Culpepper called her a cab.

"Where do you live, Yancey?" he asked as I pulled out of the parking lot. He slipped on a pair of Ray-Bans. In his dark suit, wearing those dark glasses, he looked every bit the part of quintessential G-man. I tried to imagine him in his hotdog days, wearing a white smock and a foam rubber hotdog hat. I could not.

"Clearview."

"Where in Clearview?"

"In a house in Clearview."

"Oh, I thought it might be in this car."

I glanced over at him. His face was expressionless, as it always was when he was making a joke. His face was also expressionless when he *wasn't* making a joke. This invariably led to someone getting into trouble for not laughing—or laughing, depending.

"You brought the file home?" he asked, referring to the Marsh case. So much for the small talk. He was forced to raise his voice; my air conditioner had two settings, off and arctic blast: the switch was going bad.

"Yes." I did not elaborate. One-syllable answers were the best course of action when under questioning at the hands of Culpepper.

"What's the issue?"

It was, I would learn, his favorite word. Issue. The entire world could be reduced to its myriad issues. Finding the issue was the key to everything. It was the map to the treasure and the treasure itself. The issue was the quest *and* the Holy Grail.

I had no idea how to begin, so I just began.

"Well, Laura Marsh is the owner-operator of Marsh's Playland. She's been in business four years."

"Fascinating," he said. "What's the issue?"

"She owes fifty-four grand and some change, and when Melissa—"

"You don't say! And what's the issue?"

My face was growing hot. I said, "And she can't pay it."

"*Really?* Tell me the issue."

"I—I thought I was."

"Okay. Let me help. Would you like my help?"

My knuckles had gone bone white against the dark steering wheel. I took a deep breath and didn't say anything.

"Why are we going out there today?" Culpepper asked.

"To talk to Ms. Marsh."

"No. Come on. Aren't you some kind of genius or something? That's what Gina says. Gina says you are some kind of genius, correcting Mel's grammar in your interview and acing Phase One and writing Pulitzer Prize–winning plays and all that. So come on, tell me, what's the reason we're going to see this taxpayer?"

"Because she owes taxes?"

"Jesus Christ," he said softly. "You *are* a genius." He was awestruck. "And so what's the issue? What's our problem?"

"Our problem is we have to figure out a way to get her to—"

"We don't have a problem."

"We don't?"

"No. Lesson one, Yancey: we do not have problems."

"I have quite a few."

He was staring straight ahead. Sitting this close to him I was struck by how smooth his skin was, how pink and baby-soft. This was the incongruity of Culpepper. Outside, he was boyishly cute; inside, he was a serpent-haired monster. He used this to his full advantage, but Culpepper tended to use *everything* to his full advantage.

"We do not have problems," he repeated. "The taxpayer has the problems."

"And we have the solutions?" It sounded like a advertising slogan.

He ignored me. "I'm familiar with this case. Melissa fucked around with it and fucked around with it, mostly because she felt sorry for this person, sort of like the way you'd feel about a stupid dog that runs in front of buses. There was always something going on, some tragedy striking or about to strike or that had struck ten years ago but fucked her up for life. Always a reason, always a need for another piece of paper, another extension. When

Mel got this case, this person owed ten thousand dollars. Now she owes fifty-four. This is what happens when we go with the angle that it's *our* problem. Do you blame the vet for putting down the stupid bus-running dog? Do you blame the executioner for pulling the switch on the serial killer?"

"I don't think Ms. Marsh is a serial killer," I said. "At least, I didn't get that from reading the case file."

Again I was ignored. He was in that space inside his head that Gina called Culpepperville. "Like Gotham City," she told me. "Only creepier."

" 'Pull the trigger on this one,' I told her. 'You're not doing her any favors.' But she makes up this cock-and-bull story to Gina about how vital this service is to the community and Gina backs off the seizure. If it were my case, I would have seized on first contact."

I was about to suggest that, if he wanted the case, he could have it, but we were getting close to the day care and my mind was beginning to cloud with panic. How could I possibly remember everything? Had I put my checklist in the case file, or left it at home on the kitchen table? Was there a Pub One in the file? Did I double-check to make sure she didn't have a power-of-attorney? Was she coded PDT?* One bad review from Culpepper and I was dead. My career would be over before it had begun. I was so nervous it completely escaped me that I was fretting over losing a job I professed to despise.

I patted my breast pocket, checking for my pocket commission, pen, and calculator. I ran over the three Cs† of an effective first contact. I mentally rehearsed my opening lines and imagined various scenarios—none pleasant—and how I would react to each. I was two or three blocks away when I realized that I had made a terrible mistake, I wasn't cut out for this kind of work. I was a squishy-hearted theater person, an artist type. What the hell was I doing driving around with a license to collect taxes? Dear Jesus, how did I become a tax collector? I remembered Gina's words during my second interview, after she had taken my measure: "You do know this job is in collection." At every turn of the stair, someone had warned me, pointed the way to the exit, and I had nodded and continued to climb—

---

* Potentially Dangerous Taxpayer.
† Cause, Cure, Compliance.

right up to the scaffold. What was I thinking? Culpepper broke the silence, as if he knew precisely what I was thinking.

"One day the Moment will hit you," he said.

"What?"

"The Moment. It happens to everyone. I was on my way to work and suddenly I thought, 'What the hell am I doing here?' I had this sort of panic attack. 'What the fuck am I *doing* here?' I was on the interstate and I pulled into this truck stop. I parked by a bank of pay phones and thought about calling the office and quitting right there, on the spot. I was totally disoriented. I was going into a fugue state."

I waited for the denouement. His face was turned from me; he was staring out his window. I said, "So what happened?"

"The answer came to me."

"Which was?"

"You just passed it," he said, pointing out his window.

I drove around the block. We were in a working-class section of town, where some garages and back rooms had been converted into little businesses: a small-engine repair here, a beauty parlor there, and right before me, in the little white house with the torn screening on the porch, a day care. Gravel had replaced grass in the small front yard, transforming it into a makeshift parking lot, overgrown with dandelions and crabgrass and sandspurs. A plastic toy lawn mower lay on its side in the tall grass under a stately oak tree on the northwest corner of the house. Other toys lay scattered along the front walkway and discarded in the overgrown flower bed against the front of the house. A small hand-painted sign that read PLAY LAND announced that I had arrived at the first field contact of my career. Despite the arctic chill inside my little car, I had developed a serious case of the flop sweat. My fear was unreasonable and nearly overwhelming. I reached into the backseat for the case file and, as I was bringing it toward me, the thing fell open and the papers went everywhere. Culpepper sat impassively while I hurriedly stuffed the pages, organized so meticulously the night before, willy-nilly, back into the folder. I can't say why I felt so rushed. After all, it wasn't as if Ms. Marsh was expecting us.

"Okay," I said. "Okay, I'm ready."

I stepped out of my car and closed the door. I did not feel steady on my feet. The brooding heat of late spring pressed down upon my shoulders with all the weight of impending doom. Culpepper got out and said, "You left your car running." I yanked open the door, leaned in, switched off the engine, and jammed the keys into my pocket. We cut through the yard toward the front door. The sandspurs tugged at my pants leg. Culpepper said, "You're an actor, right? So pretend this is a movie and you're Mr. RO, IRS Man, defender of justice, champion of the oppressed government. Relax and ask yourself, what's the worst thing that could happen?"

"I'm ahead of you there," I told him, as we mounted the concrete steps. "But there were so many choices, I finally gave up."

I pressed my thumb on the doorbell. Culpepper said, "It doesn't work. Knock."

I knocked. I could hear the raucous shouts of children coming from the other side of the door. From the sound of it, they numbered in the thousands. I knocked again. The door flew open. A heavyset woman in her middle forties stood in the doorway, balancing a two-year-old boy on her hip. Two other, slightly older children were on either side of her, pulling on the hem of her cutoff jeans. The children were barefoot. So was Laura Marsh.

"Yes?" she asked impatiently. It was a yes reserved for solicitors and bill collectors.

"Good morning," I replied. "We're looking for Laura Marsh."

"Well, you've found her."

I reached into my breast pocket and fumbled for my commission. I held up my sleek, brand-new pocket calculator. Laura Marsh frowned. Culpepper cleared his throat. I dropped the calculator into my pants pocket, reached into my breast pocket again, and flipped open my commission.

"My name is Rick Yancey, and this is William—Mr. Culpepper. We're with the Internal Revenue Service."

"Where's Melissa?" she asked. "I thought Melissa was handling my case."

"Melissa is gone," Culpepper said. "Mr. Yancey will be handling your case now."

She eyed me, sizing me up. I slipped the commission back in my pocket. Culpepper said, "We need just a few minutes of your time."

"Can you come back this afternoon? Around one would be good. That's nap time."

"That wouldn't be possible," he said.

"Oh."

"That's our nap time, too," I said. She laughed. Some of the tension dissipated. My tension anyway. I wasn't sure about hers. Culpepper had none.

"You people never call first," she said. She stepped back and we followed her inside. She was relaxed; she believed there was nothing to fear. After all, she had been working with Melissa about two years now and nothing too terribly bad had happened to her. The children attached to her hip stared at us with the same shocked expressions as the starving urchins featured in those commercials for famine relief. She raised her voice over the thunderous noise, calling for someone named Mary Beth. A harried-looking girl of about eighteen appeared at the end of the hall. Behind her there was a blur of motion where dozens of children cavorted in the living room.

"Take them on back with you, honey," Laura Marsh said, and Mary Beth pulled the toddler from her hip and motioned for the other two to follow. I heard her shout into the melee, "And now we're going to read a STORY!" before she disappeared around the corner.

Laura Marsh led us down the narrow hallway, turning left into her kitchen. She closed the door to shut out some of the noise. She waved her hand toward the small table shoved against one wall and offered us a cup of coffee. I wondered where the coffee machine was. The countertop was piled high with Tupperware containers, pots and pans, dirty dishes, stacks of old newspapers, a bag of cat litter, a Styrofoam cooler, roll upon roll of paper towels and toilet tissue, and a partially disemboweled microwave oven.

"I have doughnuts too."

"No, thanks," Culpepper said crisply.

"Oh, I figured you guys were like cops. You know, lots of coffee and doughnuts."

"We're not like cops," he said. He removed his sunglasses and slid into one of the rickety wooden chairs. I sat on the other side of the table. Laura Marsh remained standing. There was a heavy silence: I was up, and both were waiting for my opening lines. I had forgotten them.

Ms. Marsh jumped into the breach. "I've been meaning to call Melissa. Hadn't heard from her in a couple weeks, and that's not like her. She used to call at least once a week. Is she okay? Nothing's happened to her, has it?"

"Nothing significant," Culpepper said, and another silence settled in. There was a huge cat perched on the ledge over the kitchen sink, silhouetted against the harsh sunlight. The sight triggered a twitching response just below my right eye; I am allergic to cats. I remembered Melissa's mantra: make demand, make demand, make demand. Like all mantras, it emboldened me.

I made demand. "Ms. Marsh, we're here today for fifty-four thousand, six hundred twelve dollars and seventy-two cents."

She stared at me for a moment, and then burst into laughter, doubling over, her wide, chafed hands pressing on her large thighs. Culpepper rested his cheek against his fist and regarded her, turned his head, regarded me.

"Okay," she said, straightening, hands on the small of her back. "Will you take a check?"

Inside my head I heard myself say, "Ms. Marsh, this is no laughing matter," but that sounded so Joe Friday. I opened the case file and began hunting for the CIS,* face on fire, eye twitching. Culpepper said quietly, "Perhaps you should sit down, Ms. Marsh." Her smile disappeared. She came to the table and sat with her back to the window, and shadows gathered in the folds around her mouth, the circles beneath her eyes. The case file said she was forty-two, but she looked ten years older.

Sticking to the script, I said, "How much can you pay today?"

"Oh, Jesus, I'm flat broke. To tell you the truth, I don't even know where my checkbook is. Look, I thought I was working out some kind of payment plan."

"What made you think that?" Culpepper asked.

"That's what Melissa—"

"Melissa is no longer working your case," Culpepper said. "I think I told you that. Mr. Yancey is now working your case." He was not patronizing; he did not condescend. His voice lacked any inflection whatsoever. He was speaking so softly I could barely hear him. "Mr. Yancey has reviewed your financial statement and perhaps has arrived at a different resolution."

---

* Form 433B, Collection Information Statement for Businesses.

She looked at me, clearly expecting to hear my resolution. I had no resolution. I had no frigging idea. Where was the 433B? Was it still in my car? Why are they both staring at me like that? Why did I take this job? Why would *anyone* take this job? Why do people become garbage collectors, morticians, nuclear power plant technicians? What was the meaning of all this and what was I doing here? What the hell did I think I was doing here? I was completely immersed, drowning in the moment Culpepper had warned me about.

"I got nothin'," Laura Marsh said. "That's the God-honest truth. You're welcome to take a look."

"Who owns the house?" Culpepper asked.

"What house?"

"This house."

"I do. It's my house. You can't take my house."

"Mr. Yancey," Culpepper turned to me.

Now what did *he* want? I was busy looking for my form. Like most trainees, I was quickly developing a form-dependency. Forms gave you lots of nice little boxes to check and lines to fill out and columns to add up. Forms were the barrier between you and the banality of despair.

"Actually," I said, talking to the case file, "we can, under certain circumstances, um, enforce the tax lien against your property."

"You're gonna take my house?"

"Well, we—"

"You're not taking my house."

"We might," Culpepper said.

"You're not," Laura Marsh said.

"Tell us why we shouldn't," Culpepper said.

"Melissa said—"

"Melissa is no longer working your case. I believe we covered this. Mr. Yancey is now working your case."

"Oh, I get it. This is the IRS version of good cop, bad cop, right?"

She smiled at me, clearly the good cop in this scenario. I had located the financial statement and had confirmed that the only thing of real value to the business was the house, which had thirty-five thousand dollars in equity.

She addressed me, assuming a warm, maternal tone. "I've been to the bank. Didn't Melissa tell you this? They turned me down flat. I don't have the income right now. I'm losing money. Plus that tax lien's screwed up my credit. I thought about selling it, but if you guys take all the money from the sale, how am I supposed to start over?"

"That doesn't interest us," Culpepper said. This implied there was something that did, but he did not elaborate. I supposed that was my job.

She ignored him. She had his number. She spoke only to me, Mr. Twitchy-Eye.

"I know I screwed up. But I'm not trying to cheat anyone, least of all you guys. It's not like I got tax shelters overseas or yachts moored off Key Biscayne. Five years ago, my husband dumped me. After seventeen years. He ran off with my next-door neighbor's eighteen-year-old daughter and I was left with nothing. Absolutely nothing. I started this business because I had to eat and my kids had to eat and I wasn't about to go on welfare. It seems to me the government should reward people like me instead of coming after them like this, threatening to take away their house and . . . and everything. It seems to me the government should be going after those millionaires and celebrities who don't pay one penny because they can afford to hire big tax attorneys and CPAs who can hide all their money for them." Her desperation had given way to indignation. She enlightened us with more details on her ex-husband's philandering. There was a lengthy discussion of her myriad health problems, of the harassment she suffered at the hands of the state of Florida, of the problems with finding and keeping good employees, of the deaths of three relatives in the past two years. She just needed a little time. Things were going to get better. She was a Christian. She loved her country. She wasn't trying to stiff us. She would pay us back to the last penny. All she needed, all she was asking for, was a little time.

I made notes while Culpepper sat with his hands folded on the tabletop. He watched her dispassionately while my native empathy threatened to crush my resolve. What was I supposed to tell this poor woman? I dreaded the ending of her aria. My desperation soon gave way to outrage: How could the Service expect me to pass judgment upon this lost soul? For weeks during Phase One training our instructors had repeated over and over,

"We pay you for your judgment," but the entire system was designed in such a way as to completely remove our judgment from the process. Our training material was chock-full of flowcharts designed to determine the outcome of a case with the finality of the hand of fate. We were merely agents of the machine. We were the triggermen or, as Culpepper put it, the executioner at the switch.

"Isn't it still possible for me to get a payment plan?"

The question hung in the air. Culpepper had turned his gaze in my direction. I knew what answer she desired and I knew what answer Culpepper desired. Where did my loyalties lie? I had reached the nub of it. I must choose now, and somehow I knew that this choice was irrevocable. I must step off the cliff or turn aside.

Culpepper said, still looking at me, "Are you current with your deposits, Ms. Marsh?"

"No. No, I told you, I'm losing money. I can't afford to make any tax deposits right now. But with a little time—"

I spoke up; the flowchart answer: "We can't grant an installment agreement unless you're current with deposits."

"This is an interesting discussion," Culpepper said. "But academic. Ms. Marsh, you're asking for a payment plan at the same time you're telling us you're losing money and can't make payments."

"I'm asking for some time. I'm asking for some compassion."

"You are a operating a business. Your business is a miserable failure. You've taken the government's money to make up your shortfall and now the government wants it back. So the issue is not one of compassion on our part, but the utter incompetence on yours."

"I could pay you five hundred dollars a month," she said abruptly.

Culpepper did not miss a beat. "How?"

"I don't know. I'll do something."

"What?"

"I'll fire Justine." A sob caught in her throat. I made the following note: *She will fire Justine.* "I'll return the jungle gym—that's a two-hundred-dollar-a-month payment right there." The list grew and I scribbled it down as she dictated. Culpepper drummed his fingers on the tabletop. He shifted in his chair, clearly restless.

Finally, as she was elaborating on the absolutely necessity of a $300-per-month allowance for diapers, he rose from the chair and said, "Where's the bathroom?"

"Down the hall to the right," she told him. He shot me a look that said, *Let's wrap this up*, before abandoning me.

Laura Marsh was staring at me, waiting for my decision. I was waiting for it, too. My first case, and my OJI had left at the precise moment when I needed him the most. I had no doubt he had done this deliberately.

"So what happens now?" she asked. "Do I get my payment plan?"

I was pretending to study the financial statement. My eye, watering profusely now, was nearly closed. I wiped a tear from my cheek.

She leaned toward me and whispered, "You're new, aren't you?"

"If we give you this plan," I choked out—my throat was closing up—"how do we know you'll keep it? You've defaulted on two or three plans already."

"That wasn't my fault."

"Okay."

"I just need a little time."

"Right."

"That Mr. Culpepper doesn't understand. But you understand. I can see it in your eyes. You want to give me a payment plan, but he wants to take my house. Is he your boss?"

"Not exactly..." I did not tell her my boss probably wouldn't give her a payment plan, either.

"He has an attitude."

"Ms. Marsh, there's nothing I can do if you don't get current."

"I'll be current by the end of the week."

"If you can do that," I said, taking a deep breath, "then maybe there's something we can do."

"Oh, good. Thank you, thank you. Thank you." Her relief was palpable.

I nodded. *My* relief was palpable. Between Laura and myself, the universe had been liberated from all sorrow, all useless anxiety. Something had been decided, although I was not entirely clear what that decision was.

It was time to go, but where was Culpepper? I packed up my briefcase while she prattled about the weather, about summer colds, about unscrupulous repairmen and the untrustworthiness of human beings in general. Thinking of Culpepper wandering through her house, I agreed. I looked to my left as we came out of the kitchen and saw him squatting in the living room, staring intensely at a toddler as the child aimed a orange toy pistol at his forehead, shouting *"Bang-bang! Bang-bang!"* and Culpepper was smiling, his index finger pointing at the child's distended belly, returning fire.

We made our getaway, and Ms. Marsh was positively giddy. She even gave my hand an extra squeeze as we parted. She waved to us from the front porch. We did not wave back.

I expected a full debriefing on the way to my next case, but Culpepper was silent, quietly humming the song "Bad to the Bone." Of the many things racing through my fevered brain, the chief thought was: Why did Culpepper leave the room at the climax of the interview? What was he doing in Laura Marsh's house—was he, like Larry Simon, rifling through Laura Marsh's drawers, looking for a hidden cache of jewels? I would never know, but suspected it had something to do with the Third Protocol: *Learn what they have.*

No one was home at my next call. I checked with some neighbors, verified the taxpayer's address, and left a calling card. Culpepper told a story about Melissa digging through a taxpayer's garbage looking for bank statements, then said, "Melissa ever do a courthouse check on the Marsh case?"

"I don't think so."

"You don't think so?"

"No. No, she didn't."

"Let's go to Powell." Powell was the county seat.

"Right now?"

"Right now."

A court records check was required before reporting a case as uncollectible. It was also required prior to making a seizure. If a taxpayer tried to hide assets by placing them in someone else's name, we would know. If we were planning to seize assets, encumbrances had to be verified and lien priority established. I didn't think Culpepper saw the Marsh case as uncollectible. I also didn't think he was going to give her a payment plan.

We stopped for lunch at a hamburger joint on the outskirts of Powell, then drove downtown to the courthouse.

Culpepper said, "So what are you going to do with Ms. Marsh?"

I didn't answer at first. This was due to my verging on a panic attack. It still had not left me, the vertiginous feeling of being someone whom I was not. As if I had been thrust into an improvisational exercise against my will. Culpepper's questions usually had this effect on me. He not only expected an answer, he expected a particular answer, a perfect answer. My lunch lay like a brick in my gut. How long had it been since I'd seen a doctor? I didn't even have a regular doctor; the last doctor I'd seen was for that miserable case of the shingles a couple years back. He had laughed at me, when I expressed shock that what I actually had was a form of herpes. What sort of moron took this kind of job without having a regular doctor?

I made up my mind: as soon as I got back to the office, I was writing my resignation letter. I began to compose it in my head, then remembered Culpepper had asked me a question.

"She's supposed to get current. If she can't, I guess we don't have a choice," I said.

"Good," he said.

Court records checks are hell. In 1991, before most of the larger counties converted to computer systems, the information was transferred to microfiche cartridges and perused on bulky reading machines. The type was very small. Generally, the more delinquent the taxpayer, the greater the volume of court recordings, with multiple cross-references, judgments, releases, lien filings, foreclosures, financing statements, mortgages. Laura Marsh was no exception. Some filings had significance, some did not. I had no inkling which was which, and so resorted to copying down everything, filling up two history sheets with information. Culpepper sat beside me, silent, restless, tapping his foot. After an hour he told me to meet him outside when I was finished, and I was abandoned.

After another hour, I emerged from the courthouse, feeling utterly overwhelmed, confused, and weary beyond words. I had no idea what I had been looking at, and I was angry with Culpepper for not staying inside to explain it to me. As my OJI, that was his goddamned job.

I found him sitting on a bench under a glowering sky; it was nearly three o'clock and the afternoon rains were due. He was eating an apple, his long legs stretched out before him. The wind pulled at his shock of black hair and I had the impression of a tiny black hand, waving at me. That was all the greeting I got.

I sat beside him on the bench and together we stared across the street at nothing. I wondered if I had a parking ticket. My eyes felt as if someone had been sticking them with a toothpick. My back ached. It was three o'clock and I wanted to get back to the office to write my histories—if I could figure out what to write in them—and my tour ended at four. Now I must wait for Culpepper to finish his apple. Where had he obtained an apple? It was bright red, a Macintosh, I think, and Culpepper had shined it to a mirror finish. Its outline was exquisite against his dark blue suit. The scent of this apple tantalized me. If Culpepper had the slightest sense of the symbolic, he would have offered me a bite.

"Well," he said, "what do you think?"

"About what?"

"You up for another call?"

Once again, a simple question from Culpepper and I was on the verge of panic. Suddenly, I was bound; I was wrapped tight, writhing in indecision. What did he mean by that? What answer was he looking for? If I said no, that I needed to drive back to Lakeside and write my histories because, after all, my tour ended at four and I did not intend to work credit hours, would he consider me lacking in what he called "the fire"? But if I said yes, would he write me up for improper case management, since a good revenue officer always wrote his histories on the day of contact? He let the silence drag out, not pressing me, as if he had expected this very effect. He rotated the apple a perfect quarter turn and studied the flawless red skin before snapping into it with his teeth. He dabbed his chin with a napkin.

"Doesn't your tour end soon?" I asked meekly. A lame attempt at diversion, but it had occurred to me, as he bit into the apple with that precise, annoying delicacy of his, that his tour actually ended thirty minutes before mine.

"Good point," he said. "Let's head back. I have an errand to run—and there's something I want to show you."

He stood up and tossed the apple underhanded across his body twenty feet into the trash can, without looking. We walked in silence to my car. As it turned out, I did not have a ticket. I had two tickets. I wondered what Culpepper would do in this situation. Would he tear up the tickets, being the complete master of his universe? Or would he walk three blocks to the Powell police department and pay them on the spot, immediately? And, what was more important at the moment, what did he expect *me* to do? I slipped the tickets into the glove box.

He said nothing for the first twenty minutes of the drive back to Lakeside. The traffic was light on Highway 98. It was mid-afternoon and the sky had gone black; though afternoon thunderstorms were common in central Florida, they were not the sort of disturbances you grew accustomed to, and you did not venture into one without good reason. My reason was very good: I wanted to get back to the office and put an end to this day. I wondered what he planned to show me and what exactly his errand was, but I did not ask. He would have considered it a show of weakness if I did.

It was not until we reached the southernmost outskirts of Lakeside, with its tired strip malls, mom-and-pop video stores, small and large engine repair shops, portable vegetable stands and the inevitable check-cashing, usurious signature-loan shop, that Culpepper abruptly said, "Slow down. Take it slow through here."

The speed limit was forty-five. I slowed to thirty, as Culpepper pointed out the small business that he had worked for off and on for the past five years. This one's owner borrowed from his daughter to full-pay; that one burned his store to the ground and used half the insurance proceeds to pay him, the other half to rebuild. This one owed for every quarter, but the old man would cash in bonds every time Culpepper's shadow crossed the door. That one had a nervous breakdown and faithfully mailed her payment to him from her hospital bed. That one had been real trouble until he showed up one morning with the locks and chains and seized his prized Mercedes parked in public access. There was no hint of pride in his voice as he rattled off these anecdotal conquests. He wasn't bragging. Culpepper never bragged. I was still too green to know that he was disclosing confidential information, a serious offense in the eyes of the Service, a cause for dismissal. Years later, I heard a story, probably apocryphal, of the mid-level manager who on a Sunday drive pointed out to his wife a house his office was considering seizing. The house happened to belong to a woman in his wife's bridge club. The manager was subsequently fired. As Culpepper spoke, the dark canopy above us opened up and a torrential rain came down. My old wiper blades screeched in protest when I turned them on. I slowed to twenty-five as the lightning popped directly over the car and the thunder threatened to rattle the doors off their hinges.

"If this thing shakes to pieces," Culpepper said, perfectly deadpan, referring to my Nissan, "I call divvies on the tires." He had noticed the only decent piece of equipment on the vehicle. "Pull over."

I obeyed at once, without the slightest protest or questioning why. I eased the car off the road into the gravel parking lot of a used-car dealer-ship. BOB'S RELIABLE WRECKS, read the plywood sign by the road. I turned off the engine, and for a moment all the world was a swirling gray mass and the sound of rain, hateful in its ferocity; we had to raise our voices slightly to be heard.

"It's times like these when I think about the end of the world!" Culpep-per shouted at me. "What do you think about?"

"I worry about my roof leaking."

"You were pretty frustrated back there, weren't you?" He was referring to the court records search. "It can be confusing, but at least Powell has them on microfiche. Wait till you work Hardee or one of those smaller counties, with all the filings in these big books, handwritten, fucking nine-teenth century. I didn't understand what the hell I was doing in a court-house for my first three years."

Across the gravel lot, in a little yellow building, through a smudged win-dow, a portly man whose name was probably Bob was staring at my car. There were a half-dozen other cars in the lot, and mine seemed to fit right in.

"It's a tool," Culpepper said. "A means to an end. A necessary evil."

I nodded, though I had no idea what he meant.

"Never lose sight of the point," he went on. "Never forget why you're here. That's why I was showing you those businesses. You know, you could drive down any street in America on any given day, and I guarantee you over half of the businesses you pass would have tax trouble—whether it reached our level or not, there would be some problem with their taxes. Maybe that's because the system's too complex or people are stupid or a combination of both, I really don't care. The point is, that's why we're here."

"To help them," I said, helpfully.

"Don't be ridiculous. Oh, maybe that happens, like a happy accident, but helping people isn't your job, Yancey. You want to help people, become a social worker. Our job is to feed the beast."

"Feed the what?"

"The beast."

He pulled out his pocket commission and flipped it open. I glanced over at it, then looked away. On every revenue officer's ID, there was a drawing of the U.S. Treasury Building and, beside that, a photograph of the revenue officer. He snapped the commission closed and said, "Everything else is peripheral, even trivial. And, in order to feed the beast, Congress has given us tools that turn due process into some kind of academic exercise, like a bunch of monks debating how many angels can dance on the head of a pin. Are you following this? This is very important. If you don't get this, you're fucking doomed. You'll never like this job, and if you don't want to lose it, you better learn to like it. It's all perception, Yancey, it's all how you see yourself. You know what you are? You know what you became when you took that oath?"

I shook my head no—I had no idea what I had become.

"A fucking demigod is what you became. You think I'm being hyperbolic? You have an English degree, right? You know what hyperbole is?"

I nodded. I knew what it was. Apparently Culpepper did too, or at least he practiced it often enough.

He said, "Think about it, Yancey. If you don't think about anything else when you go home tonight, think about this. With a stroke of your pen, you can take away someone's life savings. You can take their paycheck. You can take their car. You can take everything they own except the clothes on their fucking back, and sometimes you can take that, if you do it right. It's simple: they owe taxes, you can do that. You can do all that, and on whose authority can you do that? *On your own.* Once you're out of your training year you pretty much have carte blanche. You are the only sheriff in town, the sole cock in the fucking chicken coop. You're like a medieval prince: you have the right to everything, because *you are the entire federal government.* So keep that in mind for the next eight months. Keep it in mind for your whole career. This job is about one thing and one thing only, and that one thing is not called 'government service.' You want to know what that one thing is called?"

"What?" I whispered. I didn't know if he could hear me over the roaring rain, but I doubted it mattered. Culpepper was on a roll; his eyes were burning with the fire of his zealotry, the righteousness of his cause. It was at that moment I realized that William Culpepper might very well be insane.

"Power. Power over... everyone. Think of your inventory as your kingdom and you are lord of the fucking manor. You are a prince. This job is about power and we, you and me, we are the princes of power."

He nodded, staring into the downpour, fists clenched on his thighs.

The merciful thing about Florida thunderstorms, like Culpepper's monologues, is that they eventually end. I pulled out of the lot, anxious to finish this leg of my journey into the heart of darkness, but Culpepper diverted me from my chosen path yet again, directing me down a series of residential streets, looping first west, then north, then back west, then south, and finally due east, until I was hopelessly lost in my own hometown.

"Pull in here."

I turned right into the entrance of an apartment complex called The Willows. There were no willows that I could see. The apartments occupied six buildings, all facing a common area where a fountain fitfully gurgled, its spout probably choked with algae and the remains of aquatic creatures that had the misfortune of exploring the pool's stagnant waters. Each building was two stories and contained four apartments, two down and two up. It was to Building Six that Culpepper led me. At first, I thought he was taking me home to meet his wife, but then I remembered that he lived on the far north side of town in a new development called Deer Run Creek, where neither deer nor creek ran. So it was not his wife, but someone else he was taking me to meet. I followed him up the flight of stairs to Apartment 604 and stood two steps below him as he knocked on the door. *Rap-rap, rap-rap*—it sounded like a signal. A voice cried from within, "Who is it?" A woman's voice.

Culpepper said, "Me," and the door opened.

She was young, about twenty, wearing blue jean shorts and a white T-shirt. Her feet were bare, her face, arms, and legs perfectly tanned. For an absurd moment, I was absolutely convinced he had taken me here to meet his sister. She stepped back, with a smile as dazzling as the recent lightning, and he motioned me to follow him.

She stood on her tiptoes—he was four or five inches taller—and gave him a peck on the lips.

"This is an unexpected pleasure," she said, giving his bicep a squeeze. No, definitely not his sister. My discomfort increased tenfold. She flashed a quick smile in my direction and headed for the refrigerator. Culpepper motioned to the sofa, confident I would take the hint and sit down. This, then, was his errand: a rendezvous with his girlfriend. The prince of power practicing noblesse oblige. Now, what was the point of this? A pertinent question, because I understood even at this early stage in our relationship that everything Culpepper did was calculated for effect. There was no wasted motion, no gesture not designed to manipulate or control. He was a true Zen master, applying his philosophy to every nook and cranny of his life. He had brought me here for a reason, but what was that reason? Was this a demonstration, a challenge, a threat? Or did it have anything to do with me at all? Maybe he had promised her that he would drop by for the Budweiser she now handed him. Maybe I was so insignificant in his kingdom it really didn't matter if I knew he was cheating on his wife or that he was cheating on his government—but, no; I checked my watch: his tour of duty was over. *I* was cheating on the government.

"Carrie," he addressed the girl. "This is Rick Yancey. He's my new trainee."

"Hi!" Carrie said. She knelt beside Culpepper, sitting back on her heels while he crossed his legs, very Michael Corleone–ish, in the easy chair, sipping his beer. She stroked his arm with her fingertips. The scene was so sycophantic I would have laughed if I had not been morally outraged and, if the truth were known, scared out of my wits.

"So what do you like best about the job so far?" she asked, trying to be sociable.

"The hours," I replied.

"Billy talks about it all the time," she said. I assumed she meant the job. She wrinkled her nose in distaste. She turned to Culpepper. "I'm glad you came by," she said, having fulfilled her social obligation to me. "The storm knocked out my power for twenty minutes." There was a pouting coquettishness to her voice designed to have an effect on Culpepper—or Billy. *Billy.* The name didn't fit him. It sounded immature, soft, a squishy name, and Culpepper definitely was anything but squishy. He made no move to reassure her, as she clearly expected.

"Carrie is a student at Central Florida College," he said to me. "Rick went to CFC for a year," he said to Carrie.

"Really?" She couldn't have been less interested. Her gaze—in fact, her entire being—was focused on Culpepper. She scooted closer to his legs, gripping his forearm hard. I had the impression that, if by some miracle the opportunity presented itself, she would have crawled inside his skin. I wondered if she knew he was married, then noted his wedding ring glittering on his finger. She knew, then, and it didn't matter. My moral outrage gave way to pity, as it always does when confronted with the heartbreakingly innocent or the mentally unbalanced. Now I was in the presence of both.

"A long time ago," I told Carrie. "Back then, students either had to live with their parents or on campus." This was to discourage the very thing going on before my eyes: Central Florida College was a Methodist school and, like me, suffered from frequent moral outrage.

"Oh, it's the same way now."

Culpepper said, "The school doesn't know she's living here."

"Billy and I met at Hooters," she said, as if I had asked her where they met. "That's where I work. My parents *hate* it that I work there." She pulled at Culpepper's arm urgently. "Which reminds me, the rent's due tomorrow and I'm fifty bucks short."

Without a word, Culpepper freed himself from her clutches and pulled out his wallet. She folded the cash he handed her and tucked it down the front of her white T-shirt.

"Pay you back later," she said, and kissed the tip of his nose. My stomach did a slow roll. Culpepper, who had to give the office weekly pregnancy updates (his wife and he had been trying for over a year), was this girl's sugar daddy. Dear God, I wondered, why the hell did he bring me here? It was obvious this little visit was entirely for my benefit. Culpepper was sending me a message, but what was the message?

"So how long have you two been—?" I didn't know the correct way to put it.

"Almost a year now," Carrie said. "On June twelfth, it will be a year. And Billy is going to get me something really nice for our anniversary, aren't you, Billy?"

I could guess what she wanted for her anniversary, just as I could guess what Culpepper's answer to that wish would be. In these situations, the girl always believed her man was on the cusp of a divorce. I knew now why he had brought me here, and it wasn't to parade this girl as a trophy before me and it wasn't to demonstrate what my newfound status as demigod might bestow upon me. No, William Culpepper had brought me here to lay bare his weakness, his Achilles' heel, the means by which I could destroy him. With one phone call, I could wreck his marriage and, potentially, his precious career. I could do it anonymously, so he would never know at whose hand he fell. It was the ultimate test of his power over me. He was inviting me to betray him and, by extending the invitation, creating an exit from his mad world that we both knew opened into a brick wall. The brilliance of it astounded me. It was then, with the beauty of his pristine logic making my head spin, that I realized I wanted to be just like him.

Culpepper finished the beer and declined her offer of another. "Rick has to get back to the office." He promised to call her the next day and maybe they could do something over the weekend; his wife was going to be out of town visiting her parents.

"I want you to take me bowling," she told him.

"I hate bowling," he said. "I'll take you to a Tigers game."

"I hate baseball."

"Well," he said. "I'll take you somewhere." He made a motion with his fist as if he were delivering an uppercut to her jaw, a gesture that reminded me of Jackie Gleason in *The Honeymooners*. *Bang, zoom*, Alice, to the moon! It was endearing, if not vaguely sickening.

"Come out to Hooters sometime," she said to me.

"Yancey's too uptight for Hooters," Culpepper said.

"Are you? Are you uptight?"

"I used to be," I said and, taking a deep breath to screw my courage to the sticking place, added, "But Billy's been loosening me up."

He was silent as we weaved our way through the oily puddles in the parking lot to my car. After he shut the door, Culpepper looked out the window at Building Six and asked, "So what do you think?"

"What do I think about what?"

"About Carrie."

"She's nice. Pretty."

"She's an awful lay," he said. "You know, most pretty girls are. Or did you know that?"

I started my car; some belt deep within its innards squealed, then moaned, in protest.

"One of these days this bucket is going to pop, probably while you're doing seventy-five down I-4," Culpepper said.

"Let's pray you're not with me, Billy," I said.

"Let's pray you never call me Billy again. That's the second time you've done it and there will not be a third time. If you call me Billy again I will take your narrow little head and pop it open like an peanut shell. Do you understand?"

I told him I understood.

"I guess you want to get that Marsh history down before you go," he said as I pulled into the parking lot. A loaded question. In fact, it wasn't a question at all.

"It's all right if I worked credit time?" I asked.

"Well, you could do it in the morning," he said. "But right now it's fresh."

"Yeah," I said. "I should do it now."

I worked for the next twenty minutes at my desk. As my OJI, Culpepper would write a review of my performance based on this history. Everything came down to how you presented the case. As he explained, "Always write your histories with the assumption that one day they will be used as evidence in court, because one day they might be. Remember: your history is the official government version of what happened. If it isn't in your history, it didn't happen."

I made sure to touch on all the aspects of an effective first contact: I made demand, I analyzed the facts, I weighed the taxpayer's arguments, I documented that the proper forms had been completed and publications issued. My closing lines, translated, read, "The taxpayer has been given a deadline to make a $500 payment and get current by the end of the week. If TP cannot prove she's current with this quarter's deposits, will proceed with seizure action." I reread the entire history, making sure I had covered all the bases. It was cogent, pithy, laden with devastating logic. While composing it, I tried to imagine myself as Culpepper, and in the end I was quite proud of my effort. I had, after all, graduated with honors in English. I placed the account on his desk and began to pack up my things while he read. It was ten minutes past five. I called Pam and told her I was running late but would be home soon. She was not happy. Culpepper appeared at my elbow, said softly, "Yancey," and tore the history sheets in half. He dropped them on my desk and turned on his heel.

"Try again," he said without looking at me. He sat at his desk, folding his hands in his lap and bowing his head, as if in prayer. I looked down at the torn pages on my desk and said, "What's wrong?"

"You're missing something."

"What? What am I missing?"

"Figure it out."

Okay. I read the history again, piecing the torn pages together, biting my lower lip until it burned. What was I missing? I issued Pub 1; I made demand; I updated the financial statement; I gave a deadline; I warned of the consequences; I decided what do with the case; and I laid the groundwork for executing my sentence. What was I missing—or was I missing anything? I glanced over at Culpepper, sitting cattycorner to me some twenty feet away, dozing or meditating. Was that a smile playing on his lips? The sadistic bastard, did he really think he could break my will? I played with my phrasing, carefully checking for any untoward editorial comments, which were anathema to a good history. I even pulled out my manual and looked up the elements of an effective first contact. After another thirty minutes I had a new history written. I carried it over to his desk and dropped it in front of him. He slowly raised his head, pulled the sheets toward him, flipped to the back page . . . then ripped the pages down the middle. I felt a similar tearing sensation in my stomach. He held the torn pages over his shoulder.

"Again," he said.

"I'm still missing something?"

"You're still missing something."

He was trying to break me. He was goading me into losing my temper. He wanted me to scream at him or stomp out. He wanted an excuse to write me up for insubordination. He was manipulating me toward termination. Well, fuck him. He had my ire up now; I wasn't going to let him win.

So I wrote the same history a third time. I stopped abbreviating, thinking, vainly, that he couldn't understand what the abbreviations meant. I considered typing the whole thing; perhaps he couldn't decipher my handwriting, which did happen to be poor. It was now five forty-five. The phone rang, but neither of us answered it. I was sure it was Pam. I was going to catch it when, or if ever, I got home. At ten to six I presented the third rewrite to Culpepper. I was actually swaying on my feet. If he tore this up, too, I was going to stab out his eyes with my government-issue ballpoint. He studied the first page for an agonizingly long time, then stacked the pages . . . and tore them in half.

"Jesus Christ!" I cried, losing my composure. "Can't you give me a hint at least?"

"Okay. There's something you're leaving out."

"That's it? That's my hint?"

"Not enough? Here's another: it's a moronic mistake, embarrassing, given your extraordinarily brilliant mind." He flung the torn pages into the trash can by his desk.

"Now go write this history the way it should be written and stop your fucking whining. I'm tired and I want to go home."

I started to say, *If you told me what was wrong with the history you could go home*, but I bit my lip, returned to my desk, and stared at the blank pad of paper before me. I dated the form and wrote, *Met with the deadbeat and told her we had decided she was too pitiful to live, that she was a dog and we were the bus, and asked if she had any last wishes before we pulled the switch* . . . I ripped the sheet from the pad and tore it into shreds. It would have given me some perverse comfort if Culpepper had laughed at the sound of ripping paper, but there was only silence. I wrote the history again and carried it to his desk. I was going to walk out the door before he could finish it.

I dropped it in front of him and returned to my desk and began to clean up. The sound of tearing paper was very loud in the small space. I closed my eyes and leaned on the desk. It was now six-fifteen.

A soft voice at my elbow said, "Let us reason together, Rick, shall we?"

"Nothing that's happened to me since I came here is reasonable," I said.

"One of the problems with this hiring program has been we're taking people with complicated minds and expecting simple things from them."

"Tell me what's wrong with it, Culpepper. Please." I was totally abject. He had beaten me. It was the moment he had been waiting for. He slid the pad in front of me.

"See the little block here at the top of the history sheet? You forgot to write the taxpayer's name."

I sunk into my chair. "I forgot . . . ?"

"Yep."

"That's what was missing? Her name?"

"Goes right in that little block at the top of each sheet. I'm sure you covered this in Phase One."

"That's all that was wrong?" I was having trouble processing the information.

"You bet. Otherwise, it's pretty good." He returned to his desk, whistling.

I was staring at the blank pad, shoulders bowed, hands pressed in my lap, when he called from across the room. "You see, Rick, in the real world, not the world you're from, but in this world, it's not so much what you say but the care you take in saying it."

"Go to hell," I whispered. And wrote the history again, with Laura Marsh's name printed boldly at the top of each page.

It was six thirty-five. The sun was setting. I set the history aside and wrote my resignation on a separate piece of paper. I walked the papers over to Culpepper, history in one hand, resignation in the other. I stood for a moment, to his right and slightly behind him. He did not look up. He had assumed the same meditative position, or perhaps he had fallen asleep. I hesitated for one agonizingly long moment, then slid the history sheets in front of him. I folded the resignation and stuffed it into my pocket.

The next morning I found his review on my desk. His summary ran: "Excellent work on this case, Rick. You clearly explained the taxpayer's rights and the government's position that given the circumstances we would have to seize the business's assets, including the taxpayer's personal residence. You gave the taxpayer one last chance to get current, but given the history of this TP, the possibility seems remote at best. You then made a field call to the courthouse and completed the necessary research to effect the seizure. Keep it up!"

I had successfully set the table. It was time to feed the beast.

DRAIN BAMAGED

Within the next three weeks, I made initial contact on the remainder of my cases. About a third turned out to be what Culpepper called "skimmers," cases that are easily closed by checking third-party sources: out-of-business accounts, taxpayers who have relocated out of our area, or obvious errors in assessment. More than once he emphasized: "Remember, there's only five basic ways to close a case: full payment, hardship, installment agreement, transfer, or adjustment. Don't complicate what we do. What we do is beautiful because what we do is simple."

I told Allison about Culpepper making me write an entire history six times for forgetting to record a taxpayer's name.

"I think he might be insane. I mean, really insane."

"You shouldn't say that." After two weeks under his tutelage, Allison had fallen completely under Culpepper's spell.

"Don't tell him I said that."

"Why would I tell him?" she asked innocently, which immediately convinced me that she would indeed tell him.

That night I confessed my fears to Pam.

"Why would she tell Culpepper?" she asked.

"To turn him against me." I was growing impatient with what I perceived as her lack of subtlety. "To get me fired."

"Why would she want to get you fired?"

"Because I'm her competition."

"Competition for *what*?"

"Promotion," I said with Job-like patience.

"I thought the promotion was automatic once you got through the training year."

"Not *that* promotion. The *next* promotion."

"The next promotion," she echoed. "Rick, I thought you just wanted a job to pay your bills until the writing takes off..."

"Well, they're not going to promote Caroline." I wanted to stay on the topic that was still interesting to me. "She's a moron. And Rachel is too soft and Dee is too...well, Dee is too weird."

"I know what 'moron' means, but what does 'too soft' mean?"

"You know, soft, touchy-feely; she wants everybody to be her friend."

"Oh, how horrible. And Dee's weird?"

"Well, she does have this psychology degree. I mean, she majored in *abnormal* psychology." My face was growing hot. The last I had spoken with Dee was during basic training in Tampa, the night she had invited me up to her hotel room.

"Rick, you're miserable. Quit."

"I can't quit."

"Why not?"

"You know why not."

"Pretend I've forgotten."

I said nothing. I stared into space. I had taken to staring into space, sometimes in midsentence.

"You'll find something else."

"I'm not going to live off anyone anymore," I said.

"So you get a job somewhere else."

"With a degree in English? Where else can I go and earn this much money? Even if I had a master's, which I don't, and could teach, I still couldn't make nearly—"

"So that's what it's about, the money?"

"No, it isn't just the money. I can't explain it, but this is—it's my last shot."

"Your last shot? Dear God, you're a melodramatic bastard."

"You know, it would probably help our relationship if you didn't refer to me as 'bastard.' Anyway, it's easy for you to pooh-pooh money. You don't have to work."

"Yes, how lucky I am," she said, referring to her dead husband. "How lucky for me he dropped dead one morning in our kitchen."

"Why are we fighting?"

"Because you're an asshole."

"And a bastard."

"You don't have anything to prove to me," she said.

"I know I don't have anything to prove to you," I answered.

After skimmers, the next level of cases was the hardships, which usually could be resolved after an interview and some background work, that is, verifying the financial statement wasn't purely fictional. As a Grade 7 revenue officer trainee, I had my fair share of hardships. There was the quadriplegic who deadpanned, "Just the one I'm riding in," when I asked him if he owned any vehicles. There was the out-of-work schoolteacher who failed to pay taxes on his cashed-in IRA and now worked for McDonald's. "Do you know how humiliating that is, wearing those ridiculous polyester pants and waiting on kids who used to call me 'sir'?" There was the agoraphobic trucker living on disability payments after he slammed his rig into an interstate overpass, emerging unscathed but sacrificing both his girlfriend's legs in the accident. He broke down completely during the interview, confessing that she ran off with a one-armed man she had met in rehab. "I tell you, I was goddamned tempted to cut off one of my own hands to get her back." ("Makes me want to meet the legless chick," Culpepper remarked afterward.)

And there was the man who called himself a dirt farmer—he sold and hauled topsoil from his rural property—and his wife, who sat stoically through the first part of the interview and stared blankly at me when I asked her for her date of birth. "My wife has a plate in her head," he informed me in an apologetic tone. "It's all my fault. I hit her with my scoop—with the edge of my bulldozer—came right over on top of her head. They investigated me for attempted murder," he said as he teared up. "I was cleared," he added. "I was cleared of all charges, but she's been permanently—"

"Drain bamaged!" she shouted. The words were very loud in the small interview booth. "I been drain bamaged!"

"Brain damaged," he said softly, patting her hand. "Brain damaged."

Culpepper loved this story. He repeated it often, to anyone willing to listen, delivering a perfect imitation of this woman who looked as if she might have leapt directly from the pages of *The Grapes of Wrath*. It never failed to amuse him, to shout in a high-pitched squeal, "Drain bamaged! I been drain bamaged!" It appealed to his sense of the absurd and his sense of the cruel. One day, he asked if I had told the story to Pam.

"As a matter of fact, I have."

"And she didn't think it was funny."

"No."

"You don't talk that much about work with her anymore, do you?"

"No."

"Good."

These people and the unfortunates like them troubled me during my training year. I felt horribly for them and horribly for myself for laughing at them. There was the man Allison had interviewed while he took a bath (he soaked four times a day, he explained, at nine in the morning, at noon, at four in the afternoon, and at nine in the evening, for his psoriasis— Culpepper made her rewrite her history to delete any reference to the big hairy naked man in the bathtub. Afterward, she confessed to Gina the financial statement was incomplete because she wanted to get out of there fast: the suds were dying). There was the narcoleptic who wept in our interview because it had always been his life's ambition to be a surgeon. Almost all of these people asked if we had come to arrest them. With no lawyer or CPA shielding them, and with little education, they were certain debtor's prison still existed or that the IRS was in the business of arresting every two-bit, self-employed schmuck who was too lazy, stupid, or broke to pay his taxes.

But nothing compared to what Culpepper referred to as the heart-breakers. My first heartbreaker lived with her six kids in a trailer on the north end of town. She had made the mistake of filing jointly with a truck driver who never made his estimated tax payments. It was, of course, only one of her mistakes, and a minor one, comparatively. It haunted me, the woman's florid face, bloated and blotchy from alcohol, the fresh bruises on her neck and arms, as the younger children climbed over her enormous bulk. She didn't know nothing, she told me. Her husband was gone for weeks at a time. He made too much for them to go on welfare. I noticed the small, red, circular marks on her children's arms and, seeing that I noticed, she burst into tears, pulling as many squirming children yowling *Mama!* into her copious lap as she could, running her hands over their dirty faces, along their skinny arms, caressing their legs, her mouth moving soundlessly as she stared at me, pleading with her eyes for me to understand the confession she could not speak.

An hour later, we emerged from the trailer, and I felt like an astronaut returning to an earth that was at once strange and familiar, the place I had left that had been changed irrevocably by my leaving.

In the car, Culpepper said, "Say nothing."

"What?"

"If you say anything, it's disclosure."

"What are you talking about?"

"Disclosure. I'm talking about disclosure. You know what disclosure is, don't you, Yancey? Didn't anyone in Phase One say a goddamned thing about disclosure?"

"Of course I know."

"Then why do you say 'what?' like that? Why do people do that? Why do they say 'what, what?' like that? Jesus! Listen to me. Some people might say we now have a moral obligation to report what we saw back there. How would you feel if two weeks from now you pick up the paper and find out that son of a bitch killed her or one of her kids and you told no one what was going on?"

He wasn't looking at me. He spoke dispassionately. He might have been talking about the weather. He was strolling down the streets of Culpepperville.

"Look, Rick, you're going to see a lot of things. Things that aren't meant to be seen. I've seen things—" he trailed off. He would not tell me of the things he had seen. "We come into people's homes for one reason. We aren't here to save the world."

He cleared his throat.

"We can't report any crime unless we walk in on it in progress. To report anything else is a disclosure of confidential taxpayer information. It will get you fired. It could also get you prosecuted. I knew this RO in Maitland who reported a taxpayer for child neglect. She lost her job and spent four months in jail.

"You're going to see things. These things, you'll have to find some internal way of dealing with them. We see the same things cops see, only we don't have the luxury of taking it public. Some things you see you can put out of your mind. Other things will sink right into you as far as they'll go, right into your fucking bones. You'll feel them at night, crushing you, and you can't tell anyone, except us, your brothers and sisters in the Service."

o   o   o

Gina, always attuned to the psychological health of her trainees, took me into her office the next morning, for what passes as an IRS pep talk.

"You look like shit," she said.

"I'm doing great," I said.

"Great?"

"Fine."

"Fine?"

"Okay."

"You're okay?"

I said nothing, but gave a weak smile. I think if she had smiled back I would have burst into tears.

She asked how things were in my personal life, meaning my relationship with Pam. It was none of her business, so of course I answered immediately.

"Okay," I lied. "We're great." In fact, we had barely spoken or seen each other over the past few days. Pam had taken a job at the local community theater and was gone most nights when I got home. We had begun communicating in little notes. I would come home to find one on the kitchen table, telling me when she expected to be home and I would write beneath it, "Wake me when you come in." Sometimes she did; most of the time she did not. She had taken to overeating, and her weight was inching upward.

She poked me awake at four o'clock one morning, yelling for me to roll over, "Rick, Rick, you're lying in the cookies. *You're lying in the cookies.*" At four in the morning, this seems to make more sense than in the light of day. I rose at six with chocolate chips embedded in my back; she had fallen asleep with a plateful of cookies on her lap. Battling the pounds had been a lifelong struggle, and she blamed me for her recent gains.

"Good," Gina said. "That's important." On this day, a glittering dragon-fly hovered over her left breast. Dragonflies are beneficent insects; they eat mosquitoes and other pests. Thus, I comforted myself.

"It's important to have a life outside the office," she added. "Any office, but particularly this office. I'm sure it's occurred to you, Rick, that your job here is unique. It cannot be compared to anything else in the govern-ment or even to the private sector collectors. You're charged with enforc-ing the most unpopular laws in the country. Everywhere you go, people hate and fear you. As a result, the tendency is to withdraw. It's the agency's tendency and it's our personal tendency."

I nodded dumbly. I had no clue where she was going with this.

"Relationships *outside* the IRS are critical. Especially now, during your training year. You're going to feel as if there's no one who can understand you, who can truly empathize with what you're going through. You'll begin to limit your socializing to people inside the Service. Your old friends will not understand the changes you're going through."

"I haven't changed," I said.

"You don't have a choice," she said. "I only wanted you to know that, in my opinion, there are two things you must do to succeed at this job. First, you must leave it at the office. At the end of the day, whatever is here must stay here. Do you understand what I mean?"

I gave no indication that I understood. I didn't say yes. I didn't nod in agreement. I simply stared at her. *Drain bamaged.*

"Good," she said. "The second thing is—and this is more important than the first thing—the second thing is you must have a life outside the IRS. Don't let your old life die. Find ways to keep it alive. Fight for it as if your very life depended on it. As if your very soul depended on it. Does that make sense to you?"

"I think so."

"I was married once," she said softly. "You've probably heard. It's a good thing, to be married. I recommend it—to most people. I wasn't married very long, but I wouldn't go back and *not* get married."

I said nothing. She continued, "A lot of married people aren't married by the end of their training year."

"I'm not."

"You're not what?"

"I'm not married," I said.

"You said you were engaged."

"I'm still engaged."

"How long have you been engaged?"

"Almost four years."

"Have you set a date?"

"Many times. It just keeps getting pushed back."

"She's some kind of widow, right?"

"Yes," I replied, "the only kind, really."

"Maybe she's afraid you'll die on her, too."

"I will, eventually."

"How did he die?"

"Embolism. Fell in the kitchen while he was making lasagna. He loved to cook. He was thirty-eight, in perfect health."

"It fucked her up."

"Well," I said. "If you want to get clinical about it." I was beginning to lose my temper, but there was no way to express it, not to my boss. That was what ROs' spouses, lovers, children, and "clients" were for.

"When he died she received a big payoff on the life insurance and an annuity, which she loses if she ever remarries."

"Ah," she said. "The barriers to true love."

"It isn't about the money," I said, determine to stay calm. "She thinks, well, I might have some growing up to do before we set a date."

"You never will."

"Grow up?"

"Set a date."

Her words hung in the air. Her conviction brooked no argument. She was trying to provoke me, but since coming onboard with the Service, I had added another half-inch of dermis. If I lasted the year, my hide would as tough as an alligator's.

People said Gina was a pack rat; that you had to navigate through a maze of boxes and stacks of newspapers and old milk crates, overflowing with the paperback novels of which she was so fond, to reach the sofa from the front door. Then there was the story about her cat. Culpepper had told it.

"So after Gina's divorce is final, her brother convinces her if she got a pet she could handle the grief, you know, of losing her eight-month-long marriage. Gina says no, she doesn't really like animals, at least the furry kind, except those suitable for sacrifice at a Black Mass, but one day her secretary shows up at the house with this cat she's rescued from the shelter. Now, there's a reason this cat ended up at a shelter, only Gina has no way of knowing this and Bonny swears she didn't know it, but anyway Gina says thanks, but you can keep your fucking stray cat. Well, Bonny, she bursts into tears because Gina has been giving her hell, made her life absolutely fucking miserable for the past six years, so Gina says okay, what the hell, thanks for the goddamned cat. She takes the cat and locks it in her guest bathroom. She shoves a litter box in there, and for the next two years that's where that cat lives, inside that bathroom, which is about the size of your average linen closet. Every couple of days Gina slips in a bowl of kitty chow and some fresh water and that's her pet. That's her post-divorce companion, locked up in the bathroom, yowling to beat the band. This cat screams and cries and moans from the time she gets up to the time she goes to bed, which is probably why it ended up at the shelter in the first place. It was, like, a neurotic cat. Match made in heaven, right? So Gina calls the vet and says, I got this cat that won't stop howling. And she tells the vet what's going on and the vet says, maybe, you know, maybe it's unhappy because you shut it up in a goddamned bathroom for the past year. The vet calls the humane society, and they send a couple of pet detectives over to check it out, but they report back that the cat is perfectly healthy but cries a lot, probably due to past abuse or some shit, which is like saying the cat is just on a little higher rung in the circle of hell. Gina feels vindicated and starts putting pictures of the thing on her desk, like a beloved child. You don't see those pictures now, but you wouldn't believe the expression on that cat's face—fucking haunt your dreams. That's how that whole Wiccan rumor started, if you ask me, with that cat. It had a collar with a silver bell hanging on it, like what the hell does this bathroom cat need with a bell? Anyway, despite the fact that she's decided she's in love with it, she still won't let it out of the bathroom. This goes on for another year, until finally she finds this new boyfriend who's allergic to cats, so the cat has to go. She calls her brother, because he's got some responsibility for it being in her bathroom, but he says he's already got two cats, and she says tough shit, I'm bringing you this one. Then she calls Bonny, who brought her the thing in the first place, and tells her to bring a cat-carrier over to her house right away, she's getting rid of the cat because her boyfriend can't fuck and sneeze at the same time. While they're on the way over, her brother sits his two little kids down and explains their Auntie Gina is bringing them a present, so by the time Gina and Bonny get there the kids are beside themselves, crawling the walls, dying to get their paws on the new cat. Now, Gina walks in and she sets the carrier in the middle of the room, and she launches into this long lecture to the kids about how they can't just grab at this cat, about how the cat may have to be coaxed out of its box, and how maybe they should set up a small space for it, because this cat was used to small spaces and their daddy's big house might scare this little cat. 'Don't be sad if it tries to hide from you,' she tells them. 'She's got to get used to her new environment.' Finally, when she's absolutely sure she's put a damper on all their childlike enthusiasm, she opens the box and that goddamned cat just *explodes* out of it. It was like she shot that cat out of a cannon. It flew around the room like a punctured balloon, climbing up the curtains and leaping from the fireplace and tearing around the furniture like some possessed fucking demon-cat from hell. Well, those kids went berserk. They were scared out their minds. It was a whirlwind of hair and teeth and claws, like that Tasmanian devil in those old Bugs Bunny cartoons. That cat hadn't known freedom for over two years and it was clear out of its mind! That's what it means when you hear someone around here say, 'Gina's cat,' when they get a crazy taxpayer or they finally close one of their smelliest dogs. You'll know it after you complete your training year and it takes an act of Congress to get your incompetent ass fired. That's how you'll feel—like Gina's cat."

.   .   .

Gina walked with me back to the common room. I was a full head taller than she, and I remember being struck by the total lack of pigment in her scalp: the contrast with her black hair was striking. Everyone in the office, with the exceptions of Dee and Cindy Sandifer, had dark hair. I thought of Culpepper sprouting his raven locks during his metamorphosis from Billy, Purveyor of Piggys in a Cloud, into Prince William of the castle Collect-alot. I was puzzling over the possible significance of this when Gina abruptly pulled on my elbow and said, "Allison said there was something you wanted to discuss with me about Culpepper."

My throat went dry. She must have told Gina I called Culpepper insane. Not being someone who thought quickly on his feet, I answered, "I was wondering if he liked me."

"Liked you?"

"I mean, my work. It was just something Allison and I were wondering about."

"Well, he hasn't said anything to me, and your reviews are good—you were wondering if Culpepper liked you?" She seemed amused.

"I'm assuming that—that that was what she mentioned to you about... about what I wanted to discuss with you about Culpepper." I was making no sense. Verbal dysentery, words spewing everywhere.

"Look, Bill's going to do a lot of things that might upset you. He's going to find out how far he can push you. Some things he says he doesn't really mean and the things he's trying to teach you he never really says. It's up to you and Allison to figure out which is which."

She opened the door, turning to me and saying in an abrupt whisper, "Get through this year, Rick. I have plans for you."

Before I could say anything, like "Plans? What plans?" Allison came around the corner of her cubicle and flashed a brilliant smile in my direction.

"Oh, Rick!" she said. "You don't look good! Are you feeling okay?"

I mumbled something and ducked into my cubicle. What did Allison tell Gina? More than Gina was telling me, obviously. At all costs, I realized, I had to maintain plausible deniability on the issue. It was Allison's word against mine, and anyway, any rational person would conclude it was objective fact that Culpepper was indeed insane. *You see, Rick, in the real world, not the world you're from, but in this world, it's not so much what you say but the care you take in saying it.* I massaged my temples and tried to concentrate.

It was over. I was doomed. With a single word, I had destroyed my career. And that word had been *insane*.

I dialed home. I was determined to stay grounded in something that resembled reality. I heard my own voice on the answering machine and I left the following message.

"I think you're right. Maybe I should quit. Something very bad is happening inside my head. I'm not cut out for this. I'm not sure anyone is cut out for this, but I'm pretty sure I'm not one of them—I mean, one of those people who possibly could be cut out for this. I'll try you later." I waited an extra five seconds before hanging up, in case she was screening the calls.

o   o   o

After the skimmers and the hardships, there were the cases that demanded enforced collection. These were the hot center of the revenue officer's inventory, why the American taxpayer paid us our salary. If these people were willing to pay or if it was easy for them to pay, they would have paid long before their case ever reached us. We were, therefore, the last people they wanted to see. We were below lawyers. We were below dentists. We were below proctologists. Sometimes, even their neighbors didn't want to see us—I have had doors slammed in my face more times than I can recall— but most of the time your average neighbor can't wait to rat on the person next door. No one likes to hear this, but your neighbor is not your friend. All I had to do was flash my commission and I got the life story, down to whom the wife was seeing on the side and what sort of parties they threw. Your neighbor is going to tell the IRS where you work, how long you've worked there, what kind of car you drive, what kind of jewelry you wear, what kind of valuable collections might be stored in your attic, what kind of people you associate with, and where your kids go to school. If you've moved from another city or state, they'll tell us where you're from, how long you've been at your present address, and if you have any plans for moving in the future. Drink a little too much? Seeing a psychologist? Had an abortion? Faking a disability? We'll know. And most of the time, we won't even have to ask.

"Well, Yancey, congratulations: the last one."

Three weeks after our encounter with Laura Marsh, my first contact, we were sitting in my car outside the official address of my last contact, Clausen Demolition. Clausen Demolition's home office was literally that, someone's home. Culpepper was finishing his morning banana and orange juice. I was drinking black coffee and itching for a cigarette.

"If I tossed this into the back," Culpepper said, referring to the banana peel, "do you think it would grow into a tree?" He waited for me to laugh. Then he said, "Think of the time it would save you in the field, Rick. Get hungry driving around? Just reach behind you and grab a fresh banana. If you don't like bananas, maybe some oranges or a pecan tree. You could plant a garden, have a salad."

"Okay," I said. "If I cleaned it out, I wouldn't be able to find anything."

"Your car is a reflection of your mind," he said.

"Your car," I reminded him, "is spotless, not a thing in it."

He rolled down the window and tossed the banana peel into the yard. "I'm talking about precision. Precision is the key. What do we have on this case?"

I briefed him without referring to the case file. Clausen Demolition owed $24,000 in employment taxes and had not filed an employment tax return in over two years.

"I'm figuring they're out of business."

"Never assume anything," he said.

A middle-aged, heavyset man sporting a bushy mustache answered the door. His eyes were small, lost in folds of drooping flesh. He reminded me of a hound.

"I'm looking for Clausen Construction," I said.

"Demolition," Culpepper said.

"Demolition. Clausen Demolition," I said.

"Who is?"

"I am."

"And who are you?"

I held up my commission, holding it by the right edge so he could have a clear view of my picture and the Treasury Building, the collective beast. He grabbed it out of my hand and slammed the door in our face.

"Oh, Jesus!" I whispered. My knees grew weak. Beside me, Culpepper murmured, "That was a major boner, Rick. If you don't get that commission back it's—this is not going to look good."

The door opened and the man handed back the commission. Giddy with relief, I slipped it into my pocket. For the remainder of the interview, I would tap my pocket to reassure myself it was still there.

"So you're looking for Clausen Demolition," the man said. He had the deep rasp of a lifelong smoker.

"Yes."

"All right, then."

He wasn't going to offer anything. It occurred to me he had yet to acknowledge he knew anything at all about Clausen Demolition.

"Well," I said, "we have this as the corporate address."

"Oh, well, it probably is."

"Are you Mr. Clausen?"

"Yeah."

"It's not your business, though?"

"No."

"Whose business is it?"

"My wife's."

"Your wife owns the business?"

"She's the president. It's her corporation."

"Is she here?"

"Yes."

"Can we talk to her?"

"I'll have to ask her."

"Okay."

He didn't move. He hung in the doorway, studying me. He turned to Culpepper.

"Who're you?"

"I'm with him," Culpepper said.

"Travel in packs, huh? Like wolves."

"No, in pairs. I think you need more than two to constitute a pack."

"You think so?"

"I would have to do some research before committing to it."

"Hang on," the man said, and shut the door in our face for a second time. Culpepper hummed the theme from *The Godfather*. Sweat rolled down the back of my neck and soaked into my collar.

"This is going to be fun," Culpepper said.

The door opened and the man stepped back to let us pass. The door opened directly into the family room, which was dim and thick with cigarette smoke. I breathed in deeply, grateful for the secondhand high. On the end of the sofa sat a mousy-looking woman who appeared much younger than the droopy-eyed brute standing at my elbow. Her hands were folded primly in her lap.

"Mrs. Clausen?" I asked. The room was paneled with knotted pine and seemed to devour every sound, except the labored breathing of the man at my elbow.

"Yes, this is Emily, my wife," the man said. "Honey, this man is called Yancey; he's with the IRS. Don't know this other guy's name, but he's kind of a smartass."

"Mr. Culpepper." Culpepper smiled at her, but his blue eyes were hard. "Are you president of Clausen Demolition?"

"You bet she is," the man said.

"What's your name?" Culpepper asked him.

"Clausen, just like my wife's."

"Guess I'm not the only smartass in the room," Culpepper said.

The man laughed. The laugh originated somewhere deep in his throat and only bubbled up reluctantly. I had the by now familiar vertiginous feeling that I was involved in something I had no prayer of understanding.

"Are you an officer of the corporation?" Culpepper asked him.

"Oh, no, it's my wife's business. I help out on the jobs occasionally, but it's all her baby."

Culpepper turned to Emily Clausen. "Is it all right with you if he stays?"

"What the hell is that supposed to mean?" Mr. Clausen asked.

"You aren't an officer. We want to avoid any unauthorized disclosure."

"She wants me here."

"We have to hear it from her. She does talk, doesn't she?"

After a pause, Clausen said, "You know, I don't think I like you. I don't appreciate your attitude. It's very disrespectful." This hung in the air, with no response from Culpepper. He looked at me. "And you don't even look like someone who'd be working for the IRS. That picture of you, it's not a very good likeness. It doesn't capture the real you, if you ask me."

Speaking barely above a whisper, the woman said, "It's all right. He can stay."

"See?" Clausen said. He sat beside me in a straight-back wooden chair. It groaned under his bulk. He was sitting so close I could smell his stale breath and the stench of tobacco floating about him like a fine early-morning mist. The coffee table before us was made from a cypress stump, polished and varnished to a shiny finish, the kind offered for sale along every highway in Florida.

I informed Mrs. Clausen why we had come. She made no reply. I asked her if the corporation still had employees.

Mr. Clausen said, "What do you mean by 'employees'?"

"People who worked for the corporation."

"Well, I work, but I don't take a salary."

"Does your wife?" Culpepper asked.

"Oh, she takes a draw... occasionally."

"Well, who gets on the bulldozer and knocks down the walls? Who swings the big metal ball into the building?"

"I think I just said—"

"Where are the corporate records?" Culpepper demanded.

"Some are here. Some are with our accountant," Clausen answered. He was as calm as a monk in meditation.

"We can check with the state," Culpepper informed him. "They'll tell us if you have employees. We'll check with your insurance carrier."

"Oh, I know we'll get this all worked out," Clausen said soothingly.

I pulled out the financial statement and tried to conduct a structured interview, with mixed results. Clausen answered all the questions while his mousy wife stared at me with that deer-in-the-headlights look of hers.

"Where are the business assets?" I asked.

"The business doesn't own any assets," Mr. Clausen said.

"What do you do, knock down the buildings with your head?" Culpepper asked.

Clausen ignored him. "The business leases all the equipment."

"From whom?"

"From me."

"From you?"

"Yes." He explained he had once owned a business called Burt Clausen Demolition. Thus, I discovered his first name. I scribbled it in the margin of the form. Burt Clausen Demolition was defunct and the assets from the business were being leased by Clausen Demolition, Inc., of which Emily Clausen was the president and sole shareholder. I asked for the major accounts receivable. Clausen said he would have to get back to us on that, but he did mention Maroli Construction. At that point, something changed in the atmosphere. Culpepper began to hold forth in a strained voice upon the importance of good record-keeping and proper tracking of accounts. I glanced over at him; I had never seen him like this, and after a moment, I realized that for the first time, I was witnessing fear in the face of the prince of power.

We left ten minutes later, without completing the financial statement, without developing a plan of action, without setting any deadlines whatsoever. Clausen had taken a liking to Culpepper and gave him a friendly pat on the shoulder on our way out the door. Back in the car, Culpepper scrunched down in his seat and stared straight ahead at the looming shadow of Burt Clausen in the doorway. He didn't speak until we were well on our way back to the office.

"Maroli Construction. You don't know anything about Maroli Construction, do you, Yancey? I'm going to have to talk to Gina about this. I probably should have this case. This case is too much for you. This case is way over your head."

I agreed with him, but I wasn't going to tell him that. I wasn't going to admit weakness. I had learned that much in my brief tenure with the Service. You admitted weakness to no one, either on the outside or the inside. The trick was learning never to admit it to yourself.

"It's the Mob, isn't it?" I asked.

Culpepper said nothing. He was staring out the passenger window, his face turned away from me. The morning was cloudless, the light harsh.

"He's going to call you. Put him off. Tell him you'll get back to him. If he sends you a letter or...or a package, make sure you find me before you open it."

I forced myself to laugh. "You're giving me the creeps, Culpepper." He didn't answer. Now I began to hum the theme from *The Godfather*.

"Don't act like a moron, Yancey," he said.

o   o   o

On my drive home that day, while I sat in traffic, admiring the golden afternoon light that seemed to flow over the earth in gentle waves, it hit me full force, a fear so tangible I could actually smell it; I could smell the terror rising out of me, and I pulled to the side of the road and burst into tears, sobbing uncontrollably while the traffic streamed by, cars filled with normal people on their way home from normal jobs. Jesus, how I envied them and hated them. So, what's the big deal? my little voice whispered. Quit. Call in tomorrow and tell them you won't be coming in. It was so easy, and the only answer, really. Stop being such a goddamned baby. Suddenly, I thought of the woman with the metal plate in her head, suffering from "drain bamage." I could feel her inside me, and the nervous laughter of Laura Marsh and the sound of Mr. Rose the mortician's shuffling feet on the linoleum and the gurgling laughter of Burt Clausen and the inconsolable sobs of the woman in the trailer and the desperate, secret cry for help in her eyes, and I knew in the profoundest sense that I had seen too much, I was too deep to get out. Just that morning, before leaving to visit Burt Clausen, I had opened my mail to find the check that represented my first levy proceeds. With a stroke of my pen, I had stripped a family of every penny they had in their bank account. I had signed a form, mailed it, and in three weeks had a check in my hands. It was a singular moment. I immediately ran over to Culpepper's desk and he shook my hand solemnly and said, "Ah, I see it in your eyes, Yancey. You're starting to get it now."

I had changed and, like the dirt-farmer's wife, the change was permanent. I would never be the same.

I drove home, a revenue officer. I returned the next morning as the sun rose, bloated, red, and promising brutal heat, and I was still a revenue officer.

(6)

BYZANTIUM

Culpepper enjoyed telling the story of Walter Crenshaw. Walter was a sweet man, a simple beat-cop from New Jersey, retired to Florida but bored after two years off the force. The IRS is fond of hiring ex-military and law enforcement types; they come on board with the right mind-set. According to Culpepper, he wasn't the brightest bulb in the chandelier, and would often exclaim in moments of procedural panic, "There oughtta be a handbook for this job!" Culpepper decided to oblige him, and typed the words WALTER'S HANDBOOK on a piece of paper and taped the paper to the front of Walter's copy of the Internal Revenue Manual. Walter did not last long into his training year. Culpepper was his OJI and saw to that.

"I'm not capricious," he told Allison and me after someone related a story about the trainee he allegedly browbeat until the poor bastard literally wet his pants. "It's never personal. One day, when it's your turn to be OJIs, you'll understand. The IRS is a fortress, and I am the guardian at the gate. It's my job to separate the wheat from the chaff. And anyway, that story's misleading. He did piss himself, but the sick motherfucker *liked* to piss himself. There wasn't a goddamned thing wrong with his bladder. He wore Depends—you know, those diapers for adults. He told me he liked the feeling of the warm urine spilling into his pants. He dug the idea of talking to the teenage clerk at the checkout, totally fucking oblivious, while he emptied his bladder."

Allison laughed nervously, feigning shock at Culpepper's language in the middle of the workplace. Culpepper ignored her. He was having a bad day. That morning he had undergone the first round of interviews for the frontline manager cadre, and the word was it had not gone well. The branch chief did not like Culpepper; saw him as a threat, some said.

"I'm working on your mid-year," he said abruptly, turning to me. "Conference room. Five minutes."

He stalked to his cubicle, the scent of his Obsession by Calvin Klein swirling in his wake. Allison gave me the eye.

"Ooooh," she whispered. "Lucky you."

Lucky me. As my OJI, Culpepper was required to conduct a complete review of my inventory, all thirty cases, upon my six-month anniversary with the Service. I had known this was coming, of course, but this did nothing to alleviate the distinct feeling in my scrotum that I was about to catch a hard one between the thighs.

"Bring your DIAL,"* he snapped at me as he passed my desk.

"Good luck, Rick!" Allison called.

I gave her the finger. "You're next."

"I don't anticipate any problems," she said sweetly. I considered what it would feel like to pick up the typewriter sitting on the small stand beside her and slam it over the top of her round little head. I decided it would feel good. Behind me, Rachel said, with maternal patience, "Oh, children, get along now." All morning Rachel had been working on a rap song she planned to perform at the Christmas party, which was still over six months away. The chorus went, "With a lien and a levy and a seizure and sale / We're devoted civil servants / And we hardly ever fail." Rachel could afford to be cheerful. She had it easy with Cindy Sandifer as her OJI. It occurred to me I could take out the whole office with any number of weapons easily at hand. What I lacked was the necessary willpower. The world would not miss you people, I remember thinking, as I walked down the long corridor to the conference room, where my tormentor awaited. He was sitting with the chair turned from the door, facing the blank wall four feet from his nose, his shoulders rounded, his head slightly bowed. An aura of pathos hung about him, a pall of suffering. In his dark suit, facing that blank wall,

---

* Delinquent Inventory Account Listing, a printout of a revenue officer's inventory: taxpayer name, identifying number, tax periods owing, and amounts due.

he reminded me of Bartleby the scrivener in the Herman Melville story of the same name: *I would prefer not to.* Ah, Culpepper! Ah, humanity!

I closed the door behind me. The latch went *snick.* He did not move. I slipped into a chair at the opposite end of the table, closest to the door, placing the DIAL before me, and waited.

"I have asked Gina to transfer the Clausen case to me," he said. There was a long silence. "She has refused. I don't agree with her, but I can understand her reasoning. If Burt Clausen were closely connected to organized crime, he wouldn't owe taxes."

I thought of Al Capone and said, "How do you figure?"

"Did I ask you a question, Yancey?" He still had not turned to face me.

"No, you did not."

"Then shut the fuck up. You aren't as smart as you think you are. You're smart, but not in any way that's significant, not smart in the way smart really matters. Do you have any fucking clue what I'm talking about? Do you?"

He had asked a question, which granted me license to say, "Not really." The interview must have been worse than we had imagined. He was acting as if he had just received news of a loved one's premature death. He shifted in his chair. His black hair shone in the unforgiving glare of the fluorescent bulbs above us. I wondered if the story about him losing all his hair was true or something delivered for effect. With a jolt, I realized I was feeling pity for him, this prisoner of his own ambition, this slave to the beast, this thrall to the gods of power. The outline of his dark hair was sharply defined against the blank white wall, and I thought of the apple he consumed before me that day in Powell, which now seemed so long ago. As a would-be dramatist, I was rewriting his part as we sat there, from tormentor to tragic figure, a pint-sized Macbeth, strung up by his own overweening ambition.

"Of course you don't. I'll explain. I'll use small words, nothing over three syllables: nobody truly connected to the Mafia owes federal taxes. They have enough headaches without us on their case. The mob is one of the most compliant sectors of the taxpaying public, at least when it comes to employment taxes."

"So we go after him?" I asked.

"Of course not. We're fifty-threeing it."

"Fifty-threeing" an account refers to Form 53, which is used to report taxes as currently not collectible—calling off all enforced collection.

"On what basis?" I asked.

"On the basis your OJI told you to do it. Gina will sign it."

"Okay," I said. "What about levying Maroli Construction?"

He whirled around to face me.

"Have you no conscience?" he snapped. "What do you think would happen to those two pitiful losers if the Marolis found out the taxes weren't being paid?"

"Is that our problem?"

"Spare me, Yancey."

"Our job is to feed the beast."

"You will fifty-three this account."

"You want to fifty-three Burt Clausen and seize Laura Marsh's jungle gym. Isn't that somewhat screwy?"

"We're not IRS, Inc. We're not in the business of making a profit. We aren't a business, period."

"I don't care about that. I just want what I do for a living to make sense."

He laughed. "You want a job that makes sense? Become a carpenter. What a carpenter does makes sense. He takes a few pieces of wood and some tools and at the end of the day he has something to show for it. A table. A chair. A nightstand. Something you can touch, something you can appreciate, use, perhaps something even beautiful. He has created something. What do we create?" He spread his hands apart, palms upward. "We do the opposite. We *nullify*. We confiscate. We obliterate. We take a bunch of numbers and make them go away. That's all it becomes after a while— just a bunch of numbers. You pick up a TDA* as a trainee and you think, 'Dear Jesus! This poor fucker owes five thousand dollars!' Five years later you're a Grade Twelve working million-dollar accounts. And if you're lucky—poof! you make the numbers disappear. And half the time you won't even know where they go. Your job is the black hole of occupations."

"You're getting a little too far out there, even for me, Culpepper."

---

* Taxpayer Delinquency Account.

"Then I must be pretty goddamned far."

"Why don't I just call Burt and tell him we're going to levy Maroli. Won't that get him to pay?"

"Drop this."

"Since when did you care what happens to taxpayers?"

"You drop this or I will write you up."

"Maybe you should."

"I will write you up for insubordination and you can go back to your paper route and your little faggot theater crowd."

"You're a truly pitiful human being, you know that, Culpepper?"

He took a deep breath. He placed his hands on the tabletop, splayed his short fingers, and studied his polished nails. My heart was high in my chest, my cheeks burning hot. My scalp tingled. Don't lose it, I told myself. If you lose it, he wins.

"Fine," I said. "I don't give a shit."

"You will," he said quietly. I let it pass. I had always detested confrontation and now I faced it on a daily basis. It had become the defining characteristic of my existence. Again I had the distinctly uncomfortable feeling of being a stranger inside my own skin.

"I have been waiting for the paperwork on the Marsh case," he said.

"What paperwork would that be?"

"The seizure paperwork, Yancey." He sounded weary. "Remember your plan-of-action?"

"She sent me a check for a thousand dollars."

"She did what?"

"Sent me a check for a—"

"Where'd she get a thousand dollars?"

"I don't know."

"You don't know?"

"I didn't ask her."

"It's your job to ask her."

"I didn't think it was apropos."

"You didn't think it was—apropos? Is that the word you used, *apropos*?"

"I was just happy she sent it."

"Oh, yes, I bet you were. At this rate, she'll have the debt retired by the time you're ready to. Do you begin to see the pointlessness of your argument, Yancey?"

"I wasn't aware that I was making an argument."

"You're not aware of much, are you?"

"Look," I said. "Culpepper. You're obviously upset about something other than the fact that Laura Marsh had the gall the send the IRS a thousand dollars."

"Listen to me, you little fuck, don't you ever talk to me that way again."

I laughed aloud. I didn't expect it, and clearly Culpepper didn't expect it, either.

"I'm sorry," I said. "Was that insubordinate? I was going to say that I have revised my plan-of-action in the Marsh case. My new plan-of-action is to grant her an installment agreement, and the first time she misses a payment, I am going to seize—after she signs a consent,* of course."

"Gina will never sign it," he said, meaning the installment agreement.

"I've already discussed it with her. She agrees there's some public policy considerations in seizing a day care in a depressed area of town."

"Okay," he said at length, drawing the word out. Then, very softly, so softly I could barely hear him from six feet away: "Why are you doing this, Yancey?"

I knew precisely what he meant. He did not have to explain what "this" was. I did my best Richard Gere imitation, from *An Officer and a Gentleman:* "Because I got no place else to go!"

Culpepper smiled. It was an altogether pleasant smile, and therefore altogether chilling.

"I thought paperboys always knew where to go," he said.

"How did you know about the paper route?"

"I've seen your file."

"That's in my file?"

"Your application is in your file. Remember the section about all the jobs you've held over the past ten years?" He laced his fingers together and studied me over his clenched hands. "You know, we investigate all that."

---

* Shorthand for "consent-to-enter." Under the Fourth Amendmendment, the Service cannot seize assets in "private areas" without the written permission of the taxpayer.

"The Service investigated my paper route?"

"The Service sends Inspection to former employers, family members, old lovers, present and former neighbors... then Inspection writes a report."

"Must make for some pretty dull reading."

"On the contrary," he said, "I found it fascinating."

"Can I see the report?"

"You can file a Freedom of Information Act request. Then in about two years you may get a copy, but most of it will be redacted."

"Redacted?"

"To protect the informants."

"Informants?"

"The Service must be extremely careful about who it hires. The power available to a revenue officer could be devastating in the wrong hands. We don't want morons and we don't want crooks."

I was hardly listening by this point. He was poised to launch into another of his monologues about the exalted nature of collecting taxes, and I didn't have the stomach for it. My mind dwelled on the word *informant*. Had they interviewed Pam? She was, at that time, the person closest to me— had the suits showed up at the house one day, perhaps while I was in Tampa, with their badges and shoulder holsters and dark glasses? Would she have spoken with them? Did she have a choice? And, if they had come, why hadn't she told me? And, if she did speak to them, what did she say? Culpepper was watching me, a knowing look in his eyes, as if he knew what dark weed he had planted with the word *informant*.

"You want to know how long we keep your application? For the duration of your career. See, it's a federal offense to lie on your application. Remember I told you that it practically takes an act of Congress to remove you, once you're out of the training year? If they really want to get rid of someone, they pull the application, because most people do lie on applications or they forget about a job they had for a couple of months six or seven years back. I've known several people they got that way. One was a union steward making management miserable, so they handed his file over to Inspection. Turned out he had been fired from a job, but on his app he said he had left voluntarily. After twenty-five years of distinguished service—he was a goddamned good RO, by the way—they took him out. Lost his retirement, too. Because he pissed them off. The life lesson here, Rick, is you do not cross them. You do not piss off the Service. They will find out if you've crossed them and they will find a way to get you."

Back at my desk, I dug out my copy of Form SF-171, the standard application for government employment, thinking of the day a thousand years ago when I had filled it out, remembering vividly how sad and small my life seemed once reduced to a seven-page bureaucratic form. How it appeared to me I had lived more places in the past ten years than a migrant farmworker. How my life consisted of big dreams and petty jobs. The paper route. The convenience store. The small print shop. The acting workshops for preschoolers. I had omitted the single day I worked as a telemarketer selling prescription contact lenses. That was over seven years ago. Could they find out about that one? Probably. Would they really fire me over such an insignificant oversight? Of course they would. Above my signature was the statement, in bold print, UNDER PENALTY OF PERJURY, I DECLARE THE ABOVE STATEMENTS TO BE TRUE, CORRECT AND COMPLETE. Perjury. I was a perjurer. Had Inspection already pulled my tax records and found I had not been "true, correct, and complete?" Of course they had, and Culpepper was letting me know they had and that he, too, knew they had. All he had to do, at any time, was to tell Gina he didn't think this Rick Yancey was working out and it would be best if they exiled him back to the world of his little faggot theater crowd. "Don't cross them," he had said. What he really meant was, "Don't cross *me*."

There was a note from Pam on the kitchen table when I arrived home that afternoon. "Leftover chicken and some potato salad for dinner. Have to work late. Meet me at The Cellar after rehearsal, about 10:30. Love, P." The Cellar was the hangout of choice for the theater crowd, an intimate beer joint attached to the Howard Johnson's, with an antique jukebox, stuffed parrots hanging from the ceiling, and a few tired-looking plastic palm trees in the corners. I hadn't been there in months. I decided to take a quick nap; it was only five o'clock and I wasn't hungry. I lay on the bed, still in my shirt and tie, and thought of how I hated the soft mattress and how I missed the firm mattress in my old room at my parents' house. That made me think of my parents, whom I hadn't seen in months, though they lived only twenty miles away, and the resulting guilt made it impossible to sleep. Had Inspection talked to my parents? I couldn't recall a line on the form that asked for their names, but surely they could find that out. Perhaps Pam told them. *I know I've lived with him for four years, but I really don't know him very well. He's quiet; keeps to himself mostly. You really should talk to his mom and dad. They live right over in Lakeside. Here, I'll give you their address and phone number.* Dad would tell me if they came—the visit would have disturbed him, even after assurances it was all routine and all I had done was commit a little perjury.

We've discovered he left something out on his application. This makes us wonder what else he may have left out. We need to know: What kind of person is he? What is his relationship with this Pam person? Why aren't they married? Would you say this reflects on his moral character? What are you thoughts on his moral character? We do know he's a perjurer and a fornicator—has he broken any other laws that you're aware of? And, if my mother was involved, she might tell them the story of the toy that somehow slipped into my pocket at Grant's Drug Store when I was ten. How, when she discovered my crime, I was marched back to the store to speak with the manager, a corpulent man with copious nose-hair whose name escaped me, but surely would not escape Inspection once they heard the story. *Of course I remember him, the little thief!*

A band of golden afternoon sunlight streamed across the foot of the bed, stretched itself upon the floor, and crawled up the pale blue wall on the far side of the room. In the gloaming, I had the sense of time racing toward some inescapable conclusion, to a reckoning I had not foreseen. The *why* no longer mattered. I had leapt into the river at the point of its swiftest current, and had been swept away. I wanted to reach the end; I wanted to see where the river took me. The Service had awakened something dormant within me, something that had always been there, lacking a language to give it voice, an arena in which it might triumph. Culpepper had seen this, had likely gleaned it from my file, for in my past, he had seen a reflection of his own. He was nurturing the seed through fear and intimidation—and temptation. The Service offered people like us the one thing that we would find irresistible: a world of practically limitless power, nectar of the gods to the ineffectual dreamer, for whom life was not a pursuit of happiness, but a struggle for recognition and control.

The party was well under way at The Cellar by the time I arrived a little after eleven. I kissed Pam on the cheek and apologized.

"I fell asleep."

"Rick can't stay awake past nine," she said to no one in particular. No one in particular seemed to be listening.

"I get up at four," I said.

"Why does Rick get up at four?" someone asked. So at least one person had been listening. Probably an informant. Culpepper had not said if Inspection did any follow-up after you were hired.

"Rick gets up at four o'clock in the *morning*?" someone else said.

"He goes to Denny's and writes for a couple hours," Pam said. "Or so he *says*."

"What the hell else would he be doing at four o'clock in the morning?"

The waitress stopped by the table. I ordered a beer and lit a cigarette.

"Do you have to?" Pam asked. I took it as a rhetorical question and jettisoned the smoke into the air above me. Robert Palmer's "Addicted to Love" was blaring from the jukebox behind us. She leaned over and hissed in my ear, "You look like shit. Couldn't you have at least changed your clothes?"

"You know, I don't think I've ever seen Rick in a tie," someone said.

"He looks like he's on his way to a funeral."

"I overslept; I told you," I said to Pam.

"You need a haircut."

"Must we dwell on my personal grooming, Red?"

She had recently allowed a friend from the theater (who was a hairdresser in his day job) to redo her hair. He had dyed it flaming red and spiked the top punk rocker–style. She had asked me what I thought of it, and I was forced to answer, "It's . . . challenging." Pam was a restless experimenter when it came to her hair. Since we had been together, she had gone through four distinct hairstyles, varying length, color, cut, curl. Her natural color was a mousy brown.

I forged on. "Heard a funny story today about a guy who liked to pee his pants," I said to the group, but only Pam was listening.

"Is it as funny as the guy whose dog got arrested for rape?"

"That dog wasn't arrested, it was reprimanded . . . no, it isn't that funny. It's between that and the one about the guy's twelve-year-old sticking his penis in the vacuum cleaner hose."

"That's not funny. It's disgusting."

"Hey, guess what I found out today."

"They've repealed the income tax."

"No."

"Darn."

"Inspection investigated my application."

"What's that mean?"

"Means they talked to people."

"Which people?"

I studied her carefully. Culpepper had a theory that you could always tell if a taxpayer was lying by watching the pupils. *The pupil will contract during a lie, hiding from the light . . .* The lighting was too dim for gauging pupil contraction. I took her hand to see if her palms were dry.

"They don't tell you. Culpepper hinted they talk to everyone."

"Everyone?"

"Everyone."

I waited. She extracted her hand from mine and picked up her wineglass. She sipped her wine and looked away.

Laughter exploded at the other end of the table. Tom Foster, an electronics salesman by day, actor by night, and possessor of a magnificent baritone in precise inverse proportion to his acting ability, was regaling those about him with one of his off-color jokes, of which he had inexhaustible supply. Tom was thirty-three years old and still lived with his mother. I thought of Culpepper's remark about my "faggot theater crowd." Looking around the table, I took an inventory of those who were definitely out of the closet, those still in, and those still wavering at the threshold. At least half. All were my good friends, the people I had always been the most comfortable with. I loosened my tie, rolled up my sleeves, and determined I would enjoy myself and not think about Inspection knocking on their doors and asking intimate questions about my personal life. So what if one or two at the table were giving me the eye? Or that each had turned slightly away in their chairs, or that a pair at the end of the table were whispering when Robert Palmer hardly made whispering necessary?

The waitress returned with my beer. The alcohol had an immediate, dizzying effect: I hadn't eaten since lunch. I looked about the room as it began to spin, and enjoyed the babble; it was a pleasant white noise. Pam asked why I was so quiet. I told her I had a bad day at work. She replied I always had a bad day at work. I said this day was particularly bad: Culpepper called me a little fuck and accused my friends of being sodomites. I told her about the DIAL briefing. She asked what the hell a DIAL briefing was. I tried to explain what a DIAL briefing was. She lost interest and struck up a conversation with Carl, the theater's technical director. I lit another cigarette and leaned over to speak to Pam's brother, who also acted in his spare time, looking directly into his eyes: "Time is a river and I have run the shoals!"

"What?"

"I said—has anyone from the IRS ever talked to you?"

"Just you."

I couldn't say with absolute certainty, but it appeared the pupil of his right eye contracted, ever so slightly, as he said it.

Pam drank too much and I insisted on driving her home. We would pick up her car in the morning.

"You'll be late for work."

"It's okay."

"Don't they break your thumbs for that?"

"No. The knees. But it's just one knee the first time."

We had a terrible fight during the drive home. She was sick of my obsessing over the job. I had lost weight. I was smoking too much. I ignored her. She never saw me and when she did she didn't understand what I was talking about, when I decided to talk, because all I talked about was work.

"You know, my husband had a very stressful job and he didn't bring it home with him every night."

"No, he kept it all inside until it exploded his brain."

She hit me in the shoulder as hard as she could. She told me I didn't know what the fuck I was talking about. I told her I resented her bringing up her dead husband at every opportunity; it was as if I were in competition with a corpse. I repeated my long-held belief that she had elevated his death into a kind of martyrdom; that his death had somehow transformed him into a saint beyond emulation; and that the reason she wouldn't marry me had nothing to do with my inability to provide a stable income or a lack of maturity, but had everything to do with the fact that she was still in love with him.

She screamed at me to stop the car. She threw open her door. I slammed on the brakes, throwing her forward. Her head almost smacked the dashboard. She fell out the open door, onto the road. It was one o'clock in the morning; we were on a road that wound its way through orange groves, about three miles from the house. She slammed the door and began to run, her crimson tresses swinging behind her. I pulled up beside her and called to her through the open window.

"Get in the car!"

"Fuck you!"

"Rational people do not leap from moving cars!"

"Okay. Okay." I was keeping pace with her as she walked rapidly upon the roadside. "So I'm irrational. I'm hysterical. I'm *fucked up*, Rick, so what are you gonna do about it?"

"I don't know what I can do about it."

"No, of course you don't know what to do. Poor Rick. Poor, passive little Rick, never knowing what to do. You know what I want you to do? Would that help, if I told you what I wanted you to do?"

"It might."

"All I wanted, Rick, all I ever wanted was somebody to take care of me."

"Why do you think I took this fucking job in the first place?"

"Oh, don't fool yourself, Rick. You taking this job had nothing to do with me."

"Pam, please, get in the car."

She stopped. Her head was bowed; I couldn't see her face. Her chest heaved. She climbed back into the car.

"Can't we go back?"

She wasn't talking about the house we shared. I turned and stared straight ahead through the windshield, idling by the side of the road.

"No," I said. My voice was thick from cigarettes and lack of sleep.

"Why? Why not, Rick?"

"Because I have to finish this. I can't afford another failure, Pam." I was thinking of my SF-171, how I had to attach extra pages to include all my little jobs over the past ten years—except the telemarketing gig—all the rotten places I had lived in. "If I fail at this, I'm done."

"Oh," she said. "The *drama*."

"I have to prove to myself I'm not a failure."

"And that's what success at the IRS would prove?"

"Pam, I don't even know what success at the IRS means."

"And if I told you to choose, to quit or move out, what do you think that would mean?"

I told her I didn't know what that would mean, either. There were no streetlights on this narrow two-lane road that curved lazily through the groves, its edges crumbing into the soft Florida soil. The darkness seemed to press against the beams of my headlamps, twisting them into taut ribbons of light. My hands tightened on the wheel. The river's current was strong and deep, and there was no shore in sight.

I received my write-up from Culpepper two weeks later. This review was the benchmark of my first six months with the Service. Overall, Culpepper was pleasantly surprised by my progress. He felt I made sound case decisions, conducted thorough research—though not, he noted, *exhaustive*. I did a good job protecting taxpayer rights, whatever those might be; in those days, protecting a taxpayers' rights meant handing them Publication One on first contact. During one group meeting, while Gina was reminding everyone of the necessity of issuing Pub One, Culpepper rolled one into a tube and mimed shoving it up a taxpayer's ass.

He found me lacking in two key areas: protecting the government's interest and inventory management. This was code. It meant I wasn't enforcing (I had yet to make a seizure) and I was overworking cases.

"You kept this TDI* over five weeks," he told me in my postreview debriefing. His mood was better. He was wearing his yellow tie. Culpepper's

---

* Taxpayer Delinquency Investigation: a "warrant" to collect unfiled tax returns.

moods were often reflected in his choice of neckwear. "It's pretty obvious on the face of it this TP's out of business. Don't beat a dead horse. You did everything required by the manual to locate them. You couldn't find them, so it should have been closed."

"I'll have it on your desk by close of business today," I promised.

He nodded. "I've told you before, we don't pay you to close cases in your training year. We pay you to learn the job. But—close cases. You must close cases. That's what impresses management, or are you not interested in impressing management?"

"I'm interested."

"Are you?"

"Yes."

He arched one eyebrow. "Really. Okay. The second thing that impresses management is seizures. To rise in this organization you must conduct seizures. Do you know why that is?"

"Statistics?"

"Oh, Jesus, you are growing, Yancey. You are evolving before my eyes. Pretty soon the chrysalis will split open and out will spew the butterfly."

"Spew?"

"Remember the fourth protocol. Any fucking Grade Seven sitting in Jacksonville can issue a levy. A Grade Five can file a lien. Only a revenue officer can seize. You must make that decision on a case-by-case basis, of course, but at some point, some *near and immediate* point in the future, you must conduct a seizure. It doesn't matter what you seize. Remember, you can always *make* equity." He grew wistful. "You know, in the old days we used to issue a summons and when the taxpayer showed up at the office we would seize his car. One person would take him into the booth and two others would go outside, find it, and sticker it. Didn't matter if it was ten years old riding on its rims... didn't even matter if they drove something like *your* car. In the old days, we didn't even need a consent. If we walked into the place and they pissed us off in the least, we would go, 'That's it, you're seized, asshole.' "

"Okay."

"You know, Allison has already done two seizures."

"I know."

"You have not done any. Do you think your inventory is qualitatively different from hers?"

"No."

"Do you believe you just happen to have the one set of thirty-five taxpayers that does not require seizure action?"

"I doubt it."

"Very good. Let's see. You're off to Phase Two in another four weeks. I want a seizure package on my desk twice a week, that's eight seizures before you go to Phase Two. That should keep Allison on her toes."

"I'll . . . I'll look over my cases."

"That Marsh case would be a good place to start."

"She's sending me money. Gina signed the IA.*"

"Is she current?"

"I'm monitoring that."

"Okay. So . . . is she?"

"Yes."

"Hmmmm." He brushed an imaginary wrinkle from his tie. "Speaking of Allison, in the future I would watch what I said to her."

A chill ran down the middle of my spine. "Why's that?"

"She does not have your best interest at heart. Things can get pretty nasty when promotions are on the line. They can also get nasty when they're *not*, and I would hate to see you strike out before you've even stepped up to the plate."

"I'm not following you, Culpepper."

"Christ, Yancey, aren't you the dramatist, the expert on the human condition and all that shit? Little Miss Allison doesn't just want Gina's job. She wants Gina's boss's *boss's* job. And there is very little she will stop short of to get it."

My throat had gone bone-dry.

"In the future, I would be careful what I said to her. I would not pass on any personal opinions about my coworkers, my OJI, or my supervisor. Particularly my supervisor and my OJI. I would not criticize, mock, imitate, or tattle. Particularly tattle."

---

* Form 433-D, Installment Agreement.

He smiled. His attitude toward me bordered on the paternal. If he could have reached me from across the table, he would have hugged me, stroked my brow, told me it was going to be all right. "Just remember what I told you. She cannot be trusted. I've seen it get really bad. There was one office where no one dared leave a check unattended on their desk: someone would snatch it and shred it. Or the receipt book. Do you know where your 809 book is?"

I nodded. I started to tell him where it was, then thought better of it. Culpepper was speaking earnestly now. "Don't tell anyone where it is. When you have to write a cash receipt, make sure no one's around when you put the book away. I recommend putting it in a different place each time. And never, never leave your desk unlocked, even to duck out to the john."

"You mean someone in this office would steal a cash receipt?"

"Oh, they wouldn't take the whole book. Too obvious. No RO is that stupid. No, they flip to the middle of the book and tear out one or two receipts. That way, six months down the road, a year maybe, Gina's doing your reconciliation and those receipts are gone. And I'm sure they told you what happens to you if a receipt comes up unaccounted for."

I nodded. Instant termination. An official receipt from the IRS was proof that taxes had been paid. It was the most precious form in all the Service, Form 809. The book in which they came represented literally billions of dollars in blank checks.

"I can't believe anyone in this office..."

Culpepper spread his hands, laid them palm down on the tabletop. He studied his nails. "I've known ROs who hire private investigators to tail their professional enemies. I've known ROs who have shredded entire case files. Is your desk unlocked at this moment, Rick?"

"Okay," I said. "So we can't trust the taxpayer and we can't trust one another. Whatever happened to the Service being a brotherhood?"

He smiled, all his attention still focused on his manicure. He let silence smack the end of each sentence. "You are a trainee. You are vulnerable. You will never be more vulnerable than you are right now. We can remove you on a whim. We may decide you look funny. We may decide you smell bad. Your fellow trainees will—and are doing so, even now—try to turn us against you. While you are vulnerable, you have no allies. You have no friends. You are alone."

He raised his eyes.

"Do you believe me, Rick?"

"I always believe you, Culpepper."

"This is war. Surely this simple truth has occurred to you at some point in the past six months. You are at war," he said. "All of us are. But it's a war whose front is constantly shifting. Sometimes it's before us, sometimes it's behind us. To survive this war, you have to know which way to turn and fight. You have to hear the round coming."

Indoctrination begins the moment you're hired. On your first day, everyone hails your arrival with a hearty *welcome aboard!* as if you've just set sail on the U.S.S. *IRS*. You don't go into training, you go into *basic training*. You are not an employee; you are a *frontline* employee. You do not go to your office; you go to your *post-of-duty*. You do not have work hours; you have a *tour-of-duty*. You don't go to appointments; you go to *the field*. *This is war,* Culpepper had said. And Melissa: *If it was up to me, I'd line 'em all against a wall and shoot them.* The language of war and the culture of conflict are the only means to prepare us for what is expected of us. How else could they demand what they demanded of us? You can't take their life savings, their car, their paycheck, the roof over their head and the heads of their children, without dehumanizing them, without casting yourself into a role that by necessity makes them the enemy. We occupied the front lines, and there can be no front lines without a war. Like war, our jobs consisted of hours of sheer boredom, punctuated by moments of extreme terror. And, like war, it was addictive. Blood in the water of the fountains of Byzantium.

This is war. In a moment, I would walk back to the main office, where my comrades-in-arms hunkered in their foxholes, typing levies or filling out lien requests or composing histories of their latest campaigns, covert ops, and full-frontal assaults, phones pressed close to their mouths, speaking with bankers, lawyers, spouses and former spouses, business partners and ex-business partners, current and former employers, parents, siblings, distant cousins, school principals, local cops. We have superior intelligence; we know more about our enemies' lives than they know themselves. We know where they are. We know what they do. We know what they have. We will execute what they fear.

This is war. Back at my desk, I checked each receipt in my 809 book, to make sure none was missing. None was. I slipped the book into an envelope and sealed it with tape. Now, no one could tamper with it without my knowledge. Measures and countermeasures.

This is war. The room was empty but for Henry tapping away at the IDRS* terminal. Where was everyone? I knew Allison had gone to the field. Dee had called in sick—again. Rachel might be sitting in the interview booth.Perhaps if I sat there long enough, a senior RO would breeze in and ease my mind with a war story. To talk about a particularly funny or memorable case was to tell a *war story*. I sat at my desk, not moving. Waiting for something. I had some calls to return, some histories to write, some notices to mail. I needed to check to see if Laura Marsh was indeed current with her payroll taxes—before Culpepper had a chance to do so. I needed to search for eight cases that "justified" a seizure.

This is war. I picked up my pen. I opened my file drawer. I pulled a case at random. I felt no moral ambiguity at that moment. All I felt was rage and the bloodlust of battle. That little bitch was trying to sabotage me. I could stomach failing on my own merits. God knows I had done that often enough. What I couldn't abide was thinking I might fail based on the treachery of another. I didn't make up these rules. I didn't write the Internal Revenue Code and I didn't invent the culture that grew out of it. I scoured the file for anything I might seize. I felt more alive than I ever had. I felt like a teenager, falling in love for the first time. The chrysalis was tearing open. Within it, I was poised to spew.

* Integrated Data Retrieval System: the computerized means by which all taxpayer data is organized and retrieved.

⑦

SOMETHING IN THE WATER

I had lied when I told Culpepper I always believed him. Some of his stories seemed too pat; they had a mythical feel to them, like mini–morality plays meant to drive home a point. I doubted he ever lost all his hair, although a few years later I learned that there had indeed been a Service employee, a manager, whose hair fell out due to a rare condition exacerbated by the stress of the job. I suspected this story appealed to Culpepper because it illustrated how the Service, like the military, sought to break down trainees, strip them of their individuality, so they might be remade into . . . well, the image of William Culpepper.

I don't know if a private investigator was hired in Florida to tail employees. I do know that years later an employee from the Knoxville office testified before Congress in the hearings that led to the passage of the Revenue Restructuring Act of 1998. She testified that a manager abused government time by sleeping with his secretary during duty hours. His employees had discovered this by hiring a PI, who had followed the manager and his paramour, capturing them on videotape checking into the Hilton across the street from the federal building, and in the parking lot of a popular restaurant, as the secretary mounted her boss in the front seat of the government-issued Ford Taurus, which constituted abuse of government property. The manager kept his job but was transferred to another city.

The Service is a closed society with its own language and customs. Once inside the Service, we were sealed off from the outside world and, for some, the rules of that world often had little relevance. Gina had been accurate when she told me that entering the Service could pose a serious threat to personal relationships that existed prior to joining it. The chasm is wide between the Service and the rest of society. This is not altogether the fault of the IRS. No one likes paying taxes and those with whom we dealt *really* didn't like paying taxes. All dreaded our knock on the door, our voice on the phone, our letter in the box. Everyone we met just wanted us to go away.

Sexual banter was commonplace in our post-of-duty. It relieved the unrelenting pressure of our jobs. As the training year went on, the remarks became more graphic, the line between banter and harassment redrawn, until few topics were taboo. Our relationships in the "real" world had little bearing on how we behaved in the office. Married or single, once inside the beige-colored walls of the federal building, we were citizens of Sodom and Gomorrah, indulging in innuendo with all the gleeful abandon of adolescents.

"Jesus," I said one day. "This is about the sixth abatement I've done this week."

"Rick loves to abate," Allison said.

"So does that make him a master abater?" Rachel asked.

Flirting served another purpose, closer to our emotional cores: it affirmed our common humanity, for we were still green, finding our balance; we were not yet accustomed to the schizophrenic nature of our lives. We needed assurance that we were still attractive, desirable, worthwhile people, and flirting was the straightest line between the two points. Even Gina was not above it. Once, in the middle of the work area, with several RO's present, I asked her a technical question. She invited me to sit on her lap while she explained the answer to me.

When I related this incident to Culpepper, feigning outrage, he said, "You know, this may be difficult to believe, but when she first joined the Service, Gina was one hot babe. Weighed about thirty pounds less, hair down to her ass; all the men were hot for her. I've got some pictures from a office party I'll show you sometime. She was damn good, the way she discriminated: she wouldn't go for just anybody. Then she got married and that ruined her." He did not define what "ruined" meant. "Anyway, you can report her for sexual harassment if you'd like. The Service does have a policy against it." He said this with a perfectly straight face. "But that might cause certain . . . repercussions to your career."

Revenue officers and their supervisors, who were once revenue officers themselves, understand power. If they did not, they would not be revenue officers for very long. In our Byzantine world, sex was just another expression of power, another weapon in our arsenal. Culpepper told a story about a manager who set her sights on an RO who was a poor performer. She spent two years gathering enough documentation to justify his removal from the Service. At the last moment, he came forward with an accusation that she had demanded sex in return for her dropping the case against him. It was her word against his, but the Service wanted to avoid any public embarrassment: he had threatened to take his story to the newspapers. As the most hated agency in the federal government, perhaps in the free world, the IRS constantly strives to avoid anything that would give the public more ammunition to despise it. Management backed off and the RO dropped his complaint. He continued to work for the same manager as if nothing had happened, and never lodged another complaint against her.

During our phase training, a story made the rounds of some female trainees being pulled from class by a division chief and his subordinate, a branch chief. They were taken to a meeting room at the hotel where the training was taking place. The doors were closed behind them. The women were directed to chairs arranged in the large circle in the center of the room. The division chief made a speech. He said the training period for revenue officers was the most important part of their career and if they wanted to succeed, they must learn the vital lessons of trust and bonding. "Without one another you are doomed to failure," he told them. He was going to lead them in a trust exercise. He turned to one of the women in the circle and said, "Where's the strangest place you've ever had sex?" She was too surprised to answer. Someone else laughed, thinking this must be some kind of gag. It was not. He asked the question again and she stammered, "Nowhere. I'm a virgin." The room broke up. The tension left the air. Everyone reached a tacit agreement that this *was* some kind of joke. The division chief said, "Oh no, I've heard about you. Everyone's been talking about *you*. Come on, tell us the weirdest place you've ever done the nasty." He went around the circle. Some gave honest answers. A closet. A swimming pool. On a rooftop. In an airplane. The answers grew more ridiculous as the spirit of the exercise caught on. In a church pew. On the escalator at the mall. If anyone was made uncomfortable by this bizarre ritual, she did not let on. The branch chief asked the next question: "What's the weirdest position you've ever used?" When no answer was forthcoming or not sufficiently graphic, he pressed for details. This dragged on for over an hour. The division chief asked the woman who had made love in a pool if she would mind going for a swim after the day's session. It was all conducted in a casual manner. Nobody objected. Nobody acted offended. The ones who were troubled held their tongues: they were not striving to be revenue officers because they had a burning desire to collect taxes; they were striving to be revenue officers because they had a burning desire to put food on the table. One of these trainees—the first to be questioned by the division chief—slept in her room that night fully clothed, with furniture stacked against the door. She quit the following week.

Normal boundaries can break down quickly in an environment where the most mundane task has the potential to alter irrevocably the lives of others. Culpepper wasn't the only one in the Service with a God complex. Each day, a revenue officer makes dozens of decisions that have life-changing consequences. The majority of the revenue officers I knew during my career found ways to keep this in perspective, but some became convinced of their own invulnerability. They begin as mere mortals; they end as Olympians. And, like the Greek gods, they would screw anything and everything with an orifice. A female revenue officer is reprimanded after being caught performing fellatio on two of her coworkers during duty hours. Another female RO, who is married, regularly works from a hotel room, so she can spend quality time with her lover. She gives out the hotel phone number to taxpayers in case they need to reach her. Her husband discovers the affair and is arrested for attempted murder when he tries to smash a chair over her head. The husband of another RO confronts her manager in the office, chasing him around a potted tree while the manager screeches for someone to call security. An agent with the IRS criminal investigation division suspects her husband (also an IRS employee) of having an affair. She bursts into his office one day and begins rifling his drawers. When he confronts her, she pulls her gun and tells him if he doesn't confess, she'll blow his brains out.

A district director for the IRS is forced out of his job when his secretary reports he sodomized her on his desk. Once this story hit the papers, the Service quietly moved the former director to another state—picking up his moving expenses—and paid him a six-figure salary to analyze statistics until he was able to retire. The secretary's sexual harassment claim was settled out of court—with a binding confidentiality agreement. The matter disappeared from the papers.

"Rick."

I looked up, startled. It was Gina. She was wearing a black sweater, a black skirt, and a glimmering ruby and onyx ladybug suspended just above her right breast.

"Did I scare you?"

"No, just your stealthy appearance."

She laughed. She pulled up a free chair, sat down, and said, "What are you doing?"

"Oh, working."

"Aren't you coy. Which cases are you closing today?"

I started to mumble a reply. She interrupted me. "Are you closing *any* cases today?" She didn't wait for an answer. "Have any appointments?"

"No, I—"

"Good. I'm bored."

The office was practically deserted. Henry and Bonny were in. The rest had signed out to the field or had taken leave. All revenue officers were required to sign out in the office log. The Service always wanted to know where to find you. On most Fridays, revenue officers signed out to the field, for obvious reasons. Culpepper was in Orlando, meeting with the branch chief. He had finally gotten his wish: an assignment as acting manager for a training group hired six months after our class came on board. We were no longer the new kids on the block. Culpepper was preparing the new-hires to move to their digs, across the alley from the federal building, into the same ten-story office building once owned by my father. Culpepper was technically still a revenue officer, but it had been made clear to him that he would be promoted as the permanent manager of the new group—if he proved himself.

"Come on," he said the day he got the assignment. "Let me show you my new office."

Culpepper had already hung his awards and a print of *The Scream* by Edvard Munch on his new office's wall. He was ebullient.

"It's the perfect setup," he said. "Six trainees, fresh from the street. Not one of them over the age of thirty. None have worked for the government before. I'm like a sultan with a harem full of virgins, Yancey."

"Lucky you," I said.

He leaned back in his executive chair and put his feet up on the desk. "I know I'm sort of bailing halfway through your training year, but Cindy's okay. You know enough now not to let her poison you. Just enforce. Enforce, enforce, enforce. It's the only thing anybody notices. If she tells you not to enforce, enforce anyway. Gina will back you up. Bust your ass. I don't expect to be in this job very long. I'll be the branch chief by the time you're ready to move into management. Impress me, and in another five years you might be sitting in this chair."

He folded his hands behind his head and stared at the ceiling.

"I always knew I'd be here one day," he said softly. I had the impression he was not speaking to me, though I was the only other person in the room.

Gina was rocking slightly in her chair, watching as I placed a hand over my case history to hide it from her. I wasn't sure why I was hiding it from her. "Let's go to the field," she said. "Do you have anything for the field?"

"Well, I—"

"A good RO always has something for the field," she said.

"Well, then, I am sure I could—"

"Good. Grab the cases."

She breezed from the room. I looked over and saw Henry sitting at his desk, staring at me. He called over, "Uh-oh, boy, you in trouble now." He came over, leaned on my desk, and said in a conspiratorial whisper, "You know, I didn't want them to hire you. I said it from the first; you remember it was me and Gina who did your interview? Soon as I heard you were an *actor*, I thought, Uh-oh, this gonna be trouble."

"Why's that, Henry?"

" 'Cause nobody ever gonna know when you're real."

"But how does that mean trouble?"

He hissed, "She's gonna try to take you to the house."

"What house?"

"*Her* house, dummy."

"Christ, Henry," I said.

"You wait. You'll see. 'Lemme show you my house,' she's gonna say. You watch out for that woman, Rick."

"Why, Henry?"

"Because she's evil. She's one of those, whadya call, Witchins."

"Wiccans."

He nodded vigorously. "You hit that nail right on the neck. You hear that story about the cat? Well, she didn't give that cat away—she sacrificed that cat. Bit its head off with her teeth. At one of those, whadya call, Black Mass."

I nodded. "Right, Henry. Black Mass."

"Just watch yourself, Yancey. It don't take no genius to see those handprints on the wall." He walked back to his desk and commenced to fussing with some papers, chortling to himself. Henry rarely talked to me, and when he did, I rarely had a clue what he was talking about. I dug through my file drawer and found three cases that had some potential. One was an unable-to-locate account, always good for some door-banging. Another was a missed deadline to file some income tax returns. I grabbed some blank summonses from the forms cabinet. "Oh-ho!" Henry snickered behind me. The third case needed first contact, but I was still within my thirty-day window. I double-checked my briefcase for the necessary forms: Pub One, Forms 433-A and 433-B, blank 941s and 940s. I ran to IDRS and pulled printouts of all three accounts. I was forgetting something. What was I forgetting? I would never succeed as a revenue officer if I didn't learn to keep my head in a crisis. Why this surprise attack by my manager? Had Culpepper said something to her? Had Allison? She had not suggested we go to the field on a whim. Gina did not suffer from whims.

She was waiting for me when I returned to my desk. She had slipped on a pair of dark glasses. The lenses were large, round, and opaque, dominating her face. Her jeweled pin glittered on her chest. Ladybugs bring good luck. They save crops from aphids.

"I hope there's room for me in your car," she said. "Culpepper's warned me."

"Can you give me thirty minutes admin time to clean it out?" I asked. She laughed. It appeared she had applied a fresh coat of lipstick. I stood. I was only six feet, but I towered over her; the top of her head came to a point just under my bottom lip.

"Did you know our division chief once made everyone go to the library for a week because we didn't have enough field time on our reports?"

"They track everything, don't they?"

"More than you could possibly imagine."

She sank into the passenger seat. "He's a maniac," she said, referring to Byron Samuels, the division chief. "I assume you met him at Phase One. Could you understand him? He always sounds to me like Marlon Brando in *The Godfather*, that whispery way of talking. Hell is Byron on a speakerphone." The jacked-up air conditioning blew her dark bangs from her high, rounded forehead. The bucket seat made her appear even smaller, somehow. I felt like I was driving my kid to school. In some ways, though, I was more afraid of her than I was of Culpepper. Gina was smarter than Culpepper, more subtle. She was still talking about Samuels. "He's got a terrible temper—like most people in upper management. He was doing a manager's op review and hurled the case files at him, screaming, 'These cases are *fucking shit.*'"

She looked around the confines of my Nissan and said, "It doesn't seem so bad to me." And I thought of the stories about her house, stuffed to the rafters with boxes, old magazines, bags of potting soil. Would she really invite me to her house? And what should I say if she did?

It was a typical morning for that part of the world in that part of the year. A few towering clouds, bright blue sky, ferocious sun. As I navigated through the one-way streets of downtown, Gina cranked down her window and said, "You know, all a car does is circulate whatever fetid air that happens to be inside of it?" She rested her elbow on the open window. "I didn't see you write down your mileage."

"Oh."

I punched the button for the trip odometer, which happened to be busted. She did not appear to notice. She said, "You know, occasionally Inspection comes calling and gathers up everybody's travel logs and compares them to the vouchers."

"Mine's up-to-date," I lied. I didn't even know where my log book was. Travel regulations required every field officer to keep a record of the number of miles traveled on official government business. Every month we filed a voucher and were reimbursed for our mileage.

"Has Billy ever talked to you about padding your voucher?"

"I never pad my—"

She laughed. It had a certain musical quality to it, her laugh. Like the trilling of a sparrow.

"Say you're in some outlying county and you need a map. A lot of ROs add a few extra miles to their voucher to cover the costs. Is there anything wrong with that, you think?"

Oh, she was sly. But she would have to be more sly than that. "I think you're supposed to submit the receipt for reimbursement."

"Some people hate the red tape."

"I love red tape. The red tape is why I took this job."

She trilled. She had a better sense of humor than Culpepper. I may have felt this way because she laughed at my jokes and Culpepper did not. She said, "But say you lose the receipt. Do you pad the voucher by a couple bucks or do you swallow it?"

"Swallow it," I said.

"It's funny, with ROs it's one way or the other. Either they're super-conscientious or they're totally corrupt. Do you know, Mel would actually subtract the miles she drove if she got lost?"

"Boy, you know, I think I've done that. How's Mel doing, by the way?" Melissa had recently been promoted to manager in Tampa.

"Great. Where are we going?"

"Post office. Hopefully they've got a forwarding address on this guy."

"Here's the thing about Gina," Culpepper had said. "She was a rotten RO. On a scale of ten, she was about a three. She never wrote the history until she closed the case. She never kept her cases in a folder; she kept them rolled into little tubes held together by rubber bands. She would review all her new receipts and tell her manager which ones she would work and which ones she wouldn't. She'd say, 'I'm not working this piece of shit. Find somebody else.' And her manager would, because he was afraid of her. Everyone was afraid of her, because she was smarter than

they were. She was smart enough to figure out what she could get away with and what she couldn't, which is the answer to the riddle of life, when you think about it. Then one day a new division chief comes in and looks at the stats and says, 'Jesus Christ, we need more female managers!' Because his boss in Atlanta is coming down on him, *because Washington is coming down on* him: *'We need more women in management. Promote the pussy! Promote the pussy!' So the division chief picks up the phone and calls the branch chief and says, 'I need a good woman to promote!' At that time, there were maybe seven women in the whole branch. The first person he can think of is Gina because, although she's one of the laziest goddamned ROs who ever carried a bag,* she is also the smartest. Technically, there is none better. Even I can't touch her technically. So he calls Gina into his office and says, 'How'd you like to be a manager?' Well, that's like asking the alcoholic if he'd like the keys to the liquor cabinet. And it doesn't matter one goddamned bit that Gina is the worst motivator of people I have ever seen. That's what the Service does: it rewards technical merit. It never occurs to them it takes an entirely separate set of skills to manage people than it does to manage an inventory."*

"Melissa went through a tough time here," Gina said. "When she came on board, the Service was run like a gentleman's club. Ninety-five percent of the workforce was male. You had to work damn hard—twice as hard as a man to get half the attention. Mel came on board before there was such a thing as the Outstanding Scholars Program. She started as a Grade Three clerk and worked her way up. You know, she comes from a very poor background."

"Yes, I'd heard."

She laughed suddenly. "She hates your guts, you know."

"She—?"

"She's hated you ever since the interview, when you corrected her grammar."

"That was a mistake."

"You're here, aren't you?"

"As I was saying."

---

* To "carry a bag" refers to revenue officers lugging their briefcases to the field.

· · ·

We arrived at the post office. I flashed my credentials at the clerk and showed him the name and address of my taxpayer. I leaned over the counter and lowered my voice so people behind us and in the next line couldn't hear me. I asked if my taxpayer was still at that address. The clerk disappeared into the mysterious inner sanctum of his realm. He returned after a moment with the news that indeed he had moved. He wrote down the address. I thanked him and followed Gina's bobbing black head back into the oppressive heat.

The First Protocol: *Find where they are.*

"I have a boyfriend now. Did you know I had a boyfriend? He's with the Service, too. He's a revenue agent and he lives in Fort Lauderdale. Some people tell me long-distance relationships never work, but that depends on what you want out of a relationship. He's a nerd. I mean, he really is a nerd. Right down to the black electrical tape on the eyewear. He plays chess. He has a pet iguana. I drive down once a month to see him. Sometimes he comes up here. My ex-husband was not a nerd. He was an ex-jock, dumb as a signpost. I adored him. You may be wondering why I divorced him if I adored him. Well, he had an affair. When I confronted him about it, he called me fat. He told me I got fat, so I kicked him out. I could have forgiven him for screwing around on me, but the fat remark just crushed me. Not because I'm not fat, because I am. I am fat. I'm short, fat—and so are my chances!" She laughed. "I just couldn't get over him *thinking* I was fat."

About five miles down the interstate, heading west, I realized what I had forgotten. A map. I had removed the map from the car for a reason I could not now recall. I had no idea where this forwarding address was. I pulled off the interstate and ran inside a convenience store to buy a map. I made sure to ask for a receipt. I ducked into the bathroom and sat in the stall, smoking, pulling drags as deep as I could into my lungs, until my diaphragm ached. I splashed my face with cold water. For some reason I examined the surface of my tongue. I noticed my right eye was twitching. Most likely a reaction to the cat hair that still clung to Gina's person; I went outside, climbed back into the car, and said, "I'm sorry, did you want anything?" I made a show of folding the receipt for my map and tucking it into my shirt pocket.

Gina said, "I've got some ROs who must pad their voucher by two, three hundreds dollars a month. You think I'm kidding. They think I can't figure out how they're paying for their new car."

"Can't you fire them for that?"

"What do you think?"

"Too hard to prove?"

She laughed that gentle trill. "Oh, no. It's real easy to prove. Proving it isn't the hard part. It's the appeals and the countercharges of harassment or discrimination or retaliation. That's the word you always want to remember, Rick, if you have any intention of sticking with this job, retaliation."

I was studying my newly acquired map, trying to find the street name the post office had given me. I turned my head to one side to focus my good eye; the right had nearly closed entirely.

"Any time you get a bad review," she continued, "or someone questions your ethics or accuses you of a code-of-conduct violation, cry 'Retaliation!' It'll stop the Service every time. You know, it's practically impossible to fire anybody in this damn organization. Believe me, I've tried."

"Found it!" I yelled, meaning the street.

"Mirabile dictu!" she yelled back with delight. She clapped her small hands. "For example, if I try to fire you, you can always say I'm retaliating because you refused to sit in my lap."

I pretended not to hear her. I remembered Culpepper's words: *While you are vulnerable, you have no allies. You have no friends. You are alone.*

"I'm sorry that troubled you," she said quietly. "It was only a joke."

I was back on the interstate, now heading east. Tractor-trailers roared past us, gliding by like behemoths of the deep ocean, rattling my little crustacean of a car. Gina reached up and grabbed the *Oh, Jesus!* handle, as Culpepper called it, located over her door. The wind rushed through her open window, whipping her hair into a miniature black tornado.

"Everybody's allowed to make jokes like that—except me!" she cried against the wind.

"I'm sorry!" I shouted. I wasn't certain what I was sorry about.

She yelled, "I always wanted to own a bookstore! Just a little, hole-in-the-wall bookstore, and I would buy all these out-of-print books, all these obscure titles you couldn't find anywhere else, and people would come from all over the world, because they would know if they couldn't find a book at my store, then it didn't exist!"

Neither does your store, I thought. None of us wanted to be where we were. We were all, it seemed, living defaulted lives. Plan B people. I remembered how she had laughed with delight when I said in the opening interview I had not grown up dreaming of being a revenue officer. "It's the golden handcuffs, Rick!" she yelled. "If you had any sense at all, you'll get out while you can!"

I eased onto the exit ramp. According to the map, we were only a couple of miles from the new address. The wind whimpered, dwindling. I said, "Where else can I take my English degree and make this kind of money?"

She made no reply. I turned right onto a tertiary road. It wound through towering pines, narrowing as it followed the slope of the earth. We were on the north side of town, the side bordering the Green Swamp. All the money in Lakeside seemed to flow uphill, from north to south. Revenue officers hated working zip codes on the north side; there simply wasn't any collection potential. We passed ranch homes, whose better days had long since faded, and mobile homes mounted on concrete blocks with the ubiquitous pit bull chained to a nearby tree or broken-down Camaro. Gina reached into her purse and removed a canister of Mace.

"I thought we couldn't carry that," I said.

"We can't. We are not allowed to carry guns, baseball bats, brass knuckles, knives, saps, pepper spray, Mace, or a pair of frigging tweezers. Have you run up against any dogs yet?"

"Guess I've been lucky."

"A whole pack of them attacked my car when I was an RO. They actually ripped off my rear bumper. I didn't mind the wild ones so much as the little yippy dogs the deadbeats would let jump into my lap. One day I went home looking like I had the measles from all the fleabites."

She told the story of a revenue officer in Orlando who killed a dog. The dog leapt at him from its hiding place under the front porch. He reacted instinctively with an uppercut to the dog's chin. He shattered the jaw, sending a piece of bone deep into the dog's brain; it fell at his feet, dead before it hit the ground. The Service was sued and had to pay the costs of disposing of the animal and an undisclosed sum for the owner's pain and suffering.

"So we levied ourselves for the money due the taxpayer. Got full-pay, too."

"We can levy ourselves?"

"We can levy anything. Wasn't that the address we were looking for back there?"

I made a three-point turn and returned to the address. The mailbox was leaning west as the soft ground gave way beneath it. The driveway was two ruts cut deep into the wet ground, grass growing wild between the grooves, winding through the pine trees that partially screened the house from the road.

"Well," Gina said. "We've come this far."

I turned onto the car trail, the long grass angrily rubbing the undercarriage of my Nissan. The ruts wound to the right, behind the trees. Gina clutched the can of Mace tightly in her little fist. The house slumped before us, a typical "cracker-style" Florida home, with a screened-in front porch, concrete blocks for steps, an overhang of corrugated metal attached to one side as a carport. A rusting Ford truck, a F150, sat inside the port. I stopped the car and we sat for a moment, the engine idling. It was late morning. The air outside shimmered. Dragonflies soared two feet from the ground, the sun glancing off their translucent wings. It was heartbreakingly beautiful, like sunlight glancing off the surface of the ocean. Although they are beneficent, dragonflies are predators. As are ladybugs. I waited for the pit bull to come barreling from the woods. I wasn't sure, but I did not think I had it in me to coldcock a dog, even if its intention was to kill me.

"What's this guy's deal?" she asked. She, too, seemed reluctant to abandon our little fortress.

"Owes about seven thousand dollars in self-employment tax," I said.

"Let me guess. He's a trucker."

"That's right."

The Second Protocol: *Track what they do.*

"Is he married?"

"Files single on his 1040."

"I don't see his rig. Must be on the road."

"I never assume anything," I said, trying always to impress.

"Oh, you're so . . . Culpepperish. Let's go. I've got my Mace."

I turned off the engine, unfolded myself from the car, into the blast-furnace heat. The sound of our doors closing echoed against the pines. We walked to the front porch. The wet ground pulled at our feet. On rare occasions, the benevolent universe hints to us, *Be careful*. I stood on the lowest concrete block and tried the screen door. Locked. We walked around to the carport. Another door on this side of the house. Gina stood on her tiptoes and pressed her nose against the glass. "The kitchen," she said. "Disgusting. I counted twelve cockroaches."

She walked over to the truck and squinted through the passenger window. "Rick, look."

The cab reminded me of my car. Moldy coffee. Fast-food wrappers. Stacks of bills. Old newspapers. A spiderweb, looking impossibly delicate, spread over the steering wheel. A revenue officer quickly becomes a student of entropy.

"Do you see that?" She pressed the tip of her finger against the smudged glass.

"What?"

"It looks like a pay stub."

"Sure does," I lied. To me it appeared she was pointing at a half-eaten Egg McMuffin.

"What did you find on LEVYS?"*

"I didn't check LEVYS."

"Always check LEVYS."

"Well, I do. I just don't check it before first contact."

"Start."

"Okay."

"And that piece of paper on the floorboard—doesn't that look like a bank statement?"

She pulled gently on the door handle. The truck was unlocked. She turned to me, her cheeks flushed.

---

* The IDRS Command Code LEVYS: payer information on taxpayers extracted from wage and income documents sent to the Service.

"What do you think?"

I thought of Melissa digging through a taxpayer's garbage, of revenue officers glancing in half-opened mailboxes or examining the letters on the desktop for levy sources while the taxpayer steps out to make copies, of altered histories, of the edge needed to stand out, of passing this test, of being promoted, of foreplay and her flushed cheeks, of the orgiastic Fourth Protocol, of ladybugs and how their delicate wings were protected by tough exoskeleton.

I said, "Don't we need a writ or warrant or something?"

She laughed. "Good answer. It doesn't matter anyway. I can read the bank's name from here."

I wrote down the tag number and drove to the nearest gas station. Gina waited in the car while I called the office on the payphone outside. Henry answered the phone.

"Henry, this is Rick."

"You're alive!"

"Henry, I need you to pull a tag for me."

"Where's Gina?"

"Right here. You ready for the number?"

"What number?"

"I have a tag number and I need you to pull the owner's name for me." There was a long pause.

"Henry, I'll owe you one," I said.

He whispered into the phone, "They looking for her."

"Who's looking for who?"

"For Gina. They want to know where she is."

"Who wants to know?"

"I can't talk. They right behind me." He raised his voice. "All right, I'm ready, Rick Yancey! Ready for that tag number!"

I gave him the number. He told me to hold on. The line went dead. I called back. Bonny answered the phone. I told her Henry was pulling a tag for me. She put me on hold. I glanced at Gina, sitting in the car, and thought of those little bobble-head dogs you see riding in the back of cars. Henry came on the line.

"Hey, why'd you hang up?"

"I didn't hang up, Henry. You cut me off."

"You always playing games, aren't you?"

"What's the name, Henry?"

He gave me the name. It was my guy. The Third Protocol: *Learn what they have.*

"It's him," I told Gina when I returned to the car.

"Let's go," she said.

"Okay. Where are we going?"

"To the bank, dumb-dumb. You have some blank levies with you, don't you?"

Something else forgotten. She said, "What—didn't you send him final notice?"

"It's the first thing I do."

"Good."

"I'll have to swing by the office for some blank levies, though."

"No. I'll call Bonny. She can type one up and meet us at the bank." She got out of the car. "Always have blank levies with you, Rick."

Gina directed me to a buffet restaurant for lunch, a feeding trough frequented by retirees and others forced to live on fixed incomes. She loaded her plate with mashed potatoes, bread, sausage gravy, and banana pudding. The all-white diet. I picked at my food. Gina pointed out I was picking at my food.

"No wonder you're so skinny," she said.

They were looking for her. They were standing right behind Henry, looking for her. The fear in his voice told me "they" could only be one thing: Inspection. Now I understood why she had insisted on going to the field: she knew they were coming. She probably wasn't supposed to know they were coming, but someone tipped her off. Gina had friends in high places. She had dirt on everyone. She had *leverage.* Culpepper said it was how she kept her job.

"Something on your mind, Rick?"

"Rarely."

Gina had been reported to Inspection in the past. It upset her employees, how they were expected to account for every moment of their workday when she would disappear for hours, and even Bonny didn't know where she was. There had been other, more serious, allegations. That she had cozy relationships with one or two of the more prominent powers-of-attorney in town, to whom she gave her private number and for whom she would pressure revenue officers to abate penalties or release liens. That she developed office "pets" who received the choice assignments and special awards, grooming them for advancement within the Service. That she favored women, hence Melissa had moved into management before Culpepper.

"You're doing fine," she said. "You know that."

"Most of the time I have no idea what I'm doing, why I'm doing it, and what might happen to me if I do—or don't."

"That's normal. Believe me, a day will come when you attain enlightenment. A door will open in your mind. And every day after that, you won't believe the amount of money we're paying you to do what little you do."

Only Gina could encourage and belittle in the same breath. She had stirred the contents of her plate into a single quivering, Jell-O-like blob.

"That's what Jim Neyland told me in my final interview."

She made a face. "Jim Neyland." He was the branch chief, her immediate supervisor. "Jim Neyland is a pig."

"He doesn't seem to be the only one."

"Oh, I guess not. But the world is full of pigs, Rick; we just happen to have our fair share."

She sipped her water and looked out the window. "It's easy to become cynical in this job. We tend to believe the worst *of* people because day after day we see the worst *in* people. We enter into these strangers' lives at their lowest point, at the height of their desperation, when lies and trickery and betrayal are not only easy but sometimes necessary. Don't be fooled by all the rumors that fly around. Not everyone in the Service is a depraved sex maniac. It's just that the power they give us can twist us into shapes we could not otherwise become."

She turned and leveled her eyes at me.

"We have been given great power, Rick. And to exercise power without responsibility is madness. It's worse than madness. For the ancients, the greatest sin was not lust or murder, but pride."

.   .   .

"Think of your inventory," she said. "There's probably one or two taxpayers who have a crush on you."

"I doubt that."

"Owing taxes is rarely the only problem these people have. Owing taxes is usually a symptom of some underlying neurosis. They are overwhelmed, going down the tubes, flaying around in the dark, and then you come along, and you have all this power, and you're going to tell them how to basically live their lives so they can take care of their tax obligation. Some people can't resist that. You're father figure, shrink, bartender, social worker, priest, and white knight rolled into one."

I thought of Laura Marsh, who had been calling me faithfully every week. At first our conversations were strictly business. She told me what adjustments she had made to her expenses, so gross payroll could be met. We discussed logistics of making the required monthly payment. But over the last few weeks she had called with no real issue to discuss. She talked about her ex-husband, who had reentered her life and was making unreasonable demands for visitation with the kids. She asked me for legal advice that had nothing to do with tax law. She invited me by, if I was ever in the neighborhood, for a cup of coffee. Once she burst into tears, asking repeatedly, *I am going to make it, aren't I? Aren't I?* Culpepper overheard my end of one of these exchanges and said afterward, "How much do you charge per session?"

Gina asked, "Did you know that sex is the second most offered form of currency in bribery cases?"

"What's the first?"

"Money, Rick. Money." She laughed and shook her head. Silly ol' Rick. "I'm sure Billy's told you about his bribery case. He tells everyone. It really made a name for him in the district. He leaves out some details, though. In reality, it was kind of pitiful. He was working this car salesman, and one day he asks if there's any way he can take care of his tax problem 'informally.' After six or seven conversations like this, with Billy pressing him, he finally gets the man to offer him a bribe of five thousand dollars. Only he can't pay it up front. So Billy agrees to accept the bribe on an installment basis. He gave the guy a bribery payment plan. Well, since most car salesmen are delinquents, soon everyone on the lot was calling Billy, asking

him if he can help them out, too. So Inspection wires him up. He meets
with these poor losers in cheap hotel rooms, exchanging abatement forms
for paper bags full of ten-dollar bills, while Inspection sits outside and
takes Polaroids of their comings and goings. They pleaded out and not
one served any time, but Billy impressed the hell out of the division
chief—and Inspection."

We drove to the bank directly from the restaurant. Bonny was waiting for
us in the parking lot, levy in hand. Gina said to me, "Wait for me by the
door." I waited by the door and watched Bonny whispering urgently into
Gina's ear. Gina was standing with her head bowed and Bonny, who was
three inches taller, had to bend over to relay her message. Gina nodded,
patted Bonny on the arm as if consoling her, and joined me in front of the
door. Her color was up. I misinterpreted this to mean she was upset by the
news Inspection had arrived to cart off her head.

"God, I love this part of the job! It's better than sex. Though not as
good as chocolate ice cream."

I showed my commission to the teller and handed her the levy form. I
explained what it was: we were seizing all cash in any account under the name
and Social Security number listed on the form. The teller tapped into her
system and informed us we had seized the full amount: $7,514.34. Full
payment. Gina squealed like a schoolgirl and clapped her hands.

Outside, she gave me a high five. "Doesn't it feel great? Pick up a new
case and in half a day have full payment. I wish I could be there when the
bank lets him know, just to see the look on his face."

The Fourth Protocol: *Execute what they fear.*

Gina's high lasted the rest of the afternoon. It set her afire. It loosened her
tongue. We dropped off the summons I had to serve, taping it to the taxpayer's door. Affixing it to the door was important if we chose to take the
taxpayer to court. We had to be able to attest with reasonable certainty that
he received it. On his appearance date, I would give the usual spiel. *Now,
this is your last chance to file these returns before we refer the matter to federal
court. You will have to explain to a judge why three hundred million taxpayers
have to file their returns every year, but you don't.*

Gina said, "There was one taxpayer. He became obsessed with me. For months after I closed his case he called me. When I stopped taking his calls, he would show up at the office. Sometimes he'd camp on the steps at seven in the morning. He was very nice about it, right up to the creepy line, but he never crossed it. He called me 'his little Gina.' I was a lot younger and skinnier then. Have you seen pictures of me? There's a scrapbook in the office; I'll show you when we get back. I looked like a miniature version of Cher. Imagine Cher, about ten years ago, and boil her down a couple inches—well, four or five inches, and you have me. I'm one-eighth Cherokee, hence the Pike's Peak cheekbones and black hair. You know, Culpepper was stalked once, by a hermaphrodite."

"By a what?"

"A hermaphrodite. You know what a hermaphrodite is. Someone with both, um, sex organs. Culpepper talked to him-slash-her on the phone before they met. He thought he was talking to a woman with a very bad head cold. He had decided to become all-woman, so he was going through the operations and those hormone shots—the taxpayer, not Billy—and he was still married. His wife was struggling with the decision whether to stay with him or not. He was prettier than she was, and plus she didn't like to think of herself as a lesbian. Anyway, he came in for the interview with the whole family in tow, including the two little kids. He was already dressing like a woman, so the interview was like a PBS special, you know, 'My Two Moms.' The taxpayer fell head over heals for Billy, kept talking about how ripped he was and how his eyes seem to pierce right to her very soul. 'You have ice blue soul,' he told him. It really freaked Billy out. If you ever want to really get him, tell him he has ice blue soul."

The clouds had gathered into a dark, angry mass above us. Gina breathed deep the moist air.

"The rains are coming," she said.

My final call of the day was a cabinetmaking business. A pleasant-looking man in his mid-forties met us at the door. He wore a green smock. Sawdust clung to his beard. He led us into his office, a tiny area in one corner of the building. He found two wooden bar stools for us to perch on. He sat in an executive chair that was missing a wheel. I handed him Pub One and explained why we had come. He listened politely, smiling often at Gina. The smile hardly wavered when I told him he owed $25,000 in employment taxes. I asked him if he was making tax deposits.

"Jeez, I'll tell you the truth, Mr. Yancey. I haven't been able to make a deposit in over a year now. Things are just too tight."

"We can't work with you unless you can get current with this quarter," I said. I explained how final notice worked, how a federal tax lien perfected our interest in his property, how we could—and would—levy his accounts receivable and seize his assets to satisfy the debt.

"Why would you do that?" he asked. He seemed incredulous.

"To put you out of business," Gina said pleasantly. "Do you think it's fair for you to operate without paying taxes while your competition pays every penny of theirs?"

"I ain't so sure they are."

"But they're not in Mr. Yancey's inventory. You are."

"I'm gonna show a profit. I just a need a little time."

He wasn't going to get it. Not while my manager sat beside me. Not while Allison was nipping at my heels. Not while I strained toward enlightenment.

"*Tempus fugit,*" Gina said.

"You have ten days," I said.

"Ten days to do what?" he asked.

"Get caught up with your deposits and pay us in full."

"I can't do that in ten days."

"Can you get caught up with your deposits in ten days?"

"I—I don't know. Maybe."

"We'll give you ten days to get caught up with your deposits and thirty days to pay the balance. How's that?"

"Well, to tell you the truth, that's not very good."

Behind him, on his cluttered desk, was a framed photograph of a pretty woman holding a blond, blue-eyed little boy. He noticed I was looking at it.

"That's my boy," he said. "He's three."

"Cute."

"You have kids, Mr. Yancey?"

"None that he knows of," Gina said.

"There's no way I can pull this out in forty days. You might as well shut my doors now."

We said nothing. We stared at him. It produced the desired response: he dropped his head and shrugged his broad shoulders. He said, "I got four full-time guys here. They have wives and families, too. You put me out of business and how do they put food on the table?"

"You're concerned about your employees," Gina said. I shifted on my bar stool. I knew where she was going with this. She was setting him up.

"Of course I am. This is a small company. We're—they're like family."

"Family. So why did you take money from your family to pay your creditors?"

"I'm not following you."

"She's saying payroll taxes are withheld monies. You withheld them from your employee's paychecks."

"You took their money," she said. "To pay *your* bills."

"I didn't take nobody's money. There *is* no money."

"Then you're right. We shouldn't wait the forty days," she said.

At that moment, as if on cue, the thunderheads exploded open and rain began to pound the corrugated roof. We had to shout to be heard.

"I'll take the forty days!" He raised his head. Tears were in his eyes. "I'll do what I have to do. I got a family." He turned to me and said vehemently, "You don't know what that's like."

I caught South Florida Avenue, the main north-south thoroughfare, to take us back to the federal building. The afternoon had gone prematurely gray beneath the spent thunderheads.

"Turn left up here, Rick. I want to show you something."

She directed me into a well-appointed neighborhood, not far from where my parents lived. She ordered me to slow down. I crept along at five miles per hour, wondering what was going on. She pushed her sunglasses to the top of her head. She pointed out the open window.

"There it is. Stop."

So Henry had been right. She had taken me to her house.

"That's your house," I said.

"Yep. Isn't it beautiful? I did all the landscaping myself. Look at my azaleas! I fertilize and mow, too. There is not one centimeter of crabgrass in that whole yard. Look at those palm trees in the back. Can you see them?"

"Yes, I can."

"My bedroom is in the back. I love to listen to the sound of the wind at night, rustling in the palm leaves. I close my eyes and imagine I'm on a tropical island. If I concentrate really hard, I can almost hear the sound of the waves hitting the shore. When I can't, I have this tape of sounds—you know, a meditation tape. It has Beach At Night, Rain on the Eaves, and other stuff. Whale Song, but listening to that kind of freaks me out. It's spooky."

"Why is it spooky?"

"Have you ever seen a whale? I don't mean on TV. I mean up close, in real life. I took a vacation in Maine once and went on this whale-watching boat, on which I became extremely seasick, but anyway saw a herd of whales, or I think it's called a pod. Whales are too big to wrap your imagination around. You've read *Moby-Dick*. But these were blue whales, I think. Moby Dick was a sperm whale. Would you like to see the inside?"

I tried to make a joke. "Of a whale?"

She trilled at me. "No, of my house, silly."

She actually called me *silly*. I felt no pressure from her invitation. This was no veiled threat or offer of quid pro quo. She was inviting me inside for the same reason she filled the day with her endless chatter. Gina wasn't trying to seduce me. Gina was lonely.

She turned from me and looked at her house. She sighed. "Let's go back, Rick."

o   o   o

The office was deserted when we arrived. Only Bonny had remained, like a watcher at the gate. She went directly with Gina to her office and they huddled inside behind a closed door. I sat at my desk and wrote the histories of my day's labors. I called home and got the answering machine. I hung up without leaving a message. The phone rang. I hesitated, and then picked it up.

"Internal Revenue Service, Rick Yancey."

"Rick, this is Allison. You'll never guess who was in the office today."

"Inspection."

There was a pause. Her tone changed from breathless to miffed. "How did you know?"

"I have my sources."

"They were looking for Gina."

"I know that. Gina was with me."

"I know she was with you! That's why I'm calling."

"Good. I was wondering why."

"Don't you want to hear what they wanted?"

"Isn't that why you called?"

"Well. Maybe now I just won't tell you."

"Whatever, Allison," I said. "I'm hanging up now."

"You know, Ricky, I get so sick of you and your holier-than-thou act."

"Bless you, my child. Are they going to fire her?"

"Inspection doesn't fire people, Rick," she said. Now condescending. "Management fires people."

"What's it about, her tardies and absences?"

"No, Rick. It's not even *about* her. They wanted to talk to her as a *witness*."

"A witness to what?"

She was drawing it out. She was enjoying herself immensely.

"Rick, they were here because of Culpepper. They're investigating *Culpepper*."

I was speechless for a moment. Then I said, "Investigating him for what?"

"I didn't tell you this."

"You haven't told me anything yet."

"You did not hear this from me, Rick."

"Allison, do you even know what they're investigating him for?"

She told me. I made her repeat it. I hung up the phone, shoved everything inside my desk, locked it, slipped out the back door, and walked on the rain-washed pavement to my car. I drove home. *Be proud of what you do. Be proud you're a revenue officer. Henceforward you will be held to the highest standard.* The sun balanced on the horizon beneath the lingering clouds; the world teetered on the edge between dark and light.

.   .   .

There was a note from Pam on the table, informing me that she would not be home until very late—the production was set to open that week and they were experiencing technical difficulties. I was awake when she slipped into bed beside me at one o'clock the next morning. I tried to remember the last time we had sex, but the memory that gripped me was of the first time I laid eyes on her, sitting on the steps outside the theater, waiting for a ride that never came, and how I pitied her—she seemed so lonely. Pity is the most subversive of all emotions. My job had taught me this. Culpepper said a good revenue officer is as indifferent as God. Pity softened the heart. It made the easy difficult and the difficult impossible. Pity was as corrosive as acid. Pity sucked the juice from your marrow. Pity dissembled, conned, seduced. Pity was a cheap whore, the evil twin of empathy. At least empathy did not blind you to the truth.

The truth. For weeks I had convinced myself that working for the Service had placed a strain on my relationship with Pam, but the truth was that our relationship had been tearing at the seams for at least two years before I entered Byzantium. Being there had only accelerated the rate of entropy. The Service couldn't suspend the laws of nature; it couldn't take a lamb and change it into a lion. Enormous pressure will crush ordinary rock but transform coal into diamonds. I had witnessed the passive change into self-confident, assertive people. I had also witnessed people like Gretchen Pope, who fainted regularly at her desk because she starved herself so she could afford designer dresses and her fire-engine red Ferrari. In many ways, what went on in Lakeside during my training year was an anomaly, a fantastic alternative universe, and the truth was that we were often the joke of the district. The branch chief, upon hearing the accusations against Culpepper, was said to exclaim, "Jesus Christ! There must be something in the water down there!"

Pam read for ten minutes, turned off the light, and rolled onto her side, her back to me. Pam always read at night. This night she was reading a book called *Communion*, about a man who overcomes screen memories implanted by aliens in his cerebral cortex.

I waited until her breathing grew heavy, and said, "Inspection came today."

She said, "Why?" She did not seem surprised I was still awake.

"To investigate William Culpepper."

"Culpepper? For what?"

I wondered why we never slept with our windows open. It would be nice to lie in bed and listen to the night sounds, to the crickets and cicadas, to the wind moving over the still black waters of the lake. Perhaps Pam preferred the windows closed to deter aliens from abducting her and implanting screen memories in her cerebral cortex. Growing up, I had always slept with my window open, even during the unbearable heat of summer. I had fallen asleep every night to the sound of the crickets' desperate cries for love.

"For assault."

8

GINA'S CAT

"You motherfucking sonofabitch, if I ever catch you sneaking around on my property again, I'll blow your goddamned brains out, you hear me? You are one lucky motherfucking sonofabitch I wasn't there when you criminally trespassed on my property. You people have been hounding my ass for six years now over a lousy seven thousand bucks. Seven thousand lousy fucking dollars. All I wanted was a fucking payment plan and you people come out one day and take every goddamned penny I have and now how am I gonna make my truck payment? How am I gonna buy my groceries? How am I gonna keep my fucking lights on? You people make me sick. You make me want to puke. This is America. I am an American and I love my country and what you're doing is *not* the America I know and love. It's Nazi-fucking-Germany is what it is. You should thank *God* you ain't here right now. You wanna know what I'd do to you, Mister Rick-fucking-Yancey, if you were in front of me right now? You don't want to know what I'd do. Now I want you to take that lien off my account *to*day—today, you understand me? I want that lien off so I can pay my fucking bills and not lose my fucking house."

Cindy Sandifer, my new OJI, who was listening on an extension, placed her hand over the mouthpiece and whispered, "Tell him about Form 911."

I said into the phone, "I understand you're upset."

"Oh, really? Well, you must be a fucking genius!"

"But I have a receipt from the post office, signed by you, for the letter giving you final demand."

"So the fuck what?"

"So that letter makes it pretty clear what we were going to—"

"That goddamned letter didn't say you were gonna sneak onto my property and violate my constitutional rights!"

"We've met all the legal requirements," I said. "We did everything the law requires."

"I am not a criminal!"

"No one said you were."

Cindy Sandifer cupped her hand around my ear and whispered, "Tell him he can file an ATAO."*

I said to the taxpayer, "Are you disputing you owe the money?"

"I said I wanted a fucking payment plan!"

"If you bring me certified funds for the full amount, I can release the levy."

There was a moment of stunned silence. He exploded, "And how the hell can I do that if you have all my money frozen! Jesus Christ, what do you think I do, keep a couple grand under my fucking mattress?!"

"You'd have to bring in more than a couple."

"Oh, I'm gonna bring in something, all right. You there all day?"

"All day."

"Good. Because I'm coming to see *you*."

The line went dead. Cindy hung up and looked sternly at me. "You should have told him about the 911," she said.

"It's in the Pub One."

"He has certain rights, Rick."

"And which of those did we violate? It's full payment, Cindy."

"When he comes in, give him a 911 and ask if he wants to talk to Gina."

"Okay."

She patted me on the shoulder and stood up. I said, "I should call Inspection."

"Why would you call Inspection?"

"He made a threat. He should be coded PDT."†

---

* Application for Taxpayer Assistance Order, or Form 911.

† Potentially Dangerous Taxpayer.

"I didn't hear any threats."

"He asked what time I was getting off work."

"How's that a threat?"

"He also said he was bringing something in."

"Not specific enough."

"Jesus, what does he have to do—draw a picture?"

"This happens all the time, Rick. If we coded everyone who blew their stack, everyone would be a PDT."

She left me alone with my paranoia. It comforted me that the taxpayer didn't know what I looked like; it would be difficult for him to mount an ambush. I wrote in my history, "TP irate, wants levy rel. Refused to rel. w/out cert. funds. TP stated 'coming to see me' and made unspecified threats. OJI advises to ignore, not code PDT. Advised TP of right to GM conf. and to file f. 911." I slapped the file closed and shoved it across the desk. In the beginning, such calls left me shaking with fear; now, I shook with righteous indignation. Culpepper had said, "When you think about it, it's hard to understand why so many people are afraid of the IRS. Why are they afraid of us? Say you owe thirty-five thousand dollars—that's about the average, by the way—what does the big, bad IRS do about it? It sends... *a letter*. If the taxpayer ignores that letter, it sends another one. Then another. Then another. Up to four notices, and they all say the same thing: 'Extremely Urgent! Life is about to end as you know it!' Then what does it do?" He hummed the theme from *Jaws*. "The IRS *calls you on the phone*. It tells you, 'Hey, you owe this money, and if you don't pay it, something really bad is going to happen to you.' Then, if you ignore its calls, it sends Mr. Yancey, who scratches his little head, fills out his little forms, and fifty-threes your account so it's like you never owed it in the first place." He illustrated his point with the story of the senior RO who enjoyed telling ignorant taxpayers, "Now, if you don't do what I tell you, I'll be forced to input a TC 530 on you." Transaction Code 530 was the IDRS shorthand for writing off an account as currently-not-collectible. *Oh, no, please Mr. Taxman, anything but a TC 530!*

"That's why I keep telling you to enforce. Always find a reason to enforce. Not just because it will advance your career—it will—but because it will keep you sane. It'll give you purpose, and God knows, you need that. Most of all, you'll have fun—unless pushing paper is your idea of a grand ol' time. Seizures are *fun*. Remember the Fourth Protocol. If they're afraid, do precisely what they fear. If they're not afraid, do precisely what they *should* fear."

Taxpayers often mask their fear with anger; therefore, their threats were not to be taken seriously. My policy was to let them vent their anger—interrupting them or arguing only served to escalate the tension. It served no purpose to become angry in turn; I always held the stronger position. I fully expected the irate trucker to call again that afternoon, and beg me for forgiveness, in the form of a levy release. He would not get one. I had full-payment. I had a closure, and closures were everything.

Later that morning, we assembled in the conference room for the monthly group meeting. It began as our group meetings always began, with Gina plowing through a huge stack of TDAs and TDIs, reading each name aloud. If the case was yours, you said, "Mine," and she would slide the paper across the table to you. Then Bonny distributed the latest district memos and Gina would give brief summaries of their contents. Henry would whip out his highlighter and set to work. Culpepper liked to tell the story of finding Henry in the copier room one morning not long after Henry's transfer from Miami. He was sitting at the small table with a yellow highlighter, a stack of district memos before him. Culpepper watched in silence as Henry, bent low over the paper, carefully highlighted every single line of the text. Finally, Culpepper said to him, "You know, Henry, you'd probably save time if you just put some yellow paper in the copier and copy those memos onto that."

Next came the manual updates. Every month, National Office shipped revisions of the Internal Revenue Manual to every field office in the country. The revisions reflected recent Revenue Rulings, changes in the law or tax court decisions. Often they merely reflected stylistic changes deemed imperative by some Grade 15 sitting in his cubicle on Constitution Avenue who had nothing better to do. The bottom line was the rules by which we played changed on a monthly basis. Our procedures were written in water and shifted with the political tide. This often led to professional paralysis for those ROs who did not handle change well, like Henry, who must have found comfort in his yellow highlighter.

Gina said, "I have a couple of announcements regarding the upcoming realignment of the branch, but first Toby has graciously offered to brief us on proper summons procedure."

All eyes turned to Toby. He was slouched in his chair, his large forearms resting on the table as he fingered the worn edges of his copy of the IRM. He did not acknowledge Gina, who was smiling as if enjoying some private joke. The silence dragged out and we began to shift uncomfortably in our chairs. Something was wrong here. There was bad blood in the air. It was no secret that Gina despised Toby, thought he was lazy and stupid. Behind his back, for reasons known only to Gina, she called him "Lumpy." Toby had discovered this and had stomped around the office, collaring everyone he met, saying, "You know what she calls me behind my back? Why do you think she calls me that? What's that mean? 'Lumpy,' isn't that the fat kid in *Leave It to Beaver*? Why's she callin' me a fat white kid?" No one seemed to know. He filed a grievance, asking for a transfer. Gina denied everything. He lost the grievance, but never his loathing for her.

Toby waited until the silence was practically unbearable, and then began to read from the manual. He did not look up. He did not elaborate on the text. He simply read, in a dull monotone, the entire section on issuing a summons to a taxpayer. We glanced at Gina, who was smiling blandly. He finished twenty minutes later. He closed the manual and folded his huge hands on top of it. He raised his eyes, meeting mine. I looked away. The expression in those eyes was too terrible to contemplate.

Gina said gently, "Thank you, Toby." Later, I would learn she had found an incorrectly prepared summons in one of his files during a routine case review. This had been his punishment. Once she had made Rachel fill an entire history sheet with these words: "I will not eat when I write my case histories." Gina had been disgusted to find grease stains in Rachel's files. Rachel explained she had been eating potato chips.

Gina continued, "As those of you who manage to stay awake already know, there's some changes coming to the group. We're being realigned under the Orlando branch." This meant Jim Neyland would not longer be her boss. The Service often flipped small PODs from branch to branch, for reasons known only to the Service and rarely communicated to us. "Our new branch chief will be here for a visit next week." She gave the date. We marked our calendars. "Now, as most of you know, the training group next door got a new manager effective last week. Hopefully, you'll have some free time to drop by and say hello."

"Say hello to who?" Henry asked.

"The new manager, Henry," Toby snapped at him. Toby had been trying to take Henry under his wing, with mixed results. About once a month, Toby would emerge from his office and track Henry down. We would hear him shouting at him, "Dear Jesus, Henry, you want to go anywhere in this organization, you gotta seize! It don't matter what you seize, just seize somethin'!" Henry always refused. "You're a pansy," Toby would tell him, disgusted. "Man, I seize everything. I seized a phosphate pit once, you know that? There were these guard dogs out there walkin' around with no goddamned pads on their paws. Phosphate ate 'em clean down to the bone. Ate up my best pair of shoes, too, but I didn't give a shit. Jacksonville crapped their pants when they found out I seized a damned phosphate pit. 'How you gonna secure a *pit*?' Heh, heh, heh. But I got full pay and a manager's award. Hell, I even seized a strip joint, Henry. Took everything. Took the pole. Took the wigs and the g-strings. I even took the damned tassels the girls stick on their titties."

"Pasties," Henry said. "They're called pasties." Toby frowned at him. "Don't tell my wife I know about pasties," Henry said.

"Her name is Annie DeFlorio," Gina said.

I watched as Henry wrote down the name. I wondered if he would write it down if I blurted out the word *shit*.

"Snow White," Rachel said softly, but not so softly that we couldn't hear. Allison said, "Snow White?"

"That's what some people call her," Gina said. She did not add that it was she herself who came up with the name. Gina had nicknames for everyone. Toby she called "Lumpy." Henry was "Buckwheat." Allison was "Little Red Riding Hood," which didn't seem pithy enough to qualify as a nickname. She never addressed us by our nicknames, so I wasn't sure what she called me, though I had heard it was "Tin Man," more a reference to stature than to heartlessness, I hoped.

"She's one of the chief's pets," Beth said.

"Well, I don't know about that," Gina said. "But she hasn't been an RO very long."

"She's still a Grade Eleven," Beth said.

Allison literally gasped. As the most ambitious trainee in the room, she received this news like a blow to the solar plexus. "How can they do that?"

"They can do whatever the hell they want," Henry said.

"She got a temp promotion," Beth said. She seemed to be taking some grim satisfaction in telling Allison this. Beth had been trying for years to get into management. Once again, she had been passed over, this time by Annie DeFlorio, who had joined the Service just three years before we trainees did.

"In every profession you have your benchwarmers and then you have your Michael Jordans," Toby intoned.

"I didn't think you could be a manager until you were a Twelve for at least a year," Allison said.

"It's a training group," Gina said. "So they can have a Grade Twelve manager."*

"She must be something else," Dee said.

Toby said, "She's very sharp, very on the ball. She trained under Jenny Duncan." Jenny Duncan had the reputation as the toughest—and brightest—manager in the state.

"She looks like Geena Davis," Rachel said.

"That's not fair!" Caroline said. She turned to our manager. "You're the one named Gina."

"How do you know what she looks like?" Allison asked Rachel.

"People tell me."

We looked at Gina, the one person in the room who had actually seen Annie DeFlorio. She said, "Anyway, I wanted to lay to rest some rumors that have been going around about Billy."

---

* Managers' grade levels, in all divisions of the Service, are determined by the grade levels of their employees. Gina was a Grade 13 manager, since she was supervising Grade 12 revenue officers. Annie DeFlorio was a Grade 12 manager, because no one in her group was ranked over Grade 7.

Dead silence. We had not spoken his name in weeks. Even Beth, who was the closest to him, had kept mum.

"Billy has not been arrested. He has not been fired. His reassignment is pending."

"Is he coming back to the group?" Cindy asked.

"He's got at least one offer on the table and he's taking some time off to weigh his options. Things have been blown way out of proportion. And we all need to remember that there are always two sides to every story."

Culpepper never told me his side of the story. It would be nearly two years before I would see him again, and then under circumstances that made the past irrelevant: He was no longer my OJI, we had both moved on. He had found his niche as I had mine. The most commonly accepted version of the events that led to his downfall was this: The new training group was attending Phase One in Daytona Beach, staying at a hotel two miles from the ocean. Culpepper decided to join them for a week, to better acquaint himself with his new group. His wife remained in Lakeside. There was a particular trainee, a young woman fresh from college, who had become infatuated with him, or at least pretended to be infatuated with him—she was also the most ambitious of the new-hires. She flirted shamelessly with Culpepper, had lain on the beach with him as the group sat around talking and drinking beer. She laughed at his jokes and even began calling him "Billy" during happy hour at the hotel lounge.

No one but Culpepper and the trainee know what really happened next. According to the trainee, Culpepper drank too much and made a pass at her. She rebuffed him. Later, as she was getting ready for bed, a banging commenced on her door. She heard Culpepper calling for her, demanding that she yield and allow him in. She was so frightened, she said, that she locked the door and hid under her covers, literally shaking with fear. A far cry from the rumors we had heard in Lakeside.

Culpepper would claim the opposite: that she had invited him to her room and "chickened out" at the last moment. Her story was made up to cover her embarrassment after things got too serious.

Nevertheless, two weeks later, William Culpepper was no longer the manager of the group.

○   ○   ○

They said he camped in his office and refused to pack in preparation for Annie DeFlorio's arrival. The branch chief called him and ordered him to pack up his things and move back to the federal building. Culpepper refused. The division chief called Culpepper and ordered him to move. Culpepper refused. "You want my job, come and get it," he reportedly said. The branch chief arrived in Lakeside on orders from on high, driving from Orlando with Annie DeFloria in tow. "I've brought you something, Billy," the branch chief said. The secretary stepped into the room with three large cardboard boxes. "Time to pack up," the branch chief said. Culpepper protested the accusations against him. He had been wrongly accused. He suspected the trainee was being coached, was being used as a pawn by unknown forces to destroy him. He never entered the trainee's room. He just knocked on the door. He had made an error in judgment. He was the victim here. The branch chief was unimpressed. Culpepper was nothing to him. Annie DeFlorio, on the other hand, was a rising star. Her credentials were impeccable: honors in political science, former senator's aide, outstanding revenue officer. It didn't matter that the trainee refused to press charges. It didn't matter that Inspection had recommended no official disciplinary action, calling it a he-said, she-said case. What mattered was Culpepper had made the fatal error of applying the old rules to a new paradigm: these trainees had entered under the Outstanding Scholars Program, as had we—as had Annie DeFlorio. In the span of five years, Culpepper had become a dinosaur, and the Service was hastening him and his kind toward extinction. A coup had taken place in the halls of Byzantium. The prince of power had lost his throne.

○   ○   ○

Cindy summoned me to her office after the group meeting. On her desk lay the cabinetmaker's case file, a Form 668-B* paper-clipped to the front.

---

* The form used to seize assets. Referred to as a "B" by revenue officers.

"I've reviewed the case, Rick," she began. "And I think we should talk about this before we give the file to Gina."

"Okay." I thought of Culpepper's warning about Cindy: *Cindy was trained in another state. You have to understand that enforcement is not uniform across the country. Some districts seize, some would rather have bamboo shoots stuck under their fingernails. Cindy has the highest overage* in the group because she never seizes. But if you want to be promoted in this district, you must seize. Cindy will try to stop you.*

"Don't you think ten days to get current is a little unreasonable?" she asked.

"Gina didn't."

"I was asking what you think."

"He's pyramiding taxes, Cindy. The manual is pretty clear on this."

"The CIS says he has five thousand dollars in equity. He owes twenty-five."

"But there is equity. And the manual says—"

"I've been doing this job for fifteen years, Rick. I know what the manual says."

"Well, then."

"You also told him you wouldn't do anything for thirty days."

"Only if he got current. He didn't. I need to seize on this case, Cindy."

She leaned back in her chair and regarded me. I knew what she was going to say before she said it. "Why? Because it's the right thing for the case or the right thing for your career?"

I didn't answer.

"Ten days isn't even enough time for him to talk to the bank," she said.

"Is that our concern? In another month, Cindy, he's going to owe another five or six grand. How long are we going to allow him to bleed before we put an end to it? You've seen the P-and-L.† The guy hasn't made any money since he opened the business. Whether we give him ten days or fifty, things aren't going to change."

---

* Although the definition changes with each administration, generally cases that have been in the field longer than one year.

† Profit-and-Loss statement.

"We're doing him a favor."

"That's right."

"I wonder if he'll feel that way."

"Since when do we give a damn about that?"

She relented and initialed off on the paperwork, but attached a cover memo to Gina, giving her reasons why we shouldn't seize. We both knew it was a pointless exercise. Gina had been trained in Florida, where seizures were the usual means of resolving a case. She signed the 668-B that same day. I scheduled the seizure for nine A.M. the following morning. We would arrive with the locks and chains without giving any warning to the taxpayer. Assets—and taxpayers—have a way of disappearing when people know we are coming.

°   °   °

Toby, in his never-ending quest to transform Henry from desk jockey into five-star field officer, would tell him of the glory days. "Man, when I first started I had three hundred cases. Three *hundred* cases, Henry, and you didn't need no manager's signature on the B* to seize. You didn't need no consent. You drove around with the seizure kit in your trunk and you locked 'em up on first contact. Any given day you had twenty, thirty, forty seizures going. You had to. There was no other way to stay on top of three hundred cases. My point is, you don't know how good you got it. All you got to do now is seize every month. One seizure a month, Henry, that's twelve seizures a year. You tellin' me you can't do twelve seizures in one year?" And he would say, "Henry, you're afraid of your own inventory. You think you're helping these people by not seizing them? People *thank* me when I seize 'em. They send me cards and letters. Once this lady sent me a bundt cake."

"I don't like bundt cake."

"You don't like bundt cake? Jesus, Henry, the bundt cake ain't the damn point! Most times these people are hugging a dead dog. The dog is dead and stinkin' in their arms, but they can't let it go. They love their damn

---

* Form 668-B, Levy.

dog. They fed it and played with it and took it for walks and it's part of them. But it died and it ain't our fault it died and they need us to pull the stinkin' carcass out of their arms so they can get a new dog, a puppy to give 'em the love they need."

"You crazy, Toby, you know that?" And Henry would laugh.

"You got to be cruel to be kind," Toby answered.

o   o   o

I rose at 4:00 A.M. the next morning. I showered, shaved, brushed my teeth twice, and put on the only suit I owned, the same suit I wore to my final interview with the IRS. I had trouble with the tie. Culpepper had one suit he wore to every seizure, a navy blue, with a blue-and-red-striped tie. He even had a special pen that he used to sign all the paperwork. It was possible to obtain windbreakers embossed with the Treasury logo and the letters IRS on the back. No one wore them. Culpepper said it would be like conducting a seizure with a bull's-eye drawn on your back.

By 4:45, I was sitting in my favorite booth at Denny's on Highway 92, halfway between where I lived and where I worked. On any other morning, I would have my writing binder with me, and would work until 6:45, six cups of coffee and a half pack of cigarettes later. On this morning, I walked in with the cabinetmaker's file. Beatrice delivered my coffee, black, and a glass of water. "Good morning, professor," she said. She always called me "professor." I studied the file as the earth rolled toward the sun. Dawn came cold and overcast. It was mid-November. I had just turned twenty-nine years old. I had been a trainee for eleven months, after being practically nothing for the past eleven years. The Service had hired me for this day, had trained me for it, had done everything within its power to prepare me for it. Thousands of hours, reams of training materials, hundreds of thousands of dollars. I had put it off long enough. It was time to execute the Fourth Protocol. It was time to feed the beast.

I checked to make sure I had the proper forms. Form 668-B, Form 2433, Form 2434-B. A blank consent-to-enter. Phone numbers to the towing company, the locksmith, the local police. A copy of the tax lien. A copy of the final notice. I studied the CIS. I reviewed my history,

making sure I had documented Pub 1, my deadline and warning of consequences.* If he refused consent, there would be no seizure on this day; I
would have to return to the office and prepare an affidavit for the court to
grant a writ-of-entry. I sipped my coffee, smoked, and made notes. A seizure
is carefully scripted in the Internal Revenue Manual. We must say certain
things, give the taxpayer certain documents in a particular sequence. Once
I handed the B to the taxpayer, his assets were seized, or, more precisely,
became the property of the United States government, as agent for the
American people. If he tried to remove them, he was committing a crime
called "forcible rescue." I closed my eyes and imagined myself handing him
the B, reading the paragraph in the middle of the form, requesting consent... no, I should request consent first, before giving him the B. If I gave
him the B first and he denied consent, I would have to release the seizure
immediatey. I would put the government's position in jeopardy and, more
important, look like a fool. And *I must not look like a fool.*

I slid out of the booth, light-headed from the coffee and cigarettes, and
headed for the bathroom. I splashed cold water on my face. I rinsed my
glasses. I looked at myself in the mirror. I needed a haircut. I had a blem-
ish on the end of my nose, on the very tip. Call me Rudolph. What sort of
adult man still suffers from zits? I felt the same way I did as a seven-year-
old child, when my parents made me wear a coat and tie to church.

At 6:49, I climbed into my car. I had finished my checklist for the office:
warning stickers, Scotch tape, two padlocks, chain, two "knuckle-busters,"†
seizure tags‡ for the jigsaws, the radial-arm saws, the tables saws, my 809
receipt book, a copy of the IRM. A light drizzle was falling. My old wiper
blades screeched at me. Cindy Sandifer: "A good revenue officer never gets
wet." I made a mental note to grab the office umbrella on the way out the
door. Highway 92 was already filling with commuters, ordinary people on
the way to their ordinary jobs. On this morning, somewhere far outside
our small orbits, the cabinetmaker's and mine, empires were being born.
Great fortunes were being made. Magnificent dreams were being forged in

---

* Also called WOEA (whoa-E-ah): Warned of Enforcement Action.

† A type of lock that fits over a doorknob.

‡ Notice that may be used to tag moveable assets; resembles a "toe-tag."

the fires of imagination. In boardrooms across the country, great enterprises were being launched. The fate of entire nations was being decided in the hidden chambers of the powerful. On this day, too, in this minuscule corner of the cosmos, one dream would die in service of another, if what I desired could be called a dream.

You can see it in their eyes, Culpepper had said. *Oh, how they want to believe the dream. The dream, Yancey! And you can show them, in black and white, from their own records, how they haven't made a dime since they've been in business, how they've lost every penny they've sunk into it. How every drop of blood and sweat and tears they've poured into this black hole they call a business has been a colossal waste of time, and it doesn't matter. They are* entrepreneurs; *they're living the American dream: they are the boss; they are the* man. *And it doesn't matter one damn bit they're mortgaged to the hilt, their kids are wearing hand-me-downs, they're driving ten-year-old cars with the rear bumpers dragging the ground. You know, cars like yours. Doesn't matter a damn bit the judgments filed against them, the liens, the collectors calling day and night. It doesn't even matter that you can prove to them they could make a better living flipping burgers at McDonald's for minimum wage. None of that matters. Only the dream matters.*

o   o   o

The rain fell harder as I drove west. I cracked the window to allow the cigarette smoke to escape. I was smoking too much. A pack per day now. Pam would roll her eyes when I lit up and smack her fingers against the inside of her elbow, miming a junkie getting a fix. The rain spat through the crack in the window, dotting my pants. The ash grew long on my smoke; I raised it, an offering, toward the crack, and watched the draft suck it away, so quickly it seemed to vanish into oblivion.

They revert to childhood: eternity is a day. And if they're able to turn the open sign on the door, it's a victory. It's Normandy stormed. The future becomes tomorrow, next week. Next month, next year, next five years, that's science fiction. Get through the day. This order needs to be filled. This check needs to be covered. Pull it from the savings. Cash the bonds. That IRA, who did we think we were kidding? Cash it. Cash, cash, cash. Gotta have cash. Gotta have cash in the drawer. Is that new kid I hired dipping in the drawer? Gotta call the bank, maybe they'll give me an extension on that line of credit. Just need a little time. A little breathing room. Need a new widget for the thingamabob. Maybe that widget salesman will give me credit. Gotta have credit. Can't survive without credit. These rates eat the small guy alive. Get through the day. Maybe the bank would like my receivables. Buddy of mine says you can get eighty cents on the dollar for your receivables. Cash! Gotta have the cash. Gotta get that credit. Payroll next week—dear Jesus, if only that bastard would pay me for that work I did six months ago! That would keep me through the month. The whole damn month! Heard about that home-equity line of credit. Up to 120 percent of your equity. That would carry me another month, maybe two. Gotta have the cash. Can't make payroll without cash. Cash, cash, cash. Credit, credit, credit. Bastards wait till you're down and have to have it, then slap it to you with the interest. And the deeper you get, the more credit cards come in the mail. Must have six of 'em now, at 21 percent. Must be twenty, thirty grand deep in credit card debt. Jesus, can't even think about that. Get through this day, and it's Thursday, then Friday, and you can work it out this weekend, sit down and work it all out. Think the payment on the forklift is due. What's today's date? Maybe Mom and Dad can help. Wouldn't hurt to ask. Gotta have the cash. Cash in the drawer. Can't keep the doors open without cash in the drawer.

"Well, I can't believe it," Allison said. "Rick is actually going to seize something."

She was leaning in the doorway to Cindy's office. I could easily have reached over and slammed the door into her smug little grin. Cindy and I were in the middle of an argument about whether to call the taxpayer before we paid our visit. As a disciple of Culpepper, I was adamantly opposed. Cindy thought it was the professional thing to do.

"It also makes the most sense from a time-management perspective. It's a waste of time to drive all the way out there if he won't sign the consent."

"He'll sign the consent."

"What makes you so sure?"

"I'll make him an offer he can't refuse."

Cindy frowned. "This isn't a movie, Rick."

"Oh, right."

"And it isn't a game. You're about to put this man out of business."

It was at that moment that Allison appeared.

"Don't you have anything better to do?" I asked.

"I thought maybe you'd want me to come with you. I could help with the inventory."

"There isn't that much," I said.

"I didn't think so," she said, and disappeared before I could slam the door and break her little nose.

Cindy said, "I strongly suggest you call him first."

"Call him first so he can clean out the shop? Call him first so he can run to bankruptcy court?"

"Your case closes regardless," she said calmly. Her soft tone called attention to the fact that mine was not. I was practically shouting. "I know you're anxious to make a seizure, Rick."

"No. I was just under the impression that's what the government was paying me to do. This is a really interesting discussion, Cindy, but if you're not willing to assist me on this seizure, I'll find someone who is. I'll see if Beth's here."

"I never said that. I'm just your OJI. I can't tell you what to do."

"Right. Gina is the manager, and she signed the paperwork. Let's go."

The rain had slackened to a swirling gray mist by the time we were on the road to the cabinetmaker's. The seizure kit rattled in the backseat. Cindy grabbed hold of the *Oh, Jesus!* handle and said, "You never forget your first seizure. It's like your first kiss." She told a long, uninteresting story of her first in-business seizure involving a worm-farmer, someone who actually raised earthworms for a living. "A good revenue officer never seizes anything alive," she finished. "I didn't know that then. Never seize anyone with livestock. Never seize a pet store. Because you'll have to feed the damn things." She asked if I had called Andy McNeil. I told her Andy was on standby. Andy McNeil was the towing company owner who assisted us with the seizure of vehicles in the county. Andy loved repo work. Culpepper said he was at heart a frustrated revenue officer. I found it hard to believe that anyone, in their heart, was a frustrated revenue officer. Cindy asked if I had remembered my cash receipt book. She asked if I had checked the seizure kit for plenty of Scotch tape. I listened to the odd squeaky sound beneath my hood and gave her one-syllable answers. What was that vibration in the rear? A tire about to blow? We had a good laugh when Allison blew out the rear tires on her brand-new BMW driving down the interstate; she had run over a two-by-four that had fallen from the bed of a pickup she was tailgating. She was currently wading through the Atlantic Ocean of red tape required for reimbursement for the damage. Why was I thinking of Allison? I was hyped, light-headed from the pot of coffee at Denny's, the cigarettes, and the adrenaline coursing through my blood-stream. Culpepper: *The thing about seizures is you never know what's going to happen. Things shift in an instant. I seized this gun shop owner once. He was a Viet-nam vet, an ex-marine, but a pussycat through the whole process. He went through the inventory with us and the ATF, and nobody noticed that he had left the room until we heard the shot go off in the back office. So ATF goes running back there, guns drawn, and there's the guy sitting behind his desk with the .357 on the blot-ter in front of him, and there's a hole in the wall behind him. "Missed," he said.*

Culpepper's theory, borne of years of experience, was that the most dan-gerous type of seizure was the mom-and-pop store, the sole proprietorship into which the taxpayer had invested much more than cash. *You're taking something bigger than the water cooler and typewriter, Yancey. You're crushing something precious. You're that crazy Indian bastard tearing open the chest and ripping out the heart still beating, from that* Indiana Jones *movie—not the first one, the second one, the one that sucked.*

Cindy said, "Another good reason to call is he might not be here. You have to serve the levy on him."

"The manual says I can serve it on the person in possession of his property."

"You should serve it on him."

"That's not what the manual says."

"We'll call Gina if he's not there."

"Cindy, there isn't any reason to call Gina."

"I don't think we should serve the B on an employee. I never have."

You haven't served many on anyone, I thought. Cindy was a Grade 12, the highest rank a revenue officer can achieve, but she wasn't going anywhere. Like Henry, she always found a reason to forgo a seizure. Her inventory languished; cases dragged on for years. "Baby-sitting," it was called. I did not intend to become a baby-sitter. If I was going to stick with this damn job, I was going to be the best revenue officer who ever carried a bag.

A Chevy cargo van was parked by the front door. I swung through the lot and drove to the nearest pay phone. I called Andy and told him to meet us at the business. Now, even if the cabinetmaker refused consent, I would not come away empty-handed. I drove back to the shop. The large bay doors were open. Someone on the forklift was moving pallets of material from one shelf to another. The taxpayer had valued the lift at $15,000. After taking a forced-sale reduction, that was $9,000 in my pocket. The government's pocket. The van was worth about $4,000. That was another $2,400. I was already over ten grand. We got out of the car. The mist was cold, hard-driven, icy pins pricking my cheeks. The pavement was slick, glimmering; I could feel the heat rising from the hood of my car as I walked past. Every sensation was heightened, as in the most vivid of dreams. I opened the door for Cindy and we stepped inside.

"I had my first kiss today," I told Pam after she slipped into bed beside me.

"What the hell does that mean?"

"My first seizure."

"*Grand* or *petit mal*?" she asked.

"You wanna hear what happened?"

"Not really. It bores the shit out of me."

She rolled onto her side and opened her book. I had come to bed at 9:00, my usual time, but couldn't sleep.

"I've decided something," I said.

"What have you decided?"

"I've decided that since it looks like I'm going to stick with this thing for a while, I might as well be . . . well, brilliant at it."

"Is that possible?"

"In general or for just me personally?"

" 'I don't care if you decided to be a ditchdigger when you grow up, as long as you're the very best ditchdigger you can be.' " She was being snide. My mother had said this to me when I was a child, and I had made the mistake of telling Pam the story.

"I could do it, you know. Be brilliant at it. I swear I've never felt the things I've felt today."

She yawned. "Sounds like you're falling in love."

"I think I'm . . . attaining enlightenment."

I began to tell her about the cabinetmaker seizure. Telling the story helped me to relive it and feel that odd tingling in my scalp and the sense that the room was shrinking, or I expanding to fill it. I stopped after five minutes. She had fallen asleep.

He was not, in the words of the manual, a "repeater." Nor was he one, as Gina called them, of the "hardy perennials." He had never been in business before. If he had, he might have learned some tricks to keep us at bay—at least for a while. He did not understand accounting, billing, budgeting. He understood his craft. He understood how to take a plain piece of wood and transform it into something beautiful. He understood his dream. He did not understand why we had come.

"Mr. Yancey! I was just going to call you." A common refrain when we walk in unannounced. "Hi," he said to Cindy. He led us to the little back room that was the epicenter of the dream. Sawdust crunched beneath our feet. The work area vibrated with the din of the saws. An elderly man looked up from his task as we passed. He wore blue overalls, earplugs, plastic goggles. The cabinetmaker did not introduce us. I saw two other men working in the far corner. They seemed to be having an argument. Three inside, one outside on the forklift. Four employees, plus my taxpayer. Today they would go home unemployed. He shut the door behind us, but the sound of steel teeth chewing wood still reached us as he found the stools, throwing long sheets of drafting paper onto his desk.

"Sorry for the mess," he said. "I've been working on something. Big job. Well, I don't actually have the job yet; I'm bidding on it today. That's why I was going to call you. I think I'm going to be able to . . ."

I pulled Form 668-B from the case file. I addressed him formally. My voice sounded faint in my own ears. "We're here today for $28,915.22."

"You said I could have forty days."

"I said you could have ten days—"

"Plus thirty. That makes forty."

"Ten days to make your tax deposit for this quarter. That was the first part. The most important part. Did you make that deposit?"

"That's one of the things I needed to talk to you about, Mr. Yancey."

"Did you make that deposit?"

"See, these plans here, it's for a whole subdivision. Thirty-six units. If I can land this contract, I could pay—"

"Did you make that deposit?"

His shoulders dipped slightly. In either hand he held the plans. They rattled against his thighs. He turned to Cindy.

"I'm almost there. I just need a little extra time."

"Do you have $28,915.22 to pay today?" I asked.

He sank into his broken chair. The plans fluttered to the floor. "No."

I pulled out the consent-to-enter. I dropped the case file on the stool and walked over to him. He looked up. Sawdust clung to his hair, his eyebrows. He needed a haircut. I held out the consent.

"What's this?"

"We've come to seize the assets of the business for nonpayment of—"

He waved his hand at me, then let it drop in his lap. A small sound escaped from the back of his throat, not quite a sob; his eyes remained dry. I placed the consent on his desk, next to the picture of his wife and son. He barely glanced at it. I explained what it was.

"By signing this, you're giving us permission to come in here and inventory the assets."

"Inventory my assets? You mean, take 'em. And if I don't sign it?"

"We'll go to court and—"

"You're taking me to court?"

"No. What I was going to say, we'll get what's called a writ-of-entry. Sort of like a warrant."

He nodded. He was holding up well. Better than I was. I felt as if my knees were about to give out. I focused on the mechanics; I followed the flowchart inside my head.

"You sign right here, above your name. And the date goes right here."

I handed him my pen. I was leaning over the desk, *willing* him to sign.

He whispered, "Mr. Yancey, I know I can pull this out. I know I screwed up. I screwed up big time."

"It's really out of my hands now," I said. In other words, we might as well argue about the rain.

He nodded. The pen turned slowly in his fingers. His palms were rough, calloused, scarred by old wounds, where splinters had bitten deep.

"I've known those men out there over fifteen years. That old fella you saw when you came in . . . he was my fifth-grade shop teacher. He helped me set the whole thing up."

"We really don't have a choice."

"Doesn't look like I got much of one either."

He signed the consent. I peeled off the carbon. "This is your copy." I turned and Cindy, as if we had rehearsed it, handed me the B.

"This is Form 668-B. It is our formal, written demand for payment. I have to read you this section." I read the paragraph aloud. He did not look at me. He was looking at some point over my right shoulder.

" 'The amounts shown above are now due, owing, and unpaid to the United States from the above taxpayer for internal revenue taxes. Notice and demand have been made for payment. Chapter 64 of the Internal Revenue Code provides a lien for the above tax and statutory additions. Section 6631 of the Code authorizes collection of taxes by levy on all property or rights to property of a taxpayer . . .' "

He paid no attention. I could have been reading to him in ancient Sanskrit. I finished strong, with some measure of authority, I hoped: " 'Therefore, under the provisions of the Code section 6331, so much of the property or rights to property, either real or personal, as may be necessary to pay the unpaid balance of assessment shown, with additions provided by law, including fees, costs, and expenses of this levy, are levied upon to pay the taxes and additions.' "

I separated Part 3 from the four-page form and handed it to him.

"Your assets are now under seizure," I said. I walked back to the stool and slid the consent and the B back into the case file. "Ms. Sandifer and I have to take an inventory and secure the assets."

"What about my men?"

"You're going to tell them to go home."

"Just like that? Go home?"

"We can start here in the office if you'd like," Cindy offered.

"He should stay with us," I said to her. The Service preferred it that way: there was less chance for accusations of impropriety.

"I'd like that," he said to Cindy. He walked past me. He was still holding the seizure form. He paused at the door, turned to me. "Mr. Yancey, I . . ." He gave up, turned back to the door, and squared his shoulders. He walked out. The door hung halfway open. The air was thick with wood dust and the smell of machine oil. He gestured for the men to shut off their machines by drawing his index finger across his throat. Cindy and I watched as the men stood before him, looking over his shoulder at us. The old man's face darkened. He said something to the cabinetmaker, who began to shake his head vigorously. The old man put a hand on his forearm. The cabinetmaker said something else and the old man removed his hand and dropped his head. The old man ripped off his goggles, yanked out his earplugs. He threw them into a tool kit and slammed it closed. He picked up the kit and headed for the outer door.

I moved. "Just a second."

The old man stopped. He stared at me. I turned to the cabinetmaker. "Is that his personal property?"

"These are my tools," the old man said.

A voice in the back of my head (Culpepper's?) prodded me: *Ask for proof. Assume it's a business asset unless he can prove otherwise.*

"Okay," I said.

"Come on, guys," the cabinetmaker said. "Get your stuff out of here. I'll call you later."

"What about my check?" one of them, the youngest, asked.

"You're gonna get paid, Kenny. Don't you always get paid? Come on. I'll work this out. Just get your things outta here for now. It's gonna be okay."

When they had gone, he turned back to me.

"My personal stuff."

"You better take it now."

I followed him back to the office. Cindy stood by her stool, hands folded in front of her. He found a cardboard box beside the desk. It was filled with old magazines. He dumped the magazines onto the floor and began to clean off his desk.

"So you take an inventory and then what?"

"We sell it."

"When?"

"In a couple of weeks. First, we have to advertise the sale."

"Wait a minute. You advertise?"

"Yes."

"Where?"

"The newspaper. We send fliers."

"Fliers?"

"And post notices."

"Where?"

"Here. And the post office. The county courthouse."

"Everybody's gonna know?"

"It's a public auction."

He dropped his head. He raised it. He grabbed the family picture from his desk and dumped it unceremoniously into the box. He was not going to indulge in self-pity. As for me, I had pity's neck in both hands and was choking the life out of the little son of a bitch.

"You know, I really was going to call you. If I had called you today, Mr. Yancey, would you still have come?"

"Yes."

Andy arrived with the flatbed while we were tagging the machines. I called out the model and serial numbers while Cindy recorded everything on the Form 2433. We heard the rumble of the big diesel engine through the open front door.

"What's that?" the cabinetmaker asked.

"The tow truck," I said. "We're seizing the van."

"You're taking my van?"

"It's a business asset."

"It's also my ride home."

"I thought your wife had a car."

I left Cindy to take care of the cabinetmaker while I talked to Andy.

"Rick!" he cried. Andy wasn't tall, but he was compact, like an Olympic wrestler. In fact, he had won a high school state championship in his weight class in wrestling. He wore a tight blue shirt with the sleeves rolled to his shoulders, no matter the weather. His reddish-blond hair was cut an inch from his scalp. He always reminded me, for some reason, of a Boy Scout.

He clapped me on the shoulder. Andy was one of those rare people who took an immediate liking to me. "Whadda we got?"

"This," I pointed at the van.

He laughed. "You're kidding, right?"

"What's wrong with it?"

"Allison's first set of wheels was a Beemer."

"She was just lucky."

"Better to be lucky than smart."

The taxpayer appeared in the doorway. I could see Cindy standing behind him.

"I've got some personal stuff in there," he said.

Andy looked at me. "Go ahead," I nodded to the cabinetmaker.

He opened the passenger door and began to rummage around the cluttered interior. Andy walked back to the truck and hit the switch to lower the bed. The cabinetmaker emerged from the truck holding a battered teddy bear. He stood for a moment, cradling the bear, staring at it. He turned to me. "Where are you taking it?"

"To McNeil Towing. We'll store it there until the sale."

"Can I pick up the rest of my stuff later?"

"Sure."

We heard the sound of an engine revving. It was coming from the open storage bay. The forklift.

"Oh, I forgot about Tony," the cabinetmaker said.

He walked past me and disappeared into the bay. I looked at Cindy, who was standing in the doorway.

"I'll go," I said. "Give me a tag and another 2433."

I placed a warning sticker on the van window. "WARNING: UNITED STATES GOVERNMENT SEIZURE...Persons tampering with this property, in any manner, are subject to severe penalty of the law." I scribbled down the van's make and model and vehicle identification number. A man walked out of the storage bay, carrying a paper sack, probably containing his lunch. He muttered something under his breath as he passed me. He climbed into a beat-up El Camino and roared out of the parking lot, the rear bumper slapping the pavement as he whipped onto the street. Cindy was taping a warning sticker on the office door when the forklift rumbled to life. Andy turned to me, an eyebrow raised. We trotted toward the storage bay.

The cabinetmaker was on the forklift, maneuvering it between two steel support beams. It took me a moment to realize what he was attempting. Behind me, Andy laughed. The cabinetmaker jockeyed between the two beams, experimenting with raising and lowering the long metal arms of the forklift. He was trying to wedge it between the metal columns to make it impossible for us to remove from the bay. He had placed the teddy bear between his legs. He had been holding up okay, until he found the bear in his truck. The teddy bear had broken him. I walked into the bay and shouted over the roar of the lift's engine: "Sir! Sir, what you're doing is illegal!" He spun the wheel around, cutting the front of the lift with its heavy metal arms toward me. I backed up. Andy appeared at my elbow and said, "Let me throw a chain around it. I can *drag* that son of a bitch out of there."

I kept shouting at the taxpayer, Andy kept laughing, and the taxpayer kept edging the forklift up, back, side to side, banging into the beams with such force that for a second I was afraid he'd knock one of them over and the entire structure would come crashing down on our heads. Finally, thanks to nothing I shouted, but in answer to some interior voice, the cabinetmaker gave up. He slammed on the brake, cut off the engine, and dropped his chin to his chest in a gesture of surrender.

He climbed off the seat, clutching the teddy bear by the top of the head.

"Take the damn thing," he said as he walked past.

We completed the seizure without further incident. Andy left with the forklift and truck chained up on his flatbed. Cindy and I signed the three forms 2433 we had completed and handed the cabinetmaker his copies. He still held the bear. He called his wife at work—she was a third-grade teacher—and, after a heated conversation, walked outside with us. He locked the office door and handed me the keys. I placed a knuckle-buster over the door handle and slipped that key into my pocket.

"I'll send you our minimum bid worksheet and a notice of sale as soon as they're ready," I told him.

"Take your time," he said.

There was nothing left to say, but I was reluctant to leave him. He might try to break back into the building. Then it occurred to me he could do that at any point up to the sale: the IRS did not post guards. I felt the need to say something, perhaps not to comfort him, but to help him understand that there really had been no choice in the matter. I looked at him. His gaze had turned inward. Already he was working something out. He was formulating a plan. He would redeem the dream. I could understand that. It is the universal blessing—and curse—of those who dare.

The rush from this first seizure lasted for days. What had seemed impossible just a few months before was now easy—as Culpepper promised it would be. I had crossed some threshold; I had passed through a membrane. *Enforcement—and sometimes just the* threat *of enforcement—will resolve your case.* In the month that followed, as the year wound to a close, I conducted six more seizures. Two cars. Three businesses. A piece of rental property. The only pressure I felt was from the impending holidays. It was the Service's policy not to take enforcement during the Christmas season. Some revenue officers argued this policy violated the First Amendment. I accepted it as a condition of war and planned accordingly. However, when I discovered a bank account that had not been disclosed on a financial statement, I hand-delivered a levy on the day after Thanksgiving. Gina was pleased. Allison was not. She felt I was already vying for the first choice to be the next Grade Eleven in the group.

I was walking from the parking lot to the federal building one morning when I spotted a woman standing behind a new Mercury Sable, massaging her forehead. She raised her head as I approached.

She was about my age, I judged, perhaps one or two years younger. She was wearing a red business suit and her dark, curly hair was pulled back from her face and hung in a ponytail that terminated at the small of her back. Her eyes were large and very dark, almost black. Full, perfectly shaped lips, olive-complected, about five foot eight, with long, athletic legs, she did resemble Geena Davis.

"You're Annie DeFlorio," I said.

She smiled and took my hand.

"I'm Rick Yancey."

"I know."

"You do?"

"We haven't met, but I see you sometimes wandering around the alley."

"That's my thinking spot."

"Really?" She hardly seemed to be listening. "I'm sorry. I'm running late this morning and I did a really stupid thing."

"You locked your keys in the car."

"In my trunk. How did you know?"

"I do it all the time."

She nodded as if she knew that about me. "My husband has the other set of keys but he's in Orlando."

"Tell you what, I have AAA. I'll call them and have them pop the trunk for you."

Her dark eyes widened. "Will you? That would be terrific."

"It's no problem."

"I've got a meeting in five minutes."

"Go on, I'll call and wait with the car."

"I really appreciate it."

She squeezed my forearm briefly before trotting away, her heels clicking on the pavement. I watched her.

A week into December, and six weeks until our training year ended, the new branch chief came calling. We trainees were summoned into the conference room to meet her. It was Jenny Duncan, who was a group manager in Orlando and who was feared throughout the district as the toughest, smartest, most aggressive employee Collection had ever produced, with the possible exception of William Culpepper. Jenny Duncan had been Annie DeFlorio's manager and the first to recognize Annie's potential.

Jenny's appearance belied her reputation. She was about Gina's height, but small-boned, almost fragile-looking. She was wearing a powder-blue business suit and badly scuffed heels. She shook our hands as we sat down, one by one, making eye contact with each of us and calling us by name.

"Rick," she said to me. "Gina tells me you're a man on fire."

Allison sat next to me, smoldering. She had been greeted with, "So, you're little Allison."

"My name is Jenny Duncan and I'm going to be the acting branch chief here until a new one is selected," she opened. "I wanted to take this opportunity to get acquainted and give you guys a heads-up on our expectations from now until the end of your training."

She turned to Caroline.

"Why do we seize?"

"Seize what?"

"Seize anything."

Caroline frowned. "Because people owe taxes?"

"For every dollar we collect from enforcement we write off three," Jenny said. She turned to Rachel. "Do you think it's right for us to put people out of business? Aren't we just adding to the unemployment lines? How does what we do help the economy? In other words, aren't we defeating the purpose?"

Rachel said nothing. She looked at the tabletop. Allison tilted her chin upward, a signal she was bold and assertive. "It's an issue of fairness."

"Fairness," Jenny said. "Is it fair when one revenue officer will seize and another will fifty-three under the same set of facts? None of you has been here very long, but I'm sure you've seen it happen. You all must know ROs who never seize."

She turned to Dee. "What do you think?"

"I haven't done that many seizures..." Dee stammered. In fact, she had done *no* seizures.

"Rick, you've been seizing quite a bit lately. What are your thoughts?"

"I think what Allison was getting at is the compliance aspect of enforcement."

Jenny Duncan folded her thin arms over her chest, leaned back in her chair, and said, "Explain."

I remembered a story of Toby's. I said, "In the old days, when a revenue officer was assigned a new zip code, he would hit three or four businesses, immediately seizing them, creating the biggest stir he could in the community. After a couple of months, TDA issuance in those zips would plummet."

She nodded. "Maximum impact. Shutting down these businesses encourages others to comply in order to stay open." She looked at Allison. "Fairness is a legitimate issue as well. Most small businesses struggle to stay in compliance—and there's no way of knowing if this is out of a sense of duty or a sense of fear. Probably a little of both."

She picked up a stack of printouts and flipped through them. The philosophical discussion was over. "I've analyzed your 795s* and frankly I'm a little concerned about the average number of cases worked." She asked Dee, "How many appointments do you schedule in a day?"

"Two or three. Sometimes four."

Jenny shook her head. "I don't see why. It has no effect but to drive down the closures."

Allison wrote in her calendar, "Don't drive down closures."

"Beginning immediately, I want you to schedule your appointments no more than thirty minutes apart. That's fourteen appointments in an eight hour shift, taking breaks into account."

"*Fourteen?*" Rachel asked incredulously.

"Do you see a problem with that, Caroline?"

"My name is Rachel. That's Caroline."

"Hi," Caroline said.

"I don't see a problem with that," Allison said. "I was doing more than three or four anyway. Some days I was doing eight." She had written the numeral 14 and circled it twice.

Jenny consulted another page of statistics.

"I'm also concerned about timely follow-up. Who knows how many days we have to follow-up when a taxpayer misses a deadline?"

"Ten," Allison chirped.

"That's right. Ten days. Based on the file reviews I've seen, we're missing that mark by a mile. Also, you need to be more consistent with your enforcement. If you tell a taxpayer you're going to seize, don't send a levy to the bank—seize."

---

* Form 795, also called a "daily," completed by every revenue officer each day, recording cases worked, money and returns collected, closures, type of contact (office or field).

"Sometimes that's hard to coordinate," Dee said. "And sometimes our approvals sit for over a week waiting for Gina's signature."

This sounded like tattling. Jenny Duncan was not pleased. She gave no indication she was displeased, which was a sure indication that she was.

"The manual says you have ten days to take enforcement on missed deadlines. Ten days means ten days. Ultimately, you are responsible for your inventory. In January, the Service will make its final decision regarding your employment. It's crunch-time, people. Time to show us what you're made of."

She squared the stack of prints, smacking the edges smartly on the tabletop, rose abruptly and left the room without another word.

We sat in stunned silence for a moment, and then Rachel said, "They're trying to break us."

"No duh," Allison said. "Where the hell have you been?"

Tears welled in Rachel's eyes. "I don't know how much more I can take. I've gained twenty pounds since I took this job. I can't sleep. My hair is falling out in clumps. My husband barely speaks to me. My kids come to me for help with their homework and I scream at them."

"Well," Allison said. "Being a revenue officer isn't for everyone."

"Your sympathy is touching," Dee said. "I'm not sure being a revenue officer is for *anyone*. If it weren't for the money..."

"I don't give a shit about the money," Rachel said. "No amount of money is worth this."

"I can't leave," Caroline said quietly. "I need this job."

"It's not the same for the rest of us," Rachel told Allison. "We're not like you and Rick. Gina hates us."

"I don't think she hates me," Caroline said.

"Believe me, she does. You should hear some of the things she says."

Caroline's eyes went wide. "What does she say?"

"Look at us," Rachel said. "Look at all of us. I'm fat; Rick's wasted away to a stick; Dee looks like she hasn't slept in a week."

"I feel perfectly fine," Caroline said.

"Have any of you ever stopped and asked yourself why the hell you're doing this? Why you're *allowing* them to do this?"

"You can always quit," Allison said.

"And so could you," Rachel answered. "So could all of us. That's what we should do, all of us. Just quit. That would teach them a lesson. That would send a message."

"It would be lost on them," Dee said.

"Why can't we quit?" Rachel asked again. "Really, what have we got to lose? Would things be so different for any of us? Would we be worse off than we are right now?"

"I would," Caroline said. "I need this job."

"Rick." Rachel turned to me. "You know what happens if you don't quit. You stay on another couple of years and you won't be able to. You'll be afraid to."

"I'm afraid now," I said.

"That's my point! We've been scared out of minds for the past eleven months. Is this how any of us wanted our lives to turn out? Dee, you were going to be a psychologist. Rick, you were going to be a playwright. Caroline, you were—well, I don't know what you were going to be but surely it wasn't this. Even you, Allison, you were going to be a CPA or even start your own business. *Why are we letting them tell us what we are?*"

Her question hung in the air, unanswered because it was unanswerable. Allison finally said, "Well, I can understand now why you can't sleep."

Rachel stared at her. Then she slapped her calendar closed and sped from the room, slamming the door behind her. Allison did not watch her go; she was watching me. Dee stood up.

"I'll make sure she's all right. That was really nasty of you, Allison."

"I hate this," Caroline said. "I don't understand why we're at each other's throats all the time. Aren't we all in this together?"

She followed Dee from the room. Allison was smiling now. I was not.

"Funny, isn't it?" she asked. "The one trainee among us who does the least amount of work."

"I don't think it's funny at all," I said.

"Are you going to quit, too?"

"This job mirrors my life, Allison: I'm just sticking around to see what happens next."

o   o   o

Take one appointment every thirty minutes for eight hours, with one thirty-minute break for lunch. That's fourteen taxpayers per office day. On the average field day you contact eight taxpayers. Three days in the office, two in the field, that's fifty-eight cases per week out of seventy-five in total inventory. Gina: *A good RO turns over her entire inventory in forty-five days.* Gina, who is fond of writing pithy quotes on the office chalkboard, designed to provoke fear and inspiration. *Enjoy your career: Reduce your overage!* and *Do it right the first time—Carpe Diem!* Fifty-eight cases per week. When you touch a case, do everything possible to bring it toward closure. There are no quotas, but close the cases. Close the cases. We don't track dollars collected, but collect the dollars, feed the beast. We don't track returns secured or referred for fraud, but secure the returns and ferret out the fraud, close the cases, feed the beast.

This is a Sel Code 38 TDI: Underreporter, nonfiler with over $100,000 in income. Find out why. Only when you talk to them, don't ask for the returns. Don't make demand. Be casual. Say, *Hi, I'm with the IRS, and we were just wondering why you haven't filed an income tax return for the past five years. Hey, nice Ferrari!* Remember, we want quality, don't sacrifice the quality of your work, but close cases. You want to stay with us, close cases. This small-engine repair guy who works out of the shed behind his trailer owes for six years, $32,000, he can pay $25 per month. Sign right here, sir. No, the interest doesn't stop. You'll be paying $25 per month for the rest of your days and I'll close my case. *Well, you bastards won't get me. I got nothing to take and I'm forty bucks in the hole every month, so how're you ever gonna get me?* We'll file the lien. *Go ahead, file your damn lien. What do I care about your lien?* Maybe you don't, but your children will. I understand your hatred for us, but what about your children? *Asshole... Where do I sign?*

This isn't a competition. Nobody's keeping score. How many has Allison closed this week, or Rachel, or Dee? We sing out, *Another quality closure!* so many times it becomes an office joke. *Another quality closure!*

They trudge through the door, laden with boxes and briefcases and overflowing cartons, sometimes empty-handed, *I didn't keep no receipts, Mr. Yancey.* Doesn't matter, we'll file you anyway, with no deductions. It'll increase your tax but you can always amend the return if you ever find the receipts. *That don't matter anyway; I can't pay you guys a dime.*

Fourteen per day, fifty-eight per week, the car salesmen, insurance sales-men, realtors, drywallers, wallpaperers, carpet-layers, painters, doctors, lawyers. Remarkable, no matter the profession or trade, everyone is broke. *I've got no money to pay you, Mr. Yancey.* They are not to blame; it's their husband's/wife's, ex-wife's/ex-husband's, partner's/ex-partner's fault. Some-times it's their children's fault. Most of the time it's our fault, or Congress's fault, or the president's fault. Somebody, somewhere, is definitely to blame. *I made absolutely no money those two years, Mr. Yancey. Not one blessed dime. I signed the return because my ex-husband told me to sign it.* But you lived with him at the time. *Not happily.* You enjoyed the benefits of his income. Under the law, you are equally liable for the entire debt. *But that isn't fair! Why aren't you going after him?* We may be. *Are you?* We can't tell you.

Electricians, mechanics, roofers, restaurateurs. Housekeepers, delivery-men, sign-painters, window-washers. We need the name of your nearest relative not living with you. Just as a reference. We won't contact them (unless you disappear on us, then we'll need someone to lean on). How much do you make a month? What do you spend on food, utilities, clothes, insur-ance, car payments, house payments, rent, garbage collection? What is your landlord's name? Are you current with your rent? Do you receive alimony? We'll need to see the divorce decree. You're claiming your child as a depend-ent on the financial statement but not on your last tax return. We can't allow your mother's medicine as an expense. We're disallowing your claim for $500 per month for books. Your student loans are disallowed. Your credit card payments are disallowed. Your payment on the second car is disallowed. Private school tuition, disallowed. Tithing, this is a sensitive issue, disallowed. Disallowed. Disallowed. Disallowed. Why are you spend-ing over $300 a month on food when there's only two of you? Forty dol-lars per week for gas is too much; I'll allow twenty.

Inventors, musicians, schoolteachers, firemen, offshore drillers, fisher-men. Why didn't you file the returns? *I lost my form. . . . I forgot. . . . My dog got sick. . . . I was in a coma. . . . Nobody showed me how.*

A nurse. A chiropractor. A masseuse. *I'm not a masseuse, goddamnit. I'm a massage therapist. Don't put "masseuse" on that form.* Musty papers pulled from dank corners, from attics and garages and car trunks. *This is my first audit. I guess I'm a little nervous.* I'm not an auditor. I am a revenue officer.

Then shouldn't I take the records to H&R Block? Maybe you should have thought of that three years ago.

Yes, sir, Mr. Yancey. No, sir, Mr. Yancey. Can I have two more weeks, Mr. Yancey? Mr. Yancey, I'm begging you. . . . Pulling crumpled gas receipts from a shoebox, scrubbing a runny nose with a tissue from the box conveniently located on the table. *Hurricane Andrew killed me. I haven't worked since. . . . I have AIDS. . . . She cleaned me out, took everything I have, and now you people want the rest. . . . My credit is shot; I can't borrow. . . . If I sell my concrete mixer, how'm I s'posed to make a living?* Supplicants spilling out into the waiting room. *Have mercy on me, Mr. Yancey, have mercy.* One appointment every thirty minutes, with the average appointment lasting one hour. Drumming gnawed fingernails on fat folders. Tattered blue jeans. Stained T-shirts beneath ratty denim jackets. Scuffed shoes. Scraggly hair, bad skin, yellow-toothed. Here, the shore of human detritus. Look what the tide's brought in. *I brung everything you asked for. Here's my bank statements. Here's my mortgage. Here's my W-2. Here's my electric bill and telephone and water. Here's my divorce decree. Here's my credit card statements, my payment books, my kid's hospital bills; that one's for the braces. You gonna seize the braces? Ha-ha!*

Longshoremen, dental hygienists, dieticians, physical therapists, hairdressers. *Four dollars an hour. After I pay for the rent on my space and materials, I net about $1.50. A buck fifty, Mr. Yancey. You honestly think I'm gonna report all my tips? You're damn right I do! Damn right!* Stale breath and rheumy eyes. Worn down, old at thirty. The oppression of debt. The yoke, the millstone, the cross. *That's too much. There's no way I can pay that, unless you don't want me to eat. Unless you don't want my kids to eat.*

Make demand. Set a deadline. Schedule your follow-up. Fifty-eight taxpayers per week equals forty-some deadlines. Ten days to enforce once missed, and they are usually missed. Gynecologists, surgeons, used-car dealers, chain-link fence salesmen. *You put a lien on my house!* Actually, sir, the lien attaches to everything. *Everything? Even my underwear?* Well, technically, I suppose. . . . *Why'd you do that?* Put a lien on your underwear? *This may be funny to you, buddy, but it's not funny to me. I told you I was going to get you a check.* But I didn't get a check. *Well, there's no way I can get you one now.* How come? *Because you put a lien on my house!* You missed your deadline. *Because the bank won't loan me money.* Why? *Because you put a lien on my house!* We can release the lien once you pay us. *I can't pay you until you release the lien.* I'm not going to release the lien. *And I'm not going to pay you the money, you sonofabitch!* And Toby, laughing at this, *Man, that reminds me of the time a taxpayer sent me a gift-wrapped box of shit, with this note that says, "Thought you might like the one thing of mine you forgot to take."* And Beth, saying she could top that, telling the story of the man who exposed himself to her and said, *Thought you might like to suck this dry, too.*

Feed the beast. November 19, 1991, Form 795, Revenue Officer R. Yancey, RO ID 5901-XXXX, Total Dollars Collected: $5,678.14. November 25, 1991: $10,981.74. December 9, 1991: $8,431.43. Feed the beast. Shouting out totals at the end of the day. Mark "O" for office contact, "F" for field, "C" for closure. Fill it up with Cs. No time to write the histories; clean 'em up when you're ready to close. This one needs hours of research for an abatement. Fuck it. Deny the request and let 'em file a claim. Put the burden back on them. We have no problems; the taxpayer has the problems. Enforcement closes cases. Find the pressure point and push as hard as you can. Close the case. Feed the beast.

Keep a good calendar. If you don't keep a good calendar, you're screwed. File this lien today. Send this levy. Refer this summons. Seize the car. They'll drop like ripe apples from the tree if you enforce. Give extensions, accept excuses, put off contact, and watch the dust collect on the file. By the time their case comes to you, they've had their chance. We've written, we've called; we've threatened, begged, negotiated and wheedled. Nothing left to do now but enforce. And don't beat the bushes trying to find them. Find a levy source and slam 'em. They'll by God return your calls then. Find the pressure point. Feed the beast.

The days grow short, the sky dark by six, and you, after a quick meal from the drive-thru, writing case histories at the kitchen table, just to stay above of the rising tide. *Look at you, fool,* Toby says. *Billy C. jumps somebody's bones in a hotel room and you afraid they won't keep you? Don't you know by now for every case you close they give you two?* Driving to work, startled by the wreaths hanging from the lampposts, why the hell have they hung the wreaths so soon after Thanksgiving? Then you realize it's almost Christmas and you haven't bought a single gift. Advent lends a particular urgency to the cause: in another two weeks the moratorium hits. Gotta get the levies out. Gotta file the liens. Can this seizure wait? Two weeks after January 1 comes the final review. What will they look at? Dollars collected? Cases closed? Seizures? Culpepper: *Don't fear anything, but if you must fear something, fear incompetence. Over one hundred thousand people work for the Internal Revenue Service, making it the largest employer in the federal government. During filing season, we scrape them off the sidewalk and drag them through the doors, hand 'em a calculator, and say, "Congratulations, you work for the IRS!" Remember that. The truly dangerous revenue officer isn't the one who knows what he's doing. The RO people should really fear is Henry, who couldn't find his own ass with a pickax and a shovel.*

Force them to exhaust the equity. Give us our lien interest and maybe we'll give you a payment plan for the rest. Sell it or get a loan on it. Borrow the cash from your parents, your children, your brothers and sisters. You're in our house; you will play by our rules. Ours is a monopoly; it's not as if you can go to the IRS down the street for a better deal.

The weather turns raw, like the nerves in the interview booth, beneath the poster on the wall that reads, under a glowering photograph of the man, *Only an accountant could nab Capone.* Babies wearing floppy knit hats, bouncing on laps, little fists slapping the table. Trash fires in rusting bent barrels on the cracked slab where the mobile home lists, a ship aground. Stately homes in quiet cul-de-sacs, beautiful, intricate death masks disguising financial demise. Peeking in windows, brushing back cobwebs. Squeaky doors, leaky roofs, drained swimming pools where leaves slowly rot in stagnant water. Sitting in overstuffed sofas while the family dog watches suspiciously from the corner. Openmouthed children, squawking parrots, morose fish listless in algae-encrusted tanks. Ancient grandmother, wheelchair bound, withered fingers combing thin paper-white hair, staring balefully from the corner. Flaying open, stripping bare, performing autopsies on kitchen tables, countertops, the hoods of cars, in open garages, wind biting through thin socks. They need time and there is no time. They need money and there is no money. Culpepper: *Here is the imponderable. The taxpayer claims he has no money to pay the tax. The Service claims the tax money was there and used for something else. This is the underlying philosophy behind all enforcement: "You took the people's money and now the people want it back. You can either give it back voluntarily or we will take it from you forcibly."*

Pilots, shoe repairmen, doughnut-shop owners, dog groomers, sweat-shop operators. Stacked three deep in the waiting room. So much humanity flooding through the doors we're interviewing in the hallway. On cold mornings, steam rises from the lake downtown like the mists of Avalon. We Floridians feel betrayed by cold weather. It fills us with righteous indignation. A Christmas tree appears in one corner of the waiting room, in open defiance of the First Amendment. Someone has placed, among the empty boxes wrapped as presents beneath the tree, a plastic Nativity scene bought on clearance from Wal-Mart. This one's a fifty-three. This one we'll seize after the first. Close this one as Unable-to-Locate. Transfer this one; dump it on another district. *Another quality closure!* Walking three blocks in the biting wind to the bank to convert the cash collected that day. The IRS is both recipient and remitter. There is something bitterly ironic about this. Almost there now. You didn't live through this year only to falter at the end. You must not stumble this close to the finish line. Next year your salary jumps by almost $10,000. You can buy a new car, pay off that credit card and the student loan. Maybe even get married, as remote as that possibility may seem. You are what you do, and you are a revenue officer. Almost.

"Rick, I'm leaving."

"But we haven't even ordered yet, Rachel."

She laughed humorlessly. We had just been seated at The Silver Spoon, one of the few restaurants downtown, where Cuban sandwiches and chicken with yellow rice are the specialties. Our thirty-minute lunch break had become a prize jealously guarded. It was our one opportunity in these last, hectic days of the training year to catch our breath. Rachel was not faring well. Dark circles ringed her eyes. For two weeks, she had been nagged by a persistent cough. Her sick leave was all but exhausted. Her desk was directly behind mine, and there were times when I turned around to say something to her and saw her sitting motionless in her chair, staring into space.

"I've found a job taking subscriptions over the phone. Sort of like sales, but soft pitch. You know how I got the job? I told the interviewer I was trained to sell a product everyone despises."

"I'm sorry, Rachel."

"No, I'm sorry for all of you."

Gina met privately with me after the holidays. She offered her congratulations and gave me my final review. I had qualified for the Sustained
Superior Performance Award based on my overall rating of "Exceeds Fully
Successful." In just one year, she reminded me, I could compete for the
promotion to Grade 11. "This promotion is the only freebie you get," she
said. I had jumped two grades, from Grade 7 trainee to Grade 9 Revenue
Officer. "The next one will be tough. With a territory this small, there'll
probably only be one Eleven available. You've got a year to prove to me it
should be you." She did not add, "And not Allison."

She didn't need to.

The trainees met for drinks after work. We reminisced, trading oft-repeated
war stories. Allison talked about her dream of interviewing a taxpayer while
she was naked. I asked Dee what that dream meant, since she was the psych
major, and she countered that, as Freud once said, sometimes a cigar was
just a cigar. I did not tell them about my dream. In it, I am arguing with the
cabinetmaker that the law requires me to place the teddy bear under seizure.
I have already written its description on the 2433 and to give the bear back
would be a logistical, bureaucratic nightmare. *One stuffed bear, approx. 24
inches in length, missing right eye, slight tear on left ear.* The fair market value
of the bear is $5.42. I tell the taxpayer we will accept our lien interest, or
approximately $3.25.

We toasted ourselves. Our jubilance was tempered only by our exhaustion. Dee said she felt as if she was being released from prison. We looked
at each other and shouted in unison: "Gina's cat!"

The hour grew late. We were reluctant to part. When we returned next
week, we would no longer be trainees. We would be revenue officers.

As I left the bar that night, dreading home and my erstwhile "fiancée,"
now practically a stranger to me, I thought of that day during our first week,
when Melissa took all five of us with her to seize the contents of a deceased
taxpayer's safe deposit box. A disgruntled heir had tipped her off as to its

existence. I remembered the startled look on the bank manager's face as we trooped through the door, a battalion of new recruits, wielding the full force of federal law, and how her hand shook when Melissa handed the forms to her. We followed her into the vault and watched silently as she slid the box from its chamber and set it on the table in the center of the room. She stepped back, wavering by the door. Melissa told her she didn't need to stay. "I think I probably should," was the answer. Melissa opened the box and began lifting out the contents, one by one. She separated the items into two piles: sentimental and saleable. We stood in a semicircle around the table and watched as she carefully inventoried each item. Melissa wrote on the 2433, "One diamond solitaire ring, yellow gold, approx. one-half carat." We trainees watched, acolytes attending the high priestess as she pawed through forty years' worth of a stranger's keepsakes and treasures with all the detachment of a surgeon removing an appendix. We had been granted admittance to this chamber because we were agents of the American people, acting on their behalf, endowed with a sacred trust. The significance of the moment was not lost on us. The carrier door opens and we explode from our cage, careening around the room, free.

PART TWO

The Revenue Officer

Men should be either caressed or exterminated, because they can avenge light injuries, but not severe ones. The damage done to a man should be such that there is no fear of revenge.

—*Machiavelli*

(9)

LEVERAGE

The call came two weeks after my initial receipt of the case of Paul Goodings d/b/a* Goodings Heating & Air. As with all new cases, I had immediately sent the final notice, giving the taxpayer thirty days to pay the amount in full or suffer the consequences. Usually, this notice was ignored: the type of debtor we dealt with did not respond to written notices from the Service. If they did, they would not be our type of debtor.

She sounded out of breath, as if she had sprinted to the phone from the mailbox. Her name was Alicia, and she was Paul Goodings's wife.

"I handle all the books," she explained.

"Are you on the payroll?"

"I don't take a salary or anything, if that's what you mean. But I handle all of Paul's billing and payables. He's just too busy, and frankly he doesn't have the head for it."

Neither do you, apparently. I had become accustomed to this little interior voice, an echo of Culpepper's, the bitterly satisfying mockery, the inevitable cruelty borne in the heart of the player who always holds a royal flush. I hardly noticed it anymore.

---

* "Doing-business-as," a common abbreviation within the Service, which tends to abbreviate everything. A sole proprietorship is called a "sole prop." A corporation is called a "corp." Delinquent returns are "del. rets" and assessments are "bal. dues." Group managers are "GMs." Revenue officers are, of course, "ROs." The only job title not abbreviated is that of the Commissioner of the IRS. He or she is always "the Commissioner."

I explained to Mrs. Goodings that the tax was assessed against the business and her husband, not against her. Under the law, I could not discuss anything with her.

"But, Mr. Yancey, I just told you, Paul doesn't understand any of this. He won't be able to answer any of your questions."

"Is there a separate bank account for the business?"

"Oh yes. We keep everything separate, business and personal."

"Do you sign checks on the business account?"

"No. Our personal stuff is joint, but Paul signs all the business checks... but I write them all. I write out all the bills when they come in and he just signs the check. I handle all the money, Mr. Yancey, so Paul won't even know what you're talking about."

I believed her. She had yet to catch her breath and spoke barely above a whisper. I believed her—and understood perfectly.

I said, "Where is the bank account?"

She told me.

"And is there enough in there to write me a check?"

"No. No, see, that's why I was calling. We're going to need a little time—more than the thirty days. Actually, I was calling to see if there was anything we could do to arrange a payment plan."

"Mrs. Goodings, I can't discuss anything like that with you, unless Mr. Goodings is present or designates you as his power-of-attorney. Is Mr. Goodings there right now?"

"No. No, he's on a job. It's really all he can do to keep the jobs coming in. Honestly, Mr. Yancey, just tell me what you need from us and I'll get it to you."

"What I need right now, if you can't send me the check, is to talk to Mr. Goodings."

"I just told you he can't talk right now!" she said sharply. Panic was beginning to set in. I closed my eyes and could picture her cupping the phone to her ear, her entire being focused on the receiver, willing me to acquiesce.

"I'm sorry. I'm sorry, Mr. Yancey. Things are just not very good right now. He's got so much on him. You wouldn't believe how much he has on him and this will—you have no idea what this will do to him."

"I'm sorry, too, Mrs. Goodings."

"Please, call me Alicia."

"But I really can't talk to you about—"

"If you could just give me five minutes of your time, I could bring in all our information and you'll see there's nothing we can do unless you give us a payment plan."

"I can only discuss the case with Mr. Goodings or his power-of-attorney. Do you want me to send you a power-of-attorney form to sign?"

"No. Yes. Oh, God, I don't know!" She began to cry.

"You should tell him."

"Tell him? Tell him what?"

"Tell him about the letter."

"You don't understand."

"I'm not sure you do, Mrs. Goodings. You have some time." I checked my calendar. "Sixteen days."

"What happens then? What happens on the seventeenth day, Mr. Yancey?"

"Read the letter."

I hung up. I wrote in my history, "TPW CI resp to L1058. Advsd cldnt disc case w/her. Must have POA or TP prsnt. Scrd LS. TPW advs hndl all bkkping for TP and didn't hve fnds to FP. P.O.A.: lvy bnk acct if no FP at end of not. pd."* I closed the case file and wrote in my calendar: "FC Goodings." A field call (FC) was required before recommending a seizure, and I was hoping to catch Paul before he started on his repair calls. Paul Goodings had no idea he owed over $13,000 in payroll taxes. Apparently, only two people knew: Mrs. Goodings and Revenue Officer Rick Yancey.

Culpepper had explained the principle this way: *It is not a level playing field, because it is not a game. The government takes the collection of its debts very seriously.*

---

* Translation: "[The] taxpayer's wife called in responding to Letter 1058 [Notice of Intent to Levy]. [I] advised [her that I] couldn't discuss [the] case with her. [She] must have [a] power-of-attorney or [the taxpayer must be] present [at the time we speak]. Secured [a] levy source. The taxpayer's wife advises [she] handles all [the] bookkeeping for [the] taxpayer and didn't have [the] funds to full-pay. Plan-of-action: levy [the] bank account if no full-payment [is received] at end of [the] notice period."

The Internal Revenue Code grants the revenue officer powerful tools to accomplish the Service's mission, which is, no matter how many times it is reworded over the years, to collect the tax, to get the money, to feed the beast. These tools give us an extraordinary advantage over our adversaries. This is why ROs like Henry manage to hang on to their jobs despite having almost no technical expertise or the slightest bit of sophistication: the law gives us H-bombs to take out anthills.

Alicia Goodings didn't give me a chance to make my field call.

"Is this Rick Yancey?" she asked after I answered the phone, as I always did, "Internal Revenue Service, Rick Yancey."

I told the caller I was Rick Yancey.

"Good. I was hoping I could get you before you left for the day. I'm Paul Goodings."

"You're . . . excuse me, did you say you were Paul Goodings?"

"Yes. I am Paul Goodings. You'll have to forgive me. I have a very bad cold."

She faked a sneezed into the phone.

"Sorry," she said. "I just got back to the shop and talked to Alicia. She showed me this notice."

She wasn't thinking clearly, obviously. If she had thought it through, she would have "given" the phone to herself quickly, after giving permission for me to discuss the case with her. Or him.

"I'm glad you called, Mr. Goodings."

"Please, call me Paul."

I stifled a guffaw. "Okay. Your wife tells me you don't have the cash to pay me right now."

"No. No, to be honest with you, I don't. What I'd like to propose is payments of five hundred dollars a month."

I explained I couldn't discuss "his" proposal without seeing a complete financial statement.

"The best thing to do is meet so we—"

"Meet?"

"Yes. Set up a time for you to come in."

"I'm just swamped right now, Mr. Yancey. Can't you just send the forms to me and I'll fill them out and send them back?"

It was like an episode from *I Love Lucy*, except it was more pitiful than funny.

"I understand. Well, I can meet you at the shop. Just give me a good—"

"No, I'm always on the road. Unless you want to meet with Alicia."

I explained I couldn't meet with Alicia unless he, who happened to be Alicia, was also there. But then of course I couldn't meet with just her either, but both of her. The her who was Paul and the her who was . . . her. I explained what a power-of-attorney was. I wondered if she would jump at this opportunity to commit forgery. I suspected more than one check had been signed by the feminine side of Paul Goodings.

She didn't jump. "I just don't want you to do anything in the next couple of weeks."

"She doesn't know, does she?" I asked Alicia playing Paul about Alicia.

"Who?"

"Alicia. Your wife. She doesn't know you owe this money."

"Sure she knows. She handles all the books, I told you that," said Alicia, playing Paul talking about Alicia.

"Actually, she told me that." I was better at playing the game than she was. "Maybe you and she can talk about it tonight and get back to me within the next couple of weeks. There might be something you haven't considered."

"Something like what?"

"Borrowing the money from relatives or friends. Using a nonbusiness asset to pay the tax. Skipping some payments on other debts. You know, the Service moves a lot quicker than a bank when it comes to foreclosure. Now, under the law, I can't do anything for another sixteen days." For an instant, the wicked thought of putting her on hold while I transferred her to my manager seized me. I would pick up the phone and pretend to be Gina. I pushed the thought away and now it was my turn to hunker over the receiver and will her to acquiesce.

"I promise I won't do anything until then," I said. "And I'll even think about giving you a courtesy call before I take any action." I explained I was often in the area and he could expect me to drop by at any time within the next two weeks.

.   .   .

The check for full-payment arrived in the mail the following week. I don't know where she got the money, but I suspected her husband never discovered he owed federal taxes. If he had, he would have called me. I did not make a history-entry in the case file after our second conversation. In a way, I was protecting both of us. It might raise questions about why I played along and did not confront her, why I didn't play it straight. Then the check arrived in the mail and made my omission irrelevant.

Gina enjoyed hearing this story during my monthly DIAL briefing. The issue of omitting the history-entry did not come up; rarely was Gina interested in the contents of a history. Her chief compliant about most ROs was their lack of composition skills. During our training year, she lectured us, "A history sheet is not the place for your personal opinions." She told the story of an RO, whom she had fired, who opened every narrative with a discourse on the grooming habits of taxpayers or discussed the condition of their house. *The house stank. It was very dirty. I was afraid to sit on the sofa. The taxpayer did not smell good.*

It was one of the few light moments during that particular review. Gina was in one of her darker moods. A new branch chief had taken over duties from Jenny Duncan—becoming our third chief since we had come on board—and Gina did not like him, thought him hopelessly out of touch with the field, and sincerely believed he was giving Annie DeFlorio and her training group next-door in the Wesley Building preferential treatment. She was not the only one dissatisfied by the regime change: Jenny Duncan had filed suit over the selection, claiming sexual discrimination by Byron White, the head of the collection division. Gina had asked me what I thought of the new chief, a former collection analyst from the New Orleans District named Bob Campbell.

"He seems like an equitable person," I said.

"Equitable? I don't think you can apply that word to a person."

"Why not?"

"It's not a term applied to human beings." She sounded very sure of herself and she was my boss, so I chose not to argue.

"He gives her everything and the only thing he gives me is grief," she said of Bob Campbell and Annie DeFlorio. "I know what it is. Nobody else in the branch has the guts to say it, but I'll say it: she's young, attractive, tall, and *thin*." She held forth for another five minutes about Annie DeFlorio. No one in the history of the district had risen as quickly into management. As a revenue officer in Orlando, she had the most closures, the most seizures, the most fraud referrals. During branch meetings, she snacked on cheese crackers and drank Mellow Yellow. "It'll destroy her kidneys," Gina said. "Give her stones the size of tennis balls." While in college, she had worked at Disney World, which might account for Gina dubbing her "Snow White." Annie DeFlorio was in the Wesley Building, just across the alley behind our office, but Gina rarely talked to her in person. If circumstances forced her, she would pick up the phone or fax a message.

Gina complained Campbell was skimming the best accounts and giving them to Annie's group to close, thus making us look bad. Annie had even reopened some of our old closures, written off as uncollectible, and found money where we claimed there was none. This had produced bad blood between her and Annie, and between us employees. We were resentful that Annie's trainees received only ten cases after basic training, as opposed to our thirty-five. That they had two of the best OJIs in the district jobbed in for their education. That they were being spoon-fed their inventory, with little pressure to close cases, a practice that had, ironically, produced more closures in their group. In a district where success was measured by dollars collected and cases closed, the pressure had become enormous on Gina to keep pace with Annie DeFlorio, and our DIAL reviews began to reflect this.

"Why is this still open?" she asked of one corporate case.

"I don't have any leverage," I answered. "He's a curb layer, you know, installs curbing in new housing developments. All he needs to do his job is this curbing machine."

"And he hides it from you?"

"He owes more on it than it's worth." Under the Code, the IRS cannot seize assets with no equity.

"Receivables," she said.

"He works only one job at a time."

"So issue a summons to him for the name."

"He's finished the job by his appearance date and then swears he doesn't have any pending. We'd look pretty stupid in court if—"

"Levy his bank account."

"I have—twice. Each time, he's overdrawn."

"Vehicles?"

"Brand-new truck, fully encumbered."

"Children."

I laughed. I was the only one laughing. I stopped laughing.

"Impress upon him settling up for the good of his family."

"I think he's divorced."

"Get the divorce decree."

"Actually, I'm not sure if he's divorced."

"This review might be more productive if you were better acquainted with your inventory, Rick."

"He's not divorced. I remember now. Separated, no kids."

"Are you speaking off the cuff?"

"No, I'm on the cuff."

"Everyone has something we can exploit," she said. "A pressure point."

"That's why the case is still open, Gina. I'm still looking."

"Follow him to the job site."

"I tried that. Sat outside his house the whole morning and he never left." She chewed on her bottom lip for a moment.

"Close it."

"How? He's in business."

"Fifty-three* it."

"He's pyramiding."

"Fifty-three it. I'll sign it."

"I didn't know we could do that."

"Then I've failed as your manager," she said. "I can't believe you made it through the training year without knowing what an in-business fifty-three is. There's nothing to seize, nothing to levy, nothing left to do. Fifty-three it. Close it."

---

* Reference to Form 53, used to report outstanding tax liabilities as "currently-not-collectible," with the emphasis on "currently."

"But he's pyramiding."

"Maybe I'm mumbling. I'll say it louder: *Fifty-three this case.*"

"I'll fifty-three this case."

"Any other cases in your inventory like it?"

"One or two."

"Fifty-three them. I don't want any more garbage in your inventory. I'm sick of ROs sitting on cases like chickens on rotten eggs, waiting for them to hatch. You think I don't know why you people are doing it? You think if you keep the dogs, I won't give you any new cases and you won't have to work."

"I just didn't know what to do with them."

"Now you don't have that excuse. I want those cases on my desk, ready for my signature, by the close of business today, Rick."

"You'll have them."

The cases would be shelved, and the taxpayers let off the hook, because Annie DeFlorio was making Gina look bad in the eyes of the new branch chief—or at least that was Gina's perception. She was smart enough to realize that this was probably Bob Campbell's goal, playing the two off each other, but was powerless to stop it. By pitting one manager against the other, Campbell hoped to increase dollars collected and case closures, his principal charge as leader of the branch. It was playground politics: Headquarters pressured the regions, the regions pressured the districts, the districts pressured the branches, the branches pressured the managers, the managers pressured the revenue officers, and the revenue officers pressured the taxpayers. Some taxpayers, like my curb layer, would benefit. Others would pay dearly.

"Let's talk about Marsh Day Care," Gina said.

"Well, if we must."

"I seem to recall a default letter crossing my desk."

"Yes. She defaulted again."

"I also seem to recall she has quite a bit of equity in the house."

"Yes. She has quite a bit of equity in the house."

"Hmmmm. A principle residence seizure is the single most sensitive enforcement we take. Not many ROs do them. They're usually complicated and political and therefore very, very hard to get approved."

"That's what everybody's told me."

"But if you could get one approved, that would be quite a feather in your cap."

"Right. Quite a feather."

"You know the chances of this group getting more than one Grade Eleven slot to fill is slim to none."

"That's going to make it tough."

"Not as tough as you may imagine."

"Do I have a shot?"

She laughed. "Do you care if you have a shot?"

"Odd as it sounds, I guess I do."

"Odd as it sounds, you do."

Allison waited until we were alone in the bull pen to confront me. It began pleasantly. I should have known her well enough by that point to know pleasantness from Allison was a bad sign.

"How's it going?" she asked. She pulled up Rachel's old chair and sat down. "I haven't seen much of you lately."

"It's going pretty good," I said.

"Did you hear the rumor?"

"Which one?" I knew which one.

"There's going to be only one promotion next year."

"No, hadn't heard that one. Why do you think that is? Budget cuts?"

"We're collecting too much money," she said. It was a widely held opinion in the Service that Collection was punished with budget cuts when times were good and money was flowing freely into the Treasury.

"I'll try to cut back."

"I thought Gina told you about that rumor."

"Not that I recall."

"She told me you already knew."

"Maybe she had me confused with Henry."

She leaned in, a smile playing on her lips.

"I know what you're up to."

"Okay."

"Kind of ham-handed, if you ask me."

"I really don't know what you're talking about, Allison."

"Gina told me already, Rick. You asked her if she would help you at the theater."

The community theater in Clearview had hired me to direct and adapt original stories by children into a one-act play for that summer's festival.

"Not precisely. I had to get approval from the Service for the outside employment and she was curious. I believe she asked me if I needed any help running the show."

"So of course you said yes."

"I didn't want to hurt her feelings. She has no life, you know, outside this place."

"Are you insinuating I don't either?"

"No." I frowned. "I was talking about Gina."

"You know, some people might look at this situation and say you're not exactly acting out of the goodness of your heart."

"And somebody might say the whole thing is none of anybody else's business."

"It's somebody else's business if there's influence involved."

"Influence? Did you say influence?"

"Oh, cut the crap, Rick. You know she has a crush on you."

"That's absurd."

"Everybody talks about it."

"And everybody talked about your crush on Culpepper."

"I never had a crush on Culpepper."

"My point. Everybody also says we're having an affair. You see what I'm getting at? What was I supposed to do, tell her to go to hell?"

"It's improper."

"In your opinion."

"Perception is reality," she said smugly. She had picked up the phrase from me.

"Reality is what we decide to make it," I shot back. "Why are we talking like fortune cookies? Jealously doesn't become you, Allison."

"It is improper," she said piously, "for a manager to fraternize with an employee."

"I'll try to keep my hands off her."

"It's not going to work, you know. They'll never promote a male over three females. And especially not a white male."

"Maybe I'll change my official designation to American Indian," I answered.

"It's pitiful, really. You know how things work around here. You know why Gina made manager. It's not how good you are or how much you suck up. You've got to have the right skin color and the right sexual organs. So unless you plan to have your thing chopped off, I guess you're shit out of luck, Mr. Yancey."

At the end of each month I could rely on two things: a DIAL briefing with Gina and a visit from Laura Marsh. She always insisted on coming to the office. I would lug the five-pound case file into the interview booth and listen to the latest litany of woes. On this particular visit, she was visibly upset: she had received the official notice of default of her latest installment agreement.

"I guess you're getting tired of seeing me," she said. She had gained at least fifteen pounds since we first met. The dark circles under her eyes seemed darker, her blond hair paler, her skin grayer. Although she had put on weight, Laura Marsh seemed smaller, as if she were shrinking or being slowly crushed by the innumerable sorrows of life.

"Not at all," I said. "I have a soft spot in my heart for you, Ms. Marsh. You were my first case and you'll probably be my last."

She laughed. "I think I like you better than Melissa, and I know I like you better than that Mr. Culpepper. Whatever happened to him? Did they fire him?"

"He took another job in a different division."

"I didn't mean no offense. He might be your friend."

"I'm not sure he's anyone's friend."

I opened the case file and pulled out the copy of the default letter. She averted her eyes. Her eyeliner was smudged and uneven beneath her right eye.

"You're growing a beard," she said.

"I'm trying to look more mature."

"I like it." She would not say if she thought it made me look more mature.

It was coming in patchy on the sides. I was considering growing it into a Vandyke, but wondered if that was too Bohemian for Byzantium. Culpepper would never have dreamed of growing facial hair.

"And didn't you used to wear glasses?"

"I switched to contacts."

"That's probably a good idea. You have such small eyes for a grown man. I never knew until this moment they were blue."

They weren't. I had purchased the brand of contacts that altered eye color.

"You must be in love," she said.

"I beg your pardon?"

"When my husband fell in love with my eighteen-year-old next-door neighbor, he lost twenty pounds and bought a motorcycle."

"I haven't bought a motorcycle."

"Are you? In love, I mean."

"I'm engaged."

She nodded, apparently satisfied with my answer. "Well, I'm sure she's very sweet. Does she know what you do for a living?"

"She thinks I work for the CIA."

"That's more romantic."

"She thinks my calculator is linked by satellite to Langley."

"Who's Langley?"

"Ms. Marsh, maybe we better talk about taxes now."

"Oh," she sighed. "I suppose. If we must."

"You've missed two payments. I had to send this letter."

"So what happens now, Rick? Are you going to seize my house?"

"It's like this," I said. "We usually start small and easy and work our way up to big and difficult. First we would levy your bank account. Then we would show up at the end of the day, when the parents are picking up the kids, and hand a levy to each one, to attach to the money they owe the day care. Then we would probably seize the van. The house would be the last thing we—"

"The house is the only thing I got that's worth anything."

She understood, then, where the thing must go, the terminus of our relationship. In Basic Training, I had missed a question about enforcement.

The question gave the value of each asset and asked what the revenue officer's first action should be. I had written a complicated response, involving levy on receivables and vehicles. Sam called me to the front of the class and explained the correct answer was seizure of the taxpayer's real estate. *Always go where the most equity is,* he said. *That's the asset that will be the least hassle to seize, since it's not the taxpayer's personal residence.**

"Did you ever talk to the bank?" I asked.

"Three months ago. They said come back."

"When?"

"After three months."

"So you'll go back and see what they say."

"They will say what they always say, Rick."

"Then go to another place."

"With what? You know I can't show any way to pay back a loan. I'm losing money hand over fist."

"Some secondary lenders don't really care."

"And charge credit card–type interest."

"Well, so does the IRS."

"They'll foreclose and I'll lose the house. I lose the house and I lose the business. I lose the business and I lose my children."

"Lose your children?"

"My ex is back in the picture—didn't I tell you? He's taking me to court for visitation, modification of child support, you name it. He married that little slut from next door and the minute I lose the house he'll file a motion to have me declared an unfit mother. You know HRS† has already been to the house twice in the last month? A 'confidential informant' keeps giving them reports of abuse in the day care. And who do you think that informant is? So the bottom line is, you people better hurry if you're going to shut me down, because the state just may beat you to it."

---

* A real estate seizure can be made through the mail if necessary, unlike other assets, which must be inventoried at the time of seizure. A personal residence seizure, as noted, is more difficult; it requires four levels of approval (group manager, branch chief, division chief, and district director) and is arguably the one enforcement tool (an IRS phrase) that has the greatest impact upon the taxpayer.

† Health and Rehabilitative Services, the state agency charged with child protection.

She rummaged in her purse. A pack of cigarettes fell onto the floor. Old grocery store receipts spilled onto the table. I slid the box of Kleenex in front of her.

"Thanks." The tissue came away from her face dotted black.

"We could play the worst-case scenario game for hours, Ms. Marsh," I said.

"Call me Laura. Why won't you ever call me Laura?"

"The point is I can't take this case to my manager and recommend we close it, not with this much equity in the house."

"Fine then. Fine. Just take the goddamned house. I don't care."

"You're not letting me finish."

"Jesus Christ, I've been dealing with you people for so long, I know what you're going to say before you say it!"

"What was I going to say?"

"You're going to say I've got to go back to the bank. I've got to go back just one more time."

"Can you catch up on these missed payments?"

"No. Not right now. But I am current with the deposits for the quarter. Doesn't that count for anything?"

"My manager is going to say that with this much equity you should be able to get some money to pay us."

"I've met your manager. You don't want to hear what I think about your manager."

"No. I don't. Please listen to what I'm trying to tell you. It doesn't matter who the manager is. We will not withhold collection on your account and we will not enter into another installment agreement until you give us eighty percent of your equity in the house."

She looked away. She took a deep, shuddering breath. In one hand she clutched the wadded tissue, in the other, the Marlboro Lights.

"You know it's the last thing I want to do," I said. She was almost there but, if I pushed too hard, she might break, and broken, she would lack the strength to do my will. I had to show her the only unlocked door in the black corridor and ensure she had enough energy to walk through it. "As the letter says, we can't do anything for thirty days. But as long as you have a commitment from someone to lend you the money, we can give you extra time."

A strand of blond hair had come loose from her bun and hung over her forehead; the tip swayed and brushed her cheek. She had pushed herself away from the table and was resting her elbows on her broad knees, her shoulders hunched, her back bowed. She rocked slightly back and forth in the chair.

"Would you really take my house, Rick?"

"The Service would."

"That's not what I asked you."

"Even if we did take it, the sale wouldn't be final for six months. At any time you can get it back."

"If I had the money."

"If you had the money."

"But if I had the money, you wouldn't take my house."

"I'm telling you what your options are. You and I both know this is bigger than just you and me. I represent the United States government, and you represent someone else, too."

"Who?"

"Your children."

She nodded. "That's right. None of this is their fault. I screwed up bad. They shouldn't have to pay for that."

"It's going to be okay. You're going to be able to do this."

"Do you really think so?"

"If I didn't think so, I would have already seized the house."

"Thank you, Rick. Thank you."

"You're welcome," I said. I remembered Toby telling Henry how taxpayers would thank him for stripping them of their possessions. She slowly straightened in her chair and brushed the hair from her forehead. She was going to do it. My mentioning the children had been the coup de grâce. The maternal instinct is primal, like fear, lust, jealously, rage. Learn to exploit these and you can rule the world.

Are you in love? she had asked. And I answered, *I'm engaged.* She lacked the subtly to understand what my answer meant. Mine was a perpetual betrothal, an eternal commitment to commit at some unspecified point in the future.

Pam and I met at dinnertime the following week. I was heading into town and she was heading out: Pam had recently taken a new job at a theme park in Orlando, a job that demanded she work most nights and weekends. She slid into the booth opposite me and said, "What the hell happened to your hair?"

"I got it cut today."

"Why's it so short?"

"I'm going for the G-man look."

"Why's it so shiny?"

"Sean put this stuff in it."

"Who's Sean?"

"My hair guy. You know Sean."

"I don't know who the hell you're talking about."

"I told him I wanted something different. He said short was better."

"Guess if he said shave it off, you would have shaved it off."

"Don't start on me about hair, punk rocker."

"Well, I don't like it. And what's it with the beard?"

"You don't like it? I've gotten a lot of compliments."

"Contacts, beard, new haircut. What's going on here, Rick?"

"Nothing."

"It's someone else, isn't it? You can tell me. It's that little what's-her-name from the goddamned office, the Infernal Revenue Service, Allison. Is it Allison?"

I laughed. "I'm not having an affair."

"Then what are you having? You're a little young for a midlife crisis."

"Really, sometimes you just want a change. You get bored with yourself. Haven't you ever gotten bored with yourself?"

"It's pretentious," she said. "I understand the contacts—you do look better without the glasses, but why did you change your eye color?"

"I wanted to look like Mel Gibson."

"You don't look like Mel Gibson."

I was losing my patience. "I know what you're trying to do. You're trying to manipulate me."

"Oh, save it, Rick. Telling someone how you feel isn't manipulation. What is it with you, lately? Every time we have a disagreement, you accuse me of trying to manipulate you. Make your eyes purple, I don't give a shit."

She stood up.

"What are you doing?" I asked.

"I'm going."

"Our food hasn't come yet."

"You eat mine. You need it more than me."

"Pam, we've hardly seen each other in a month."

"That isn't my fault."

"I'm not blaming you. I'm stating a fact."

"Only you could be so goddamned moody and so goddamned detached at the same time." She flopped back down and snapped her napkin. "I'm fat," she said.

"You're not fat," I said wearily.

"I am fat. Don't tell me I'm not fat. I know I'm fat and it's insulting when you lie and say I'm not. I catch you looking at me. I see the disgust on your face. Maybe that's why you're doing this whole makeover thing with the beard and the hair and the eyes. You want someone else."

"No."

"Because I'm fat."

"No. I don't want someone else."

"Then what do you want?"

Our food arrived. Neither of us touched it. I looked out the window to the highway outside.

"To feel more normal."

"You got blue contacts to feel more normal?"

"This isn't about the contacts. It's about feeling I'm on the outside looking in. Like I'm sitting in the stands watching something I can't participate in. Most people, you know, have benchmarks, you know, like their first kiss, their first job, the day they got married."

"We're not going there, Rick."

"We don't seem to be going anywhere."

"I've had a wedding. Believe me, you're not missing much."

"My point is, I don't want to miss anything. I only get one life."

She said, "Now who's manipulating?"

"Don't knock manipulation. If it weren't for manipulation we wouldn't be here."

"What the hell are you talking about?"

"If not for manipulation, neither one of us would have been born. What's copulation but the culmination of one grand—or not so grand—manipulation? Everything is driven by it, everything that happens happens because of it, and everything that doesn't happen happens in spite of it: economics, religion, politics, culture. We're manipulated from the second we're born to the moment we die, by our parents, schools, churches, newspapers, television, books, movies, magazines, radio . . . *everything* is manipulation, everything is propaganda, to pressure us, push our buttons, to leverage us into buying something, believing in something, loving something. The binding force of the human condition is manipulation."

"You . . . are you okay, Rick? I mean it. Are you okay?"

"I'm off on a tangent."

"You're off on something."

"Is it about the money? I've been at this job almost two years now, Pam. I make more than you do, not counting the annuity."

"I can't marry you, Rick."

"Why can't you?"

"Because I don't even know you anymore."

I didn't argue with her. "Is that my fault?"

"Oh, now you're going to put this back on me? I never told you to take this goddamned job. In fact, I begged you not to. And when you ignored me and took it anyway, I told you to quit. Why didn't you? Why did you— why are you doing this?"

I decided to tell the truth. "Because I'm good at it."

She laughed. "And Ted Bundy was good at picking up girls."

I leaned in, speaking in a fierce whisper. "That's fine, good for you. I'm sure it makes you feel better to equate what I do with serial killing. What's so wrong with being proud of myself for once in my sorry little life? You don't know what it's like to fail at everything. You don't know what it's like to feel like a loser. Well, you know what, Pam? I'm not going to be what I was before I took this job. That person is dead, as dead as the man who collapsed in your kitchen, and if that's who you're in love with, then I guess we never will be married."

She fled from the table. I did not chase her. I watched her jump into her car and whip out of the parking space, almost ramming the parked car behind her. I lit a cigarette and thought of Newton's first law of motion. Allison had told me repeatedly that nothing would change with Pam, the deal being too sweet: Pam got all the benefits of marriage without any of the responsibilities. At any time, she could walk and still keep the annuity. Meanwhile, I paid Pam rent for living in the house and gained nothing. When the relationship ended—not *if*, according to Allison, but *when*— Pam would have the house and all its contents, and I would be right back where I started five years ago. A car, some old books, and clothes. "Think about it," she said. "What's in it for her? But the bigger question, is what the hell is in it for *you?*"

I had no answer to that question. Except it was unfinished business. I had grown accustomed to wrapping things up neatly. *Another quality closure.*

I stabbed my cigarette into the ashtray. I felt ashamed, as if I had failed an important test. I silently told her I was sorry, but Culpepper's face was in my mind's eye. Somehow, I had failed him, too: I still wasn't the revenue officer I could be. I still had not found the revenue officer inside. If I had, the paperwork to seize Laura Marsh's house would be on Gina's desk. If I had, the curb-layer would have been out of business months before my DIAL review. Intellectually, I had become a revenue officer. It was emotionally that I had failed to make progress. I had mastered the mechanics of the job, but not its soul.

Sitting in that restaurant, I was nearly overcome by a blinding, choking, impotent rage. The force of it startled and baffled me. I could see the curb-layer's face before me, hear his whiney good-ol'-boy accent, *Well, I guess you're just gonna have to come on and git me, Mr. Yan-Say*. I imagined stabbing out his eyes with my steak knife. As I swung the knife, his face metamorphosed into the face of Laura Marsh. Then every taxpayer in my inventory. Then Gina. Then Allison. Then Pam. *We're coming after these bastards dull as butter knives when we should glitter like daggers!* I was slicing off layers, peeling back the faces before me, to reach the center, the ultimate ground, the source of all my frustration and rage. At bottom, I expected to find the face of William Culpepper. But as my knife tore away his face, I caught a glimpse of someone else's eyes, bright blue and glassy as fish eyes, fixed and staring. I had applied the principle of leverage to everyone in my life with one exception, the only person whose will I had left inviolable. It was time to take the irrevocable step over the threshold, to enter the sanctum sanctorum of Byzantium. Pam assumed I had changed my appearance in response to love. But I did not love anyone; not even the wielder of the knife, butcher and victim, owner of the blue fish eyes that now went dark as the blade plunged home.

I was not in love, but it was time to fall in love. And, in Byzantium, there is only one sacrament where love might be found.

War.

(10)

IS IT SAFE?

The opening salvo arrived in the form of a letter, addressed to me, with copies to the commissioner of the Internal Revenue Service, the District Director, Bob Campbell, Gina, our local congressman, the two senators from the state of Florida, and the president of the United States. The letter was mailed certified, return receipt requested. It read:

Dear Sir!

We have recently come into knowledge of your illegal activities against us and our property! This is your OFFICIAL NOTICE to CEASE and DESIST all ILLEGAL activity you are THREATENING us with in your Letter 1058 dated 07/12/92. If you do not CEASE and DESIST your PROPOSED ILLEGAL ACTIVITY, we will have no choice but to SUE your Agency and YOU PERSONALLY under the BIVENS ACT for the maximum amount allowed under law, up to and including the sum of ONE MILLION DOLLARS. We are providing this OFFICAL NOTICE under AUTHORITY of the Uniform Commercial Code which clearly inacts [sic] all your so called AUTHORITY as NULL and VOID. If you and your cohorts insist on coming onto our PROPERTY again we will have no choice but to PROTECT OUR PROPERTY TO THE FULL EXTENT OF THE LAW.

YOU HAVE BEEN WARNED!

We declare ourselves to be SOVERIGN NON-CITZENS [sic],

and by this document fully EXCISE and REMOVE Ourselves from the Social Security System, SOVERIGNS ONLY of the state of Florida, subject to the rule of LAW, which to say the POSSE COMMITATUS, under which YOU have no authority, under the Common Law, or right to harass us.

We also declare and aver we are not citizens of the provinces of the United States, its commonwealths or protectorates, of Puerto Rica or the District of Columbia, nor are we employees, heirs, assigns or subjects of the United States Government, its allies or lackeys.

We do also by this document state we do not earn "income" as defined by the Internal Revenue Code and are not subject to the "tariff tax." We do also by this document challenge the authority of the Sixteenth Amendment, which was NEVER properly radified [*sic*] by the States, and therefore has no RULE OF LAW.

We would be happy to comply with your demands, however, if you will provide to us, within thirty (30) days of date of this letter, by registered mail, the following information. Failure to provide this information will constitute your ADMISSION that you have no AUTHORITY over us as SOVEREIGN NON-PERSONS as defined by your own so-called INTERNAL REVENUE CODE:

1. Copies of all delegation orders giving you authority to commit the acts of fraud listed in your letter.
2. Copy of your "pocket commission."
3. RELEVANT documentation establishing we are "taxpayers" as defined by the IRC (Internal Revenue Code)
4. Your home phone number (as DEMANDED by the UCC (Uniformed [*sic*] Commercial Code)
5. Your home address.
6. Your full name, not your "pseudonym" under which you perform your ILLEGAL operations.
7. Your "employee" number.
8. Your Social Security Number.
9. Your official "post-of-duty," work hours, and full names and

addresses of those engaged in similar activities within your immediate "sphere of influence."

If you do not provide this information within the thirty (30) days
specified in this letter, you are admitting to the aforementioned
statements as to their FACTUAL BASIS, that we are NOT nor
have we ever been, SUBJECT TO Title 26 of the United States
Code (USC).

We do not wish to provoke you, but we are tired of this FRAUD
and ABUSE heaped upon the American "taxpayer." We WILL NOT
HESITATE to exorcize [*sic*] our GOD GIVEN RIGHT to protect
our LIVES, OUR PROPERTY & OUR SACRED HONOR.

The signatures had been notarized, above the words, "In Sui Juris."

I carried the letter into the suite of offices occupied by the senior revenue
officers. The only one in was Beth. She smiled pleasantly at me. Beth had
always impressed me as unflappable and I was glad she was the one I found
first.

"What is the Bivens Act?" I asked.

"Never heard of it," she said.

I placed the letter on her desk. She read the first page and said, "Tell
'em you'll see their Bevins Act and raise them a Writ of Replevin."

"What are you talking about?"

"They're protestors."

She held out the letter, but I didn't take it.

"ITPs.* You studied it in Phase Training, didn't you?"

"Can they really sue me for a million dollars?"

"Henry was sued once," Beth answered. "By a protestor. Took him to
small claims court. The moron—Henry, I mean—didn't tell anyone. He
hired a private attorney and went to court. The ITP was suing for recovery of a bank levy. He lost. Inspection investigated Henry for not telling
anyone. If they do sue you, Rick, make sure you tell someone."

---

* Illegal Tax Protestors.

"What do I do?"

She raised an eyebrow. "What do you mean?"

"I mean, do I answer this letter? Do I have to give them all this personal information? What is a posse commitatus?"

Beth laughed. She waved me toward a free chair.

"Okay," she said. "I guess the doctor is in. Tell me about the case."

He was a dentist. On my field call, he explained he had never had tax troubles in the past, but he was confident he could work his way out of the mess. He took full responsibility for the mess. He owed employment as well as personal taxes. His wife worked in the office with him. They were both in their mid-sixties. He reminded me of my grandfather. She offered me fresh oatmeal cookies. The place was run-down; he offered low-cost dentures to retirees on fixed incomes and Medicare. He owned a big X-ray machine and I conducted the interview in his "lab," where he made the molds for the dentures—surrounded by set upon set of teeth, on tabletops, on chairs, lining bookshelves, everywhere I looked, toothy wax grins. Both had been gracious, apologetic, even abashed at running afoul of the IRS. I had set a deadline and hand-delivered the final notice, giving them thirty days to borrow on the dental equipment to full-pay me.

"And instead of full-pay, they send this," she said, indicating the letter. "Well, they're obviously not hardcore. It may still be early enough to knock some sense into them." She explained that someone who found our tax lien recorded at the courthouse probably contacted them. This person or organization sold them an "untaxing" package of which this letter was a part. They probably assured my taxpayers this letter would remove them from the tax system and wipe out any existing debt they owed to the government.

"The funny part is, the people who sold this garbage to them are probably in full compliance."

"It's a scam?"

"No, Rick, it's for real. The Social Security system is completely voluntary, the Sixteenth Amendment was never ratified, and the IRS is a private business incorporated in Delaware."

"I don't remember the letter saying that. About the IRS being a corporation."

"I didn't read the whole thing. That's one of the arguments they use."

"So, I don't have to answer this?"

"Sure, you're going to answer it. How much time is left on the final notice?"

"About ten days."

"You have a levy source?"

"Bank account."

She shook her head. "I guarantee you that account is closed or now under a different name. What about his MPN?"

I shook my head, mystified.

"Medicare Provider Number. All Medicare doctors have one, and we need one to levy the Medicare billings. That's okay. With protestors you want maximum impact anyway."

"Maximum impact?"

"Write them a letter, reminding them of the deadline, and give them a date you'll be out there. Don't call them. At best you'll end up in a pointless argument. At worst, they'll record you, edit the tape, and the next thing you know, you'll be on the six o'clock news saying, 'I'm gonna nail your ass to the wall!' "

"Wait a minute. I'm going out there?"

"You're going to seize them."

"And the warning about coming onto their property again?"

"Don't worry," she said. "I'll assist, if you want."

The person I was thinking of was the massive Toby Peterson. But Beth had the experience and expertise to handle anything these protestors might throw at us. In the end, I decided to opt for brains over brawn.

"You sure we can't be sued?"

"Of course we can. It happens all the time. But the law protects us and the Service will defend us, as long as we were acting within the scope of our official duties. Don't look so worried, Rick. You're lucky. Protestor cases are fun. A lot more fun than the usual shit we deal with."

She told the story of a protestor who chased her around his kitchen table three times before she bolted for the door, remembered she still had a summons in her hand, then ran back to the table and slapped it down before racing from the house.

"There was a revenue officer killed by a protestor," I said, remembering a story from Basic Training.

Beth nodded. "Michael Dillon, the only revenue officer ever killed in the line of duty. The highest award you can get is named after him."

"I just hope it's never renamed the Dillon-Yancey Award."

She laughed. "He sounds like a cream puff, and remember, they've just become protestors. That's the point where they're easiest to turn. They haven't invested thousands of dollars in the scam; they don't have their life savings riding on it. The worst protestors I ever worked was this group of old men at a nursing home. Now, those bastards were hardcore. It was all just a game to them. More exciting than *The Price Is Right* and Wednesday-night bingo and they were so goddamned old, what did they have to lose? It made them feel powerful, battling Uncle Sam. What a nightmare. They buried me in paper and frivolous lawsuits and harassed me for weeks."

"How did they harass you?"

"Back then I was listed in the phone book. They'd call two, three o'clock in the morning. They wouldn't say anything, just held the phone long enough to make sure I was completely awake. They sent pizza to my house. They subscribed me to *Hustler.* They filed liens against me. That one really got me mad, because I was trying to buy a house at the time and it really screwed up my credit, even though the Service filed suit and had the lien expunged. They published ads in the paper. They picketed the office. You name it."

"How did it finally end?"

"The leader of the group died."

"Did we ever collect anything?"

"Not a penny."

"So what was the point?"

She frowned. "What do you mean?"

"What did we get out of it? Why even try to collect from a bunch of crazy old men?"

"Gee, I don't know, Rick. That's a question for Billy. I'm just a grunt. I do what they tell me. In seventeen years, I don't think I've ever asked why we were doing something. I just did it."

.   .   .

Gina summoned Beth and me to her office for a briefing on the case. Protestor cases were considered "high-profile" and could generate coverage in the local papers. More important, for Gina's sake, it had the potential to raise her group's profile in the branch and in the district. Rumors were flying that Byron White was working to fire Gina. When word of this reached her, she allegedly said, "If Byron White wants my job, he can come down here and get it." It is nearly impossible to fire someone within the Service, except in cases of gross negligence or criminal conduct, but even those cases are difficult to prosecute. Managers were more vulnerable, however, because they did not have the protection of the union. Usually, managers who had fallen out of favor were not fired, but demoted to the field—"busted down," in the lexicon of the Service. Gina did not want to be busted down.

"He owns the real estate," she said. "Why aren't we seizing that too?"

"No equity," I answered.

She looked at Beth.

"Can we make some?"

"It would be a stretch."

"Without the real property, you'll need consent," Gina said. If we didn't seize the building, we couldn't take control of the assets inside it without the taxpayer's written permission. The odds were long indeed that a protestor would voluntarily sign a consent-to-enter.

"There's always public access," Beth said.

"What, the waiting-room chairs and old magazines? Let's get real. Why don't we just go ahead and get the writ?*"

"Counsel† won't go forward until consent is denied," Beth answered. This was a requirement of the manual.

"They may make an exception with protestors."

"They never deviate with protestors, Gina," Beth said. The two did not care for each another. Beth thought Gina was brilliant, but lazy and arrogant. Gina thought Beth wanted her job. They were both right.

---

* Writ of Entry, a court order to enter a private area to seize assets.

† District Counsel, the legal arm of the IRS that represents Collection in the courts.

"So you drive out there and when he denies consent, you turn around and drive back, forcing you to make a second field call once you've got the writ. That doubles the risk, Beth."

Beth pointed out we were not dealing with hardcore protestors. Just our showing up with the locks and chains might turn them. It was conceivable we might not even have to seize.

Gina cut her off. "No, we are going to seize. We are going to send a message." She probably meant a message to the "protestor community," as it was called, but she could also have meant a message to Bob Campbell and Byron White.

She continued, "Speaking of risk, let's talk about escort."

"We don't think it's necessary," Beth said. "The taxpayer is in his sixties."

"If he can pull teeth he can pull a trigger," Gina said.

"And, I was going to say, he hasn't made any overt threats."

Gina turned to me. "Did you call CI?" The Criminal Investigation division was charged with providing armed escorts for revenue officers in risky seizures.

Beth said, "I ran it by Howard." Howard Stevens was the manager of the CI group in Tampa, which covered our post-of-duty's territory.

"Did you? *You* did, Beth? Excuse me, I'm confused. I thought this was Rick's case."

"It is Rick's case."

"Rick is a full-fledged revenue officer now. He doesn't need an OJI." She turned to me. "Why isn't CI in on this, Rick?"

"We want to move fast," I said. "You know the red tape we have to wade through to get approval on an armed escort."

"Wade through tape? You're mixing metaphors, Mr. English major. Well, we could always call in the locals." She was referring to the Lakeside police department.

"It's overkill," Beth argued. "And imagine what the papers will do with it, the IRS and cops swooping down on this little old man."

"So what's the plan? You and Rick show up, confront him, ask for consent, and leave?"

"He may sign."

"Yeah, right."

"I've gotten them to sign before," Beth said.

"Not under my watch you haven't."

"I haven't always been under your watch, Gina."

"What do they say in the movies? I just don't want anything to go hinky."

"Come with us," Beth said, knowing what Gina's answer would be.

"I'd rather have a root canal." Gina laughed. "Hey, I made a dental joke!"

She signed the levy. Her signature was an illegible scrawl. "Rick," she said, "I want you to white out my name on this form. These people *will not* know who I am."

After we left her office, Beth turned to me and said, "Our fearless leader."

It was the height of summer, the temperature in the mid-eighties by ten o'clock. I lugged the seizure kit to my car. Beth walked beside me with the case file.

"They may try to goad you into losing your temper or saying something you'll regret later," she advised. "Stay professional. If they get personal, don't you get personal. If they refuse consent, don't argue or try to trick them. Just tell them you'll be back with a writ. Are you nervous?"

"A little."

"There'd be something wrong with you if you weren't. I've been doing this a lot longer than you and I still get nervous. You never really know."

I cleared a place in the debris inside my trunk for the seizure kit. The chains within it clattered as I set it down.

"Don't pull right into the parking lot," Beth said. "We'll circle the building first."

"What are we looking for?"

"Escape routes."

By ten-forty, I was circling the parking lot of the dentist's office. There were three cars in the lot. Beth told me to drive slowly so she could jot down the license plate numbers. Later, if we survived, we would run them through the DMV records to identify other possible protestors. She explained protestors often rallied to one another's defense when the Service called. Strength in numbers.

"Don't pull into a space," she told me. "Back into it, that one right over there, closest to the road. And don't lock the car."

"Should I leave the keys in the ignition?" I asked, imagining fumbling in my pockets as I sprinted to safety.

"No." She had her keys in her fist, the door key to the federal building poking up between her index and middle fingers. For the first time, I was seized with real fear. *They give us H-bombs to take out anthills.* No, they deny us any reasonable means of self-preservation. I backed into the parking space she had pointed out and turned off the car. A silence descended. The morning was sunny. The warm air shimmered over the asphalt. A blue jay sitting in a live-oak tree beside the car turned its head in our direction and studied us with black, lidless eyes. The adrenaline was making me light-headed.

I asked, "You ever hear those stories about mothers being so hopped up on adrenaline, they're able to lift cars off children?"

"No."

We got out of the car. Dear God, I remember thinking, how beautiful the world is! My heart was pounding, my palms were sweating, my eyes were watering behind my sunglasses, but I felt like Lazarus emerging from the tomb after three days of darkness, light bursting through the linen wrappings over his eyes. Most of humanity, I thought, sleep-walked through life, brains muddled by petty concerns, daydreams, the numbing mediocrities of the day-to-day. Most of us, if not already in the tomb, waver on the threshold, afraid to step into the light, afraid we might actually prefer being half-dead to fully alive.

I started toward the building. Beth said, "Rick, you forgot the seizure kit."

"Oh, right."

I had not forgotten it. It weighed at least forty pounds, and I couldn't imagine myself sprinting across the parking lot with it.

On the glass door was a hand-printed sign that read,

NOTICE! PERSONS TRESPASSING UPON THESE PREMISES WITHOUT THE EXPRESS PERMISSION OF THE OWNERS WITHIN WILL BE PROSECUTED WITHIN THE FULL EXTENT OF THE LAW! YOU HAVE BEEN WARNED!

"That's redundant," I said. "By definition, trespassing is entering without permission." I was trying to comfort myself as best I could.

"Okay, good point, Rick," Beth said. "There's someone right on the other side of the door. I count three bodies."

"We're outnumbered," I said.

"One of them is holding something."

"Let's call the cops." The safety manual I received in Basic Training had admonished us to observe NO TRESPASSING signs and consider returning with an armed escort.

"It looks like a box."

"I'd be less than honest if I said I didn't feel a little ridiculous standing here."

"It's your case, Rick. Your call."

I took a deep breath. "We go in."

The box turned out to be a stenographer's machine. A card table had been set up in the middle of the waiting room, and the person holding the machine was a court reporter hired by the taxpayer to record our conversation. The two other people Beth had seen were the taxpayer and his wife.

"Halt!" the old man cried. "You are to cease and desist this illegal entry!"

Beth said, "We're on official business."

She handed the case file to me. I set the seizure kit on the floor behind me and pulled the consent-to-enter from the file.

"Doctor," I said. "We're here to place the assets of the business under seizure—"

"Like hell you are! You people are criminals—"

"—for nonpayment of internal revenue taxes—"

"—and you are perpetrating a criminal trespass against my sovereignty!"

The stenographer's fingers flew over the keys. The taxpayer took a step toward us, his index finger extended toward my nose. From the safety manual: *Maintain at least an arm's length distance from the taxpayer.* I backpedaled, my heels hitting the seizure kit behind me. I had placed it directly in front of the door. *Leave yourself an escape route.* How was I going to hand him the form and maintain the proscribed distance between us? Slide it across the floor? Fold it into a paper airplane? I mentally rehearsed hopping over the kit, backward, in case he made a diving leap for my throat. Beth was on her own. An alternative fantasy presented itself: the taxpayer lunges at Beth and I heave the heavy seizure kit upside his head. This daydream was more satisfying.

"I held up the form. "This is a consent-to-enter."

"I'm not giving you bastards consent to do a goddamned thing!"

"Let's go, Rick," Beth said quietly.

"We'll be back, Doctor," I said, "with a court order."

"Your kangaroo courts have no jurisdiction over me! I am a sovereign citizen of the state!"

"And the next time you won't know we're coming." This was provocative, but my color was up.

"You come out here again and I will protect my property! I am warning you! I will exercise my inalienable right to life, liberty, and the pursuit of happiness!"

I picked up the seizure kit. Beth was behind me, holding the door open. It bothered me that I didn't have a parting shot at hand; I wanted the last word. From the safety manual: *Don't ask, "Is that a threat?" This question often incites violence.*

"Let's go, Rick," Beth said again. "He's denied consent."

"You're goddamned right I deny your consent! I categorically deny you and if you come out here again I will use force to protect my rights! You hear me, Yancey! *I will use force.* You have been warned!"

o   o   o

Howard Stevens folded his hands behind his head, leaned back in his chair, and stared at the ceiling. The twenty-year-old piece of furniture groaned in protest. Howard Stevens was a big man, 210 pounds and most of it muscle. The first feature that struck me, however, was his enormous head. He had played football in college and at forty-two still worked out four times a week, at the government's expense. Howard Stevens was the head of the Criminal Investigation office in Tampa. The night before, he had driven to Lakeside with another agent. He had taken a personal interest in the case and wanted to be in on the next phase of the campaign. It was seven

A.M. We were meeting in the bullpen, now called "the war room" by Gina. Allison sat at her desk, pretending to work, and glowering.

"We ran a check on this guy," Stevens told Gina. "He's clean. No priors."

"That's encouraging."

He turned to me. "What exactly did he say again?"

"He warned me that he intended to protect his property."

"And he..." Howard Stevens consulted my three-page memo. "He shook his finger at you?"

"That's right."

"Did he do this?" Stevens pointed his index finger at me, thumb upright.

"I didn't notice the thumb."

"Okay. Okay." He massaged the back of his neck. He was making sure there were no lingering jurisdictional issues. If a clear threat had been made, Inspection would be charged to escort us back into enemy territory. We had asked, but Inspection decided the threat had not been specific enough.

"There's one thing that troubles me," Stevens continued. "I know we're going after the contents. The, um, X-ray machine and molding equipment and that, um, stuff, but what about the building?"

"What about the building?" Beth asked.

"Why aren't we seizing the building, too?"

"There's no equity," I said.

"Then you can't lock him down," Stevens said. "You can't secure what you've seized." We could not deny the rightful owner access to his property. Beth, Gina, and I looked at one another. This minor point had totally escaped our attention. Allison hid a smile behind her hand.

"The one thing you can count on with protestors," Stevens said, "is they know the law as well as we do. You're going to have to make arrangements to move the stuff out."

"It'll eat up the equity," Beth said. She meant the cost of moving and storing the meager contents of the dental office would offset any profit the government might hope to realize at sale.

Stevens shrugged. "As far as I know, Beth, the manual still prohibits no-equity seizures. If we can't take the building, this one's a no-go."

"You could have told us that over the phone," Gina said.

"I would have, but this is a protestor," Stevens said in a mild tone. "You sure we can't find some equity?"

"Rick." Gina turned to me. "Where's your workup on the building?"

I handed her my calculations on the real estate, the comparison of what the building was worth to what was owed on it. Stevens studied it over Gina's shoulder.

"This is zoned commercial?" he asked.

"Yes."

"How did you arrive at the value?"

"Tax assessor's, plus twenty percent," I said. This was the rule of thumb and the minimum Gina required.

Stevens shook his head. "Good location?"

"Yes."

"What about comparative sales?"

"No," I answered.

"I think maybe we've lowballed this," Gina said. "The tax value is good as a starting point, but it is a good location and they're usually low when it comes to commercial property."

"I'd up it at least thirty percent," Stevens said.

"Forty," Gina said.

"Let's go with thirty-five," Stevens said.

"Thirty-five, Rick," Gina instructed me. I punched the numbers into the calculator.

"Well?" Stevens asked. "Do we have equity now?"

"Not much," I said.

"But it's there."

"With a magnifying glass." I recalled Culpepper's words: *Remember, we can always make equity.*

"I'll type up another B," Beth said. Procedure required two levy forms, one for the real estate and another for the personal assets.

"Then we're a go?" Stevens asked.

"We're a go," Gina said. Stevens looked at me. His eyes were deep-set and dark, almost black. I nodded.

"You and Beth are there for the assets," he told me. "The taxpayer is mine. The only contact you're going to have is handing him the forms, the writ-of-entry, the levy, and the Notice of Seizure. Do not engage him other-wise. Let us do the talking. If things go sour, your job is to find the nearest exit and get the hell out of there. If you're not near an exit, hit the floor, find cover. Wait for an all clear from me before you do anything else. We've notified the locals and they're on standby, but we want to avoid bringing them in; it just muddies the waters. These people need to under-stand it's the federal government they're screwing with. He's got no regis-tered weapons, but that doesn't mean granddaddy's shotgun isn't behind the counter. We did a drive-by last night, and there's only two ways out of there: that glass door in the front and the door in the back." He nodded to the man in the dark suit standing by the doorway, who had not spoken a word during the meeting. "Greg will cover that door and I'll go in with you and Beth. I'm going to introduce myself and let him know why I'm there, and then you do your thing. Are you absolutely sure he has no knowledge of us coming today?"

"I told him we'd be back."

"But he doesn't know it's today."

"Not unless we have a double agent in the office."

Stevens glanced at Allison. It was an extremely gratifying moment. Stevens rose from the chair, and kept rising until I had the impression the top of his head would brush the ceiling. His coat came open and I glimpsed his shoulder holster. It hit me then that it was entirely possible we might be walking into an ambush. Jim Neyland had told me in my final interview that I would come to see the job as a game, a battle of wits between the taxpayer and me. He was wrong. The gun hanging under Howard Stevens's left arm meant this was no game. I wondered, if I had known in the begin-ning this was coming, would I still have taken the job? It was impossible to answer that question. The person who had said yes to Jim Neyland almost two years ago was not the same person who now followed Howard Stevens out the door and to his Ford Taurus, illegally parked in the loading zone. It was probable that the person who existed two years ago would have been paralyzed with fear. I had the odd sensation of being outside my own body, watching myself slip into the passenger seat beside Stevens. Rick Yancey pulling the dark glasses from his coat pocket. Rick Yancey check-ing his pocket commission. Rick Yancey with the sky-blue eyes and dark goatee and curly, slicked-back hair and brand-new silver-coated ballpoint in his pocket and Florsheim shoes shined to a mirror finish. Rick Yancey, like Richard Cory of the poem, glittering as he walks.

"Deja vu," I said to Beth as we stepped out of the car. We waited for Howard and Greg to don their blue windbreakers embossed with the words U.S. TREASURY SPECIAL AGENT on the backs.

"I'll take any patients that might be in there," Beth said. She was all business.

"Did you bring some levies?" I asked. We would serve them on the patients for payment.

"They're in my briefcase."

We followed Stevens across the parking lot. Greg broke from the group to take his position by the back door. His coat was unbuttoned. Stevens had hooked his badge on his lapel; the morning sun glinted off its gold surface.

"Have you ever fired your weapon in the line of duty?" I asked.

"Never even drawn it. Came close once."

"What happened?"

He paused, his hand on the door. He was reading the NO TRESPASSING sign.

"I changed my mind."

There were no patients inside. The receptionist rose from behind her partition as the door came open, her mouth opening soundlessly as Stevens heartily wished her a good morning. I set the seizure kit down and flashed my commission at her. I asked her if the doctor was in.

"He's in the back."

"We need to see him," Stevens said.

"I'll get him."

She disappeared through the door behind her desk. Stevens turned and leaned on the partition, a half-wall separating the receptionist's work area from the rest of the room. A trickle of sweat ran down the middle of my back. What was the protocol? Do I make introductions? I glanced at Stevens, whose mouth was open in a cavernous yawn. He caught me looking and said, "If I push you, you go down."

"What's that?" I found myself whispering.

"If I push you, go down. Don't argue. Don't ask questions. If I can't reach you, I'll shout 'Down!' "

"Okay."

"You never know."

The inner door swung open and my dentist stood in the doorway, the receptionist a couple of steps behind him. His face was dark, his eyes ringed by black circles. We stared at each other for a few seconds, until I heard Stevens's voice in my ear.

"Rick, you're on."

"Hello, Doctor," I began.

"Cindy!" he yelled at the girl behind him, keeping his eyes on me. "Call the police!" He stepped into the room, closing the door behind him, leaving her inside the examination room. He came around the partition, into the waiting room. His hands were on his hips. His nostrils were flared. His bushy salt-and-pepper eyebrows were drawn together. He smelled of alcohol.

"Doctor, I'm here today for $32,415.23."

"I don't owe you a penny!"

"Can you pay that today?"

"You're not listening to me!"

Beth handed me the writ-of-entry.

"Doctor, this is a court order authorizing us as federal agents to enter these premises and seize the contents of your business for nonpayment of internal revenue taxes." I held it out to him. He took it from me and glanced at it. Then, with exquisite deliberateness, he tore the papers in two and allowed them to fall from his hands. They fluttered to the floor around his feet.

Beth handed me the next document. The routine reminded me of a surgeon and his assisting nurse—or a dentist and his hygienist. I fought the urge to laugh.

"This is Form 668-B. You need to read this paragraph, in the middle of the form."

He folded his hands over his chest and glared at me.

"I do not recognize your illegal forms."

"I'll put it right here," I said, balancing the paper on the partition. "You can look at it later."

"I intend to piss on it later."

"This is another Form 668-B. We are serving this form in order to seize the building. This is Form 2433. It is your formal notice of seizure. This one has the legal description of the real property. We'll be giving you another Form 2433 once we complete the inventory of the assets."

"I don't have any assets. I don't have any possessions under the definition of the very so-called laws you profess to enforce."

Beth had left my side to begin listing the assets in the waiting area: the battered sofa, the overstuffed arm chairs, the two end tables.

"I intend to have you arrested and I will sue all of you personally for a writ of trespass and suspension of my habeas corpus. I will file suit against you for violating my civil rights as a sovereign citizen of the state of Florida, under which your so-called revenue statutes have no jurisdiction over my sovereignty."

"How's that?" Stevens asked.

The dentist jumped, as if just noticing Stevens's bulk taking up half the room. "Who're you?"

"I'm Special Agent-in-Charge Howard Stevens. How are you?"

"Special Agent-in-Charge, huh? Well, la-de-da. Let me ask you something. What is the section of the Internal Revenue Code that requires me to file a tax return?"

"I would have no idea."

"You have no idea of the law you purport to enforce? You've answered my question, Mr. Special Agent-in-Charge. There is no law, because by definition I am a nonperson."

"I'm sorry, you're a what?"

"A nonperson. A nonperson, as defined by the Internal Revenue Code."

"Is that so?"

"You're damn right that's so! And I got the evidence to prove it!"

"Rick," Beth said. "I'm done here."

"Okay," Stevens said. The bemused look on his face fell away and his dark eyes lost their sparkle. "This is the deal, Doc. These folks have served you with papers that authorize them to take full possession and control of your property. You're going to let them do that. You're going to allow them to do their job with no interference. If you chose to interfere in any way with the performance of their official duties, I'll have no choice but to place you under arrest—in violation of Title 26 of the United States Code, Section 7212(a) and/or Title 18 of the United States Code, Section 111 . . . in case you want the citation."

The dentist stepped around me and jabbed a thin finger into Stevens's chest.

"You bastards take one stick of furniture. You touch one piece of equipment. You lay one filthy Nazi paw on my molds, and I'll have you arrested for breaking and entering, assault and battery, trespassing and grand theft."

"We're willing to take our chances," Stevens said dryly. He nodded to Beth and me. We walked into the reception area. Behind me, I heard Stevens cry out, "*Down!*" And I hit the floor, Beth falling with a thud beside me. I folded my hands over my head and waited for the bullet to tear through my body. So this is how it ends, facedown on a threadbare carpet that smelled mildly of dog urine, and for what? What was my life worth? $32,415.23. I could hear the sounds of a struggle, of someone grunting and someone else shouting. I took a deep breath and rolled to my side. Stevens had taken a position between us and the doctor, blocking his way into the reception area, one hand gripping the partition, the other pressed against the wall. The slight dentist was slamming his body into Stevens, shoulder first. Stevens was grunting with each blow; the doctor was shouting incoherently, nearing a falsetto as he began to sob. Stevens took him by the shoulders and pushed him straight back.

"You've got to settle down!" he shouted. "I don't want to arrest you!"

He released him, and the dentist kept backing up until his knees hit the sofa and he collapsed onto it, burying his head in his hands. Stevens watched him for a moment, one hand inside his jacket. He glanced back at us. His face was flushed and his dark eyes shone brightly. He was pumped. He nodded to us.

"If that girl's back there, send her out the through the back. Get Greg in first to check out the interior before you get to work. I'll stay with him."

"You okay?" I asked Beth.

She nodded. Her lips were wet and her eyes were shining brightly, too.

"Let's go," she said. "I'm good."

"Come on!" the dentist screamed as we went into the back room. "Come on and fucking arrest me, you Nazi fucking bastards!"

"Shut up or I will," I heard Stevens say, wearily.

We completed the seizure without further incident. I signed the second 2433 and Beth signed directly below me: under the law, two IRS employees must attest to the accuracy of the seizure. I found the dentist sitting in the waiting room, Stevens standing by the door, watching the traffic pass outside. Beth placed a warning sticker on the front door while I handed the taxpayer his copy of the Notice of Seizure. He wadded it into a ball with great deliberateness and threw it at my nose.

"I will see you in court," he promised me.

Stevens left his post and joined us.

"We all done here, Rick?"

"All done."

"Oh, you're done all right," the dentist said.

"I've given you a lot of rope here, Doc," Stevens said. "Don't use it to hang yourself."

There was a rapping on the door. An elderly man leaning on a cane was standing outside, cupping his hand against the glass.

"That's my eleven o'clock," the dentist said.

Beth unlocked the door and stepped outside. The dentist watched, open-mouthed, as Beth handed his patient a Notice of Levy. This reminded me of something.

"The patient files."

Stevens asked, "What about them?"

"We can't place them under seizure."

"Doctor-patient confidentiality?"

I nodded. "You'll have to take them with you," I said to the dentist.

"I'm not taking them with me because I'm not going anywhere."

Stevens turned to him and said with exaggerated patience, "You will be leaving, because we are leaving, and you are here with our permission. This is now the property of the United States government."

"Which has no jurisdiction over me."

"Whatever. You should consider yourself lucky you're not under arrest. You've committed at least two felonies this morning, so my advice to you is to shut your mouth, pack up your files, and live to fight another day."

We watched him drive away in his Toyota Camry.

"You know," Stevens said. "For a nonperson, he packs quite a wallop."

"Why didn't you arrest him?" I asked.

Stevens shrugged. His expression was as impenetrable as a Buddha's. "We all have a role to play, Rick. I might have done the same thing, if some assholes came to take away everything that mattered to me."

o   o   o

A week later the dentist called and asked to meet with me in the office. I brought the request to Gina.

"Of course you'll meet with him," she said. "But prepare for the worst."

"I know what my idea of the worst is," I said, remembering the dive into the carpet. "What's yours?"

"Video cameras. Tape recorders. Picketers. An army of protestors camped on the steps. Use the booth with the panic button." One of the interview booths was fitted with an emergency button located under the table. It was linked directly with the police department. In larger posts-of-duty, the panic button rang in the offices of Criminal Investigation, which would send at least one armed agent to the rescue. Our button also rang in Gina's office, a fact that did not inspire confidence. Toby scoffed that Gina would dive out the window if the panic button ever was hit.

"At the very least, expect him to tape-record the meeting. So we will record as well. There's an office tape recorder around here somewhere. Ask Bonny. But make sure you check the batteries; I don't think it's been used since Billy was here."

On the morning of our meeting, there was no army at our gates. Just my taxpayer and his stern, thin-lipped wife. Neither of them looked well. I led them into the booth, located in a room just outside Taxpayer Service. I left the door open and slid behind the panic-button side of the table. The tape recorder was loaded with fresh tape and batteries, but the dentist had not brought one, unless he was concealing it beneath his seersucker coat.

"Mr. Yancey," he began. "This is difficult for me. I have ... *we* have ... made a terrible mistake."

He wiped his hand over his face. His nails were long, yellow, and broken at the ends. His hand was shaking. I thought, *And this man is a dentist.*

"We want to know how we can make this right," his wife said.

"That depends on your definition of right," I said. "Can you pay the full amount?"

"We—" the dentist began.

"No," she said. "We can't. Not all at once. We would like for you to consider letting us open the doors for a few more months."

"They've cut off our electricity!" the dentist shouted. He began to weep. Following my instincts, I abandoned my native caution and closed the door. When I returned to the table, he had composed himself enough to add, "We were suckered, Mr. Yancey. Five hundred dollars. Five hundred dollars we don't have. Five hundred dollars."

"That you could have given to me."

She said, "Without the business we'll lose our house. We'll lose everything. It's all the income we had."

"So you know we can't pay all of it." He was growing impatient. "Tell us our options."

"Well, they're pretty limited right now. We can release the seizure if you pay us the full amount. We can also release it if you give us the minimum amount we expect at sale."

"How much is that?"

"With the real estate, about five thousand dollars."

He moaned. She lowered her head. No one said anything for a moment. Then she said, "We don't have five thousand dollars, Mr. Yancey. Isn't there some program—doesn't the IRS have something that can help people like us?"

"You can file a Form 911. That's an appeal to overturn our decision based on the hardship it's created."

"Well, it's certainly created a hardship," he said bitterly.

"That's debatable," I shot back. "We were working on an installment plan before you sent that letter."

"We were suckered," he repeated. "We were conned."

"We made a mistake," she added. "Can't you take that into consideration?"

I tapped my pen on the desk. I let the silence drag out.

"You keep saying you were conned. Who conned you?"

They exchanged a glance. He looked at me. His eyes were bloodshot. It was ten o'clock in the morning, and he smelled of alcohol. He knew immediately where I was going and was hesitant to follow me there.

"We got this letter, about a week after you first came," he said slowly. "Making all sorts of promises. I don't know how they got our name or knew we owed taxes."

"The tax lien," I said. "It's filed at the county courthouse. It's public record."

"Yeah, I guess so. Anyway, this letter made all these promises. Said it was going to 'untax' us, get rid of you—not you personally, but the IRS. I meant the IRS. And all we had to do was send them five hundred dollars."

"So you gave them five hundred dollars."

"You got to understand, we were desperate. And when you read their stuff, well, it kind of makes sense."

"It didn't make much sense to me," she said.

"Well," he said.

"What did you get for the five hundred dollars?"

"This packet full of letters to send, instructions how to send them, who to send them to. Mostly it was copies of these magazine articles."

"From magazines I never heard of," she said.

"And court cases. Court papers where the judge ruled against the IRS. God, there must have been four or five hundred pages of this stuff. It all made it sound simple, and—"

"Too good to be true," she said.

"Do you still have this material?"

"Yeah."

"Can I see it?"

"Don't you . . . the IRS probably already knows all about these guys?"

"Did anyone contact you? Over the phone or in person?"

Again, they exchanged a look. She said, "Surely you understand, Mr. Yancey. This isn't easy for us."

"I do understand," I said. "And if you had come to me with this stuff before we actually seized . . . the seizure changes everything. We can't make it go away or pretend it never happened."

"We don't know these people," the dentist said. "We don't know what they're capable of. They said once we posted that sign on our door, we could shoot you on the spot. We could blow your brains out and nothing would happen to us!"

She spoke his first name sharply. He dropped his head and resumed his weeping.

"We would like to see the material," I said, speaking gently to him but looking at her. She was the level-headed one. She was the one to present the deal to. Whatever she decided, he would acquiesce to it. "We want the name of the organization that contacted you. We want the name or names of the people within this organization you may have spoken to."

She nodded slowly. "And if we do that?"

"I'll see what I can do."

"What does that mean?"

"It means I will see what I can do. The final decision isn't mine. But I will plead your case to my boss."

"I wasn't trying to hurt anybody," he cried out. "I swear before God I never wanted to hurt anyone!"

"Oh, shut up," she said to him.

"That doesn't matter now," I said.

An hour later I met with Gina behind closed doors.

"What's this?" she asked when I handed her the form.

"Form 911."

"Ahhh. The protestor seizure. Well, they should be able to turn this around quick." She started to pick up the phone. She was going to call the Taxpayer Advocate's Office. Once filed, an Application for Taxpayer Assistance Order (ATAO) was assigned to a caseworker, who was required to make a determination in twenty-four hours. In protestor cases, the decision was always in our favor. The Advocate's Office understood these applications for what they were: a delaying tactic, an attempt to tie up the bureaucracy with frivolous requests.

She slowly lowered the receiver. Something about the form troubled her. "You know, it's funny, Rick, but isn't this your handwriting?"

"It is."

"You helped them fill out the form?"

"I filled it out for them."

She studied me for a long moment. "Why are you grinning like the cat who swallowed the canary?"

I explained my strategy. If we released the seizure, the branch chief—or even the division chief—might question our decision. But a decision from the Advocate's Office was binding on Collection. If they determined the seizure created an undue hardship on the taxpayer, we would be compelled to release it.

"So? We can release, too. *We* can say it's creating a hardship."

"We don't want to say that."

"We don't?" she asked.

"Because we're not gonna go easy on protestors."

"When you came in here you said they weren't protestors. Now you're saying they are. Which is it, Rick?"

"They're not, but they must appear to be."

"Come again?"

"It has to look like we didn't have a choice. It has to look like they've won the battle."

"Look like that to whom?"

"They're prepared to give me names, Gina."

"Ah." She understood immediately.

"And they won't give me names unless—"

"Unless they feel safe." She began to scribble something on her notepad, thought better of it, tore off the sheet, and tossed it into her shred drawer. "You'll have to be careful how you construct the history."

"I'll show you a draft before I put it in the file."

"Okay. Okay." She was smiling. She had not been smiling when I entered the room. "I'll write a cover memo to ATAO to fax with the form. I'll be properly stern but leave the door open. Is Beth here?"

"She's waiting."

"I'll call them, too," she said, meaning the Advocate's Office. "Tell the taxpayers we'll have the seizure released by the end of the day."

"Good."

"Rick," she called softly. I turned at the door. "Excellent work."

o   o   o

I went outside and walked in the alley behind the federal building, my favorite place to think and smoke. Gina had never used those words before, at least not in reference to me. *Excellent work.* It really had been a brilliant, bloodless campaign that benefited all the combatants. The taxpayer would retain his practice. Gina would earn points with her boss and maybe even save her job. And I would emerge the clear front-runner for the next promotion. At each juncture of the battle, I had used leverage to its fullest advantage. The dentist's letter had freed me to act with no compunction whatsoever, nothing like my interminable ethical wrestling match with the Laura Marsh case. There was no moral ambiguity to this kind of war, a war against protestors, whose sole purpose was to defeat our tax system, which would cripple our government and threaten the very existence of our nation. Long ago Culpepper had warned me that I must find a reason to like the job if I wanted to preserve my sanity. I had finally found the reason.

Since there was no one with me, I said to a nearby pigeon, "War is insane, but to keep my sanity, I must make war." The pigeon, intent on his intricate dance to seduce a nearby female, ignored me. That was okay. He was a pigeon, that's all he was and all he was ever going to be, and he was doing his thing.

For the first time since Jim Neyland shook my hand in Tampa, I did not feel like a stranger inside my own skin. I was there. I had reached the moment of enlightenment Gina had promised would come. I had spewed from the chrysalis in an explosive, ecstatic epiphany, my wings dazzling bright against the sky. He was finally awake, the person who had always dwelled within me; indeed, who dwells within everyone, furiously alive yet dead asleep, wrapped in layers of linen, waiting for someone—or something—to call him forth. The call had come and I had answered it. I was awake now.

W A R

Two months later, Gina and I were on a conference call with Bob Campbell, the branch chief.

"Bob," Gina began, "Rick has an idea for a RCP."*

"I'm listening."

"Protestor groups often advocate changing W-4s† to claim exemptions from their withholdings," I said.

"True."

"We'd like to target the major employers in the area, as well as those segments known for protestor 'clumpings.'"

"Nothing worse than a clump of protestors," Bob Campbell said.

"We would review the W-4s on file to identify possible protestors, then research IDRS to see if we have assessments or unfiled returns on the probables."

"Then?"

"Then? Well, then we ... enforce."

"You know, the Service Centers have this program," Bob Campbell intoned. Gina rolled her eyes. "Employers are required to send questionable W-4s to them for review."

---

* Return Compliance Program, term for special projects outside the normal range of day-to-day collection.

† Form W-4, provided by wage earners to their employers, for computation of the amount to withhold for federal income taxes.

"Yes," I said. "But only those W-4s that have ten or more exemptions. At least one protestor group is on to this and advises its members to list nine exemptions."

"How do you know that?"

"I've seen some material and heard it from my informants."

"Your what?"

"The dentist," Gina reminded him.

"Oh, right. Okay, so what's the idea here?"

Gina and I looked at each other.

"The idea, Bob," Gina said, "is to conduct a compliance project to review W-4s in targeted industries in order to identify possible illegal protestor activity."

"Uh-huh, uh-huh. And then what?"

"Bring 'em back into the fold or give 'em a little jail time. Make an impact. You know, Bob, compliance stuff."

"I see. Well, it sounds pretty good. Send up a memo and I'll run it by Byron."

"Bob," Gina said, "as branch chief, you can approve an RCP."

"Well, how many people you think you need for this project? Not the whole group, do you think?"

"I was thinking Rick and maybe two other Grade Nines."

"Okay, put that in the memo, too."

After some pleasantries (Bob's golf game was off; Gina had dropped out of aerobics for the fifth time), the call ended. Gina muttered something under her breath that sounded like "asshole" and flashed a smile at me.

"You write the memo and I'll send it up," she said. "My only concern is overgraded cases in your inventory." Under the contract, only a certain percentage of my inventory could exceed the Grade 9 level. "But I'll keep an eye on it."

I took a deep breath. I had waited for one of Gina's good days to ask about the project. Her good days were becoming less and less frequent. She was M.I.A. for hours at a time. Some said she was at home brooding. Others said that she was papering the town with résumés. Byron White was nearing retirement and had made it clear he would not ride off into the sunset without Gina's head in his saddlebag.

"There's something else I wanted to ask you," I said.

"Go ahead."

"I want every protestor case in the Queue*."

"What, for the whole country?" She thought I was joking.

"I thought I'd start with just our territory."

"Protestor cases do not produce high yields."

"I'm not interested in harvesting."

She laughed. "What are you interested in?"

"Slash-and-burn."

"Stop, you're scaring me."

"I'm serious. How many are there in the Queue?"

"Rick, I'm not giving you an entire inventory of protestors."

"That's what I'm asking, Gina. How many can you give me?"

"Gee, aren't you all gung ho."

"*How many?*"

She flinched. "I will . . . I will look into it, Rick."

o   o   o

With minor variations, a typical case radiated from the taxpayer outward. Upon receipt, I checked IDRS for additional assessments or missing returns still in notice status, then hit the street to contact the taxpayer, make my demand, secure the financial information, set my deadlines. Everything that followed depended upon the taxpayer; every action I took was merely a reaction to their response, whether that response was to ignore me, put me off, or struggle to comply with my demands. I quickly discovered that this method could not be applied to illegal tax protestors. Approaching them on the front end only tipped them off and gave them the opportunity to launch a counterattack. By definition, protestors had no regard for the law; the only thing they understood was brute force, the Service's power to inflict harm upon them. Nothing so banal as physical harm, but financial, emotional, and psychological harm. The worst thing you can do to a protestor is make him feel powerless.

---

* Special repository of cases that are waiting assignment to a revenue officer.

So I waged my war in these stages: *Intelligence*, *Reconnaissance*, and *Attack*.

STAGE ONE: INTELLIGENCE

The couple owed about $20,000 on a return filed for them by the Internal Revenue Service*. They had not filed their personal income tax returns for three years. Yet IDRS showed that the husband had received over $50,000 for each of those years. He owned an insurance business; she appeared to be a homemaker. Two children, according to their last filed return. They lived in a rental house. He had some investments in the market, but nothing significant. His business was located in a strip mall on the east side of town.

DMV records showed two vehicles registered to the taxpayer: a white '89 Ford pickup truck and a red '68 Chevrolet. The truck was fully encumbered by a note to Ford Motor Credit. The '68 Chevy had no lien against it. DMV records indicated the model of this car was a Chevette.

There was no record of real estate in either of their names at the county tax assessor's office. Nor did I discover any record of transfers of property within the last five years. Often, protestors will try to protect their assets by transferring title to their children or other nonliable parties, such as dummy corporations or bogus trusts. The evidence they leave behind is always obvious, making it easy for us to "reach the asset," the Service's euphemism for seizure.

The bottom line was there was precious little I could do to collect the twenty grand. The only asset immediately available was the Chevette. I was not encouraged. If I was lucky, I might clear a couple hundred bucks at sale. But, as I tried to tell Gina, protestor cases were not about yield.

STAGE TWO: RECONNAISSANCE

I drove to the strip mall and slowly cruised the parking lot. There was no white Ford pickup and no Chevette. His office appeared to be open, and I

---

* Section 6020(b) of the Internal Revenue Code provides that the Service may file a return on behalf of a taxpayer if the taxpayer neglects or refuses to file voluntarily.

wondered if he had disposed of the assets and was now leasing his vehicles. There were twenty or thirty cars in the lot, and I wrote down all the tag numbers. I would run them through DMV when I returned to the office and look for a link between the owners and the taxpayer. I pulled into a parking place and looked up the taxpayer's address on my map. Perhaps the Chevette was parked in the driveway, in which case I would not need a writ-of-entry to seize it. I was leaving the lot when something red caught the corner of my eye, and my spirits soared.

STAGE THREE: ATTACK

I raced back to the federal building, whipped the car into the loading zone, jumped out, leapt four feet onto the platform, remembered I had left the car running, hopped down, turned off the car, jumped up again, flung open the side door, remembered I had forgotten to lock the car, decided I had left nothing in it worth burgling, yanked open the door to the suite of offices for the senior revenue officers, sprinted down the narrow hallway, ducked my head into each room, swung around at the end of the hall and ran back, hung a sharp right to the bullpen door, bruised my index finger punching in the security code, and fell into the room shouting, "Where the hell is everyone?"

I heard a small cry from the IDRS cubicle. Cindy Sandifer's head appeared over the partition, eyes wide, mouth ajar.

"Rick! What happened?"

"It says Chevette, one 1968 red Chevrolet Chevette, but it's wrong; DMV got it wrong or he pulled something or paid somebody off, but that doesn't matter, it's free and clear, we're first, we've got it. What are you doing? Are you free?"

"Free for what?"

"Where's Gina? Please, please God, tell me Gina's here. Is she here? She hasn't gone home to mow her lawn or anything, has she? I need a B and a 2434*. It's right there, right there in the parking lot, Cindy, in fucking public access. The sonofabitch even has a FOR SALE sign on it, can you

---

Form 2434-B, Notice of Encumbrances, required by Gina before seizure approval.

believe that? And it's perfect; it's absolutely fucking *perfect*." I was at my desk, flipping through my address book. "I'm calling Andy. You never answered me."

"Which question? You asked about fifty."

"Is Gina here?"

I found the number for Andy's Towing and began to dial.

"Yes, but she's locked in her office with Bonny. She's having one of *those* days, Rick. I wouldn't bother her if I—"

"She's still the goddamned manager, isn't she? I'll get her to sign the fucking B if I have to shove it under—Andy, Rick Yancey. How's it going, man? I'm gonna need a driver to meet me in about a half hour...Cindy, here's the TIN.* Pull the accruals on his account...Yeah, I'm still here, Andy." I looked at Cindy. She was standing next to me. "Can you please print the accruals on his account so I can type the B?" I turned my back on her. "No, I was talking to Cindy. Listen, I need a truck. It's right off 98, next to that drive-thru convenience store. Yeah, that's the one. You got a flatbed available? I don't want to hook this baby up and drag it down the road. I don't want to risk a single fucking scratch. Well, I guess you're gonna find out when I get there. I'll call you back." I hung up. Cindy had not moved.

"It's a protestor, isn't it?" she asked.

"Yes. Yes, it's a protestor." I stepped around her and went to the forms cabinet. "Are you free?"

"When?"

"Right now."

"You're going to go right now, at three o'clock in the afternoon on a Friday, to seize a protestor?"

"Jesus, it's three already?"

I sat down at the typewriter. It groaned at me and I smacked it hard in the side.

"What about escort?"

"I'm not bringing escort."

"Why not?"

"Because there's nothing to indicate I need one."

---

* Taxpayer Identification Number, or SSN.

"What has the protestor said?"

I slammed my fist on the typing table. "Christ, Cindy, you aren't my fucking OJI anymore! You don't have to question every single goddamned bit of esoterica in my case file!"

"What's esoterica?"

"I'm asking you if you're free to assist me in this seizure. If you are free, pull those accruals, find your commission, and pack up your desk. If you aren't free or you don't want to help, then leave me alone! It's three o'clock and if I don't get back out there it might be gone!"

"What might be gone?"

"The car! The car! The car! Christ, what the hell have I been talking about since I walked into the room? DMV says it's a 1968, red Chevy Chevette. Well, it's a 1968 and it's red all right, but it's no Chevette. It's a *Corvette*, it's in mint condition, it's parked in public access, the taxpayer has no clue I know about it, and it's three o'clock on a fucking Friday afternoon! Is that enough for you?" I pulled the completed levy form from the typewriter and slid in the 2434-B. "Oh! And it's a convertible. Did I mention it was a fucking convertible? Cherry red with black leather seats. It's the most beautiful goddamned thing I've ever seen in my life, and I'm going out there to get it, even if I have to take Henry with me. I'm going to get it."

"Henry isn't here."

"Henry isn't the point!" I shouted.

"Why are you shouting at the top of your lungs?" she shouted back.

I took a deep breath. We stared across the room at each other.

I said in a measured tone. "So, are you free?"

"Call in the locals," Gina advised.

"The locals, right," Cindy said. She had joined us in Gina's office for the impromptu briefing.

"Gina, he's an insurance salesman," I said.

"John Wayne Gacy ran a successful construction company."

"And he was a clown," Cindy added.

Gina nodded gravely. "And he was a clown."

"If things go sour, I'll back off. Andy will be there."

"Good, he can wrestle him to the ground, put him in a half-waddyacallit."

"Nelson," Cindy said.

"Nelson, right."

"Andy'll tear off his head and shit down his neck," I said.

"Why Rick, how colorful."

"Sorry."

"He's a little excited," Cindy said.

"Yes, but could he tear off John Wayne Gacy's head and shit down his neck?"

"Who?" Cindy asked. She was getting lost. "Rick or Andy?"

"Rick doesn't look like he could tear off a chicken's head."

"How did we get from a protestor seizure to me tearing off a chicken's head?" I asked.

"He could bite it off," Cindy said. "I had an uncle in Shreveport who could do that."

Gina laughed and signed the levy form. "Okay, it's almost four. If you're going, I guess you better go. Rick, you never fail to make my day. Have you by the way?"

"What?"

"Ever bitten off a chicken's head?"

Andy met us at a gas station two blocks from the taxpayer's parking lot. He had brought the massive flatbed tow truck. The engine was running and the air was thick with diesel fumes. A toothpick jutted from the side of his mouth and he twirled the gnawed piece of wood with his tongue.

"Cherry red 'Vette, way to go, Ricky!"

"Don't hook it up until I give you the signal," I said.

"Oh, yes sir, like I haven't done this a thousand times before. Hey, Cindy, how's it going? Look at Rick, willya? Like a virgin in a whorehouse."

Cindy sighed. "I love working with men."

o   o   o

He followed us to the parking lot. I parked next to the Corvette and stepped out of the car with the case file and a roll of tape. Andy pulled the truck into the far corner of the lot, leaned his arm out the window, and gave us the thumbs-up. I pulled a warning sticker from the case file and Cindy said, "What are you doing?"

"I'm stickering the car."

"You can't sticker the car yet, Rick."

"Watch me."

"You haven't given the taxpayer the levy."

"Don't pester me with details, Cindy."

"It isn't a detail, Rick, it's the law."

"It isn't a law, Cindy. It's a procedure. There's a difference."

I placed the sticker on the driver's side window; the taxpayer had been kind enough to leave it rolled up for me.

"Rick," she said. "You're putting a warning sticker on an asset that isn't seized yet."

"Look, Cindy, see that big glass façade over there? That's his office. How far is that? Fifty feet, a hundred? How fast do you think he can run? Or send somebody else out here to rescue the thing once I hand him the B?"

"Stickering it won't stop a rescue, Rick."

I ignored her and headed for the building. She trotted to keep up.

"I don't feel right about this. You've never had contact with him. You don't know what he's like, how he's gonna react."

"I have to take that chance," I said. "I didn't have time to write a fucking three-page memo to pass through Gina up to Howard, then back down to me."

We were at the door. I placed my hand on the metal bar across the front.

"Where's your commission?"

"Right here."

"Cindy, no offense, but let me do the talking. They only understand one thing."

"And what would that be?"

"The Fourth Protocol."

"What the hell is the Fourth Protocol?"

I went inside.

.   .   .

There was a small office area and a half-wall partition near the back. The two desks up front were empty. I rang the little metal bell sitting on the partition. The door in the rear wall opened and a middle-aged woman poked her head out.

"Hi!" she called.

"Hi!" I called back. "We're looking for Mr.—"

"Just a sec. Can I tell him who's here?"

"Rick Yancey." Cindy raised her commission; I placed a hand on her forearm and forced it down. "And Mrs. Sandifer."

"Okay. Have a seat and he'll be right out."

She closed the door behind her. I turned back and looked into the parking lot. If he caught a whiff of us, he might sneak out the back of the building and make for the car.

"When he comes out," I told Cindy, "turn around and keep an eye on the parking lot."

"Why?"

The inner door opened again and he came out, followed by the woman. Her hair was in a bun, a few loose strands falling over her high forehead. She was probably in her forties, the right age, and she hung close to him; the body language was right, too. The wife. He was wearing his salesman's smile and approached the partition with the glad hand extended. Auto, home, health, whatever your insurance needs, you are in good hands with me. He had no frigging clue.

I held up my commission. He stopped in his tracks, hand still toward me, smile frozen.

"My name is Rick Yancey. This is Mrs. Sandifer. I have something for you."

I laid the levy form facedown on the partition. His hand dropped on top of it. She started to say something, and he said, "Carol!" and she shut her mouth.

"We're seizing the Corvette. You need to read that paragraph in the middle of the form."

"I don't owe this."

"This is Publication One. It explains your rights. Read it, and if you have any questions, I'll be happy to answer them."

"Carol," he said. "Call the police."

I said to Cindy, "Told you I didn't need to call them."

I turned my back on him and walked to the glass door. I leaned out and gave Andy the thumbs-up. The gears of the tow truck screamed. Carol had not moved to call the police.

"We're taking the car," I said. "We're going to have another form for you when we're done. Please don't leave."

"I'm calling my attorney."

"Good idea. Probably something you should have done a long time ago," I said. "Mrs. Sandifer."

I held the door for her and we walked across the parking lot. The car glistened in the late afternoon sunlight. Its chrome shone like diamonds.

"Rick, lemme tell you," Andy said as he lowered the truck bed. "I've been hauling for you guys for ten years. Busted up old clunkers, broken-down rusting hunks of sheet metal, bald tires and bad transmissions and pieces of shit that shouldn't even be on the road, but this is the finest thing on four wheels you've ever yanked. Congratulations."

The taxpayer banged out the door and sprinted across the parking lot. Andy watched him, a bemused expression on his face. "What a dumb-ass," he said. "You know, it just blows me away, how these people think they can get away with it." Cindy muttered something under her breath.

"Hold on! Hold it right there!" the taxpayer cried. He arrived out of breath. He bent over, hands on his knees, trying to catch his breath. His shoes were scuffed. There was a thin line of dirt beneath each fingernail. Desperation consumes us by degrees, taking small bites until there is nothing, no joy, no hope, no love, only the desperation, ravenously chewing.

"This car is not mine!"

"That's your phone number on the FOR SALE sign," I pointed out.

"I mean, there's a lien on it. I owe more than it's worth."

"Not according to my report."

"Well, your report is wrong. Hey!"

Andy had drawn the taxpayer's attention by crawling under the car to hook up the chain. He was ignoring our conversation. I had given him the signal and he would not back off unless I told him to.

"He's gonna scratch it!" He pointed a finger at my nose. "You put so much as a dimple in this car and I'm suing your ass for damages."

"I would think you of all people would be fully insured." Beneath the car, Andy guffawed. Cindy frowned. She held a clipboard with the Notice of Seizure attached and was writing a description of the car, including the VIN,* the odometer reading, the make and model, color, accessories.

"I'm getting this car back," he said. "I'm getting it back and it had better be in the same shape you took it or by God you're gonna hear about it. I can already see where you've scratched it. I can see it right there, right there on the right bumper. That scratch wasn't there before. Jesus Christ! You're tearing apart my car!"

He turned on his heel and sprinted back to the building. Andy rose and wiped his hands on his jeans. His drivers always wore gloves to hook up a car. Not Andy.

"He's going for the gun," Andy said.

"Probably just his copy of the Code."

"I never should have come here with you," Cindy told me. We ignored her.

"If it's a gun," Andy said, "you're my human shield."

The glass door flew open and my taxpayer trotted back, carrying a legal pad.

"Oh, God," Andy whispered. "It's worse than a gun."

"I'm going to write down every ding, every scratch, every chip, and you're going to initial next to each one and then you're gonna sign that that's all there is."

"I'm not signing anything," I said.

"I'll sign it," Andy said.

"You're not signing anything," the taxpayer snapped at him.

"Mrs. Sandifer is preparing the Notice of Seizure," I said. "We've got plenty of space on it to—"

"We can always attach yours," Cindy offered. The good cop. "How's that?"

---

* Vehicle Identification Number.

"As long as it's signed."

"The notice will be signed," she said.

"Fine. That's fine."

They walked around the car. From time to time he dropped to his knees with a little cry and pointed at something in the finish. Cindy would go down beside him and squint, shaking her head, and he would run one of those dirty fingernails along the shimmering red paint. I lit a cigarette and stood next to Andy. It was getting late. Andy told me he was hungry. After they had made a third circuit around the car, I decided to put an end to it.

"Okay," I said. "We're loading her up now. Step away from the car, Mr.—"

He had filled one page of the legal-sized paper with notes. He tore off the page and handed it to Cindy. Andy threw the lever and the car jerked onto the bed of the truck. The taxpayer gave a small cry and turned away. He folded his hands across his chest and watched the thickening commuter traffic crawling along the highway. He worked the muscles in his jaw. He would not watch the car as it slowly ascended the bed, or when the bed lowered, or when Andy hopped on to secure the car for the drive back to the towing company. I signed the Notice of Seizure and Cindy signed below me.

"If you want the car back," I said as I handed him his copy, "we'll need the full amount that's listed on this form."

He took the form, crossed his arms again, and turned away.

"Do you have any questions before we go?"

He turned and spat in my face.

I followed Andy to the lot. Andy's bill would run about a hundred bucks for the tow and $8 per day for the storage. His bill would be added to the taxpayer's; the IRS never paid seizure expenses out of its own pocket. I had thought to grab the office Polaroid before I left; I wanted pictures to print on the Notice of Sale. I worked on the ad copy as I drove. *This is your chance to own a classic!* Cindy wasn't talking to me. Andy pulled around to his back lot. I parked and ran over to the truck before he could get out.

"Don't drop it outside," I said.

"What's that?"

"Don't you have a place you can put it where it won't get wet?"

"I was going to put the top up."

"The rain will dot it."

"You serious?" He rubbed his chin slowly. "Okay, I guess I could put it in the bay. But that'll cost you an extra five bucks a day."

"That's fine. Put it in the bay."

After he dropped the car, I took pictures, chortling, climbing on top of mounds of old tires to get a better angle, tripping and almost falling on a pneumatic hose someone had left across the concrete floor. Andy leaned against the wall and watched me, laughing. Cindy sat in my car, waiting.

On Monday they were sitting in the interview booth. Carol seemed relieved. She smiled often and kept patting his hand. He refused to look me in the eye. He handed me a cashier's check for the full amount due on the levy as well as the tax returns they had not filed, with another check for the total due on those. I informed him he would receive a bill for the penalty and interest he would owe on the delinquent returns. He was beaten. I had won a total victory. Still, I felt dissatisfied; I didn't want to lose that car.

"You took his baby, you know," she said.

"I know."

I could not expect all protestor cases to be resolved as easily. The vast majority of ITPs are middle- to lower-class tradesmen with little or no college education. Many are retirees exercising their constitutional right to be royal pains in the ass. Only a few are hardcore, paramilitary, separatist types bent on the destruction of the government. Like the insurance salesman and the dentist, most protestors are merely gullible saps who have fallen on hard times and are conned by unscrupulous promoters into parting with money they don't have for a "product" that doesn't work. Consequently, when the case came to me, there were few assets to seize and what I could seize had minimal value. The goal, however, was never full payment of the tax. The goal was compliance. The goal was changing a protestor's heart and mind. Like the early missionaries plunging into the darkest corners of Africa, I was charged not so much with collection as with conversion. It was not enough for them to obey Big Brother. They must love him.

.   .   .

I found the ad in the classified section of the Sunday newspaper. In two weeks, a "convention" of "freedom-loving Americans" would meet at the Lakeside Civic Center for a day of rallies, speeches, and dissemination of "patriotic" literature. The event was sponsored by something called The Pilot Connection, a national organization based in California and a known protestor group. "Learn your rights! Discover what the IRS doesn't want you to know!" There was no admission charge, but donations were welcome and appreciated.

I showed the ad to Gina.

"So what?" Dark circles ringed her eyes. Rumors were flying that blood was in the water and Bryon White was circling for the kill. On those days when she came to the office, Gina huddled for hours with her secretary, Bonny. Some days Bonny would emerge in tears, but she never told us what was said behind the closed door. Whatever Gina was plotting, Bonny would not divulge. She was the keeper of her boss's secrets.

"I want to go."

"For what purpose?"

"The first rule of war is to know your—"

"Oh, cease and desist with that nonsense, Rick. You're trying to wear Culpepper's clothes and it's an ill fit. You want me to authorize you to rub elbows with these nuts at the government's expense? What's your plan, anyway? Are you going to set up a booth, participate in a debate, hand out tracts like a Jehovah's Witness?"

"I was thinking incognito."

She laughed harshly. She reminded me of one of the witches from *Macbeth*. "Oh, a covert op. Let me guess, you're going to write down tag numbers and take lots of clandestine shots."

"Getting some tag numbers did occur to me. But I was thinking I might get some leads on any new schemes they may be promoting."

"You've been working protestors for a couple of months now—what if you're recognized by one of your 'clients'? No, *recognized* isn't the term. 'Made.' What if somebody 'makes' you? Are you going to wear a disguise? I have an old pair of Groucho glasses, if you want to borrow them."

"I guess you're not going to authorize this."

"You guessed right. We don't do undercover work. Write a memo to Howard in CI."

"He never responds to my memos. I think he's filing them in the round filing cabinet."*

"You know why he doesn't respond, Rick? He doesn't respond because the IRS has the highest rate of compliance in the entire world, higher even than those countries that throw their deadbeats into prison. Ninety percent of those required to pay taxes do pay their taxes. Protestors, in particular, the bottom-feeders you're chasing, make up only a tiny fraction of the remaining ten percent who don't."

"In other words, I'm wasting my time."

"*Your* time?"

"Okay. The government's time. Thanks for setting me straight, Gina. I would hate to labor under the false impression that what I was doing had any significance."

"Rick, Rick, now don't go stomping out of here with that scrunched-up little troll-face. Don't you hate those little trolls with the primary-colored hair? Sit down. I want to tell you something... there's something I've notice about you, something I've known since you came here, and that is you tend to view this job as some sort of drama, some kind of great conflict that you're the center of and well, that just isn't the case. I don't know everything about your personal life and frankly I don't want to know everything about your personal life, only I'm a little jealous because you happen to *have* a personal life. I'm rambling, but my point is, don't get so full of yourself that you lose all perspective. The Service is... well, it sure as hell isn't the universe. And me and you and everybody else here aren't engaged in some kind of titanic struggle between good and evil." She looked away. Her window had a nice view of the little plaza a stone's throw from the federal building, but she usually kept her blinds drawn. In a gentler tone, she said, "I never thanked you for inviting me to help you with that show you wrote. It was fun. I had a really good time." She turned back to me. "When is this rally?"

---

* A trash can.

"Next Saturday."

"Saturday? This is still America, Rick. Do whatever you want."

I wore the same flannel shirt I had worn to the open house. Blue jeans. A Chicago Cubs baseball cap. My new Ray-Bans. A pair of old boots from the back of the closet. I looked the part of a good ol' boy, except for the Ray-Bans. It would have been smarter to leave my contacts at home, but vanity forbade.

"I still don't see the point of this," Pam told me that morning.

"You know, it would make for a better cover if you came along."

"You were supposed to take me shopping this weekend."

A local department store had recently sent me a charge card with an astounding $5,000 credit line, more money than I had grossed in 1986. Pam wanted to replace the living-room furniture.

"We'll do it next weekend," I said.

"I'm going to New York next weekend."

"Oh, that's right."

"You never listen to me."

"What's that?"

"Very funny. Don't you think you're taking this Elliot Ness act a bit too far?"

"Elliot Ness didn't work for the IRS."

"I saw the movie. He worked for the Treasury."

"So does the Secret Service and Customs."

"Really, Rick, you're starting to freak me a little."

"You're going to New York for your job and I'm not freaking."

"I'm not going to spy on people."

"I can't help it if my job is interesting and yours isn't."

"Your job is weird and it's made you weird."

"Does this cap make my head look too small? I have a very pinched face; it's not a good hat-face."

She walked out of the room. Screw her. Since I had come home to myself—to the revenue officer inside me—we had barely spoken. She had begun staying over in Orlando two or three nights a week because, she said, she hated the forty-minute commute from her house in Clearview. Whatever.

By ten o'clock that Saturday morning, I was sitting on the steps leading to the main auditorium and convention floor of the Lakeside Civic Center, smoking a cigarette and sipping lukewarm coffee from a Styrofoam cup, bored out of my mind. I had recorded some tag numbers and some copy from several interesting bumper stickers (HITLER BELIEVED IN GUN CONTROL TOO; GET UNTAXED 800 555-6767; DOWN WITH THE TAX OPPRESSORS!). I had wandered the main floor, where booths had been set up with tables loaded with pamphlets, survivalist training manuals, flyers, and innumerable petitions for sale and on display. The middle portion of the room was devoted to firearms. I entered the auditorium and sat with about fifty other people while a rotund bald man lectured that the income tax system was completely voluntary and therefore you could voluntarily leave the system and there was nothing the IRS could do about it. I started taking notes, then gave up. I had heard the same tripe a dozen times before from my taxpayers. He displayed a dollar bill on an overhead projector and proceeded to explain that all currency in the United States was printed with a built-in tracking system. The government could track down any citizen it wished using this system. I wrote in my notebook, *But how does the govt know who's carrying any particular bill?* I toyed with the idea of raising my hand and asking him, just to fuck with him, but thought better of it. He went on. There was a hidden code in our currency. Our money was worthless since the United States abandoned the gold standard and therefore the paper money could not be considered legal tender for payment of taxes. Only income is taxed and your paycheck is not income; it is barter (he spelled the word out: "b-a-r-t-e-r"), an even exchange of goods (money) for services (labor). The Internal Revenue Code, which is the IRS Bible, after all, says only people living in Puerto Rico, the Virgin Islands, and the District of Columbia are subject to the income tax. For each claim, he cited a reference from the IRC. He sounded very sure of himself. Again, I was tempted to raise my hand and tell him it all sounded great, but if everybody did this, wouldn't our government collapse, our armed forces disperse for lack of pay, and the United States become a province of Canada? Again, I restrained myself. Now, on the overhead was his ten-step plan guaranteed to remove anyone who wished from the tax system or, as he put it, "remove you from the IRS's master file." He bragged that he had not paid taxes in ten years and there was nothing the IRS could do about it. I circled his name on my program and wrote in the margin, *Pull him on S***D.* Check with Howard.* Odds were CI and the Department of Justice already had a case on this guy. I left the auditorium before he got to the important part, the cost of his "master file plan," with a slight headache and the desire to smash somebody into a wall. I considered some of his arguments near treasonous but, after listening to the same dreck for months, I was numb.

I stopped by a display on the convention floor on my way out. I picked up a book entitled *The IRS: The Greatest Lie Ever Told.* The fellow manning the booth came over and said, "That's a great one. Real eye-opener."

"Pithy title."

"Seventeen-fifty."

"If I give you my money, the government might mistake you for me and ship you off to the gulag."

"Huh?"

"You have *Civil Disobedience*?"

"That a book or a tape?"

"It's an essay, actually, a very famous essay by Henry David Thoreau."

"Never heard of him."

"He's sort of the founding father of tax protestors."

He said nothing, but his eyes narrowed. Protestors did not call themselves protestors. They were patriots. Sovereigns. Nonpersons. But never protestors. My pulse quickened. If I had $17.50, I would have bought the book, to allay his suspicion. But I didn't have $17.50, so I made a hasty retreat. On the steps, I sipped my coffee and smoked my cigarette and wondered why I was planning to buy $5,000 worth of furniture for a house that wasn't mine, for a woman I wasn't sure I loved anymore, if I ever had, to incur a debt with nothing to show for it when I moved out and left the furniture for her and her new lover to enjoy. Did she have a lover in Orlando? Did it matter?

People were wandering around the plaza. The fountain had been turned off for the winter. Children played on the concrete steps, running up and

---

* IDRS command code that cross-references names to Social Security numbers.

down, screaming in that hysterical way of children who are on just this side of boredom. I could follow her to work. Or show up unannounced at this coworker's apartment she claimed to be sleeping in. Occasionally I would answer the phone and the person on the other end would hang up. What if she had taken another lover? Should I feel betrayed or relieved?

A large man sat down beside me. He asked me if I had an extra cigarette. I shook one out of the pack for him. He asked if I had a light. I handed him my lighter. He lit the cigarette, handed back the lighter, and leaned back, inhaling deeply, resting his huge forearms on the step behind him.

"So what do you think, brother?" he asked.

"Real eye-opener."

"Your first time at one of these?"

I nodded. He said, "How'd you find out about it?"

"Saw the ad in the paper."

"Is it on your back?"

I assumed he was either talking about the government in general or taxes in particular.

I nodded again. "It sure is."

"Not an easy burden, brother."

"No. No, it isn't."

"How long?"

"Almost two years."

"Oh, man, that ain't nothin'. They been coming after my ass for twenty." He offered me one of his enormous paws. "Mac Brewster."

"Henry. Henry Thoreau."

"Nice to meet you, Henry. So what do you do?"

"I'm a carpenter."

"You don't say. I'm a drywaller. Work for anyone?"

"Just myself."

"See, that's what the fucking IRS doesn't understand. They beat the shit out of us, backbone of the fucking economy. Don't get me wrong, I don't buy all the shit they're selling in there. I just want to keep what's mine. What I earned with my own sweat and blood and fucking tears, you know what I mean, Henry?"

I nodded emphatically. "I do know what you mean, Mac. I love my work."

"Damn straight."

"You know why I love my work, Mac? Because I take a few pieces of wood and some tools and at the end of the day I have something to show for it. A table. A chair. A nightstand. Something you can touch, something you can appreciate, use, maybe something even beautiful."

"Amen to that, brother."

"Damn straight," I said.

I am a carpenter, and I build ships of paper to sail on seas of red, amid currents of black and green. My tools are pen, paper, envelopes, padlocks, chains, and a ferocious will. I navigate by instinct and the inescapable logic of brute force. Days become weeks, weeks become months, winter gives way to spring, and I sail on through heavy fog, far from friendly shores, gathering sailor's tales from the unforgiving sea, of husbands deceiving wives, wives deceiving husbands, both deceiving themselves; of secret bank accounts in dead men's names; of houses deeded to two-year-olds, to phony corporations, to the family dog; of millions of dollars lost in refunds when accounts are paid with worthless money-orders drawn on fictitious bank accounts; of a man clever enough to hide all his assets but not so clever that he remembers to hide the flowerpots containing marijuana in his backyard; of hands gnarled and callused from thirty years of hard labor, the skin on the knuckles cracked and dry, pounding on a table or as a fist shaking in the air; of tattered copies of court cases, highlighted, underlined, cross-referenced, annotated; of dog-eared paperback volumes of the IRC, tabbed, indexed, notes scrawled in the margins, punctuated by ??? and !!!; of rural fortresses, mobile homes, and shotgun shacks and "cracker" houses on concrete blocks sinking slowly into the wet Florida soil, surrounded by barbed wire and padlocked gates, guarded by Dobermans and German shepherds and pit bulls, and the hand-painted signs tacked to trees, to fence posts, to screen doors, POSTED NO TRESPASSING: THIS PROPERTY PROTECTED BY SMITH & WESSON, KEEP OUT! TRESPASSERS WILL BE SHOT!; of the fear that lurks behind the veil of rage and righteous indignation, fear of losing their possessions, and the greatest fear of all, the fear of being wrong; of the lunacy borne of poverty and despair and greed, but most of all of greed, that no Amendments after the Tenth are valid, including those following the Civil War, that the Service is a private corporation incorporated in Delaware, that there is no moral obligation to pay taxes to fund war or welfare queens or abortion, never mind that morality and taxes have nothing to do with each other, that the IRS is part of a twelve-nation Zionist conspiracy to control the world, that "income" is a legal fiction and has no real meaning; that a true follower of Jesus does not pay taxes, since he paid no taxes, though he did say, "Render unto Caesar"; of pulling into a driveway escorted by two police cruisers and hanging back while the cops went inside to ask if there were any weapons in the house and hearing, "Put down that knife!"; of anonymous phones calls and letters that begin "Dear Criminal!"; of my home state of Florida having the honor of being the protestor capital of the world; of death threats and stalking and hang-ups and headlights appearing from nowhere on lonely country roads at dusk; of filing phony liens against yourself and doctored court papers indicating you're exempt from income tax; of screaming toddlers on hips and the stale smell of urine and cars on cinder blocks rusting in the moist air and obscenities shouted through locked doors, over phone lines, scrawled in letters; of whole families bound together by the faith that they alone have access to the truth and they, behind their barbed-wire fences and padlocked gates, are liberated; of ill-used roads and tiny ponds and drainage ditches filled with slime-encrusted water and the sad loping gait of underfed cats; of the construction worker, the fireman, the cop, the barber, the retiree, the carpet-layer, the divorcee, the car salesman, the TV repairman, the landscaper, the architect, the evangelist, the wedding planner, the Amway salesman, the night watchman, the Wal-Mart clerk, the professional gambler, the broker, the antique dealer, the Laundromat owner, the dishwasher, the telephone repairman, the mechanic, the real estate salesman: true believers and conmen, desperadoes and fools, ludicrous, pitiful, maddening, duplicitous, sincere, predictable, surprising: humanity.

o   o   o

I checked my watch. 5:42. The stars were fading and the eastern horizon had begun to glow a fiery red. Beth sat beside me in the car, wincing and shifting in the tiny bucket seat, trying to get comfortable. Her makeup appeared to have been hastily applied and her hair was pulled back from her face. We both sipped coffee from twenty-ounce Styrofoam cups. I had parked on the shoulder of the two-lane road, about a hundred yards from the small house. We could see the black Camaro, which we called a "white-trash Cadillac," parked in the driveway. The tag matched the DMV report; I had the right house.

"Don't tell me," Beth said. "The car isn't his."

"It's registered to his girlfriend. This is her address, too."

"Put the house in her name?"

"It's a rental."

"Shame about the car. Those things sell great around here. Camaros, Trans-ams, pickup trucks. Is she the nominee?"* She was referring to the car.

"She bought it way before the tax was assessed."

She nodded, sipped her coffee. I asked her if she minded, holding up a cigarette. She shook her head; she didn't mind. I rolled down my window and lit up.

"You know," she said, "I live around here."

"I didn't know that."

"A couple of miles that way. And my ex lives a couple of miles the other way."

"So this guy lives in the middle."

She laughed. "I guess."

"He's been driving me nuts. There's nothing to latch onto. Soon as my levy hits he quits and finds another job."

"You've followed him before?"

"No. Just worked off leads from his former employers."

"Girlfriend?"

"Can't go near her."

"How come?"

"He's been arrested twice for domestic assault."

"But she dropped the charges."

I nodded. "True love has no boundaries."

"What makes you think he's going to work this morning?"

---

* Legal term for someone who holds an asset "in name only."

I shrugged. "It's near the end of the month, bills are coming due."

Abruptly, she said, "I'm hungry. Is Pam still on that Jenny Craig thing?"

"She dropped that. Now she's on the cabbage diet."

"What's the cabbage diet?"

"You eat cabbage every day. Cabbage soup, raw cabbage, cabbage sandwiches."

"Cabbage sandwiches?"

"I'm kidding about the cabbage sandwiches."

"I've never heard of the cabbage diet."

"Neither had I."

"Does it work?"

"No idea."

"How was her trip to New York?"

I flicked my cigarette into the drainage ditch. "She did the usual tourist thing. Tavern On The Green, Empire State Building, Statue of Liberty, Radio City Music Hall, Macy's. She loved Macy's, and Saks. She brought me a souvenir." I showed her my new key ring: a picture of the Manhattan skyline encased in plastic.

"Wow. That must have cost her a buck fifty at the airport."

"It's the thought that counts."

"You should have gone with her."

"I wasn't invited. It was a business trip."

"What is her business exactly?"

"She chaperones the characters from the park around. Sort of like their handler."

"Fascinating work."

"If you can get it."

The front door of the little house flew open and a tall, skinny girl with an explosion of dyed-blond hair jumped over the two concrete steps and trotted toward the car. She was wearing a black leather jacket, blue jeans, and black boots. She walked with her arms folded over her chest, her head down; we couldn't see her face.

"The girl exits the house," I said. "She seems in a hurry, or upset, or both."

The door flew open again, and he bounded down the steps after her. He was wearing a white T-shirt, blue jeans, cowboy boots, a greasy baseball cap pulled low over his forehead, his shoulder-length hair bouncing as he walked.

"She is followed closely by the boy. She keeps her back to him and huddles by the passenger side of the car."

Beth asked, "What are you doing?"

"He goes to her. He is clearly upset. He jabs a finger in her face. 'Doncha ever run out on me agin, woman, y'understand?' She raises her head. For a moment she is tempted to grab the finger shaking in her face and bite it off, down to the knuckle. 'I'll run out when I want, Ronnie. Watcha gonna do about it?'"

"Stop it," Beth said, but she was laughing.

"He takes her by the shoulders. 'You do it agin and I'll rough you up, worse'n last time. You remember last time, Rondine.'"

"Rondine?"

"'Git your stinkin' hands offa me, you brute!'"

"'Doncha call me a brute! I'll show you brute!' He goes to his side of the car. Drops his keys. Curses. 'Look what you made me do, bitch!' He gets in, but she hesitates. Now is her chance! Make a break for it, Rondine! You can do better! He's a loser! Go!"

"Run," Beth murmured. "Run, Rondine."

I started the car. "But at last she decides, 'What the hell, he bought me this Harley jacket, he's cute, and I do love him. Oh, I do love him so.'"

The Camaro's rear wheels spun in the muddy ground, throwing divots five feet into the air as Ronnie whipped the car onto the road. I pulled behind him and quickly we were matching his speed of sixty miles per hour.

"Ronnie's in a hurry," Beth said. "Your car sounds like it's about to disintegrate."

"Are you kidding? I've had this baby up to sixty-five before."

We could see their heads through the rear window of the Camaro. The fight appeared to be escalating. He looked more toward her than the road, and the car was swerving over the center line, then careening toward the right shoulder, coming dangerously close to the drainage ditch. She began to punch him in the right shoulder, her stringy blond hair whipping back and forth, and he was trying to catch her fist as it came toward him.

"This is getting bad," Beth said.

"The dumb-ass is going to run up a light pole."

"Oh, my God!"

The passenger door had come open. Now Ronnie was punching her in the left arm, alternating his fist with the flat of his hand; he was trying to shove her out the open door. She had opened it, of course, but apparently had changed her mind about bailing, so Ronnie decided to facilitate her original desire. My speedometer inched toward sixty-five.

"Rick, you've got to back off. If she comes out of that car—"

The Camero was now whipping back and forth as Ronnie employed physics to hurl his lover from the car. Beth screamed at me to slow down as the girl's body fell out of the car, hit the right shoulder of the road, and rolled into the drainage ditch, coming to rest facedown in the four inches of standing water.

Ronnie kept going.

So did I.

o   o   o

I kicked open the bull-pen door; it crashed against the opposite wall. Caroline rose from her desk. Allison and Bonny appeared in the doorway of the secretary's office. Henry looked up from the IDRS desk. Beth was close on my heels.

"She could have died, Rick!"

I flung the case file onto my desk and sat down, my back to her. Beth stood in the middle of the room and shouted at me.

"What the hell is the matter with you?"

"What happened?" Allison demanded. "What did Rick do?"

"I didn't do anything."

"That's my point!" Beth shouted.

"Who died?" Caroline asked.

"Nobody died, for Christ sakes!"

"How do you know that, Rick?" Beth asked. "How the hell would you know what happened to her?"

"We couldn't stop."

"Did Rick hit someone with his car?" Caroline asked.

"And why couldn't we?" Beth asked.

I swung my chair around to face her.

"Because it's disclosure."

"Oh, that's bullshit. If you were so worried about disclosure, why didn't you stop at a pay phone? Why didn't you make an anonymous call to the police?"

"He's a protestor, Beth."

"So what?"

"So he knows the rules! He would use disclosure to get me fired!"

"You didn't stop because you thought you might be fired?"

"No, goddamnit!" I was on my feet now, shaking with rage. I jabbed my finger toward her nose. "I didn't stop because stopping is against the law!"

She took a deep breath, then laughed. "You're incredible, you know that? You are absolutely—"

"I saw her in the rearview mirror, Beth. I saw her get up."

"I didn't see her get up."

"Well, I did."

"Damn it, Rick, the point isn't whether or not she got up!"

"Then what is the point? Regardless, this would have happened, Beth. Regardless! Think about that. And the next time it happens, the next time he beats the shit out of her, where will we be? Where will *you* be?" I whirled on our audience, pointing at each of them in turn. "Or you? Or you? Or you? Or you?" I turned back to Beth. Tears were running down her cheeks. And her tears only intensified my rage. "You think any of us can do anything to stop it, this, this, this *shit*?"

"He's lost it," Henry said.

"Dear God, for two fucking years I've had to wallow in it. For two fucking years I've been turning over rocks and wallowing in the nasty shit that lives underneath them, and there is nothing I can do about it! That's my point, Beth. We can't stop Ronnie if he wants to kill her; we can't stop any of it because we're not in it for that. We're not in for *that*." I waved my hand at the window beside Caroline's desk. I grabbed a levy form from my desk and held it high. "This is what I'm in for! This is it! This is why I'm here! I'm here for this, not to pull some cheap piece of trailer trash from a drainage ditch. Whatever happens to that girl has nothing to do with me. Nothing to do with me and nothing to do with you and nothing to do with any of us, and it sure as hell has nothing to do with taxes!"

"Oh, my," Caroline whispered.

"You're right, Rick," Beth said quietly. "It doesn't have anything at all to do with taxes."

I drove home in a hard rain. My wiper blades were shot, smearing the dirt over the windshield, and between the water and the earth, I could not see.

Don't you ever wash this bucket, Yancey?

I'm afraid to.

How come?

The dirt's the only thing holding it together.

The traffic on Highway 92 was light, and I shifted into fifth gear and stamped my foot on the gas pedal. Sixty. Sixty-five. Sixty-eight. Racing eastward to an empty house. The shock of lightning directly overhead, raindrops hurling shadows. Seventy. Seventy-four. Let some deputy dog pull me over. I'll get out of the car with a tire iron. She had rolled limp as a rag doll into the ditch, her body bouncing on the rocky shoulder. I saw her push herself up; I know I saw it. I could remember the water flying from the ends of her stringy blond hair as she shook her head back and forth. Eighty-two. The front tire was vibrating violently now. Before me, the flat bellies of the anvil-shaped clouds roiled, tortured shapes in the flickering explosions deep within. Thunderheads had always reminded me of great ships, with masts soaring hundreds of feet into the sky. As a child, I wondered what made them pause at a particular place and time to unleash their fury. My face was wet.

Ronnie had driven on to work. I got the name from the construction company he was working for from one of the trucks parked at the site. That wasn't the point, though, according to Beth, who was a seasoned acolyte of Byzantium. She should know better.

The point was Ronnie went to work. And so did I.

VENGEANCE

Toby dropped the note on my desk on his way out the door. It was written on a single sheet of typing paper, folded into eighths, addressed to me and marked CONFIDENTIAL, in Toby's neat handwriting. The bull pen was empty, but I took a furtive peek around the room anyway. I unfolded the note and read: "Meet me outside on the dock in two minutes." I opened the desk drawer containing the day's shredding and dropped the note inside. Almost four minutes had passed; I was already late.

"What are you doing tonight?" he asked me, inscrutable behind his dark glasses. A stiff breeze from the south ruffled his pants legs, folds of material moving laterally pushed by the wind, breaking on his inseam like waves.

"You asking me on a date?"

"No bullshit. This is official Union business. Are you free tonight for a meeting?"

"Sure, I guess. What's it about?"

"You know what it's about."

I didn't reply. Of course I knew.

"Everybody's gonna be there," he said.

"Even Allison?"

" 'Specially Allison. Yes or no, Rick."

"I'll be there."

He nodded. There was something about me that made Toby uncomfortable. I had sensed it the first day, when he had pointed at the ceiling and held up the sign that read THEY'RE LISTENING.

"Six o'clock, Bennigan's on South Florida. You know where I mean?"

"Sure."

"Six o'clock. Don't forget."

The conversation was over, but neither of us moved.

"I'm gonna go in first," he said. "You stay out here and have a smoke in the alley, or whatever you do out here in the alley. Don't come in right behind me."

I nodded. I, too, had slipped on my dark glasses. It was a conversation suited for dark glasses. Bennigan's was a pub styled as a restaurant or a restaurant styled as a pub, depending on the tastes of the patron, dark-paneled, smoke-filled, and intimate. In other words, the perfect place to plot an assassination.

"She gotta go," Henry said.

We were sitting at a large round table in the back of the restaurant, the entire Lakeside group, with the exception of Bonny and, of course, Gina. Bonny, Toby felt, could not be trusted, though she was a dues-paying member. Bonny's most admirable quality, loyalty, disqualified her, in Toby's eyes, as a member of our conspiracy.

"We all gotta remember one thing," Toby rumbled. "What we're doing here is unprecedented in the history of the Service. No revenue officer group has ever presented an ultimatum to upper management."

"Which is why ours has to be perfect," Beth said.

"Not only perfect," Toby said. "But we all gotta speak with one voice. So I gotta know, right now, who's in and who's out. If you got any reservations at all, better speak 'em now or forever hold your peace."

"It's pointless if just one person drops out," Beth said. "We can't go forward with just three or four names. 'No one else in the group's complained,' they'll say. They'll blow it off."

Toby nodded. Caroline said, "They'll blow what off?"

"Our grievance," Toby said. As Union steward, Toby was proposing a formal allegation of contract violations that warranted immediate action on the part of management. The grievance would also contain a suggested remedy. In this case, the remedy was extreme and, as Toby said, unprecedented.

"I thought we were just going to sit down with Bob and Byron," Caroline said.

"Sit down and what? Curl at their feet and beg for a bone? We tried all that. Me. Beth. Culpepper, when he was here. It never does any good. They nod and say, 'We'll look into it,' and Byron White stomps around head-quarters poundin' on the walls and swearing he's gonna have her head, but what changes? Huh? What ever changes around here?"

"I just want to understand what we're asking for," Cindy said. "We're asking them to fire her?"

"That's going too far," Beth said. "We're asking them to remove her as our manager."

"If we asked them to fire her, they'd tell us to take a short walk off a long pier," Henry said.

Beth sighed. "That's a long walk off a short pier, Henry."

"But back to Beth's point," Allison said. Her voice was shrill, an indica-tion that she was agitated. "I don't think we should say anything else until we've all committed to this."

"She's right," Henry said. "Maybe we all should sign something, like a pledge."

"Maybe we should all prick our fingers and make a pinky swear," Dee said.

"I ain't prickin' nothin'," Henry said.

"We'll all be signing the grievance," Toby said.

Allison shook her head violently. "No. No, tonight we're deciding if there's even going to be a grievance. As Beth said, if we're not all in, then we're all out." She looked in my direction. I was tracing the tip of my fin-ger in the water sweated from my glass of beer. "Let's start with Rick."

"I want to hear what everyone else has to say."

"Of course you do," she sneered. "Gina's pet."

"Rick ain't nobody's pet," Toby said.

"Everybody knows. Gina's not keeping it a secret. I heard she was going around Orlando, telling everybody at branch headquarters what a terrific RO Rick is. Bringing it up at branch meetings."

"Well, at least it's clear how Allison will vote," I said. Two weeks before, Allison, Caroline, Dee, and I had submitted our applications for the next promotion, the sole Grade 11 that would be rewarded sometime in the spring. Although, officially, Gina was not the selecting official, a group manager's opinion carried enormous weight with the branch chief. Never had a branch chief ignored a manager's wishes regarding a promotion. Allison saw her only hope of defeating me in the ouster of Gina Tate as our group manager. Perhaps a new manager would favor her instead.

"Lay off Rick," Dee said. "He can't help it that he's better at it than you are, Allison."

Allison was flabbergasted. "He's no better than me."

"I wasn't speaking about being a revenue officer," Dee said. Cindy and Beth laughed. Toby frowned.

"We're getting offtrack here. We'll come back to Rick. Allison, I guess you're in."

"I'm in."

Beth said, "I'm in."

"This is fun," Dee said. "It's so devious and . . . Machiavellian. I'm in."

"I guess I'm in," Cindy said, and finished her piña colada in a single swallow.

"You bet your ass I'm in," Henry said. "I'm sick to death of her shit."

"Goes without sayin' where I stand," Toby said.

It was down to Caroline and me. Caroline was clearly struggling; she had a military background and this was foreign to her. It felt like mutiny. Finally, with tears in her eyes, but with a steady voice, she said, "I'm in."

It was my turn. I looked at Beth. I had guessed that Beth wanted Gina's job. I wondered if she has acting on behalf of Byron White. Tonight or tomorrow morning, would she be on a pay phone to White, reporting on the progress of our conspiracy? Was White, unable to remove Gina on any procedural or ethical grounds, using the Union to place her head in his saddlebag? I wondered if Toby knew he was being used, and whether he would even care. I decided he probably wouldn't care. He detested Gina, as did Henry. Together, they accounted for 80 percent of Gina's withering remarks, her cruel jokes, her gleeful degradations. I remembered the day she forced Toby to read the manual section on summons enforcement. Her flippant and insensitive, to say the least, reference to Henry as "Buckwheat." Dee probably didn't care who her manager was; she had her own, all-consuming issues to deal with. Caroline was terrified of Gina, but not to the point of blind loyalty. She would follow the lead of the rest of us. Everything came down to manipulation. It seemed possible to me that White was manipulating Beth by subtly implying the job was hers, if only Gina could be removed. Beth could be manipulating Toby by allowing him to think the Union was wielding the power. She could also be manipulating Allison by allowing her to think she had a shot at the promotion if Beth became the manager. Allison probably pushed Caroline and Dee toward the coup with the argument that under Gina they had no chance of being promoted. I could almost hear her say it: "If Gina goes, I have no idea who'll get the next promotion. But if she stays, I *guarantee* you it will be Rick."

And I—how did I feel about assassinating Gina? Wasn't it professional suicide to attack her now? Beth and Allison were close. If Gina fell, there was a real chance Beth would give the promotion to Allison and I would spend months, perhaps years, in Grade 9 purgatory. Even Henry—Henry! was a Grade 11.

A grievance can take months. Some have even dragged on for years. If management slammed Gina, she could fight; she could file appeals that might take years to resolve—plenty of time for her to decide the next promotion. But if she didn't fight, if she simply resigned or returned to the field, what then? What chance did I have if I backed out now that everyone had voted yes? Would Beth—or even Cindy, if she became the new manager—reward my disloyalty to the group by promoting me? As this struck me, I looked at Beth with new admiration. Even William Culpepper could not have orchestrated it better. There was only one answer I could give. Beth was already smiling. She knew. She knew what I was thinking! She nodded at me. She had been counting on me to see that this was no choice between "in" or "out." The choice had already been made for me.

I said, "I'm in."

Toby passed out our assignments. He and Beth would write the formal grievance to present to Bob Campbell and represent the group at the hearing. Allison and Dee would compile the individual recollections of Gina's excesses: her personal jibes in the workplace, her harassment, her preferential treatment, her cozy relationships with powers-of-attorney and other third-parties, her tactics of intimidation, called "fostering a hostile work environment" in the contract. I would proof the final document for any factual or grammatical errors. Henry, Caroline, and Cindy were not given assignments beyond making notes of Gina's verbal assaults upon them personally.

"We have to move fast," Toby said. "The longer this takes, the greater the chance of leaks."

"Speakin' of leaks," Henry said, and left the table.

"I'm worried about Henry," Allison said.

"Why?" Caroline asked. "Is he sick?"

"I'll take care of Henry," Toby answered.

"Okay," Allison said. "And I'll keep my eye on Rick."

"Rick's okay," Beth said. "Rick is going to be just fine."

When I arrived home, my head was still a little foggy from the beer. I did not hold my liquor well. Once safely there, however, I decided to have another drink. I made a gin and tonic and sipped it while I smoked on the porch. The backyard sloped a hundred feet to the shore of the small lake, and I watched the moonlight dance on the black water. A bird called from the rushes. A lone frog harrumphed. *I never thanked you for inviting me to help you with that show you wrote. It was fun. I had a really good time.* Once, during one of the latter rehearsals, I looked up from my seat in the front row and saw her standing stage right, her hands crossed primly in front of her, staring at me from the shadows. *You know she has a crush on you.* In the beginning, she counseled me to have a life outside the IRS, but she did not seem to have one. Even her boyfriend was in the Service. *I always wanted to own a bookstore! Just a little, hole-in-the-wall bookstore, and I would buy all these out-of-print books, all these obscure titles you couldn't find anywhere else, and people would come from all over the world, because they would know if they couldn't find a book at my store then it didn't exist!* She was expendable now. She had failed to help Beth advance into management. She had alienated Toby and, by alienating him, alienated the Union. By making it clear that she intended to promote me, she had turned Caroline, Dee, and Allison against her. And, ironically, her favoring me gave me no choice but to join the others.

Within the Service, the ultimate sin is vulnerability and only strength inspires loyalty. Gina was vulnerable because upper management had turned on her. There was no way she could survive with Byron White *and* the group against her. Revenue officers are like sharks, and when there is blood in the water we are merciless.

My drink was gone. I crunched the remaining ice. I did not believe the rumor that she was looking for a job outside the Service. Gina would never leave the Service. *It's the golden handcuffs, Rick! If you had any sense at all, you'll get out while you can!*

"It's too late, Gina," I said aloud. "It's too late."

"What's too late?"

I yelped, jerking forward and spilling the ice into my lap.

"What are you doing out here at eleven o'clock at night talking to yourself?" Pam asked.

"You scared the shit out of me," I fussed at her, brushing the ice from my pants. "I thought you were staying in Orlando tonight."

"I changed my mind."

"Checking up on me?"

"Hardly."

"Boyfriend has other plans?"

She stared toward the lake and didn't answer.

"We're taking out Gina."

She laughed. "You IRS types kill me. Talking like some B-grade gangster movie. I thought you liked Gina."

"I do like Gina."

"So why do you want her fired?"

"It's complicated."

"Too complicated for simple ol' me."

"Maybe not complicated. Just a long story."

"And telling me is not worth your time."

"Oh, I get it now. You drove forty miles just to pick a fight with me."

"Don't flatter yourself. The most I would drive to pick a fight with you is five, ten miles tops. Why are you drinking, anyway? You never drink."

"That shows how little you know me, Pam. Every night I pass out in a drunken stupor."

"Tell me, seriously, what did Gina ever do to you? Wait. Let me guess. 'It isn't personal; it's just business.'"

"You know, I can't tell you how much I've enjoyed this. Three years of you mocking and ridiculing and sneering at what I do."

"What do you expect, Rick? Really. I'm supposed to be proud of you? I'm supposed to brag on you and tell you what a wonderful person you are since you became a tax collector? I hate that place. And I hate what that place has done to you. And I hate you for working there, for totally disregarding my feelings about you working there, for totally disregarding *any* of my feelings, for totally disregarding *me*. I've been thinking a lot about this lately, and I think maybe—maybe it would be best if you moved out of the house."

" 'My house.' You almost said it, 'my house.' "

"That's right, asshole. My house. I want you out of *my* house. I'm sick of you and I want you out."

"Well," I said. "At least now I know why you came home."

"And get it all in one trip, Rick, because anything you leave behind I'm throwing in the goddamned lake."

I moved into an unfurnished apartment on the north side of Lakeside. I bought a bed and frame from Sears, a coffee machine and AM/FM alarm clock radio from Service Merchandise, linens and cookware and cleaning supplies and a television from Wal-Mart. I was broke, maxed out on my credit cards, and, looking around the empty rooms of the apartment, had precious little to show for it. I didn't even have a kitchen table and chairs. I bought a set of TV trays and ate my meals sitting at the foot of the bed, three feet from the new television.

A week after I moved, Caroline and I were alone in the bullpen. I was doodling on a history sheet and punching numbers into the calculator. One leather sofa with matching leather chairs, $2,670. One coffee table, $415. One end table with lamp, $75. Rent for twenty-four months at $365 per month, $8,760. One designer hand-crafted diamond-and-pearl engagement ring, $525. Total cost, excluding miscellaneous expenses, $12,445.00.

Caroline was arguing on the phone with a taxpayer. The name was familiar; she had been baby-sitting this case for months.

"I can't do anything for you if you don't make your tax deposits...we have very strict guidelines . . . you can't stop at one lender . . . have you tried factoring your receivables?"*

There was something I was forgetting. I chewed on the end of my pen and tried to concentrate. Caroline's voice assumed a whiney quality when speaking to taxpayers, as if she were trying to annoy them into paying. Pam was the beneficiary on my life insurance policy, with a face value of $54,000. There was a dismemberment clause; around $35,000 if, say, a taxpayer poked out my eyeball. Then there were the EE Savings Bonds deducted from my paycheck, to which she was also the beneficiary. Two $50 bonds every month for twenty-four months, $2,400. Grand total thus far, $68,845, not counting the miscellaneous expenses. I wrote a note to Bonny to pull the forms I would need to remove Pam as my beneficiary of these various assets.

"Well, how much more time do you think you need?" Caroline asked.

She sounded resigned. That's what slays us: resignation, weariness, inertia, the black despair of monotony. I threw down my pen and went to her desk. She cast her eyes in my direction and gave a little helpless shrug. If I had had a heavy object, I would have smacked her on top of the head with it. She finished the call and said, "Sorry," as if she were interrupting me.

"It's the nurseryman, isn't it?"

"He does landscaping, too."

"What's the deal with him, Caroline?"

"Well, I can't get him current."

"It isn't your job to get him current, Caroline. Where's the financial?"

She opened the case file and handed the form to me. She did not hesitate. She seemed relieved.

"There's equity here."

"Not enough. For the bank, I mean."

"We're not a bank and you're not a loan officer." I handed the form back to her. "You're a revenue officer. Why don't you seize him?"

"Well," she drawled out the word, trying to arrange her thoughts. "Cindy said—"

"Cindy said? Cindy said. We're not trainees anymore, Caroline."

"I know that, but—"

---

* That is, selling the accounts receivable to a third party to raise cash quickly.

"Unless she has a related case, you're not supposed to be talking about it with her. That's disclosure."

She became defensive. "She's a Grade Twelve. It's part of her job description to help lower-graded..."

"Lemme guess, she told you to give the guy a little more time."

"It's a big operation, Rick. Forklifts and trucks and ten thousand dollars' worth of plants and trees and shrubs and... and things like that. Cindy said we never seize anything that's alive."

"Bet she even told you not to file the lien."

"She did not."

"Did you?"

"Of course I did. You know—" her thoughts had finally caught up— "Talking about disclosure, you just looked at the financial statement."

"Let's seize him."

"What?"

"Let's seize the bastard."

"Oh, Rick. Don't call him that. He's a very nice man."

"You want me to assist?"

"Assist what?"

"The seizure."

"But I'm not doing a—"

"Jesus, Caroline, I saw the date on the financial statement—you were three months into your training year. This thing has moss growing on it."

"It's my case, Rick, and—"

"Did you put in for the promotion?"

She looked blankly at me for a moment. Caroline did not normally make conversational leaps.

"Because there is only one thing that impresses management, Caroline. You and Dee have done maybe four seizures between the two of you. Four seizes in two years. What was your rating last year? What'd you get in 'Protecting the Government's Interest'? What'd you get for 'Case Decisions'? Do you think it's as high as what Allison got—or what I got?"

"Well," she drawled, thinking again. When uncomfortable, Caroline tended to grin. Now she was smiling widely. "I've only seized a car and a piece of rental real estate. I've never done an in-business seizure."

"I'll help you," I said.

"You'll help me?"

"I'll assist, if you want. Is the file ready?"

"Ready for what?"

Two days later we were sitting in her car, parked in a church parking lot, which happened to be the parking lot of the Methodist church I attended as a boy. We were waiting for Andy McNeil to meet us. The nurseryman had several trucks: pickups, delivery vans, flatbeds, as well as three forklifts, according to Caroline's financial statement and DMV records. It was going to be a good seizure.

"That lake down there," I told Caroline. "That's where I used to hang out every Sunday when I was a kid."

She was a bundle of nerves; the fear radiated off her like the stench of alcohol off drunks. Did it radiate from me on the morning I seized the cabinetmaker? I couldn't remember; it seemed a thousand years ago.

"Oh, did your mother bring you out to feed the ducks?"

"No, she brought me to Sunday school. That's where I would play hooky."

"You played hooky from Sunday school?"

"I was an adolescent agnostic."

"Oh, I'm so sorry. That's so sad. Did you get over it?"

"As best I could," I said. Talking seemed to ease her anxiety, but she was still grinning from ear to ear. She opened the case file and began to review it, the fourth time since we had parked ten minutes ago.

"Everything's going to be fine," I said.

"I sure hope I remembered everything."

"It doesn't have to be perfect, Caroline."

"Oh, I know."

"You remember what they told us in Basic? 'Don't worry about screwing up. Everybody screws up. And we can fix almost everything you do.'"

"Yes, I remember that."

"'Make a decision. Just make a decision and go with it. We want you to make decisions; that's why we hired you.'"

"I remember that! I remember them saying that! Who said that?"

"Sam."

"That's right." She closed the case file. In two more minutes, it would be open again. She said, "It's a family business. His father started it and now his two sons work there."

"It won't even go to sale."

"It won't?"

"We're going to scare the living shit out of him. And in two weeks, three, tops, you'll have the money. You'll have full-pay."

"How do you know?"

"You're taking his baby." I looked out my window, at the sunlight glancing off the rippling water of the lake. "Find what they love, Caroline. Find what is most precious to them and take it."

Andy arrived, in convoy with two other drivers. Andy was driving the big flatbed; he would haul the forklifts. I stepped out of the car to have one last smoke.

"You're gonna need more trucks," I said.

"You know, Rick, I do get other work, now and then, from other folks. I'll call in some backup, if we need it. This isn't your case, right?"

"Right. Why?"

" 'Cause after last time, I ain't comin' on any more of your cases." He was referring to the protestor seizure that went bad, when the daughter almost took his head off while he was hooking up the '82 Monte Carlo. "Hey, did I tell you I know this guy? He does the landscaping at my sister's church."

"I didn't know you had a sister."

"This is because I don't want you to know a goddamned thing about me, taxman." He was laughing. He clapped me hard on the shoulder. "Gettin' warm, ain't it? Two weeks of winter, a week of spring, then hello motherfucking summertime."

I climbed back into Caroline's car. She was gripping the steering wheel with both hands.

"You get out of the car," I said. "You walk over to the taxpayer. You tell him why we're here. You hand him the B. You read the paragraph on the B. We sticker the stuff. You fill out the 2433. You hand him the 2433. We load up the trucks and the forklifts. We put a lock on the gate, and we leave. Simple."

She nodded, staring straight ahead. "Simple."

o   o   o

And it was, until the son got a call on his cell phone from his frantic mother. He was at a job site. He dropped his shovel and jumped into his pickup truck and raced to the nursery, to his father's rescue. The truck he drove belonged to the family business; he was bringing it right to us. Behind his seat, stuffed in a crumpled paper bag, was the Saturday night special he kept with him, for emergencies. Beside the bag was a plastic baggie containing ten ounces of marijuana.

Caroline handed the taxpayer the B. I stickered the forklifts first, recalling my first seizure and the teddy bear that haunted my dreams afterward. I walked into the yard, under the hot afternoon sun, and stickered the passenger-side window of the old Ford pickup parked there. I was walking around the front of the vehicle when I heard a terrific crash. I looked up. The back gate had been ripped from its post by the barreling truck driven by the taxpayer's boy. It was coming directly at me. I froze. The front bumper of the old Ford pressed against the back of my knees. There was nowhere for me to run.

At the last second, he swung hard to the right, skidding to a stop, throwing up huge clods of wet earth. I stepped away from the Ford. He leapt from the cab and came right at me. He gave me no chance to speak. And he raised both hands as he came for me, screaming obscenities. I was a motherfucking-sonofabitch. Then a bastard. By "asshole," he was on me. He slammed his hands into my right shoulder, knocking me off-balance, but I managed to stay on my feet. Behind me, Andy shouted, "Hey!" and a young girl appeared as if from nowhere and wrapped her thin arms around the kid's waist. He struggled in her grasp, and she screamed at him to stop, to not be crazy, to calm down. Andy appeared at my elbow, his sleeves rolled up to his biceps. He was itching for a fight. "You okay, Rick?" he asked. I nodded. I held up my commission for the boy to see.

"My name is Rick Yancey," I said. "I am an agent of the Department of Treasury, and you have just assaulted a federal officer."

"So fucking arrest me, asshole!" he screamed.

"That's later," I said.

·   ·   ·

He was arrested the following week, charged and released on $25,000 bond. I drove to Tampa to meet with the Assistant U.S. Attorney in charge of prosecuting the case, and with Inspection. Inspection investigated threats against, assaults upon, and harassment of Service personnel, in addition to investigating the personnel itself. The Inspector assigned to my case was running late. He called and told the AUSA to start the meeting without him. The AUSA was a man named Gunderson. We met in his office in the federal building, the same building in which Jim Neyland conducted my final interrogation.

Gunderson entered the room with one hand over his eye.

"Sorry," he said. "I was in the hall and some kid poked me in the eye."

"Really?"

"Look." He dropped his hand. His right eye was swollen nearly shut. "Little bastard could have blinded me."

"Why did he do it?"

"How the hell should I know? Little bastard." He punched his intercom button and shouted at his secretary to get him some ice and a towel.

"Where the hell is Inspection?" he asked. The question seemed rhetorical, so I didn't answer.

"Well, I've seen the report, and lemme tell you, Rick, there's some problems with this one." He jabbed the button again and shouted, "Ice, ice, ice!" He flopped into his chair and leaned his head back and massaged his eye with the heel of his hand. "I'm gonna be frank with you. We got zero jury appeal. Zero. Nada. Zilch. First, his age. He's an eighteen-year-old kid. He flew off the handle to defend his old man. Second, his lawyer says the kid didn't know you were a Fed. You didn't identify yourself."

"Then why—"

He held up his left hand. The right remained over his eye. "Then why did he shove you? That's a good question, but the answer won't help much. Third, you are the IRS. It isn't right, it isn't fair, it shouldn't matter, but it does matter. You are the IRS, and no matter who I put on that jury, no one's going to raise their hand and say, 'Hey, I love the IRS!' And last, you didn't leave."

"I was supposed to leave?"

"Immediately. Forthwith. Without hesitation. It's kind of hard to make our case if you stick around to complete a seizure. I mean, how scared could you have been? Forget scared. How hurt? How threatened? How serious was it anyway? A little shove from an immature eighteen-year-old, defending the honor of his daddy. Why *did* you stick around? Tell me the truth."

"I was angry."

"Because he shoved you."

"It was a punch."

"Really? A punch is better."

He picked up Inspection's report and squinted at it with his left eye. He quoted, " 'At which point the subject violently placed both hands on Revenue Officer Yancey's right shoulder and forcibly pushed him backwards several feet.' You didn't fall down."

"No."

"It would have been better if you had fallen down."

"I'll remember that next time."

"Doesn't sound like he punched you. Did he ball up his fist? Did he hit you with a fist?"

"He sort of lunged at me and hit me with the heel of his hands."

"So it wasn't a fist."

"Halfway to a fist."

"Halfway to a fist? You're gonna get up on the stand and say that? 'He punched me with his hand halfway to a fist?' "

"I heard there was a gun in the truck."

"There was. Did he take it out while you were there?"

"No. He left with his sister."

"He left?"

"Yes."

"And you stayed."

"Yes."

"Ah. So the threat was gone. That's why you stayed."

"He hung around for about thirty minutes."

"The threat was gone. That's why you stayed to complete the seizure."

"Right."

"Where the hell is Inspection? Where the hell is my ice? Okay. So, you complete the seizure. Why didn't you call the cops?"

"He seemed calm."

"What about the gun?"

"I didn't know about the gun."

"Forget about the gun. The gun has nothing to do with it. He has a license."

"Okay."

"What were you doing when he busted through the gate?"

"Stickering one of the trucks."

"Putting a warning sticker on it?"

"Right."

"Where did you put the stickers?"

"I had just placed one on the passenger-side window."

"Did he see it?"

"The sticker?"

"Was the door open? Was it open, like, facing toward him as he came toward you?"

"No."

"He came from your right, though. He could have seen the sticker."

"Why does it matter if he saw the sticker?"

"Because if he saw the sticker he could assume you were the IRS. It helps if he knows you're the IRS. Why didn't you identify yourself?"

"I did."

"After he hit you."

"Right."

"Always identify yourself before they hit you."

"I will."

"He tested positive for dope, you know."

"I didn't."

"Found some in the truck, too. We can't introduce any of that unless he gave some kind of indication to you at the time of the assault."

"He wasn't smoking anything when he came at me."

"But his demeanor? Drooling, eyes rolling in his head, slurred speech? Anything to indicate to you he was high?"

"He just seemed pissed as hell."

"That's it. That's their defense in a nutshell. He gets this frantic call from Mommy, 'They're takin' Daddy's trucks!' and here he comes. He claims she didn't tell him it was the IRS. Says all he knows is he was defending his property from trespassers. Lost his head. Big misunderstanding. You're going to hate to hear this, Rick, but we're gonna plea this one out to a lesser charge. I can't go to a jury with this one. They'll roll it into a hard little ball and stick it up my ass."

"So let me understand you," I said, my temperature rising. "You're saying, first, I should have shouted 'Halt! IRS!' at him when he jumped out of the truck. Second, he should have smacked me with a fist. Third, I should have fallen down. Fourth, once I got up I was supposed to jump into the car and haul ass out of there. And fifth, I should have examined him carefully during the assault for any clues that he might be stoned. And sixth, none of the above makes any difference, because no one likes the IRS. But number six aside, if I had done all that, then you'd have a perfect case?"

"No, I'd have a perfect case if he had pulled out the gun and shot you."

At that moment there was a knock on the door.

"Christ," he said. "My ice. About goddamned time."

He opened the door and growled, "You're late. And you better have some goddamned ice with you."

"I've got the ice if you've got the bourbon," William Culpepper said.

"Look, Yancey, you made the paper."

After the meeting, Culpepper had invited me down to the cafeteria for some coffee and doughnuts. It was two o'clock in the afternoon and the coffee was thick as maple syrup. He ate one glazed doughnut and was now working on an apple, "for balance," he said.

It was the lead story in the local section of the Lakeside paper. The headline read, IRS AGENT ASSAULTED DURING SEIZURE.

"Don't look so glum, Yancey. There's no such thing as bad press. When he cuts the deal they'll put it on page six. What matters is the arrest. Your taxpayers will read this and think twice before they take a swipe at you."

"I'm heartened."

"I just wish I could have been there."

"You miss being a RO?"

"No. But if I was there, I'd have this."

He pulled back his jacket to reveal the shoulder holster. All Inspectors were authorized the carry firearms. *Great*, I thought. *Culpepper with a gun. I can sleep tonight.*

"They told me you'd changed," he said.

"Who told you?"

"New haircut. New beard. New wardrobe. Blue eyes. Why blue?" His own blue eyes sparkled. Culpepper was feeling his oats. "Now if only you could gain thirty-five pounds. You want to join my gym?"

I tried to imagine myself as Culpepper's workout buddy, and failed.

"And Rachel quit," he went on. "I knew she wouldn't make it."

"You didn't think I'd make it."

"You haven't made it."

"You can't provoke me, Culpepper."

"Okay." He laughed. "Heard about the group's grievance. Too bad."

We had lost. Gina was still our boss. Her victory had emboldened her; she was nastier than ever, in her own cheerful way. Toby had fallen into a deep depression. When he came to work, he sat at his desk and played reggae on his Walkman, listening through earphones so we had to shout at the top of our lungs at him, "Toby! You have a phone call! YOU HAVE A PHONE CALL!"

"What a bunch of fuckups," Culpepper said. "You went about everything ass-backward."

"What do you mean?"

He was glowing. He lived for such pontifical moments.

"Look, they hate her. Upper management, I mean. They've always hated her. But she's too smart for them. Always had the goods on somebody, always covered her tracks, always outsmarted them at every turn. Two division chiefs, two district directors, and four branch chiefs, she's outlasted them all. They would love to get rid of her, but they have no leverage."

"That's why we filed the grievance."

He shook his head. "Tell me something. Did you get blue contacts because of the statistic that blue-eyed people are smarter than the general population?"

"Reading *Mein Kampf* again, aren't you?"

He smiled. "No. *The Prince*. See, you broke the rules. You don't tell management what to do with one of their own. You stepped onto their territory and they blasted you back over the DMZ. Because when it comes right down to it, incompetent and lazy as she is, she's still one of them, and you're still one of *you*."

"I guess the only alternative then is to kill her."

"You need to listen to me. I'm telling you how to do this. To get rid of Gina, you have to wank the dog."

He told the story of the dog breeder he had worked as a Grade 11 revenue officer. On his first field call, she revealed her secret for keeping her males in top breeding condition.

"She jacked them off. You know, gave them a hand job. So I asked her, 'How often do you have to masturbate these animals?' And she says, 'Oh, about once or twice a day.' That seemed a bit excessive to me. I mean, these must be some incredibly horny dogs. I say, 'What kind of dogs do you breed?' And she goes, 'Chihuahuas.' And I said, 'Well, that must be a very delicate operation. I can see how someone in your position might find it difficult to keep on top of the taxes.' "

When I finished laughing, I said, "I don't see what wanking a Chihuahua has to do with getting rid of Gina."

He ignored me. "She took me out back to the kennel and those were some of the happiest goddamned dogs I'd ever seen in my life. There was this one that could jump five feet straight up into the air, I'm not kidding." He finished his coffee and said, "Management is the lonely dog-breeder. You are the horny Chihuahua. You don't relieve yourself, you come to Mamma for relief. Employees don't tell management what to do with management. Employees tell management what do with *them*."

"I still don't get it."

"You're smart, Yancey. You radiate intelligence. You're the fucking Rasputin of the IRS. Think about it on your drive home. You'll get it. Only you didn't get it from me."

He comes at me, his shoulder lowered like a running back busting through the line, and the early afternoon sun casts his face in shadow. He wears a dirty T-shirt and cutoff jeans; his legs are tanned and muscular, his body toned from years of hard physical labor in the brutal Florida heat. Motherfuckingsonofbitch! And his hands come up, dirt packed tight beneath his chewed-up fingernails, my face his target: he will claw out my eyes; he will jab his fingers into my eye sockets, hook his knuckles inside the ocular cavity, and rip off my face. I spread my legs wide, planting myself to absorb the impact. At the last possible second, I duck beneath his flailing arms and smash an uppercut into his solar plexus. Stepping to one side, I bring up my left fist and let it fall against the side of his head. I hear a voice behind me say, "Holy Jesus, Yancey," as the nurseryman's son collapses face-first into the gravel driveway, out cold before he hits the ground. I turn. It is Andy, looking at me with newfound admiration.

"My God, you're skinny," Toby said one day at lunch. "How can you eat a big fat burger like that and still stay so skinny?"

"Metabolism," I answered.

"Metabolism?"

"And I'm an ectomorph."

"What the hell is an ectomorph? Sounds like some kind of worm."

Henry laughed. "Rick's a worm."

"Somebody with a lean body-type," I said. "Hard as hell to put on weight."

"If you're an ectomorph, what am I?"

"You're an endomorph. Someone with, uh, a lot of tissue."

He gave one of his deep belly laughs. "Gotta helluva lot of that." He placed both hands on his stomach and jiggled it up and down.

"I've tried everything," I said. "Milkshakes three times a day, weight-gain supplements."

"That don't mean shit," Toby said. "You gotta stop smokin' so much and guzzlin' the coffee. It's the caffeine and nicotine doin' you in, my man."

"Need to pump," Henry said.

"Listen to you," Toby said. " 'Need to pump.' "

"Pump iron. You know, lift weights, like Arnold Schwarts-a-whatever."

"The only thing Rick do liftin' weights is break his skinny little arms."

"Still, rather be skinny than a fat-ass like you, Toby."

"You watch it, Henry, or I'll take my straw and ram it up your nose."

"When I was seventeen, I enrolled in that Charles Atlas course," I admitted. "You ever see that in magazines? Ninety-eight-pound weakling gets sand kicked in his face and he takes Charles Atlas's course and just six weeks later he comes back and beats the shit out of the guy who stole his girl?"

They both stared at me, expressionless.

"It used to be in all the comic books."

Nothing. I sighed. "Anyway, I ordered this thing and it comes in these tiny pamphlets, about this big with real tiny writing and these little diagrams, and it all works on the principle of resistance—you don't lift weights, you just kind of push on different parts of your body."

"Well, that's the biggest load of bullshit I ever heard in my life," Toby said.

"It didn't work," I conceded.

"Join a gym and pump some iron," Henry said.

But I couldn't picture myself strolling around in a gym, my chicken legs exposed for all the world to see.

"You cut out the cigarettes, you'll gain ten pounds at least."

"I need to gain about thirty."

"We never satisfied," Henry said, growing philosophical. "Toby wants to be skinny; you want to be big."

"And you want to be smart," Toby finished.

"And I want to be *single*." Henry was the only one laughing. It didn't bother him, he usually was.

Headquarters in Jacksonville dispatched Fred Newberry to Lakeside in response to our complaint. Fred was something called an Occupational Development (OD) Specialist. Fred had a handlebar mustache and a hound-dog face. He wore the unofficial uniform of headquarters, clip-on ties and short-sleeve dress shirts, complete with pocket protector. He loved flipcharts and buzz words like *group dynamics* and *team building*. Fred was like one of those overly enthusiast people regularly seen on infomercials and at used-car lots. He was interminably upbeat. He also enjoyed full-body hugs, especially from every woman he met.

Gina was gracious, apologetic, kind, and optimistic. It was a show for Fred's benefit: he would be making a full report directly to Byron White

and she had no intention of giving him any ammunition. For our part, the
day was spent in glum recalcitrance. Toby barely spoke, wallowing in his
despair. At one point, Fred asked Gina to leave the room so we could openly
discuss our concerns. Fred got nowhere with us. He decided to leave the
room, too. "Just write down what you got. Nobody has to put their name
on anything. If this is going to work, we've got to have full and honest
communication."

No one said anything for a while. I was looking at Beth and thinking,
Wank the dog. Go on, Beth. Wank the dog. I hadn't felt proud when I figured
out Culpepper's riddle, just relieved. "Wanking the dog" was the only hope
left.

"You know," Beth said quietly. "I've been thinking about this, and I
think maybe we've been going about it all wrong."

Still no one said anything. She went on. "You don't tell management
what to do with one of their own, even if one of their own is Gina Tate."

"I don't know what the hell you're talking about," Toby said. "We lost.
End of story."

"I say we file another grievance."

"I ain't filin' another grievance. I ain't sittin' another day in a room
with that man." He was referring to Fred.

"No. Listen. We made a mistake. We told them to remove Gina. What
we should have done was ask them to remove *us*."

There was a stirring in the room. Henry was frowning. Toby lifted his
head, staring hard at Beth. Allison had begun to nod.

"We file another grievance, with the same facts, but we ask for a different remedy. Don't transfer Gina—transfer us."

"We all ask to be transferred to a new GM?"* Toby asked.

"I don't see how that's different," Cindy said.

"The end result is the same," Beth said. "But we aren't dictating to
Byron what to do with her."

"They take us out, she don't have a group no more." Henry was nodding. Even he got it.

"I'll file the damned thing tomorrow," Toby said.

---

* Group manager.

"We still all have to speak with one voice," Beth cautioned. "Is everyone willing to give it one more try?"

Five minutes later, Fred stepped back into the room. A few crumbs from the morning's coffee cake clung to his mustache. He clapped his hands and cried, "So are we making any progress?"

"You bet we are," Toby said.

I called in sick a few days later. That afternoon, a big truck pulled into the driveway and two burly men unloaded a cardboard container about twice the size of a refrigerator box. I directed them to put it inside the bare living room. "Still moving in?" one of the men asked me. I told him I was. I worked late into the night, sitting cross-legged, surrounded by huge metal poles, pulleys, and steel cables, puzzling over a fourteen-page pamphlet, Charles Atlas to the tenth power.

It was state-of-the-art, top-of-the-line, the Cadillac of home gyms. It worked by creating resistance with the pulleys and gears buried inside a plastic control panel. The workout guidebook promised a full bodybuilding program that worked all the major muscle groups. The men in the commercials had flexed mightily, their golden skin glistening...talk about demigods! It had cost over $1,400. I put it on my new American Express Gold card. In just six weeks, the ad had promised, I would begin to see results. In the guide I read, *In order to build muscle, you must destroy it. Weight training literally rips the tissue; it is the healing of the muscle that makes it grow. This is why you must determine the maximum resistance your body can bear. You must find the "breaking point" of your body and reach it with each workout, but never go beyond it.*

Two weeks later we were ordered to report to a nine o'clock meeting with the branch chief. Attendance was mandatory. No fieldwork. No taxpayer appointments. All requests for leave were denied. Bob Campbell was driving over from Orlando to make an announcement. Bonny informed us that Gina had called in sick; she would not be attending the meeting.

He began without preamble, refusing to look at us. He referred to a single sheet of paper.

"We have decided to honor your request to be transferred to another group within the branch," he said. His tone was neutral, but the vein throbbing on his forehead betrayed him.

It was a stunning victory, unparalleled in the annals of the Service. An entire group had ousted its own manager, had imposed its will upon the powers of Byzantium. If this was possible, what was impossible? For Byzantium was immortal: as long as the nation existed, Byzantium was indispensable. Congress might change the name, the agency might reorganize, the means of assessment and collection might vary with the political climate, but taxes have been and always will be the lifeblood of the nation. Byzantium was immortal, and we had dictated to its high priests. For the first time, I began to understand what Culpepper meant when he referred to us as demigods.

"Effective next pay period, Allison, Caroline, Cindy, and Henry will be transferred to Doug Michaels's group." Doug Michaels was a group manager in Orlando. "Rick, Toby, Beth, and Dee will go to Annie's group across the street."

They were breaking us up. I felt foolish; I should have anticipated this. You don't leave a cabal intact to strike again. I glanced at Beth. Her objective had not been getting rid of Gina, that was merely a means to an end. But they were not going to reward her treachery with a promotion to manager. This, too, should have been anticipated.

"What's going to happen to Gina?" Allison asked. Bob Campbell lashed out at her. "That's our business," he snapped. "If she chooses to tell you, fine. But you're not going to hear it from me." He wanted to say more, but chose not to. You didn't reach his level of management by speaking your mind.

Caroline, Allison, and I met later in the conference room to draw up the battle plan for my W-4/Protestor project, which had been green-lighted by Bob Campbell, after two memos and three conference calls. It was April 15, tax day. I had been with the Service for two years, three months, and two days.

We would work as a team to impose the least burden on the employers as possible. Some larger employees had hundreds of W-4s on file. I was explaining what to look for on the form that might indicate a protestor had completed it. Allison interrupted often, arguing that many alterations could simply be a mistake on the part of an ignorant taxpayer. She was surly. I had not wanted her on the team, but that wasn't my call.

We were poring over a map of the county when Gina entered.

"I have an announcement," she said. She spoke quickly, without looking at us. "Rick has been selected for the Grade Eleven promotion."

She left the room. Caroline congratulated me and reminded me of the tradition of the selectee bringing in doughnuts to celebrate.

"Congratulations, Rick," Allison said. She was making a valiant effort to hold it together. Convinced she was the better revenue officer, Allison knew the promotion had been hers for the taking, but the timing was wrong. The coup had come too late.

That night, I stripped down to my underwear and studied myself in the full-length mirror, a model of self-absorption, front view, side view and, looking over my shoulder, rear view. *Look at you, you have no ass. The amazing butt-less man and his lifelong quest to find his missing ass.* I turned to face the mirror again and spread my arms straight out from my sides. *Eli, Eli, lama sabachthani!* The bathroom scale had read 135 pounds. I was six feet tall and weighed 135 pounds. I could hide behind a light pole. The chart that came with my home gym indicated my optimum weight was 175–190 pounds. I squinted my eyes and tried to imagine 40 pounds of lean muscle added to my slight frame, and failed. I began to flex my muscles, such as they were, trying out different poses, feeling a little ridiculous, berating myself, the cheapest personal trainer I could find, because I was never going to see this through unless I was angry; only anger could motivate me in the long haul.

"Look at you! You're no thicker than a fucking blade of grass. There are corpses that look better than you, you desiccated, knobby-kneed, emaciated motherfucking son of a bitch. There ain't much on the outside, so you better pray there's something substantial on the inside. What's inside you? Huh? Huh?" I gripped my wrist with my left hand as I pushed my right arm upward, grimacing at the bicep balancing on the bone like an small apple. "Your body is only a manifestation of your inner being. Inside you're just as starved, because you won't let yourself believe that anything you believe is believable. You don't have faith in your own dreams. You're like a theologian who doesn't believe in God. It is the ultimate hypocrisy, to act like a demigod while refusing to become one. Become one! Be! Do you believe you are a god? Do you believe in perfection? Do you believe in the hundred-seventy-five-pound man inside you?" And so on.

I popped a Simple Minds CD into the player and jacked up the volume. I reread the section of the guidebook that talked about working individual muscle groups: *Remember, you want to work the muscle to the point of exhaustion, but never past it.* Sounded like my day job. I punched in the code for the particular muscle group I wanted to work (biceps/triceps), input the number of reps and total weight, and set to work.

An hour later I was done, dripping sweat, my arms feeling light and rubbery. I walked past the mirror without looking and took a long, hot shower. Tomorrow I would pay for my efforts, but for now I felt pretty damn good. I had embraced something, and it had felt holy. I wrapped a towel around me and went into the kitchen and mixed my weight-gain powder in eight ounces of whole milk. I finished it in four swallows, feeling bloated and slightly nauseated. I lit a cigarette. The guidebook didn't mention it, but smoking probably wasn't recommended when starting a body-building regimen. I noticed a slight quivering in my fingers.

"There," I said to the empty room. "It's begun."

D E M I G O D

My new office was just across the alley from the federal building, but a world away from the milieu in which I had come-of-age as a revenue officer. Located on the sixth floor of the Wesley Building, my cubicle overlooked Main Street, with a view of Mirror Lake, where Blinky the alligator had resided when I was a child. Blinky had only one eye and was the unofficial city mascot. I grew up, moved away to attend college, and when I returned, Blinky was gone, destroyed: he had become too tame and had lost his fear of humans. Big mistake.

The floor had been renovated recently and still smelled of drywall and fresh paint. The carpeting was new, the furniture was less than five years old, the computer systems were state-of-the-art. We moved across an alley and six stories into the air, but it was as if we had stepped over the chasm separating the nineteenth and twentieth centuries. Allison, Caroline, Cindy, and Henry were jealous: only those of us transferred to Annie DeFlorio's group moved into the Wesley. They would remain in the federal building, to be managed "off site," as it was called, by Doug Michaels in Orlando. We, however, would be integrated into Annie's existing group, the trainees, now full-fledged revenue officers, who had come on board six months after we did.

Gina had been offered a transfer to Jacksonville. It was a face-saving gesture on the Service's part. The only alternative was to be "busted down" to RO and work side-by-side with those who had forced her out. She took the job, an advisory position that required no case work and no supervision of employees. The Service was, in effect, putting Gina Tate on ice, where she could do no one, including herself, any harm.

Beth and I met with Annie DeFlorio during that first week to get better acquainted. Her office was twice the size of Gina's, the same office in which Culpepper had hunkered down, refusing to leave until the branch chief arrived with his marching orders.

"I don't know everything that happened next door and, frankly, I don't want to know," she began. "I've heard there are some concerns about Gina poisoning the well, trying to influence my opinion of you, and I want to assure you that I don't judge employees by what's said about them. I look at their work and how they conduct themselves while they're doing it." Meaning Gina had indeed been poisoning the well. I wondered what, if anything, she had told Annie DeFlorio about me.

"I don't like gossip," she continued. "I won't listen to it and I don't expect my people to listen to it—or spread it. Our jobs are tough enough as it is."

I glanced at Beth. She was staring expressionlessly at Annie DeFlorio.

"I will not tolerate hypocrisy. In this group, we do not say one thing and do another. We do not pay lip service to the manual while we bypass procedure or the law. We do not act like someone's friend to their face and gossip about them the second they leave the room. The only time I want to hear you complain about someone else is when you suspect some kind of integrity issue, and then you better have the evidence to back it up."

There's a reason we've never had our own TV show or movies made about us, Culpepper had said one day while we were driving around in the field. *And it's not because we don't have interesting jobs. In a lot of ways, our jobs are more interesting than cops' or doctors'. The reason there will never be a movie or TV show about revenue officers is, as a group, you will not find a homelier bunch of people working in a particular profession. Present company excluded, of course. I mean, we're ugly as the attendees at a plumber's convention. And Hollywood knows this. Or they understand nobody in America is going to believe anybody in the Service could look like Rob Lowe or Michelle Pfeiffer. It just strains credulity. Now, that's not to say I haven't seen some pretty hot ROs. They're just damn few and far between. I have noticed, since they began this Outstanding Scholars Program, the quality has improved. For example, wait till you get a look at Annie DeFlorio. Anybody passing her on the street would be flabbergasted to learn she worked for the IRS. They would laugh in your face. No one will ever believe we could be beautiful, because the perception is that all that we do is ugly.*

"Beth, you had asked about my expectations. Let me tell you what I don't expect. I don't expect perfection. I don't review cases looking for mistakes. I don't review time sheets looking for irregularities. I don't live by quotas or keep count of the number of seizures you've done. I don't check the clock every time you go to lunch or take a break. If your work is flowing, if you're closing cases and turning over your inventory and doing the right thing on each case, I don't slam you for taking twenty minutes on a break or an hour for lunch or calling in sick when you need a 'mental health' day. I intend to treat you as human beings first and employees second, and whatever happened in the past, whatever was said about me or my group, is forgotten. All of us are going to start with a clean slate."

"She called you Snow White," Beth said.

"I know what she called me," Annie DeFlorio said. "And it's mild compared to some of the things she called you, Beth. This is an example of the hypocrisy I talked about. Would you tattle on her if she was sitting here now?"

Beth smiled humorlessly. Already, Annie had an enemy, owing to several factors. Her looks. Her position as manager. Her intolerance of an entire way of life for Beth and the "old hands" who had come on board long before the Outstanding Scholars Program. I had a feeling, however, that Annie would not be as easy to depose as Gina, if Beth should ever conspire to take up the dagger again.

Every morning, before checking her messages, before jumping on the phone to fellow managers or the branch chief, before going through her mail or the contents of her in-box, Annie DeFlorio poured herself a cup of coffee and toured the room, stopping at each cubicle and chatting a few minutes with any RO who happened to be in that day. She never directed the conversation. Sometimes we talked about cases; sometimes, if the RO was comfortable with it, about our personal lives. She seemed genuinely interested in us, but never intruded upon our privacy. Her training was in political science, not tax or business administration; her professional background included a stint as a U.S. senator's aide. She always made eye contact and possessed an astounding memory of the most esoteric fact about us. She confessed it had once been her ambition to be a prosecutor.

She never pried into our personal lives, but would offer glimpses into hers. When we first moved in, she told us she had recently reconciled with her husband of eleven years, a successful restaurateur based in Orlando. They had two children, both boys, the younger just starting preschool. Their pictures were displayed prominently on the filing cabinet in her office and on her desk.

She was serious about her job, and she was serious about *our* jobs. She considered it an honorable profession and a sacred trust, vital to the functioning of our government. Politically, she was conservative—the senator she had served had been a Republican—but lacked the intolerance found in so many conservatives. She regularly lectured on the subjects of diversity and sexual harassment in IRS conferences.

And she scared the hell out of me.

About a month after my transfer, Annie summoned me to her office. It was the first time I had set foot in there since her meeting with Beth and me. What had I done? Was it the Marsh case, which I had allowed to fester during my protestor crusade and the internecine war between Gina and the group? Was it the hockey team that owed two years' worth of employment taxes, the first professional team to play in Lakeside, and its evasive Canadian owner? *Only a damn Canadian would think he could make a hockey team successful in Central Florida*, Toby had said.

I had learned early in my career that the best defense is self-abasement.

"My overage is creeping up," I said, before I even sat down. "But I'm gonna get a handle on it. I don't have an excuse, except all that stuff that went on next door."

She laughed. "Rick, I didn't ask to see you to talk about your overage."

Her hair was loose and flowed over each shoulder, a cascade of tight curls that shimmered under the fluorescent lights. She had a habit of twirling the ends of her hair around her index finger as she talked. I found the practice extremely distracting.

"Somebody told me you thought I didn't like you," she said. "They weren't trying to cause a problem," she added quickly. "I just wanted to tell you that I think you're wonderful. You have an excellent reputation, and the work I've seen reflects this."

"Thanks, Annie."

"Do I frighten you?"

"Excuse me?"

"They said I scared you."

"I don't think I used the word *scare*. Maybe intimidate."

She laughed. Annie laughed more often than anyone I knew in the Service. She pulled her finger from her hair and now ran this same finger along the flesh just below her bottom lip.

"Why?" she asked.

I looked away. I had always been hopelessly tongue-tied in the presence of attractive women.

"That's okay," she said. She wasn't trying to embarrass me. "You've got to understand, I'm not like Gina. If I have a problem with anything you do, I'm not going to make snide comments in group meetings or ambush you in a review. You're going to know in plenty of time to get your act together."

"I had an idea for this hockey team case." I was determine to find some way to impress her.

"Go."

"The owner is Canadian."

"Right."

"He doesn't have a Social Security number."

She nodded.

"So we can't assert the penalty.* At least, that's what I thought. But I checked the IRC and with SPf† and we can create a Social Security number for him, for the express purpose of asserting the penalty."

"Great. Let's do it. Can we collect it?"

"I'm sorry?"

---

* The Trust Fund Recovery Penalty, called the "100%" Penalty then, a means by which the Service collects payroll taxes from responsible individuals within corporations. The penalty assessed under the individual's Social Security number is equal to 100 percent of the taxes withheld from the corporation's employees.

† Special Procedures function, technical advisers in district headquarters.

"We're not putting money on the books we can't collect. We must be rational, Rick. I know that must seem strange to you, using the word *rational* in the same context as collection. I can't control what the entire IRS does, but I can have a small say-so in my own little corner of the world."

"I'll see what he's got."

"Why don't you just seize the team?"

"I'm sorry?"

"Seize the hockey team."

"There's no assets—well, there's some hockey sticks and equipment and the uniforms and the, um, pucks, but—"

She shook her mane of curly hair. I caught a whiff of White Diamonds.

"No, Rick. Seize the *team*. The franchise. Seize it as an ongoing concern. With something like this, the whole is greater than the sum of its parts."

"I—I hadn't thought of that, Annie."

"And once we've seized it, we'll fax the notice of sale to *The Journal*," our local newspaper. "They'd love to run a story. We'll get more bidders at the sale and some great press on the compliance side." The paper had been running stories for over six months, playing up my Canadian taxpayer as an intrepid, if Quixotic, dreamer, in an effort to rally civic support for the team. To notify the paper was not disclosure. Once we seized and advertised the sale of the assets, our actions were public record.

I left her office, my head spinning. She had solved in the space of two minutes a thorny problem I had been wrestling with for months. Her solution demonstrated a quantum leap in thinking—in essence we would be seizing an *idea*—that was humbling; my brilliant plan had been to give the guy a Social Security number and assess tax against him that we might not collect. But how do you place a value on a team that was losing money? How do you factor in the money owed to the investors? I had no clue and was afraid to ask her, not because I feared she might ridicule me, but because I didn't want her to discover I wasn't quite as wonderful as she thought I was.

I was standing in the doorway of Annie's office, chatting about the latest news from England, of the mysterious bacterium that was causing an outbreak of what the press had dubbed "the flesh-eating disease." For some reason, we both found this morbidly fascinating.

"Have you ever heard about the Ebola virus?" she asked. "It turns your insides into soup. It melts you and when you die, all the blood pours out of every orifice in your body. Nobody really knows where it came from or what causes it or how to cure it."

Toby's voice rumbled behind me, "CIA."

I jumped a little. Toby slid past me and sat down inside her office. The chair groaned in protest.

"Oh, you see a conspiracy behind everything," Annie teased him.

"Child, you've led sheltered life, so I don't hold it against you. CIA's behind Ebola and this flesh-eating thing, just like it was behind AIDS."

"I thought AIDS came from monkeys," I said, a little annoyed that he had interrupted.

"They were gonna use it against the Russians."

"Africa is a long way from Russia," I said.

He waved his huge hand in my direction. "Africa was just their staging area. Why Africa? Because nobody in the world cares if a black man dies. Then the experiment got outta hand. Genie popped outta the bottle."

"I thought it was a plot to kill all the homosexuals."

"Well, you would." From early in our relationship, Toby had suspected I was gay. I was from the theater, after all, and dressed well. And what real man would change his eye color?

"They cookin' up somethin' all the time," Toby said, meaning the CIA, not homosexuals. "Labs all over the world. Who you think come up with Agent Orange? You wait. This is nothin' compared to what they're workin' on now."

"What are they working on now?" Annie asked, her eyes growing wide.

"State secret," I said. "If he told you, he'd have to kill you."

"As long as it's not Ebola," Annie said, and shivered. Today she was wearing a sleeveless yellow dress that terminated three inches above her knees, a summery frock.

"You wanted to see me?" Toby asked her.

"Yes. There's a taxpayer coming in today for a conference, and I need your help."

"It's that doctor, isn't it?"

"Dr. Pierre, yes."

The Pierre account belonged to Beverly Underwood, one of the original trainees under Annie. Dr. Pierre was an odd little man, of French ancestry, who alternated his strategy between feigning ignorance of taxes and claiming Bev was acting out a personal vendetta. He was unpredictable, as was his wife.

"His wife called yesterday," Annie explained. "And right in the middle of the conversation she starts calling Beverly all sorts of horrible names and accuses her of being pregnant with her husband's child."

Toby laughed.

"And then she tells her she's prejudiced against Europeans because she's married to a racist."

"Who is?"

"Beverly."

He laughed again.

"It wasn't enough to get Inspection interested," Annie said.

"Hell no. Inspection only cares about bustin' ROs."

"Bev and I would feel a lot better if you were here. Might keep things calm."

"You want me in on the interview?"

"Oh, no. Just, I don't know, maybe sitting outside the door. I'll leave it open so you can hear. I would—well, I'd just feel more comfortable with a big guy like you nearby."

He nodded. "No problem. What time tomorrow?"

I backed out of the doorway and returned to my cubicle. My skinny little cubicle. I sat down at my desk. *I'd feel more comfortable with a big guy. . . .* Dr. Pierre was not a large man. He was shorter than I, but had about twenty pounds on me: Rick the ectomorph; Rick the worm.

The next day, Dr. Pierre had come and met with Annie and Beverly in Annie's office. Toby sat just outside the door, leaning against the wall with his eyes closed, as if he were just taking a quick nap. I pretended to work at the IDRS terminal, located ten feet from Annie's door. I could hear Dr. Pierre saying, "Please, please, Ms. DeFlorio, I am begging you," in a heavy French accent. "I am *begging* you."

When he left, an extremely frustrated little Frenchman, Annie stepped out her door and touched Toby on the arm, mouthed the words *Thank you,* and disappeared into her office without acknowledging my presence. I rose from the terminal, walked to my cubicle, and kicked my desk as hard as I could.

I walked with a limp for the rest of the day. I did not realize it at the time, but my slow descent into madness had begun. A true friend might have seen the signs, been able to read the portents of the coming storm, but I had no true friends left. I had drifted away from my friends in the theater. My relationship with my family had been strained for years. I didn't go to church and I didn't frequent bars. Each day after work I picked up a three-piece chicken dinner from the KFC drive-thru and ate at the foot of my bed. I would watch the nightly news, then prepare for my workout. I was breaking Gina's first rule of survival: there was no life outside the Service for me, no distinction between Rick Yancey the revenue officer and Rick Yancey the human being. My goal was nothing short of *perfection*. The perfect human body, the perfect revenue officer. I should have foreseen the outcome; I should have known what lay on the other side of my desire.

In the twilight, after my preworkout high-carb bar ("for an EXPLOSIVE workout!"), I strip to my underwear and face myself in the mirror. I see him emerging, the one who has always dwelled inside me, straining for release, struggling for birth. One hundred and fifty-five pounds now, and gaining. The chest is broader, the ribs less pronounced. An attractive, intricate lacing of veins runs down my forearms, my biceps. I can actually see definition, a distinction of line and shadow, on my arms, my legs, my stomach. Abs are the most difficult muscles in the human body to isolate but, being an ectomorph, I am blessed with a foundation to build upon. One night, on a whim, inspired by the gleaming images found on glossy muscle magazine covers, I stop by the store and pick up some baby oil. I slip off my underwear to pose, slickly naked, before the mirror. I throw a towel over the padded seat of the exercise machine; otherwise, my naked glutes will slide right off and I might crack something precious on the leg bars beneath. With the music blaring, I reach an easy, almost mechanical rhythm. The desire, the longing and the rage, exists symbiotically with the will: nothing is possible through intellect alone. I abandon the Kafkaesque *The Fly* as my paradigm and pick up William Hurt in *Altered States*, floating in that pod, that modified hot tub, denied all sensory input, blind, deaf, mute, numb, then leaping out as that wicked caveman, primordial man, or whatever the hell he was, leaping, cavorting, turning over cars. Or better, Kier Dullea in *2001: A Space Odyssey*, evolving into the Starchild with those bulbous eyes and disproportionally shaped head. Thus, men may become gods and gods men.

So, thrusting, lunging, pulling, squatting, crunching, I watch the needle rise, 155, 157, 160, limbs shimmering with sweat and oil in the bright bathroom lights, after darkness has come, to the point of exhaustion but never beyond it, for God dares not give us unbearable burdens; rising at four, feeling little soreness now, but a kind of kinetic force leaking like gas from a bottle; walking in Annie's office every morning to find her eating her regular breakfast, peanut butter cheese crackers with Mountain Dew to drink; stomping through the office, shouting for anyone who would listen to hear, "If I were in charge, no more IBIAs!* No more IAs period! All first contacts would be seizures!" unsure if anyone heard or cared if they did; watching the needle rise to 162, 164; seizing the rental house, the motorcycle, the '89 Ford Taurus, the Lincoln Towncar with the busted-out brake light, the mortgage, the earth-moving equipment; sitting for hours in her office over the course of several weeks, swapping stories from our childhoods ("I always wanted the next thing. The day after Christmas I couldn't wait till Easter. After Easter, my birthday. After my birthday, Thanksgiving. Graduated from college when I was twenty. Married at twenty-two. First child at twenty-five. Always rushing ahead, wanting the next thing, wanting *everything*."); staring into the yawning abyss of the Self, now at 167 and all of it hard muscle, people—some of them young, attractive women—noticing me, this blue-eyed buff demigod, and the abyss opens wider, sucking me down into aggrandizing cynicism, as the cute girl at the sandwich shop who ignored me for months begins to flirt with me; stuttering in Annie's office, "I thought for Valentine's Day . . . well, I was wondering if it would be all right if I got you something," and her, nodding absently, "Yes, that would be all right," as she turns her head to hunt for something in the file cabinet. "Yes, that would be all right. Yes, yes," as she turns her head away; sneaking the card and Godiva chocolates into her office before

---

* In-Business Installment Agreements.

she comes in, forgetting to sign the card in my nervousness; reading this in my operator's manual: *You want short reps of the maximum weight you can bear. The key to building muscle is forcing the muscle past its normal capacity;* watching her walk to her car from my sixth-floor window, keys already in her hand, for he has been stalking her, and she is afraid; telling her, half in jest, "One day your prince will come," and her answer, "Well, I wish he'd hurry up and get here," to me in my white Oxford shirt with the collar that was now too tight; kneeling naked before a mirror, staring at this face that now does not seem to belong to me; slamming my fist into poles, drywall, desktops, at the slightest provocation; consuming four thousand calories a day; spinning like a Dervish without the underlying premise of faith; crouching in the shower as the water slams down on my bowed back; screaming obscenities into dead phone lines; whistling in the dark; shedding the old skin like a Gila in the sun; taking myself to the outer edge of my capacity and pushing, pushing, pushing, pushing, until I can bid welcome to the god within.

o   o   o

The man on the telephone was not happy. I had just levied the bank account he had successfully hidden from his creditors for the past six years. I was doodling on a history sheet and barely listening. Beside the pad of paper was a stack of phone messages, six of them from Laura Marsh, all marked "urgent."

I was a criminal. He was going to sue me. According to my own Internal Revenue Code, he didn't exist. I watched the whitecaps on Mirror Lake; it was a blustery day in mid-March. He began to read from the Code. I interrupted him.

"Shut up."

There was a shocked silence on the other end.

"What did you say to me?" he choked out at last.

"You people, all I hear from you is talk. You say you're going to do this and promise you'll do that, but you never do any of it. You have this idea that you can bluster and bully your way through every problem and somehow that will make the problem go away. Well, let me tell you something, buddy, this is one problem that is never going away. Never."

"I'm recording this conversation, I'll have you know."

"Good! Check the tape after we're done and if you've missed anything, let me know. I'll be happy to repeat it. We are never going away. We will be here until there is no *here* anymore. The IRS is *forever*, and you can duck and jive, you can threaten and argue, you can register your sovereignty and declare your nonpersonhood and hunker in your bunker, and we will still come after you. We are relentless, implacable, indefatigable. We will show you no mercy. We will rip that American flag you have wrapped around yourself, wad it up, and stuff it up your treasonous, hypocritical ass. I happen to know for a fact you spend two or three days out of your week at the VA hospital—who do you think pays for that, you ungrateful sonofabitch? I pay for that. Me and about a hundred million others, so you can drag your worthless deadbeat ass down to the VA for your cortisone shots and your angiograms and your bypass operations, when you haven't paid your fair share in twenty goddamned years. Are you getting all this? Should I slow down? God knows I wish you were right; I *wish* you didn't exist. I wish it every time I pick up your case file, so in my own small way, I help you out, chisel away at the edges, cut off as much of your miserable life as I can, so bit by bit I narrow your existence to the smallest possible space a human being can occupy. You think about that the next time you drive to the bank to cash your Social Security check."

"You ain't touchin' my Social Security check!"

"It's my Social Security check!" I shouted. "I'm paying for it!* You're living on my dime! You owe me a total of fifty-seven thousand dollars and I want it back."

I slammed the phone down. My collar was soaked with sweat and my hands were shaking. One of the messages from Laura Marsh fluttered to the carpeting. I knew why she was calling. She had defaulted her latest installment agreement and wanted yet another audience with the prince, another opportunity to abase herself.

---

* The average American receives the total amount paid over his or her lifetime into the Social Security system within three years of retirement, plus all interest. The rest is funded through current workers' contributions.

.   .   .

"You shouldn't have come down here, Ms. Marsh," I told her. It was 4:45; my tour-of-duty was over. "You don't have an appointment."

"Well, I didn't know what else to do, Rick. You won't return my phone calls."

"I didn't return your phone calls because there's nothing left to be said. You're not making your payments, you're not making your deposits. There's nothing left to negotiate, Ms. Marsh."

Tears welled in her eyes. I slid the Kleenex box toward her. She was not wearing makeup. I had never seen her without makeup. I decided she was not the kind of woman who should venture into public without any makeup.

"At any rate," I snapped, "you're here. Here you are. Again."

"I lost six clients. That's why I couldn't make my deposit, Rick. If you could give me just a few more weeks."

"No," I said.

"No?"

"I can't give you a few more weeks."

"I've done everything, Rick. I've done everything you asked me to do. I can't help it if the banks won't loan me the money. I can't help it if my kid needs braces. I can't help it that my competition undercuts me."

"For three years I've heard this. I've heard the same thing, over and over, and now there's nothing left to say. What could you possibly have to say to me, Ms. Marsh, that can change anything?"

Tears flowed copiously down her fleshy cheeks; it was amazing, the amount of liquid that was draining from her eyes. She didn't bother with the Kleenex.

"Have mercy on me," she whispered.

"This isn't about mercy. And it isn't about your ex-husband or your sick children or your unreliable employees or even about you. It's not about you and it's not about me, so don't beg for mercy. Do you know what this is about, Ms. Marsh?"

"No."

I leaned in. "Taxes."

"Oh."

"It's about taxes, Ms. Marsh. You owe them, I collect them."

"Please, Mr. Yancey. Rick, you know you can't do that to me."

"Three years ago—no, more than that, five years ago, you had a decision to make. You were losing money. You barely had enough to feed your family and keep a roof over your head. But instead of making a rational decision, cutting your losses, closing the business, finding a real job, and moving on with your life, you chose to chase...well, I'm not exactly sure what you were chasing, but you must realize by now what you're chasing is a ghost, a phantom, Ms. Marsh. You've dug yourself into a hole halfway to China and, as the sides crumble in on you, you just dig faster. You don't try to claw and scramble up the sides to daylight. You just dig the pit deeper."

She stared at me for a moment before saying, "Is everything okay, Rick? Are you feeling all right?"

"What I feel is irrelevant."

"You're still a human being."

"That's irrelevant, too."

"Oh, that's horrible. If that doesn't matter...can you tell me what does?"

"I've been trying to tell you that for the past fifteen minutes. Taxes. Taxes. Taxes."

"I know you better than that, Rick. I know you don't believe that. We'll get through this. We'll figure out some way to get through this."

"I am seizing your house, Ms. Marsh."

She began to shake her head. "Oh, no. No."

"I'm preparing the paperwork next week."

"You would take my house? You would take away the only thing of value to me in this world? You would take away the roof over my children's heads?"

She went on, but I had stopped listening. It seemed as if she were sitting in another room and I was overhearing a conversation to which I did not belong. I was in Tampa; it was the fall of 1990; and Jim Neyland was saying, *You see, Rick, the kind of people I'm looking for seize houses even if it means they can't sleep at night.*

I looked at Laura Marsh. To Laura Marsh, I mattered. To Laura Marsh, I was everything. I held her fate and the fate of her offspring in the palm of my hand. With a stroke of my pen, I could take away everything she had struggled for in the world. I was more than a human being to Laura Marsh. Laura Marsh rested her elbows on the table, wringing her hands before her face in supplication. If I had ordered her to her knees, I had no doubt she would have knelt before me.

But it was a sham. It was so transparent as to be laughable. I wondered how often this scene had been repeated throughout history. We were playing out a drama older than those of Euripides, a drama as old as civilization itself. And this tired epic was still being played, and would be played, as long as there was civilization, in drab cubicles and musty warehouses and cramped living rooms across the country, and I wondered how often those in my position were seduced into believing they were Olympians, sons and daughters of the gods, dispensing justice. We were not gods. There was only one god in our cubicle and that god Culpepper had called *the beast*. For three years we had allowed it to deceive us, to enthrall us, inspire our imaginations with fear and wonder. It appealed to our common feeling of impotence: offering remedy to me, validation to her.

"I'm taking your house," I told her.

The next day, after three hours of intense labor, I completed the seizure request package for the Laura Marsh case, including the cover memo to the District Director, explaining why the Service had no choice now but to seize the house and the contents therein. I placed the folder in Annie's in-box. I had no doubt the seizure would be approved by the District Director. I knew my reputation preceded me.

I met him for drinks in a smoky little bar on the outskirts of town. It did not exist on any map, but I had no trouble finding Culpepperville; I had been there many times in the past four years. To get to Culpepperville, I had only to close my eyes. It existed only in Culpepper's imagination and, in his benevolence, he had decided to share it with me.

He was waiting for me, as always, sitting at the far end of the bar, nursing a Bud Lite and watching a Bulls game on the TV hanging from the ceiling. The bar had no name and the patrons no faces. Like shades in a dream, they floated, dark shadows amid the swirling cigarette smoke, their voices far away and muffled, as if coming from another room. It was a comfortable place; it reminded me

*of the neighborhood bars on the north side of Chicago, where I had dwelled a life-
time ago. There was a dart board and a pool table and dark-paneled nooks and
crannies where sinister men and desperate women hatched plots, struck deals,
pledged their sacred honor—only to betray one another at the crucial hour. In
other words, his kind of place.*

*He did not look over as I slid onto the stool beside him. He was transfixed by
the basketball game. A drink appeared before me, gin and tonic, my usual. I lit a
cigarette.*

*"Look at that, Yancey," he said. "Look at him. He isn't human. He defies the
ground rules. Everything about his game says, 'Take your physics and stuff them
up your ass.'"*

*We watched as Jordan seemed to float toward the goal, right arm extended
over his head, cupping the ball, his mouth frozen open in an astonished O. "Son of
a bitch," Culpepper said approvingly as Michael acquiesced to gravity and came
down. He shook his head and sipped his beer with that same delicacy he employed
on the day in Powell when he ate an apple and informed me I had become a
demigod.*

*"I thought I'd see you tonight," he said. "Here," sliding a bowl of roasted
peanuts toward me. "Biggest nuts in town."*

I asked him, "Did you see today's paper?"

*He nodded, eyes still on the flickering blue television screen. I had read some-
where why televisions always seem to shine blue light, but had forgotten the
reason.*

I slid the newspaper in front of him. He barely glanced at the headline: LOCAL
WOMAN COMMITS SUICIDE; BLAMES IRS IN NOTE.

*"I know," he said. He slapped his open palm on the dark mahogany and
yelled, "Come on, goddamnit, defense! Where's the fucking defense!" He finished
his beer and motioned to the featureless bartender for another. "I've been following your evolution with great interest, Yancey. I mean, you're practically unrecog-
nizable. What have you put on, thirty pounds?"*

"Thirty-five."

"And all of it hard muscle. What a stud! Wanna arm wrestle?"

"Not really."

He shrugged. "It's your time."

"Do you remember her?"

"*I remember everything, remember?*" *He watched the game go to commercial. Michael Jordan for Nike. He shook his head and smiled. "You know what's wrong with our society, Yancey? We all want to be like Mike but nobody wants to work like Mike. We sit our fat asses in the La-Z-Boy, crack open our Buds, eat the popcorn from bowls balanced on our jiggly bellies, and fantasize about being Michael Jordan. Of course, it's not just a physical thing; it's bigger than that. We can't all be superhuman athletes. But the fat ass on the La-Z-Boy could be the Michael Jordan of bus drivers—you see what I'm getting at? I'll tell you a secret, Yancey. I always knew you had it in you. That's why I was so hard on you. It was a compliment, really.*"

"*You talk too much,*" *I said.*

He shrugged. "Thought that's why you came."

"*That is why, but now I can't.*"

My empty glass was whisked away and a fresh drink placed before me. I lit another cigarette. A clean ashtray appeared at my elbow. I immediately flicked an ash into it, hating the shining purity of the glass.

"*Then I will,*" *Culpepper said. "I'll pose it as a hypothetical. You have this revenue officer. He's hired for one reason. He's smart. He's a total fuckup in every other department, but he's got brains. And ambition, despite his ludicrous résumé and the way he skims the surface of life, like one of those bugs you see in summertime, sliding along the flat water on a still day. That's all he needed, really, to become what he was already, that and the line the Service drew for him in the sand. 'There! And no further!' Only with a wink and a nod, because this is sand we're talking about, and the line can be moved. Did you know the term we use all the time in our jobs,* deadline, *comes from war, too? That was the line the prisoners of war could not cross or they'd be shot.*

"*So they show him the line and they say, 'These are the rules. These are what you may do and may not do, but within these parameters of what is possible,* everything *is possible.' Are you with me so far, Rick? I don't need to give you an example, do I? Sketch a picture on your cocktail napkin? Why do you consume those dainty-assed drinks anyway? You're a big, beefy piece of man-cake now.*

"*So little by little, this hypothetical revenue officer of ours discovers that within the protocols the Service has laid out for him resides a force akin to no other in the universe: the power to impose his will upon others, the strong and the weak alike, the willing and the unwilling, the king and the jester, the sage and the fool. This power they have given him, there is no other like it, though there is one power greater than it is. Would you like to know what that greater power is?"*

"Yes. I would."

"I'm not going to tell you what it is." He was still looking at the television. "Yet. Anyway, one day he is given the opportunity to stretch forth his hand and unleash the full force of his will, the epitome of his power, the ability to force his own misery upon another human being. All his cowardice, his rage, his feelings of insecurity and impotence, he can focus on some poor, helpless soul like sunlight through a magnifying glass—did you ever notice when you were a kid the funny way burning ants smelled, like the smell of burning hair?"

"You're a sick man, Culpepper," I said.

He laughed. "Sick. But you see where I'm going with this hypothetical, Yancey. You could have posed it yourself. You knew where the road ended that day in the interview booth with her. You knew it the very first day, when you took Jim Neyland's hand and said, 'Yes.' Don't flatter yourself. Don't run around with the big, black MEA CULPA, MEA CULPA! *tattooed on your high forehead. You have an extraordinarily high forehead, by the way. I mean, you could rent out space, like a billboard."*

"I didn't know where the road ended. I—you said yourself, we can't be held responsible."

"You interrupted me. You always interrupt me right when I'm getting to the good part. You think this has never happened before? You run around like a virgin after his first lay, convinced nobody's ever had sex quite like that *before. Get over yourself, Yancey. The Service expects from you what you did. And she expected it, too. See, that's the brilliance of our system: 'Execute what they fear.' For if we fail to execute what they fear, the beast will die." He had lost me and, in his frustration, slapped his open hand on the bar. "Christ, Yancey, it's what I've been trying to teach you from the very beginning. Laura Marsh was waiting for it and your job was to give it to her."*

"I'm going to leave the Service."

He laughed again. "That's a nice idea, Yancey. You think about it every day. You take it out every night, like a little toy, and you play with it. 'Oh, woe is me. What good is this?' Three years ago you had a decision to make. You made it, and since then you've been chasing a ghost, a phantom. You've dug yourself a hole halfway to China and, as the sides crumble in on you, you just dig faster. You don't try to claw and scramble your way to daylight: you just dig the pit deeper. Relax,

Yancey. There are no more lines now. You stepped over the last one. You wanted to be perfect and now you are. You are the perfect revenue officer."

I stubbed out my cigarette. The ashtray vanished and a clean one took its place, compelling me to light a third cigarette.

"You aren't comforting me, Culpepper."

"Oh, is that why you came tonight? Look at you," he said, not looking at me. "All blubbery and squishy. You're like an insect, Yancey: tough on the outside and just a bunch of mush on the inside."

At last he turned to face me. His face shown with all the benevolence of his wisdom. In that moment, I might have embraced him. In that moment, as he smiled gently at me, his blue eyes soft and compassionate, I might have loved him.

"Do not suffer yourself, Rick. You are on the other side now." He patted my hand. "I told you there was something greater, and you know me well enough by now to believe I don't lie when it comes to the issue of power. I am its prince, you may recall."

"What is it?" I was desperate to know.

He was smiling. He looked almost angelic, bathed in the blue glow of the television screen, the smoke twisting and spinning around him like zephyrs bearing him to heaven.

"The ultimate power, Rick, the one thing the Service can neither give you nor take from you, the greatest power in the universe is the power to save the dog."

"What the hell does that mean? What's it with the dog metaphors? First it's wank the dog, now it's save the dog—why are we always talking about dogs?"

He threw back his head and howled with delight. He laughed until tears ran from the corners of his eyes. He clapped me hard on the shoulder.

"You kill me, Yancey! You fucking kill me! Oh, sorry. Poor choice of words. Hey, don't get up."

"I'm leaving."

"You just got here."

"I've had enough. Goodbye, Culpepper."

"Okay. See you later."

"I'm not coming back."

"Sure. See you then."

"You're not listening to me, Culpepper. I'm never coming back here."

"Said the turtle to his shell."

(14)

ANNIE

M y tour was over. I dropped by the pet store before hitting the KFC drive-thru. It was okay: Mr. Riley, the owner, was in Chapter 11 bankruptcy, and therefore no longer my concern.* He had filed the day before I arrived at his shop to close it down. When I walked through the doors that day, a tarantula in its ten-gallon aquarium habitat made a lunge for me.

Mr. Riley had expected me on that day. He was not expecting me on this day.

"Mr. Yancey! Is something wrong?"

"Actually, I was thinking about getting a pet."

"Really?" He seemed surprised that an IRS agent might want something to care for.

"Got any specials going?"

He recovered nicely from the shock of seeing me and said, "Well, let me see . . . what kind of pets do you like?"

"Dogs—but I can't have a dog."

"How about a nice kitten?"

"I'm allergic."

"Tropical fish . . . we have a special on guppies."

---

* Under the Code, the IRS, as well as other creditors, are prohibited from taking collection action outside the auspices of the bankruptcy court. If a taxpayer files for bankruptcy, the Collection Division passes the case on to the attorneys and the Bankruptcy Advisory Section in district headquarters.

"I'm no good with fish. I had an aquarium when I was a kid and the fish always died. What I need is a low-maintenance kind of pet."

"Ah, turtles."

"No turtles."

"No turtles?"

"Definitely not turtles."

"You know, iguanas are very popular now."

"Aren't they poisonous?"

"Now, Mr. Yancey, do you think I'd sell you something poisonous?" His dark eyes twinkled. "Say, how about a guinea pig? Wonderful little creature, very tame."

"I don't want a rodent."

"Well, technically, I'm not sure if—"

"And I can't have anything that'll mess all over the apartment."

I was following him through the store. I stopped by a large raised pen.

"What are these?"

"Ah, now these are top sellers, a perfect pet for a single person. Very low maintenance, sociable, and these happen to be hand-raised. Go on, stick out your finger."

I slipped my hands into my pockets.

"Do they talk?"

"You can teach them. They're very intelligent birds."

"How long do they live?"

"Well, that's the amazing thing. Some have lived to be a hundred."

"I'm not comfortable with a pet that'll outlive me."

"Have you considered an ant farm?"

I held out my index finger and the bird hopped onto it. I raised my arm slowly, bringing the bird closer, but not too close. I didn't want to lose an eyeball.

"Scratch under his chin. They love that. But gently. Gently."

A long feather rose on top of its head, waving in the air. How delicate this creature was! I could snap its neck with my fingers.

"Cockatiels make wonderful pets," Mr. Riley said, closing in for the kill. "And since it's you, I'll take twenty percent off."

"I can't do that, Mr. Riley."

"How about a free bag of seed? And you'll need a cage, of course."

"I can't accept any gratuities."

He rung up my items. He recommended a book on cockatiel care and I bought that, too.

"It likes you," he said approvingly. "Did you know birds are gender-specific?"

"Aren't most vertebrates?"

"I mean, they usually like either men or women."

"What sex is it?"

"Oh, um ... well, let's see."

"That's all right. I'll give it a gender-neutral name.

"We include lifetime clipping on all our birds."

"You do bird grooming?"

He explained that cockatiels, like all birds, have something called flight-feathers. Once these were clipped, the bird could not fly.

"They grow back," he said. "Once a month you'll need to bring it back in."

I studied my receipt in the car. He had neglected to ring up the book and the bird seed. I looked up and saw him standing just inside the glass doors of the pet store. He gave a little wave.

"Okay, bird," I said. I would work on its name later. "Let's go home."

"You got a what?" Annie asked.

"A bird. A cockatiel."

"Oh, God." She shuddered. "I hate birds. My father kept some chickens when I was growing up in Crossville." Crossville is a tiny village atop the Cumberland Plateau in eastern Tennessee. "And the roosters would chase me and my sisters around the yard." There were two parakeets in the house, too, which her father would release, and she and her older sister would hide in the bathroom, screaming, until he relented and placed them back into the cage.

"I guess there weren't too many Italians in Crossville, Tennessee," I said.

"I'm not Italian," she said. "I married an Italian. I'm German, Dutch, English, Irish—with some Cherokee thrown in."

"I don't know what I am."

"You don't know what you are?"

"I'm adopted."

"Oh."

"Some have guessed I might have Cherokee blood."

"Why would they guess that?"

I didn't know. I couldn't even remember who told me they thought I was part-Cherokee. I said, "But I'm thinking I'm mostly Croat."

"Croat?"

"You know, Croatian." Croatia had recently been in the news. "I see pictures of those people on TV and there's a resemblance." She laughed. This encouraged me. It convinced me she was interested and amused. "When I was a kid, I used to fantasize that John Wayne was my biological father."

"Why John Wayne?"

"Oh, he was, you know, big and tough."

She laughed again, saying, "I seriously doubt John Wayne was your father," which discouraged me.

"Allison and Dee have a theory I'm the love child of JFK and Marilyn Monroe."

"Do you ever wonder about it?" she asked. "Who your birth parents are?"

We had been talking for fifteen minutes. I was still leaning in her doorway. This kept me close to the exit, in case something went awry and I had to make a quick getaway. I slid into the chair opposite her desk and said, "Sometimes."

"What do your adoptive parents say?"

"That my mother was a student at the University of Florida—they don't know anything about my father. My dad—the man who raised me—was good friends with this doctor in Miami who placed babies."

"Placed babies?"

"He treated unwed mothers and found homes for them, the babies, I mean, if he could. If he couldn't, he would abort them."

"Have you looked for them? Your birth parents?" She was careful not to say "real parents."

"I've never wanted to."

"Oh, I would. If I was adopted, I'd have to meet them. I'd have a million questions. Doesn't it kill you, not knowing where you came from?"

"Sometimes I do feel a little . . . alone, like I dropped out of the sky."

"No," she said. She knew what I was trying to say. "Not alone. Rejected. That's the first question I would ask, if I found her. 'Why did you give me away?' "

"Uh-huh."

There was a gentle tap on the door. Beth stood in the doorway, a case file in her hand. I rose quickly as she said, "I'm sorry. Am I interrupting something?"

"No, just chatting with the Croat," Annie said.

"I gotta get to work," I said.

" 'Bout time," Beth muttered under her breath as we passed.

I walked back to my desk. My phone rang. I let it ring. I stared out the window two blocks east toward Mirror Lake. If Blinky were still alive, I might be able to see him, sunning himself on the concrete promenade that ringed half the lake. It's all politics, I thought. Her background is politics. She applies it to everything. Don't go overboard. Don't misinterpret what happens between you. Didn't *politics* and *politeness* share the same Latin root?* Why was I spending less and less time in the field? Why were my cases gathering dust? Why did I just spend thirty minutes talking about chickens and parakeets and Croatians and the deep groanings of my rejected soul, when I should be working? And how the hell could she presume to know what I was trying to say? Plenty of people in my life had finished sentences for me; none that I could remember knew what I was thinking. None ever had the temerity to say, *I know you're saying this, but what you're really feeling is* this.

"Rick, do you have a minute?"

"Huh?" I turned from the window. Allison was standing in my cubicle. She was smiling pleasantly.

"Let's go for a walk. I need a break."

---

* Actually, "polite" is from the Latin, *polire*, meaning to polish. "Politics" is from the Latin, *politicus*, meaning political.

"I just took a break."

"I know. Take another one with me."

"I'm expecting a phone call."

"You just ignored a phone call."

"That wasn't the one I was expecting."

"How do you know?"

"I don't want to take a walk with you, Allison."

"Let's take a walk."

I followed her into the main hallway. We rode in the elevator to the ground floor without speaking. When I was in high school, the elevators in the Wesley were still hand-operated and part of my summer job was running the tenants and their visitors to their floors. It required a light touch, expert timing, and an ironclad stomach. We walked outside into the bright sunlight. I slipped on my Ray-Bans. It was midmorning and about eighty-five degrees. It was July.

"You know what everyone's talking about," she said.

I lit a cigarette and said, "I don't give a shit."

"You know what they're talking about and you don't give a shit, or you don't know and don't give a shit?"

"Both."

"Understand, I'm only bringing this up because we're friends."

You're not my friend. "Sure."

"She's married, Rick."

"Who?"

"Okay. Let me just add this. She's got two kids. And the guy who fathered them happens to be Italian."

"She isn't."

"Who cares? He is. And he's from New York."

"What are you implying?"

"And I hear he has family connections in the *garment industry.*"

"How do you know so much?"

She sighed. "And one more thing. She happens to be your immediate supervisor. Do you know what the Service does to people who have affairs with their immediate supervisors?"

"I can guess, but I'm not having an affair with my immediate supervisor."

"How can somebody so fucking naive beat me out of a promotion? That's the question that keeps me up at night, Rick. Look, it doesn't matter if you are or not. What matters is what people believe."

"I can't control what people believe."

"You spend hours in her office. Everybody complains about it. Nobody can get in to see her. Everybody sees the way you look at her; *I've* seen it."

"Allison, I appreciate your concern, but we're not having an affair, and nothing I can say or do will change anyone's mind about that. They're gonna think what they're gonna think."

She laughed. "My God, you are so self-centered."

"What are you talking about?"

"Think about her. You don't care what a rumor like that would do to her career? They'll *crucify* her, Rick."

"They didn't crucify Alan Randall." Alan Randall was the District Director accused of sodomizing his secretary.

"Alan Randall had sex, Rick. The Service will always tolerate sex, especially between a male boss and a female subordinate. This is different. The roles are reversed and it's something a bit more serious than some horny old pervert raping a clerk."

"Oh, how you go on," I said, to goad her.

She shook her head. "You live in a fantasy world, Rick. I guess that's why you're so good at this job. Why you ripped into protestors and never think twice about seizing. It never feels quite real to you, does it?"

"And it does to you?"

We had completed our circuit around the building and were standing before the front doors.

"Who put you up to this, Allison? Beth or Dee or both of them?" I asked.

"In spite of everything, I always considered you a good friend, Rick."

"You aren't my friend," I said. I left her standing on the sidewalk. I could feel her eyes on my back as I walked to the elevator. I wondered why they chose her to deliver the warning. As I rode up to the sixth floor, I remembered the elements of an effective taxpayer contact. *Make demand. Warn of consequences.* And, if the demand was ignored, *take enforcement action.* Allison had hinted at what form that enforcement might take.

Crucifixion.

.   .   .

I had seen him only once, when he dropped by the office one day, not long
after my transfer to her group. He barreled past me in the hallway, wearing a yellow Polo shirt, topsider shoes (no socks), and green shorts, the
quintessential preppy. He barely glanced at me. He walked straight to
Annie's office and slammed the door behind him. I looked over at Bonny
sitting at her desk and said, "What's it with Mr. Greenjeans?"

"That's Annie's husband," she said. We could hear the shouting, mostly
from him, behind the closed door.

I stood by Bonny's window and watched him exit the building and walk
to his car. She had filed for divorce shortly before Gina's ouster, reconciled, and now was having more trouble.

"He calls here sometimes fifteen, twenty times a day," Bonny told me.
"Screams at me when she's on another line or in a meeting. You know what
he told her once? 'Sure you're a superstar at the IRS. It's full of idiots.
You're just less of an idiot than the rest of them.'"

One day Annie was reaching for a case file and the sleeve of her dress
drew up, revealing an ugly bruise on her right shoulder. Later, I took Bonny
aside and asked, "Does he hit her?" She knew who I was talking about.

"You saw it, too."

I nodded. "I oughtta bash his fucking fat hairy face in."

"Should we say something?"

"What if we're wrong?"

"It's the right spot."

"What is?"

"On the shoulder, where a sleeve will hide it. Batterers know where to
hit you so it doesn't show."

Annie buzzed me at my desk.

"Hey," she said. "Do you have a second?"

She asked me to close her door.

"I'm afraid." She nodded toward the phone. "He just called me. Well,
first the bank called me. He went to work for a bank, did I tell you that?
Right after we separated. He lied on his résumé. Said he could speak

Spanish, said he had banking experience, said he graduated cum laude from college—all of it a lie. Rick, the man never even graduated from college. They hired him pending a background check. Well, a few days ago they called me. I'm still not sure why they called me, but I told them the truth. So they confronted him, and he tells them it's a nasty divorce and he's got restraining orders against me and I won't let him see his own children and he swears everything on the application is true and then he must have called the college and had them seal his records, because the bank called the college and the college told them his records had been sealed."

She was gasping for breath. I asked her if she wanted anything; I could fetch a glass of water. She shook her head.

"I'm not finished. The bank called me back. After they fired him. He blew up and said things, apparently some pretty terrible things, and one of the VPs was so concerned, she called me from the airport. She said she couldn't get on the plane without calling first. She wouldn't tell me what he said, but she was calling to tell me she had concerns for me. She kept saying 'Be careful. Be careful.'"

"You should be careful," I said.

"I'm not finished. That was him just now on the phone. He asked about the kids and he asked about me and he apologizes for all the crap he's been putting me through and then, Rick, then he *asks me out on a date.* And I say, 'Well, how's the job going?' And he says, 'It's going great, it's going really great, they love me there and I love banking,' and he's begging to meet me for dinner…he's begging me."

She could contain herself no longer and began to cry. My instinct was to touch her. I sat down instead.

"He's going to kill me."

"No, Annie."

"You don't understand, Rick. I haven't told you all of it. You would not believe what I've been through the past twelve years."

"Tell me."

"He promised he would kill me if I ever left him. 'Because I love you so much,' that's what he said. Then he changed his mind. He decided if I left him, he wasn't going to kill me; he was going to throw acid into my face.

'One day you'll be walking down the street and some stranger will pass you and you won't even know who it is and the next thing you know, you'll be blind and disfigured for life.'" She sank into her chair, overwhelmed. It struck me, in that moment, how utterly alone Annie DeFlorio was.

Immediately after she served the divorce papers on him, her husband filed for bankruptcy and took a job as a waiter in a diner. He began stalking her in earnest. He refused to pay the court-ordered interim support for his children and was thrown in jail for contempt. She laughed when she told this story. "He called me and screamed for me to come get him out of jail, 'and when you get down here I'm gonna kill you.'"

"And you think that's why he called you just now?"

She nodded. I stood up and took a step toward her.

"What do you want me to do?"

She looked surprised. "There's nothing you can do, Rick."

"Annie. Annie, listen, you gotta get a restraining order."

She laughed. "A restraining order? I've had restraining orders on him before. Restraining orders are worthless, Rick."

"There's must be something we can do."

"There is one thing, but I don't know if I can do it."

I asked her what that one thing was, but she refused to answer. Annie DeFlorio kept her own counsel.

o   o   o

I worked with the bird every night, but it refused to talk. It chirped when I came home from work and went berserk when I exercised, dancing on its little wooden perch, hopping from foot to foot, head feather at high mast and waving. Perhaps my nudity disturbed it, but I suspected it was the Simple Minds CD playing at high volume. It enjoyed riding on my shoulder, and I quickly learned to change into an old shirt before allowing it to come aboard. Occasionally it stretched its thin neck out and chewed affectionately on my earlobe.

I couldn't decide on a name for it. I liked Horatio, but worried the bird was a "she" and didn't want to humiliate it with a masculine name.

One day it exploded from my shoulder, flew crazily about the room, then banked and slammed into the window. With a cry I ran to it and scooped it off the floor.

It fussed at me, as if its accident were somehow my fault. Its flight feathers had grown back.

Annie called me into her office to review my outside work request. All employees needed management's blessing before accepting a second job outside the Service.

"So you'll be writing for the newspaper?"

"Theater reviews and features."

"I knew you did some theater; I didn't know you were a writer."

"Not many do, sadly."

"I loved the theater when I was in high school. My drama teacher told me I should consider an acting career. But acting wasn't my passion at the time."

"What was?"

"Writing."

Her husband failed to show at the final hearing. The judge awarded Annie custody of the children and set child support at $600 per month, based on the financial statement submitted by her husband's attorney, and despite his history of earning more than $100,000 a year as an entrepreneur during their marriage. There would be no alimony. Her lawyer told her not to fight it; it was time to cut her losses and get on with her life. To contest it might also place her in danger. He gave her one last piece of advice before submitting his bill.

Leave.

Allison brought me the news.

"Annie's taking a hardship* to North Carolina."

"You're lying."

"Go ask her."

I rose from my desk and started for her office.

---

* An agency-approved transfer to another post-of-duty based on dire circumstances of the employee.

"It's already approved, Rick," she called after me. "She's leaving in a month!"

I stopped outside her office. The door was closed. I walked slowly back to my desk, slamming my fist into a support beam on the way. I heard her door open, turned on my heel, and walked quickly to the side door leading to the hallway, to escape. I heard her ask, "What's wrong with Rick?" and Allison saying in that prissy little voice, "Well, what do you think?"

o   o   o

That night I drove to Orlando to see a touring show of *Evita*. On the drive home, an enormous weariness overcame me. I pulled off the interstate and bought a large cup of coffee that could not have been less than six hours old. I was on International Drive, and hotels towered on both sides of the thoroughfare. I thought of my bare apartment and the nameless bird hunkered in its cage, no doubt wondering where Daddy was. I set the coffee on the hood of my brand-new car and tapped out a cigarette; I had taken a pledge not to smoke while driving. One day in the field, I dropped a lit cigarette into my lap and nearly ran up a tree while I slapped at my smoldering crotch. I had been awake since four that morning and I knew I wasn't going to make it back to Lakeside that night.

I checked into the Hilton. In the room, I undressed and caught a glimpse of myself in the mirror by the closet. There seemed nothing left to do. This body, from all angles, was perfect. I had reached the other side of something, but I wasn't sure what that something was. I dressed, feeling more ashamed of my body than I did when I was skinny. I sat on the edge of the bed and smoked, another solitary man in a white shirt in a hotel room.

That Monday I had received my annual performance rating. In each of the critical elements of my job, I was given an overall score of "5," the highest possible. Straight fives was practically unheard of in the Service. It left no room for improvement. Byzantium was declaring me perfect. The perfect revenue officer.

Mine was a nonsmoking room, and I tapped my ashes into an inch of tap water in one of the little plastic cups. The remote control for the television was anchored to the bedside table. The television was chained to a bolt inside the cabinet. The clock radio and the lamps—and I—were the only things not nailed down. I remembered a news show about hotels spying on their guests with hidden cameras. They hid the things in the lamps, the TV, even in the overheads in the bathroom. Somewhere in corporate headquarters, a little guy had watched me examine myself in the full-length mirror.

Annie's parents lived in Greensboro and she needed them now. She was leaving. She had even considered leaving the Service; she had submitted applications to both senators from North Carolina. Jim Neyland had already removed her from the group; she was no longer my boss. She was no longer my boss, no longer married, and in another month, no longer in town. She would be seven hundred miles away.

I dropped the cigarette into the cup and lay back in the middle of the bed, my arms stretched out, my feet dangling over the end. I thought of my first day on the job, after taking the oath of office to protect the nation from all enemies, foreign and domestic, of Toby pointing at the ceiling and flashing the sign, THEY'RE LISTENING. Of course, no one was listening then and no one was watching me now, but that was not the point. The Service's power was not limited to its hold on the public's imagination. It held us, too. Even those of us in the Service didn't think of ourselves as part of it. We were not *it*. *It* was something outside us. *The beast*, Culpepper had called it. That was the farce I had been playing, the farce we all played: no matter how frightened our taxpayers were, we were twice as terrified, because our fear was based on the truth. We *knew* Byzantium for what it was. That night, in that hotel room, I realized something else: I knew Byzantium for what it was, and Byzantium was me.

o   o   o

A week later I was sitting across from her desk. Her door was closed. "There's something I wanted to tell you, before you leave."

"Okay." She folded her hands on the desktop and leveled those luminous brown eyes at me.

"And I wanted to take this opportunity." I trailed off. This was starting to sound like an acceptance speech. I cleared my throat. "I know you're going to be busy…that you *are* busy, getting ready to move, finding a house in Greensboro, getting your kids into school, and…all that. And we're not going to have much time to—I mean, time is getting kind of short."

She nodded. Her phone rang. She ignored it. When it stopped ringing, she said, "If you're worried about your departure rating…"*

"I don't. I mean, I'm not. I mean, I guess I care, but that's not what I'm trying to say."

"I'd be interested to hear it. What you're trying to say."

"I just wanted to say that I guess it isn't much of a secret around here, to anyone, except maybe one or two, like Henry, that I…well, that over the past eighteen months I guess you've noticed I've been sitting across this desk quite a bit, and I wanted to tell you why."

"Okay."

"Okay?"

"Okay, tell me why."

"Because I've…well, the truth is, I've grown quite…um, fond of you."

She smiled. "Fond of me?"

"Oh, yes. Quite…fond."

"So have I, Rick."

Her phone rang again. This reminded her of something. She laughed, and her laughter and the ringing phone shattered the moment past retrieval.

"Well," she said brightly. "You can always call me in Greensboro, if you want to talk." The phone stopped ringing. "Of course, I can't guarantee you I'll take the call." Again she laughed.

It was early spring, and the warm air brought the rains at dusk as I drove to the bare apartment in my spotless new car, for, as Culpepper once told me, your car is a reflection of your mind. I continued my punishing workouts, but the fierce joy was gone. At work, I picked up case files and thumbed listlessly through their pages before placing them back in the filing cabinet. Headquarters rotated a series of acting managers through the office,

---

* Whenever a supervisor—or one of her employees—changes jobs, the Service requires a performance rating be completed for the benefit of the new supervisor.

refusing to appoint anyone from the group to the position. Beth was livid. Jim Neyland appeared in town one morning and summoned the revenue officers into the conference room, for a private interview, with one exception: he did not talk to me. Henry, who was in the army reserves, took off for two weeks of training in the processing of battlefield casualties. "What exactly will you be studying?" Bonny had asked, to which Henry barked, "Tag-toe!" It was a favorite office anecdote. Dee transferred to the Tampa office. Day after day I sat in my little cubicle and looked out the window while my cases aged and phone calls went unreturned, letters unanswered. Bartleby had his brick wall; I had Mirror Lake. I appreciated the irony of that. Mirror Lake.

I was waiting for something.

It came on a Wednesday afternoon, on my way back to the office, tie loose, shirtsleeves rolled to my elbows, legs gelatinous with fatigue, stinking of cigarettes and stale coffee and garbage.

Normally I would not have returned to the office after a day in the field. A good revenue officer never does. But I had found something and wanted to get out a levy as soon as possible.

My discovery lay on the passenger-side floorboards: a bank statement and two statements from a Merrill Lynch money-market account, the papers stained by what appeared to be red juice, perhaps Hi-C or cranberry. They were last month's statements; the money might still be there. I wasn't sure if the money belonged to a protestor. The assessments I was trying to collect were over five years old. He had filed his returns for the past two years, but had been dodging me for a month, refusing to return my phone calls or appear on his summons date. He had been coded ITP five years ago, but may have had a change of heart. I would levy these accounts to find out.

He lived on the far west side of town, in a prefab unit indistinguishable from the others that lined the street. It was a dry, treeless wasteland of saw grass and sandspurs, of cracked sidewalks and fire-ant mounds that dotted the sandy front yards, of leaning mailboxes and wandering mongrel dogs marking their territory, of sullen, shirtless children riding their trikes or cutting through the yards of gnarled earth, dragging sticks in the dirt, and the hot air shimmered over the tarmac.

I pulled into his driveway and walked to the front door. I left my car door open and the engine running. I held my commission in one hand and the case file in the other. The carport was empty, the interior of the house dark. I did not leave my card. I had already left a summons, which he had ignored. I stood for a moment in the meager shade of the front stoop and looked down the street. I counted four dogs and seven children. Surely, in one of these cracker boxes, an adult was cooped. *Grab my shotgun, Ethel! Gotta Fed at the door!* I sighed, went back to the car, threw the file into the passenger seat, and backed out of the drive. I slammed on the brakes. How had I missed it? Sitting by the curb were three large black Hefty trash bags. It was garbage day.

I sat for a moment in the idling car, tapping my index fingers on the wheel, staring at the garbage. Melissa, Culpepper once told me, often dug through people's trash. At the time, the thought disgusted me. I shifted the car into neutral and set the parking brake. I looked down the street. I looked up the street. Two dogs, no children. The coast was clear. I reached down and pulled the release to open the trunk. I stepped quickly from the car and grabbed two of the bags, walked to the back of my car, and threw them in. I slammed the lid closed. I did not take the third bag; somehow, it felt not quite so bad, leaving one. As I came around the car, I almost ran into a boy, about seven, standing by the left front bumper, wearing a pair of ragged cutoff blue jeans and nothing else, skin a glistening ochre, hair shaved to his scalp, scowling in that self-righteous way of children who believe they have caught an adult up to no good. A long scar ran from his hairline, down his nose, terminating at his chin. It looked as if someone had cut his face in half and sewn it back together. His arms were folded over his chest and his stomach hung over his waistline. As far as belly button types go, he was an outi.

"Whatcha doin' here?" he demanded.

"I was looking for—," I said. "Does he live here?"

"Why'd ja take the garbage?"

"I'm the new garbageman."

"You don't look like a garbageman. You don't drive a garbage truck."

"We got unionized," I said. It felt as if we were playing a scene from a perverse version of *The Grinch Who Stole Christmas*. "I gotta go." I slid into the driver's seat and he came around the open door. He wasn't done with me yet.

"I'm tellin' you stole the garbage."

"I'll give you a quarter if you don't."

"A dollar."

"You gotta be kidding."

"You're rich," the kid said. "You got a tie on and it ain't even Sunday."

"I don't have a dollar. How about fifty cents?"

"I like your pen."

I pulled the ballpoint from my pocket and handed it to him. Too late, I realized it was a government pen, with the words *U.S. Treasury* etched upon its sleek black surface.

"Okay," I said. "It's a deal, right? Mum's the word." A shrill voice in my head hissed that now he would use the pen to write down my tag number, but that seemed an incredibly savvy move for a seven-year-old. I pulled a U-turn in the middle of the street and gave him a little wave as I drove away. He didn't see me. He was staring at the pen.

I drove to a gas station, parked by the Dumpster behind the building, rolled up my sleeves, and tore open the first bag. In the blistering heat, the stench of rotting food almost overwhelmed me. Old lettuce, apple cores, a half-eaten piece of chicken breast, eggshell, a mysterious white substance that had the consistency of curdled milk, several banana peels, coffee grounds, used feminine napkins, wadded tissues, empty Bayer aspirin containers, two issues of *Field & Stream* from three years ago, corn husks, the remnants of spare ribs, the grease congealed along the ragged pink edges of the meat, a broken pencil, four days' worth of newspapers. Useless. I heaved the bag out of my trunk and hurled it into the Dumpster, my gut contracting in an effort to control my nausea. I stared at the remaining bag for some time, my hands slick with grime and probably crawling with a billion pathogens. Fuck it. I tore open this bag and three quarters of the way to the bottom found the statements. Pay dirt. I tossed the second bag into the Dumpster without finishing the search. I'd had enough.

I ducked into the station bathroom to wash up. The tiny room stank of urine and the mirror over the sink was cracked, from top left-hand corner

to bottom right, and I thought of the tanned urchin's face, the boy who
had taken my pen in exchange for his silence. Undoubtedly, he would
betray me. First he'd tell one of the dogs, then a friend playing hopscotch
in the road, then his mamma or daddy, proudly showing his Treasury pen
to all. Scrawled on the walls were the banal obscenities found in rest rooms
all over the world, some racist, most sexual, with a few graphics thrown in
to aid the literarily impaired. I scrubbed up to my elbows, like a doctor
preparing for surgery, while I read these missives, struck by how unutter-
ably lonely or bored their writers must have been. It is this desperation for
the human touch that shapes our destiny, I thought. It saves or damns us,
there's no in-between. The paper towel dispenser was empty; I had no way
to dry my hands. I returned to the car, shaking the water from my hands; it
dripped from my fingertips and spotted the hot pavement, evaporating
before I closed the car door. I rolled down the windows and jacked the air
to high, but could still detect a hint of garbage rising from my skin, as if
the stench had been absorbed and was now leaking from my pores.

I was two miles from the office when I came upon what I had been waiting for, the answer to the Culpepperean riddle that had been vexing me
for weeks.

It began when the car directly in front of me slammed on its brakes. I
reacted at the last second, jerking to a stop only inches from the bumper in
front of me. My windows were still down, so I heard the inhuman shriek,
the high-pitched wail of an animal in pain. Out of the corner of my right
eye I saw a large black shape lurch to the shoulder of the road, still yowling in pain. The traffic began to inch forward. It took me a moment to
realize that whoever had hit the dog had no intention of stopping. The
animal had collapsed on the side of the road; through my rearview mirror,
I could see its ribcage heaving as it lay on its side, head flat on the ground.

"Maddie! Oh my God! Maddie! Maddie!"

I continued to edge forward, watching the scene through my rearview
mirror. A woman raced across the street to the dog's side. A young child, a
girl, or it might have been a boy with long hair, hung on to the woman's
shorts as she dashed across the street.

"Oh my God! Somebody! Somebody help us!"

I whipped the wheel hard to the right. The car behind me lay on its horn. I parked on the shoulder and ran fifty yards to where the dog lay dying. I had hesitated; it was my intention to continue on to the office—the levy sources I had would not be good for long. That little miscreant would rat on me and the taxpayer would figure out my intentions with his garbage. The woman lifted her head at my approach. I was surprised by her appearance. She was much younger than I had thought when I first saw her run across the street. She could not have been older than twenty. The child—a girl—was hiding behind her.

"You killed my dog, you son of a bitch!" the young woman screamed at me.

I knelt beside the dog and placed my hand on its rib cage.

"Your dog isn't dead. And I wasn't the one who hit it."

It was a large animal, a mutt. Black Lab, German shepherd. Maybe some collie. It had a Lab's face, but tall, pointy ears, like a shepherd.

"I was doin' my laundry," the woman said, and pointed to the Laundromat across the street. "Cassie was supposed to be watching her."

"I was watchin' her, Mamma!" the little girl cried.

"What kind of person would just hit a dog and keep on going?" the young woman demanded. I had no answer for her, so she repeated the question. "What kind of person would just hit a dog and keep on goin'?"

"You've got to get this animal to a vet," I said. "I'll carry it to your car."

"We don't got a car," the woman said. "My boyfriend's got the car. Oh, my God, she's gonna die, ain't she?" And her daughter—I assumed it was her daughter—burst into tears.

"That's okay," I said. "I'll take her. You go back to your clothes."

She looked at me without comprehending. I said, "Call your boyfriend and have him come pick you up—you can meet me at the vet's."

"What vet?"

I gave her directions. It was less than a mile from where we stood. I slid my arms beneath Maddie's body. Her large brown eyes rolled in her head and she growled deep in her throat.

"You can't take her to the vet," the woman said. Panic was giving way to harsh practicality. "He'll kill me if you do. He didn't want the dog in the first place. We can't afford the bill."

"Don't worry about that now. I'll wait for you at the vet's."

I carried the dog back to my car, stumbling a bit on the uneven ground. I looked down and saw its blood on my white Oxford shirt. I was forced to lay the dog on the ground to open the passenger door. She whined in protest or from pain. I flipped the passenger seat forward. The car was spotless and I had nothing to cover the rear seat. It didn't matter. I had no responsibility toward this dog and yet had every responsibility toward its life.

I turned and picked it up. Again the eyes rolled and the tongue lolled from the mouth.

"I order you not to bleed all over my new seat," I told her. I gently laid the dog across the seat. Its breathing was shallow, but even. I placed my hand on its head. The eyes were losing focus, and it seemed a terrible injustice somehow, that its last sight might be of a stranger, the entire front of his dress shirt stained crimson, her hairs sticking to his hands, tacky with her blood. In a benevolent universe, the last thing Maddie saw would be the face of Cassie, the little girl who adored her.

I drove to the vet's.

I knew of this veterinarian because this veterinarian had been a "client" in my training year. The receptionist recognized me as I came through the door. I never learned if her sharp intake of breath owed to recognizing me or to the blood covering me from neck to groin.

"It's okay," I said, in case it was due to the former. "I'm off duty. I've got a badly injured dog in my backseat. I'm afraid to move it again because I'm not a professional."

She disappeared into the back room. After a moment, she reemerged, followed by the doctor.

"Mr. Yancey, Angie here tells me you killed a dog."

"No," I said. "Somebody hit a dog and I'm trying to save it. It's in my backseat."

They hustled the dog inside. I sat in the waiting room, and realized I never got the owner's name. All I had was the dog's name. Maddie. The receptionist came into the room. The dog was getting X-rayed. There was a form she wanted me to fill out. Breed. Age. Shot record. I told her I didn't know any of these things. The only thing I knew was the dog's name. Maddie. She asked how it was spelled. I asked her what possible difference could the spelling of the dog's name make? Would it live? She didn't know. Who were the owners? I didn't know. I told her what had happened. She didn't understand why I had brought the dog in. I told her I didn't understand either. It was easier to lie at that point. The vet came into the room, still wearing the rubber gloves, fingertips glistening with Maddie's blood. I stood up.

"Is she going to live?"

"It's got a broken leg. Contusions, lacerations, can't detect any internal bleeding, but the next twenty-four hours will tell us a lot. I'm really glad you brought her in, Mr. Yancey. Many people who hit dogs just keep going."

"I didn't hit the dog."

"No, of course you didn't."

"I'm serious. I did not hit that dog."

"Well, in any case, you should seriously consider putting it down."

"Putting it down?"

"Particularly since it's not your dog. Best thing to do in the case of a stray."

I explained Maddie was not a stray. I told the story again. The vet seemed dubious.

"I want you to save this dog."

"That's up to the owner."

"Believe me, she wants you to."

"Why didn't she drive it here herself?"

"She doesn't have a car."

The vet and Angie exchanged a look.

"Don't worry about the bill. I'll cover it."

"We're talking six to seven hundred dollars, minimum," the vet said. "And even then there's no guarantees."

"I don't care. I'll pay it. I'll give you my credit card number right now." I was shoving my card toward him. He laughed.

"Oh, no. Angie takes care of that."

"Good, and you take care of that damn dog. I am not authorizing you to put it to sleep. This dog is going to live. If this dog doesn't live, I will personally bring a malpractice suit against you. I brought her to you alive and now it's your responsibility to make sure she stays that way."

He studied me for a moment. "You know, maybe we've got you IRS types all wrong." He disappeared into the back.

"You want to go back and see her?" Angie asked.

"Who?"

"The dog."

"No."

"Sometimes people do. You know, in case..."

"That dog is not going to die," I said.

I turned to a little display of dog accessories hanging by the front door. I selected a long red leash and a pink collar. Angie gave her opinion that the red and pink clashed, so I switched the pink collar for a blue one. She informed me Maddie was a girl dog, and probably would prefer a matching collar; blue was a boy color. I paid for the items and told Angie to make sure the owners got them when they came to pick up the dog.

"What happens if the owners don't show for her?"

"Well, assuming she lives, we'll put her up for adoption, then it's to the Humane Society if we can't place her."

"And if no one adopts her there? What happens there?"

She shrugged. "What always happens there, Mr. Yancey."

I handed her my business card. "If they don't show up, call me. I'll adopt her."

"Oh, that's so sweet."

"No, it's karmic."

I drove to the office. Bonny rose from her desk.

"My God, what happened?" she asked, staring at my blood-soaked clothing.

"Where's Annie?"

"In her office, I think."

I strode into her office without knocking. She was standing at the filing cabinet behind her desk, the late afternoon sun streaming through the window glistening on her dark hair. Boxes were scattered over the room and the walls were blank, the pictures of her children packed away. Annie was leaving.

" 'Would you like to make more money?' " I blurted. I paced as I talked, never looking in her direction. " 'Sure, we all would!' You ever see that commercial with Sally Struthers? You know, Gloria from *All in the Family*? Well, she's going to be in Orlando next Tuesday; she's in a touring show of *Grease* and I have to review it and I have an extra ticket and I was wondering if you wanted to go with me. I know it's short notice, but—"

"Of course."

"Excuse me?"

"Yes."

"Yes?"

"I would love to go."

"You would?"

"I just have one question. Why are you covered in blood?"

I bought a new sports jacket, a new shirt—one of those collarless numbers that was all the rage—and a new pair of shoes. The jacket was white; the shirt black-and-white checkerboard. I checked it out in the mirror and thought I looked like a waiter. The shoes were a half-size too small: after gaining all that weight, my feet still looked too big for my body. I drank half a pot of coffee; it was going to be a long night. When touring shows came through town, the paper wanted to run the review the morning after the opening, which meant I had to write the review on the same night I saw the show. That morning, Annie gave me directions to her house, after asking, "Are we still going to see this play?" I had avoided her since I asked her out. I answered only if she wanted to: I was determined to leave the door open for a graceful exit.

"Of course I still want to," she answered.

o   o   o

She answered the door wearing a sleeveless black dress that accentuated her long legs.

"Hi," she said. "You look nice."

"You think so? I think I look like a waiter."

She laughed. "You want to come in?"

I looked at my watch. "Actually, if we're going to make it to Orlando by curtain..."

"Okay. Let me grab my purse."

·   ·   ·

I barely paid attention to the show. Occasionally my shoulder brushed hers, and I could see her hands folded in her lap, and at some point in the first act I reached over, my heart slamming in my chest, and took her hand, and Annie DeFlorio let me hold it.

As the lights came up at the end of the first act, I leaned over and whispered in her ear, "I guess you've figured out by now, I'm just crazy about you."

She smiled and nodded. I put my arm around her and she leaned her head against my shoulder and her hair was soft under my chin. Her hair smelled like raspberries. I closed my eyes and breathed her in. She was going to leave me and, after a few awkward phone calls, she would be lost to me forever. Another man would hold her hand. Another man would stroke her hair and breathe her in and bring her to his bed. I stroked her bare shoulder and thought this might be the last time I touched her.

After the final curtain, as we walked to the car, she asked, "Do you believe everything happens for a reason?"

"I never thought about it."

She laughed. "Liar."

"Okay, I have, but the implications terrify me."

"Why?"

"Because some pretty terrible things happen, Annie." Her name sounded different to my ears, felt different on my tongue, now. I said it again, softly, "Annie."

She stopped walking. We were almost to the car. I thought she had stopped so I could open her door. I turned.

"Sometimes," she said, "sometimes, though, wonderful things happen."

I walked back to her and kissed her. She opened her eyes and said, "I honestly had no idea, until tonight."

We stopped at an all-night diner for coffee. We both took ours black. "I never knew a man who didn't take cream or sugar," she said. I realized at that moment how deep into the well I had fallen when this remark, spoken in a tone of admiration, made me swell with pride. I ate a piece of apple pie. Annie listened to my confession, smiling while I babbled. She was beautiful. She was the most beautiful woman I had ever known. I recalled all the times I sat in her office, distracted past all reason by the twirling of the ends of her hair and the running of her finger along her lower lip. She laughed and said she wasn't even aware she was doing it.

I kissed her in the car and again on her front porch. She did not invite me in. "I had a wonderful time."

"You said I didn't look like a waiter just to be kind, didn't you?"

She laughed. "Okay, maybe you do look a little like a waiter."

"You never lie, do you? Well. I guess I'll see you tomorrow then. At work."

For some reason, we both laughed.

Three days later, on March 17, St. Patrick's Day, we drove to Sarasota to see another play. Annie wore a green sweater and a short green plaid skirt.

"Green is your favorite color," I told her.

"How do you know that?"

"You told me. A long time ago."

"Okay, smart guy, what's my favorite kind of food?"

"Easy, French. Gimme something tough."

"My favorite day of the week."

"Thursday." I was guessing.

She gasped. "Is that yours, too?"

"I've always loved Thursdays."

She was smiling. "Why?"

"Because it's the day after Wednesdays."

"What's your birthday?"

"November fourth."

"Mine's in November, too. November nineteenth."

"Both Scorpios. You know, they say Scorpios are sexual demons."

"I know." She took my hand.

"I feel absolutely great," I told her.

"Me, too."

After the show, we drove to a restaurant in Tampa. We sat in the parking lot and talked. We kissed. I stroked her hair, whispered in her ear, "Annie." An hour went by.

"Are we going in?" she finally asked.

"I'm not hungry," I said.

"Neither am I." She sounded relieved.

"Let's drive back to Lakeside," I said. "We'll stop somewhere on the way."

On the interstate, the conversation lagged. She took my hand and gently kissed my fingertips. I drove straight to her house. She invited me inside for a drink. Inside, the drink I requested was a glass of ice water. We sat on the sofa in the living room. We were alone; her children were visiting with their father. Neither of us had eaten since lunch. Neither of us was hungry.

Later, long after it had become March 18, she clung to me, running her fingers over my bare chest.

"Why did you do it, this bodybuilding thing? Not that I mind exactly."

"I wanted you to notice me."

"Seriously."

"I wanted to be perfect."

"Nobody can be perfect, Rick."

"You are. I'm in love with you, Annie."

She placed a finger on my lips. "I need to tell you something. I never cheated on him."

"You're not cheating on him now."

"No, I mean, I was faithful in my marriage. And I married very young, Rick; I don't have much experience."

She was lying on her back, the covers pulled to her chin, her hair a shimmering brown halo beneath her head, her face a pale, exquisite outline against the darkness. I leaned over her and ran my fingertips along her brow, across her eyelids. She shuddered.

"I'm afraid," she whispered.

Beth sat on my left at Annie's farewell luncheon. Annie sat on my right. After our orders were taken, Beth leaned over and whispered, "You're holding Annie's hand under the table, aren't you?"

"Yes," I answered. I should have lied.

During the meal a man walked into the restaurant. He was alone. He sat down and chatted with the waitress. He looked vaguely familiar. At first I thought he might be one of my tax protestors; I had definitely seen him somewhere before. I nudged Beth and said, "That guy over there, sitting by himself, I've seen him somewhere before."

"That's Peter Watson," she said casually, without looking up from her salad.

I remembered him now. Peter Watson was Culpepper's boss, the head of Inspection for the North Florida District.

Annie summoned me to her office that afternoon and closed the door. I tried to kiss her and she pushed me gently away.

"It's begun," she said.

"We haven't done anything wrong."

"That isn't the point, Rick. You've been here long enough to know that."

"It's just a scare tactic."

"Beth called Culpepper, or maybe she called Peter. They're friends. I just got off the phone with Jim Neyland. He spent twenty minutes screaming at me."

"Why?"

"He asked if we were dating. I told him the truth. I wasn't supposed to tell the truth. He said, 'Come on, Annie, you're supposed to laugh and roll your eyes and say nothing.' He wants me to overnight him a copy of your EPF."*

"Why?"

"Because he's started a file on us, for referral to Inspection. He's interviewing everyone in the group, and they're telling him we've been having an affair for months."

"I'll call him," meaning Jim Neyland.

---

* Employee Performance Folder, containing reviews, memos, copies of evaluations, awards, commendations, reprimands, and nationally mandated forms such as acknowledgments of receipt of official documents.

"That would be an incredibly stupid thing to do, Rick."

"I'll talk to Peter Watson."

"You will not. In another week, I'll be gone and all this—"

"Don't say it, Annie."

"You've been here long enough to know this would happen. We crossed them, Rick. You don't cross them," she said, echoing Culpepper. "They are going to do whatever they're going to do, regardless of what we do now."

"Then I know what to do."

I kissed her hard on the mouth, my hand on the back of her neck. Her hair was up and thin strands fell on either side of her face.

"It's going to be all right," I said. "They don't understand what they're dealing with."

Jim Neyland called me a few days later to counsel me. It was a typical Jim Neyland counseling session.

"You know, when I heard about that assault, Rick, my first thought was, 'Well, Jesus, that poor kid just ruined his life,'" referring to the nursery-man's son. "But then I decided, for your first assault, you did okay."

I thanked him. From Jim Neyland, "doing okay" was the highest praise.

"But I didn't call to talk to you about that. I actually called to talk to you about Annie."

"I have nothing to say to you about Annie."

"Well, I have something to say to you."

"Not without the Union present, you don't."

"This isn't a contractual matter," he said. "Far as I know, there's nothing in the contract about plugging your boss."

"You know, Mr. Neyland, just when I thought you couldn't be more offensive, you surprise me."

"Don't mention it. Look, kid, here's the deal. Nobody is going to believe this story. Nobody in the Service is gonna buy you and her hooking up right as she's leaving. I mean, what kind of nutcase does that?"

You would, I thought, remembering the rumors about him and women in the service, the pending sexual-harassment suit against him filed by three female managers, and Annie's story of his making a pass at her one day in Jacksonville.

"And now I hear you're going to put in for a hardship to North Carolina."

"What if I am?"

"Well, that would be an incredibly stupid thing to do!" He finally lost it. "Christ, you wanna talk contract, let's talk contract. Under the contract you can't get a hardship based on the fact that you have the hots for someone!"

"You can if those hots lead to marriage."

"Oh, yeah, right, you're gonna marry her."

"Maybe I am."

"Look, Rick, you're coming dangerously close to proving me wrong. Nobody I hired has ever proved me wrong. Didn't I tell you that once? I'm trying to give you some friendly advice, for your own damn good and for hers, too. A lot of damage has already been done, but this thing will all blow over without much more trouble if you break it off now."

"Dear Jesus," I said, more to myself than to him. "Who do you people think you are? Who the hell do you think you are?"

"I'm the goddamned branch chief, that's who I am, and I can and I, by God, will do everything in my power to stop you two from—"

I hung up on him. I had never hung up on a branch chief before. It felt good.

She put her children on a plane to Greensboro; they would live with her parents for a week before she joined them. I would arrive at her house after sunset, cook a meal for her (anything with chicken, her favorite), a bottle of cabernet by the fireplace, then make love, holding her afterward as she slept, nestled against my shoulder. She had thrown away the bottle of sleeping pills prescribed during the divorce and its aftermath. There were things about her marriage she would never tell me. She was the most honest person I had ever met, but also the most private. Though she had opened herself to me as she had to no one else, she remained aloof, mysterious, a naked riddle curled in my arms. And she was smarter than I was, smart enough to fear the future. I pressed my lips against her cool forehead. Under the bed was the short iron bar from my exercise machine: a few days before, a neighbor had seen her ex-husband parked in the driveway, standing on the hood of his car, trying to peek through the garage door windows.

.   .   .

I drove her to Greensboro and helped her move into her rental house. She drove me to the airport and waited with me for the plane to board. The terminal was practically deserted; I was taking the red-eye to save money. She cried. I held her. She asked when I would be coming back. Soon, I told her. I flew home. My vision was coming true: we talked for hours on the phone, running up hundreds of dollars in long-distance charges. I passed on news from the office. She talked about the Greensboro POD and the single Exam manager who kept hitting on her.

Then, one night, she ended the call with "Goodnight, sweetie." The next morning I typed my hardship request and faxed it to Jim Neyland's office.

Around this same time, I received a card in the mail with a return address I didn't recognize. As I opened it, I thought of Toby saying taxpayers sent him thank-you cards for putting them out of business. The card wasn't from a taxpayer. It was from a dog.

It read: "Thank you for saving my life!" There was a picture included of that large black mutt with the ridiculously big ears lolling on the bed with Cassie, her thin arms wrapped tightly around its neck.

Why are you covered in blood? Annie had asked the day I saved the dog. It was unavoidable, I had explained. Sometimes it is inevitable, the blood on our hands. We cannot choose. But there are times when we can. I had a dream in which I shared a drink with William Culpepper in a place that existed only inside our heads, where I imagined the unimaginable: a human sacrifice upon the altar of my ambition.

The seizure file was returned to me, reviewed and approved by the District Director. Byzantium had blessed my decision to take Laura Marsh's house. It was paid for, after all, with money belonging to the American people and the American people wanted it back. *Imagine you're IRS Man, champion of the oppressed government*... The manual recommended I deliver the paperwork in person, but it wasn't a requirement. I only had to sign the form and drop it in the mail. It was like dropping a laser-guided missile on a hovel half a world away. There was no alternative except to fifty-three the case.

I did not hesitate. The time for agonizing over Laura Marsh had come to an end. Finally, we were at the terminus of our journey together. She was done and so was I.

I carried the seizure file to the shredder, and fed the culmination of three years' hard work into the ancient grinding maw of the machine. I returned to my desk and in five minutes prepared Form 53, Report of Currently-Not-Collectible Taxes.

Feed the beast, indeed.

Four hours after faxing my hardship request to Jim Neyland, my phone rang. I didn't answer. I knew it was Neyland and I was busy typing a memo to the division chief, accusing Jim Neyland of making threats against me and Annie, accusing Inspection of launching a campaign of intimidation and harassment based on my relationship to Annie, and accusing the employees of my POD of creating a hostile work environment because of my relationship with Annie. I informed the division office I would be submitting a Freedom of Information Act request to obtain the secret file and would be reporting Neyland's conduct to Inspection. I was faxing this memo when Bonny handed me the message from Jim Neyland to call him ASAP.

"What the hell is this?" he shouted at me.

"My hardship request."

"You're telling me you and Annie DeFlorio are *engaged*?"

"That's what I'm telling you."

"Maybe I'll just see what Annie has to say."

"Maybe you should read the memo first."

"What the hell are you talking about? I'm holding the friggin' memo."

"Not that memo. The other memo."

"What other memo?"

"The memo I just faxed to the division chief. I'm sending you a copy, by regular mail."

There was a silence.

"What's it say?"

"I don't feel comfortable telling you that."

"You don't feel comfortable telling me that? Jesus! Well, let me tell you what I feel comfortable telling you, Rick. There is no way in hell I'm signing off on this hardship. It's bullshit. Pure bullshit."

"I don't care."

"You don't care!"

"The division chief has the final authority over hardship requests. You know that, Jim."

"And what the hell do you think the division chief is going to say after I tell him what I know about you two?"

"I think he'll base his answer on the facts."

Jim Neyland laughed. "The facts? Look, kid, people are going to talk. They're going to believe the worst because that's what people do. People will always believe the worst. Always. You go through with this and it's over for both of you. It's professional suicide, Rick. Your careers are *over.*"

"I was referring to the facts in my memo."

"This memo?"

"The other memo."

"The other memo?"

"The memo to the division chief."

"You can't just write a memo and send it directly to the chief."

"I just did."

"Well, you can't. It isn't standard procedure."

"Oops."

"What's it say?"

"That's the second time you asked me that."

"And this time you're gonna give me an answer or I'll fire you for insubordination."

"It's the chief's memo, Jim. If he wants you to see it, I suppose he'll show it to you."

"Okay, well, I see where this is going. I guess you think you're pretty clever, huh?"

"Whatever I am, Mr. Neyland, you made me."

I hung up. Three days later I received by fax the division chief's response. It was a copy of my memo, with this scrawled in the margin: "Ain't no secret file. Ain't no campaign. Am working on your hardship now." I laughed when I read it. I could picture Jim Neyland stomping around the office, cursing my name.

Now all I had to do was propose.

.   .   .

I called the vet's, since the vet had not called me.

"You'll be happy to know they picked up the dog."

"I know," I said. "The dog sent me a card."

He laughed. "The dog sent you a card?"

"Don't misconstrue me here, Doc, but if there's anything you need tax-wise, just let me know."

"Sure will, Rick. Thanks. Oh, and I had Angie send you a copy of the bill."

"I got it." $783.43. I had laughed aloud when I opened the envelope. I had gotten off cheap.

I rented a Ryder truck, the smallest available, because I did not have many things available to put in it. I hitched my car to the back and sat the bird in its cage beside me for the seven-hundred-mile journey north into the mountains.

"Well, bird," I said. I had given up on finding a name for it. "Let's go."

EPILOGUE

In 1998, as any CPA, tax attorney, or conscientious taxpayer will tell you, the world of taxes and tax collecting suffered a seismic shift. The job of the revenue officer changed forever with the passage of the Revenue Restructuring Act of 1998 (RRA '98), which redefined the mission of the Service, making the incidents that are described here nearly impossible to repeat. Included in that legislation is a section referred to inside the Service as the "Ten Deadly Sins," violations of the Code for which termination is the only remedy. One section deals with harassment and intimidation of taxpayers. It is hardly surprising, then, that seizures, liens, and levies are at an all-time low.

As a result, today's new-hires will not suffer as my class did in the early '90s. There won't be the unrelenting pressure to collect dollars, to conduct seizures, and to close cases. There won't be the "cowboy" attitude of the old days, so seductive because it was so effortless. Many of the old hands retired or left the Service after RRA '98 became law. Now, revenue officers are a dying breed. When I was hired in 1991, there were over nine thousand revenue officers. Today there are fewer than thirty-five hundred. There is legislation in Congress to contract out many collection functions to the private sector. There was even a movement to change the official title, from "revenue officer" to something like "compliance assistor."

I have left the Service to write this book, but the Service has not left me. It will always be a part of me. What I experienced within the fortified walls of Byzantium has gone too deep to be exorcised. Yet I am grateful. I am grateful to the Service for the skills it taught me and the lifestyle it granted to me and my family. It was within the Service, after all, that I discovered what Culpepper called "the greatest power in the universe." It was within the Service, after all, that I found love.

I style this as a confession, but it is no apology. I leave proud to have served, for I turned a corner in the Service. I might have ended up like Culpepper, gnawing the dried bones of my ambition. Instead, the Service brought me to a place where I could see what truly matters in life. That is the ultimate irony of my experience: The Service woke things inside of me that only being in the Service could redeem. It brought me to the edge of the chasm so I could step over to the other side. Without the Service, I would not have been able to "save the dog."

And as for the rest...

Of the five trainees hired in 1991, only Caroline remains with the Service.

Allison eventually earned her CPA and now works in the private sector.

Rachel quit during the training year. Dee left the Service five years later.

Gina sends me Christmas cards and calls me occasionally to catch up. She is still employed by the IRS.

Jim Neyland took an assignment to teach tax administration to Third World countries.

Byron White retired and now represents taxpayers before the Service.

Jenny Duncan left the Service on a disability discharge.

Beth and Melissa are managers in what is now called "The Small Business/Self-Employed Division (SB/SE)," the Service's new name for Collection.

Toby, Henry, Cindy Sandifer, Sam Mason, and Larry Simon remain with the Service as revenue officers.

William Culpepper's whereabouts are unknown.

Laura Marsh closed her day-care business to take a job as a substitute kindergarten teacher.

Annie married me.